Programming
the 29K RISC
Family

Prentice Hall Series in Innovative Technology

Dennis R. Allison, David J. Farber, and Bruce D. Shriver   *Series Advisors*

Bhasker	*A VHDL Primer*
Blachman	*Mathematica: A Practical Approach*
Johnson	*Superscalar Microprocessor Design*
Kane and Heinrich	*MIPS RISC Architecture, Second Edition*
Kehoe	*Zen and the Art of the Internet*
Lawson	*Parallel Processing in Industrial Real-Time Applications*
Mann	*Programming the 29K RISC Family*
Nelson, editor	*Systems Programming with Modula-3*
Nutt	*Open Systems*
Rose	*The Little Black Book: Mail-Bonding with OSI Directory Services*
Rose	*The Open Book: A Practical Perspective on OSI*
Rose	*The Simple Book: An Introduction to Internet Management (2E)*
Shapiro	*A C + + Toolkit*
Slater	*Microprocessor-Based Design*
SPARC International Inc.	*The SPARC Architecture Manual, Version 8*
Strom, et al.	*Hermes: A Language for Distributed Computing*
Treseler	*Designing State Machine Controllers Using Programmable Logic*
Wirfs-Brock, Wilkerson, and Weiner	*Designing Object-Oriented Software*

Programming the 29K RISC Family

Daniel Mann

Advanced Micro Devices

P T R Prentice Hall
Englewood Cliffs, New Jersey 07632

Mann, Daniel.
  Programming the 29K RISC family / Daniel Mann.
      p. cm. -- (Prentice Hall series in innovative technology)
  Includes bibliographical references and index.
  ISBN 0-13-091893-8
  1. RISC Microprocessors.   I. Title. II. Series.
QA76.8.R5M35   1994
005.265--dc20   93-10610
                                                                CIP

Editorial/production supervision: *Ann Sullivan*
Cover design: *Tom Neary*
Cover photo: *Ron Victor, Technagraphy®*
Buyer: *Mary Elizabeth McCartney*
Acquisitions editor: *Karen Gettman*
Editorial assistant: *Barbara Alfieri*

Published by P T R Prentice-Hall, Inc.
A Simon & Schuster Company
Englewood Cliffs, New Jersey 07632

29K, Am29000, Am29050, Am29030, Am29035, Am29200, Am29205, EZ030, SA29200, MiniMon29K, ASM29K, AM2902, ISS, SIM29 and UDI are trademarks of Advanced Micro Devices, Inc.; Fusion 29K is a service trademark of Advanced Micro Devices, Inc.; AMD is a registered trademark of Advanced Micro Devices, Inc.; XRAY29K is a trademark of Microtec Research Inc.; High C is a registered trademark of Microtec Research Inc.; i960 is a trademark of Intel, Inc.; MC68020 is a trademark of Motorola Inc.; UNIX is a registered trademark of UNIX System Laboratories

The publisher offers discounts on this book when ordered in bulk quantities. For more information, contact: Corporate Sales Department, PTR Prentice Hall, 113 Sylvan Avenue, Englewood Cliffs, NJ 07632, Phone: 201-592-2863, FAX: 201-592-2249

Printed in the United States of America
10 9 8 7 6 5 4 3 2 1

ISBN 0-13-091893-8

Prentice-Hall International (UK) Limited, *London*
Prentice-Hall of Australia Pty. Limited, *Sydney*
Prentice-Hall Canada Inc., *Toronto*
Prentice-Hall Hispanoamericana, S.A., *Mexico*
Prentice-Hall of India Private Limited, *New Delhi*
Prentice-Hall of Japan, Inc., *Tokyo*
Simon & Schuster Asia Pte. Ltd., *Singapore*
Editora Prentice-Hall do Brasil, Ltda., *Rio de Janeiro*

To my wife
Audrey
and my son
Geoffrey

Contents

Preface . . . . **xix**

Chapter 1
Architectural Overview **1**
  1.1   A RISC DEFINITION 3
  1.2   FAMILY MEMBER FEATURES 5
  1.3   THE Am29000 3–BUS MICROPROCESSOR 7
      1.3.1   The Am29005 10
  1.4   THE Am29050 3–BUS FLOATING–POINT MICROPROCESSOR 10
  1.5   THE Am29030 2–BUS MICROPROCESSOR 13
      1.5.1   Am29030 Evaluation. 15
      1.5.2   The Am29035 15
  1.6   THE Am29200 MICROCONTROLLER 16
      1.6.1   ROM Region 17
      1.6.2   DRAM Region 19
      1.6.3   Virtual DRAM Region 19
      1.6.4   PIA Region 20
      1.6.5   DMA Controller 20
      1.6.6   16–bit I/O Port 21
      1.6.7   Parallel Port 21
      1.6.8   Serial Port 21
      1.6.9   I/O Video Interface 21
      1.6.10 The SA29200 Evaluation Board 22
      1.6.11 The Prototype Board 22
      1.6.12 Am29200 Evaluation 23
      1.6.13 The Am29205 Microcontroller 23
  1.7   REGISTER AND MEMORY SPACE 24
      1.7.1   General Purpose Registers 25

	1.7.2	Special Purpose Registers	27
	1.7.3	Translation Look–Aside Registers	38
	1.7.4	External Address Space	39
1.8		INSTRUCTION FORMAT	41
1.9		KEEPING THE RISC PIPELINE BUSY	42
1.10		PIPELINE DEPENDENCIES	44
1.11		ARCHITECTURAL SIMULATION, sim29	46
	1.11.1	The Simulation Event File	51
	1.11.2	Analyzing the Simulation Log File	57

Chapter 2
Applications Programming 61

2.1		C LANGUAGE PROGRAMMING	62
	2.1.1	Register Stack	63
	2.1.2	Activation Records	64
	2.1.3	Spilling And Filling	65
	2.1.4	Global Registers	66
	2.1.5	Memory Stack	67
2.2		RUN–TIME HIF ENVIRONMENT	67
	2.2.1	OS Preparations before Calling start In crt0	69
	2.2.2	crt0 Preparations before Calling main()	72
	2.2.3	Run–Time HIF Services	73
	2.2.4	Switching to Supervisor Mode	75
2.3		COMPILER FEATURES	78
	2.3.1	Metaware High C 29K Compiler	79
	2.3.2	Free Software Foundation, GCC	79
	2.3.3	C++ Compiler Options	79
	2.3.4	Linking Compiled Code	80
2.4		LIBRARY SUPPORT	82
	2.4.1	Memory Allocation	82
	2.4.2	Setjmp and Longjmp	82
	2.4.3	Support Libraries	84
2.5		C LANGUAGE INTERRUPT HANDLERS	86
	2.5.1	Using an Interrupt Context Cache	89
	2.5.2	Using Signals to Deal with Interrupts	91
2.6		SUPPORT UTILITY PROGRAMS	94
	2.6.1	Examining Object Files (Type .o And a.Out)	94
	2.6.2	Modifying Object Files	96
	2.6.3	Getting a Program into ROM	96

Chapter 3
Assembly Language Programming 99

| 3.1 | | INSTRUCTION SET | 100 |

3.1.1   Integer Arithmetic 100
3.1.2   Compare 102
3.1.3   Logical 103
3.1.4   Shift 103
3.1.5   Data Movement 107
3.1.6   Constant 110
3.1.7   Floating–point 111
3.1.8   Branch 111
3.1.9   Miscellaneous Instructions 115
3.1.10 Reserved Instructions 115
3.2   CODE OPTIMIZATION TECHNIQUES 116
3.3   AVAILABLE REGISTERS 117
3.3.1   Useful Macro–Instructions 119
3.3.2   Using Indirect Pointers and gr0 119
3.3.3   Using gr1 120
3.3.4   Accessing Special Register Space 121
3.3.5   Floating–point Accumulators 122
3.4   DELAYED EFFECTS OF INSTRUCTIONS 123
3.5   TRACE–BACK TAGS 124
3.6   TRANSPARENT ROUTINES 127
3.7   INITIALIZING THE PROCESSOR 127
3.8   ASSEMBLER SYNTAX 127
3.8.1   The AMD Assembler 128
3.8.2   Free Software Foundation (GNU), Assembler 128

Chapter 4
Interrupts and Traps 131
4.1   29K PROCESSOR FAMILY INTERRUPT SEQUENCE 132
4.2   29K PROCESSOR FAMILY INTERRUPT RETURN 133
4.3   SUPERVISOR MODE HANDLERS 135
4.3.1   The Interrupt Environment 135
4.3.2   Interrupt Latency 136
4.3.3   Simple Freeze-mode Handlers 137
4.3.4   Operating in Freeze mode 137
4.3.5   Monitor mode 139
4.3.6   Freeze-mode Clock Interrupt Handler 139
4.3.7   Removing Freeze mode 141
4.3.8   Handling Nested Interrupts 144
4.3.9   Saving Registers 145
4.3.10 Enabling Interrupts 147
4.3.11 Restoring Saved Registers 149
4.3.12 An Interrupt Queuing model 151
4.3.13 Making Timer Interrupts Synchronous 157

4.4   USER-MODE INTERRUPT HANDLERS 157
    4.4.1   Supervisor mode Code 159
    4.4.2   Register Stack Operation 161
    4.4.3   SPILL and FILL Trampoline 163
    4.4.4   SPILL Handler 164
    4.4.5   FILL Handler 165
    4.4.6   Register File Inconsistencies 166
    4.4.7   Preparing the C Environment 170
    4.4.8   Handling Setjmp and Longjmp 171

Chapter 5
Operating System Issues 173
5.1   REGISTER CONTEXT 174
5.2   SYNCHRONOUS CONTEXT SWITCH 177
    5.2.1   Optimizations 179
5.3   ASYNCHRONOUS CONTEXT SWITCH 184
5.4   INTERRUPTING USER MODE 185
    5.4.1   Optimizations 188
5.5   USER MODE SIGNALS 189
5.6   INTERRUPTING SUPERVISOR MODE 193
    5.6.1   Optimizations 195
5.7   USER SYSTEM CALLS 196
5.8   FLOATING–POINT ISSUES 199
5.9   DEBUGGER ISSUES 200
5.10 RESTORING CONTEXT 201
5.11 INTERRUPT LATENCY 203
5.12 SELECTING AN OPERATING SYSTEM 204
5.13 SUMMARY 207

Chapter 6
Memory Management Unit 209
6.1   SRAM VERSUS DRAM PERFORMANCE 210
6.2   TRANSLATION LOOK–ASIDE BUFFER (TLB) OPERATION 215
    6.2.1   Taking a TLB Trap 220
6.3   PERFORMANCE EQUATION 220
6.4   SOFTWARE CONTROLLED CACHE MEMORY ARCHITECTURE 222
    6.4.1   Cache Page Maintenance 227
    6.4.2   Data Access TLB Miss 228
    6.4.3   Instruction Access TLB Miss 230
    6.4.4   Data Write TLB Protection 231
    6.4.5   Supervisor TLB Signal Handler 232
    6.4.6   Copying a Page into the Cache 234
    6.4.7   Copying a Page Out of the Cache 236

	6.4.8	Cache Set Locked	237
	6.4.9	Returning from Signal Handler	238
	6.4.10	Support Routines	239
	6.4.11	Performance Gain	240

Chapter 7
Software Debugging 243

7.1		REGISTER ASSIGNMENT CONVENTION	243
7.2		PROCESSOR DEBUG SUPPORT	244
	7.2.1	Execution Mode	244
	7.2.2	Memory Access Protection	245
	7.2.3	Trace Facility	245
	7.2.4	Program Counter register PC2	246
	7.2.5	Monitor Mode	247
	7.2.6	Instruction Breakpoints	247
7.3		THE MiniMON29K DEBUGGER	248
	7.3.1	The Target MiniMON29K Component	249
	7.3.2	Register Usage	250
	7.3.3	The Debugcore	251
	7.3.4	Debugcore installation	252
	7.3.5	Advanced DBG and CFG Module Features	256
	7.3.6	The Message System	258
	7.3.7	MSG Operation	258
	7.3.8	MSG Virtual Interrupt Mechanism	259
7.4		THE OS–BOOT OPERATING SYSTEM	260
	7.4.1	Register Usage	260
	7.4.2	OS–boot Operation	261
	7.4.3	HIF Services	262
	7.4.4	Adding New Device Drivers	263
	7.4.5	Memory Access Protection	263
	7.4.6	Down Loading a New OS	267
7.5		UNIVERSAL DEBUG INTERFACE (UDI)	268
	7.5.1	Debug Tool Developers	269
	7.5.2	UDI Specification	270
	7.5.3	P–trace	272
	7.5.4	The GDB–UDI Connection	274
	7.5.5	The UDI–MiniMON29K Monitor Connection, MonTIP	274
	7.5.6	The MiniMON29K User–Interface, MonDFE	275
	7.5.7	The UDI – Instruction Set Simulator Connection, ISSTIP	277
	7.5.8	UDI Benefits	278
	7.5.9	Getting Started with GDB	279
	7.5.10	GDB and MiniMON29K Summary	282

Appendix A
HIF Service Calls 285

| | A.1 | Service Call Numbers And Parameters .... | 285 |

A.2   Error Numbers 340

Appendix B
HIF Signal Processing **347**
B.1   User Trampoline Code 347
B.2   Library Glue Routines to HIF Signal Services 353
B.3   The Library signal() Routine for Registering a Handler 354

Appendix C
Software Assigned Trap Numbers **357**

References and Bibliography **359**

Index **361**

Figures

Figure 1-1.   RISC Pipeline *3*

Figure 1-2.   CISC Pipeline *4*

Figure 1-3.   Processor Price–Performance Summary *6*

Figure 1-4.   Am29000 Processor 3–bus Harvard Memory System *9*

Figure 1-5.   Am29200 Microcontroller Address Space Regions *18*

Figure 1-6.   Am29200 Microcontroller Block Diagram *18*

Figure 1-7.   General Purpose Register Space *26*

Figure 1-8.   Special Purpose Register Space for the Am29000 Mircoprocessor *29*

Figure 1-9.   Am29000 Processor Program Counter *33*

Figure 1-10.   Additional Special Purpose Registers for the Am29050 Microprocessor . . .   *35*

Figure 1-11.   Additional Special Purpose Registers for the Am29030 Microprocessor *35*

Figure 1-12.   Additional Special Purpose Register for the Am29050 Microprocessor *38*

Figure 1-13.   Instruction Format *41*

Figure 1-14.   Frequently Occurring Instruction–Field Uses *43*

Figure 1-15.   Pipeline Stages for BTC Miss *45*

Figure 1-16.   Pipeline Stages for a BTC Hit *46*

Figure 1-17.   Data Forwarding and Bad–Load Scheduling *47*

Figure 1-18.   Register Initialization Performed by sim29 . . . .   *50*

Figure 2-1.   Cache Window *64*

Figure 2-2.   Overlapping Activation Record Registers *66*

Figure 3-1.   The EXTRACT Instruction uses the Funnel Shifter *107*

Figure 3-2.   LOAD and STORE Instruction Format *109*

Figure 3-3.   General Purpose Register Usage *117*

Figure 3-4.   Global Register gr1 Fields *121*

Figure 3-5.   *Trace–Back Tag Format* *125*

Figure 3-6.   *Walking Back Through Activation Records* *126*

Figure 4-1.   *Interrupt Handler Execution Stages* *132*

Figure 4-2.   *The Format of Special Registers CPS and OPS* *133*

Figure 4-3.   *Interrupted Load Multiple Instruction* *145*

Figure 4-4.   *Am29000 Processor Interrupt Enable Logic* *149*

Figure 4-5.   *Interrupt Queue Entry Chaining* *152*

Figure 4-6.   *An Interrupt Queuing Approach* *153*

Figure 4-7.   *Queued Interrupt Execution Flow* *155*

Figure 4-8.   *Saved Registers* *159*

Figure 4-9.   *Register and Stack Cache* *132*

Figure 4-10.   *Stack Upon Interrupt* *167*

Figure 4-11.   *Stack After Fix–up* *170*

Figure 4-12.   *Long–Jump to Setjmp* *172*

Figure 5-1.   *A Consistent Register Stack Cache* *175*

Figure 5-2.   *Current Procedures Activation Record* *176*

Figure 5-3.   *Overlapping Activation Records Eventual Spill Out of the Register Stack Cache* *181*

Figure 5-4.   *Context Save PCB Layout* *183*

Figure 5-5.   *Register Stack Cut–Across* *198*

Figure 6-1.   *Average Cycles per Instruction Using DRAM* *211*

Figure 6-2.   *Average Cycles per Instruction Using SRAM* *212*

Figure 6-3.   *Block Diagram of Example Joint I/D System* *213*

Figure 6-4.   *Average Cycles per Instruction* *214*

Figure 6-5.   *Probability of a TLB Access per Instruction* *215*

Figure 6-6.   *TLB Field Composition for 4K Byte Page Size* *216*

Figure 6-7.   *Block Diagram of Am29000 processor TLB Layout* *217*

Figure 6-8.   *Am29000 Processor TLB Register Format* *218*

Figure 6-9.   *TLB Miss Ratio for Joint I/D 2–1 SRAM System* *221*

Figure 6-10.   *Average Cycles Required per TLB Miss* *222*

Figure 6-11.   *PTE Mapping to Cache Real Page Numbers* *224*

Figure 6-12.   *Software Controlled Cache, K bytes paged–in* *226*

Figure 6-13.   *Probability of a Page–in Given a TLB Miss* *226*

Figure 6-14.   *TLB Signal Frame* *230*

Figure 6-15.   *Cache Performance Gains with the Assembly Utility* *240*

Figure 6-16.   *Cache Performance Gains with NROFF Utility* *241*

Figure 6-17.   *Comparing Cache Based Systems with DRAM Only Systems* *242*

Figure 7-1.   *MinMON29k Debugger Components* *249*

Figure 7-2.   *29K Target Software Module Configuration* *250*

Figure 7-3.   *Vector Table Assignment for Debugcore* *253*

Figure 7-4.   *Processor Initialization Code Sequence* *253*

Figure 7-5.   *Operating System Information Passed to dbg_control( )* *255*

Figure 7-6.   *Return Structure from dbg_control( )* *256*

Figure 7-7.   *Typical OS–boot Memory Layout* *265*

Figure 7-8.   *Currently Available Debugging Tools that Conform to UDI Specification* *271*

Figure A-1. *HIF Register Preservation for Signals* *332*

Tables

Table 1-1.   Pin Compatible 3–bus 29K Family Processors   7

Table 1-2.   Pin Compatible 2–bus 29K Family Processors   13

Table 1-3.   Micorcontroller Members of 29K Processor Family   17

Table 1-4.   3–bus Processor Memory Modeling Parameters for sim29   52

Table 1-5.   3–bus Processor DRAM Modeling Parameters for sim29 (continued)   53

Table 1-6.   3–bus Processor Static Column Modeling Parameters for sim29 (continued) ..   53

Table 1-7.   3–bus Processor Memory Modeling Parameters for sim29 (continued)   54

Table 1-8.   2–bus Processor Memory Modeling Parameters for sim29   55

Table 1-9.   Microcontroller Memory Modeling Parameters for sim29   56

Table 2-1.   Trap Handler Vectors   71

Table 2-2.   HIF Service Calls   74

Table 2-3.   HIF Service Call Parameters   76

Table 2-4.   HIF Service Call Parameters (Concluded)   77

Table 3-1.   Integer Arithmetic Instructions   101

Table 3-2.   Integer Arithmetic Instructions (Concluded)   102

Table 3-3.   Compare Instructions   104

Table 3-4.   Compare Instructions (Concluded)   105

Table 3-5.   Logical Instructions   106

Table 3-6.   Shift Instructions   108

Table 3-7.   Data Move Instructions   108

Table 3-8.   Data Move Instructions (Concluded)   109

Table 3-9.   Constant Instructions   111

Table 3-10.   Floating–Point Instructions   102

Table 3-11.   Floating–Point Instructions (Concluded)   103

Table 3-12. Branch Instructions *104*

Table 3-13. Miscellaneous Instructions *105*

Table 4-1. Global Register Allocations *177*

Table 4-2. Expanded Register Usage *200*

Table 7-1. UDI–p Procedures (Version 1.2) *272*

Table 7-2. ptrace( ) Services *273*

Table 7-3. GDB Remote–Target Operations *274*

Table A-1. HIF Open Service Mode Parameters *288*

Table A-2. Default Signals Handled by HIF *331*

Table A-3. HIF Signal Return Services *33*

Table A-4. HIF Error Numbers Assigned *340*

Table A-5. HIF Error Numbers Assigned (continued) *341*

Table A-6. HIF Error Numbers Assigned (continued) *342*

Table A-7. HIF Error Numbers Assigned (continued) *343*

Table A-8. HIF Error Numbers Assigned (continued) *344*

Table A-9. HIF Error Numbers Assigned (concluded) *345*

Table C-1. Software Assigned Trap Numbers *357*

Table C-2. Software Assigned Trap Numbers (concluded) *358*

Preface

This book brings together, for the first time, a comprehensive collection of information required by the person developing software for the Advanced Micro Devices 29K family of RISC microprocessors and microcontrollers. It is useful to the computer professional and student interested in the 29K family RISC implementation. It does not assume that the reader is familiar with RISC techniques.

Although certain members of the 29K family are equally suited to the construction of a workstation or an embedded application, the material is mainly applicable for embedded application development. This slant shall be appreciated by most readers; since early in the 29K's introduction AMD has promoted the family as a collection of processors spanning a wide range of embedded performance. Additionally, in recent years, AMD started a range of microcontrollers, initially with the Am29200. The inclusion of onchip peripherals in the microcontroller implementations resulted in this particular extension to the family being well received by the embedded processor community.

The success of the 29K family, and of RISC technology in general, has created considerable interest within the microprocessor industry. A growing number of engineers are evaluating RISC, and an increasing number are selecting RISC rather than CISC designs for new products. Higher processor performance is the main reason cited for adopting new RISC designs. This book describes the methods used by the 29K family — many of which are characteristic of the RISC–approach — to obtain a performance gain vis–a–vis CISC processors. Many of the processor and software features described will be compared with an equivalent CISC method; this shall assist the engineer making the CISC to RISC transition.

Because the 29K family architecture reveals the processor's internal pipeline operation much more than a CISC architecture, a better understanding of how the software can control the hardware and avoid resource conflicts is required to obtain the best performance. Up to this point, software engineers have had to glean information about programming the 29K family from scattered application notes, conference proceedings and other publications. In addition much of the necessary information has never been documented. This has lead to a number of difficulties, particularly where the most efficient use of the RISC design features is sought.

The material presented is practical rather than theoretical. Each chapter is in a somewhat standalone form, reducing the need to read earlier chapters before later chapters are studied. Many of the code examples are directly usable in real embedded systems rather than as student exercises. Engineers planning on using the 29K family will be able to extract useful code sequences from the book for integration into their own designs. Much of the material presented has been used by AMD, and other independent companies, in building training classes for computer professionals wishing to quickly gain an understanding of the 29K family.

This book is organized as follows:

Chapter 1 describes the architectural characteristics of the 29K RISC microprocessor and microcontroller family. The original family member, the Am29000 processor, is described first. Then the family tree evolution is dealt with in terms of each member's particular features. Although all 29K processors are application code compatible they are not all pin compatible. The ability of the 29K family to be flexible in its memory requirements is presented. In addition, the chapter shows the importance of keeping the RISC pipeline busy if high performance is to be achieved.

Chapter 2 deals with application programming. It covers the main topics required by a software developer to produce code for execution on a 29K. Application coding is done in a high level language and the chapter assumes the C language is most widely used. The dual register and memory stack technique used by the 29K procedure calling–convention is described in detail, along with the process of maintaining the processor's local register file as a cache for the top of the register stack. Application programs require runtime support. The library services typically used by developers make demands upon such operating system services. The Host Interface (HIF) specifies a set operating system services. The HIF services are described and their relevance put in context.

Chapter 3 explains how to program a 29K at assembly level. Methods of partioning and accessing a processor's register space are described. This includes the special register space which can only be reached by assembly level instructions. The reader is shown how to deal with such topics as branch delay slots and memory access latency. It is not expected that application programs will be developed in assembly language, rather, that assembly language coding skills are required by the operating system developer. Some developers may only be required to utilize assembly coding to implement, say, a small interrupt handler routine.

Chapter 4 deals with the complex subject of 29K interrupts. Because 29K processors make no use of microcode, the range of interrupt handler options is extended over the typical CISC type processor. Techniques new to the reader familiar with CISC, such as lightweight interrupts and interrupt context caching, are presented. Most application developers are moving toward writing interrupt handlers in a high level language, such as C. This chapter describes the process of preparing the 29K to handle a C level signal handler after taking an interrupt or trap.

Chapter 5 deals with operating system issues. It describes, in detail, the process of performing an application task context switch. This is one of the major services performed by an operating system. A detailed knowledge of the utilized procedural–linkage mechanism and 29K architectural features is required to implement a high performance context switch.

Chapter 6 describes the Translation Look–Aside Buffer (TLB) which is incorporated into many of the 29K family members. Its use as a basic building block for a Memory Management Unit (MMU) is described. This chapter also demonstrates the use of the TLB to implement a software–controlled cache which improves overall system performance.

Chapter 7 explains the operation of popular software debugging tools such as MiniMON29K and GDB. The process of building a debug environment for an embedded application is described. Also dealt with is the Universal Debug Interface (UDI) which is used to connect the user–interface process with the process controlling the target hardware. The use of UDI introduces new freedom in tool choice to the embedded product developer.

Although I am the sole author of this book, I would like to thank my colleagues at Advanced Micro Devices for their help with reviewing early manuscripts. I am also grateful for their thoughtful suggestions, many of which were offered during the porting of 4.3bsd UNIX to the Am29000 processor. I would also like to thank Grant Maxwell for his review and comments on Chapter 1. Thanks also to Embedded Systems Programming for allowing the use of material describing the GDB debugger which first appeared in their volume 5 number 12 issue. Finally I would like to thank AMD for the encouragement to complete this book. I have enjoyed the experience and learned much on the way.

Chapter 1

Architectural Overview

This Chapter deals with a number of topics relevant to the selection of a 29K™ family member. General RISC architecture characteristics are discussed before each family member is described in more detail. A RISC microprocessor can achieve high performance only if its pipeline is kept effectively busy — this is explained. Finally, the architectural simulator is described; it is an important tool in evaluating a processors performance.

The instruction set of the 29K family was designed to closely match the internal representation of operations generated by optimizing compilers. Instruction execution times are not burdened by redundant instruction formats and options. CISC microprocessors trap computational sequences in microcode. Microcode are sequences of *internal* processor operations combined to perform a machine instruction. A CISC microprocessor contains an on–chip microprogram memory to hold the microcode required to support the complex instructions. It is difficult for a compiler to select CISC instruction sequences which result in the microcode being efficiently applied to the overall computational task. The myopic microcode results in processor operational overhead. The compiler for a CISC can not remove the overhead, it can only reduce it by making the best selection from the array of instruction options and formats — such as addressing modes. The compiler for a 29K RISC can exploit lean instructions whose operation is free of microcode and always visible to the compiler code–generator.

Each 29K processor has a 4–stage RISC pipeline: consisting of first, a fetch stage, followed by decode, execute and write–back stages. Instructions, with few exceptions, execute in a single–cycle. Although instructions are streamlined, they still support operations on two source operands, placing the result in a third operand.

Registers are used to supply operands for most instructions, and the processor contains a large number of registers to reduce the need to fetch data from off–chip memory. When external memory is accessed it is via explicit load and store operations, and never via extended instruction addressing modes. The large number of registers, within the processor's register file, act effectively as a cache for program data. However, the implementation of a multiport register file is superior to a conventional data cache as it enables simultaneous access to multiple operands.

Parameter passing between procedure calls is supported by dynamically sized register windows. Each procedure's register window is allocated from a stack of 128 32–bit registers. This results in a very efficient procedure call mechanism, and is responsible for considerable operational benefits compared to the typical CISC method of pushing and popping procedure parameters from a memory stack.

Processors in the 29K family also make use of other techniques usually associated with RISC, such as delayed branching, to keep the instruction hungry RISC fed and prevent pipeline stalling.

The freedom from microcode not only benefits the effectiveness of the instruction processing stream, but also benefits the interrupt and trap mechanism required to support such events as external hardware interrupts. The preparations performed by 29K hardware for interrupt processing are very brief, and this *lightweight approach* enables the programmer to define their own interrupt architecture; enabling optimizations to be selected which are best for, say, interrupt through put, or short latency in commencing handler processing.

The 29K family includes 3–bus Harvard memory architecture processors, 2–bus processors which have simplified and flexible memory system interfaces, and microcontrollers with considerable on–chip system support. The range is extensive, yet User mode instruction compatibility is achieved across the entire family [AMD 1993a]. Within each family–grouping, there is also pin compatibility. The family supports the construction of a scalable product range with regard to performance and system cost. For example, all of the performance of the top–end processor configurations may not be required, or be appropriate, in a product today but it may be necessary in the future. Because of the range and scalability of the family, making a commitment to 29K processor technology is an investment supported by the ability to scale–down or scale–up a design in the future. Much of the family's advantages are attained by the flexibility in memory architecture choice. This is significant because of the important impact a memory system can have on performance, overall cost, and design and test time [Olson 1988][Olson 1989].

The microcontroller family members contain all the necessary RAM and ROM interface glue–logic on–chip, permitting memory devices to be directly connected to the processor. Given that memory systems need only be 8–bit or 16–bit wide, the introduction of these devices should hasten the selection of embedded RISC in future product designs. The use of RISC need not be considered an expensive option in terms of system cost or hardware and software design times. Selecting RISC is not only the *correct* decision for *expensive* workstation designs, but increasingly for a wide range of performance and price sensitive embedded products.

1.1 A RISC DEFINITION

The process of dealing with an instruction can be broken down into stages (see Figure 1-1). An instruction must then flow through the pipeline of stages before its processing is complete. Independent hardware is used at each pipeline stage. Information is passed to subsequent pipeline stages at the completion of each processor cycle. At any instant, the pipeline stages are processing several instructions which are each at a different stage of completion. Pipelining increases the utilization of the processor hardware, and effectively reduces the number of processor cycles required to process an instruction.

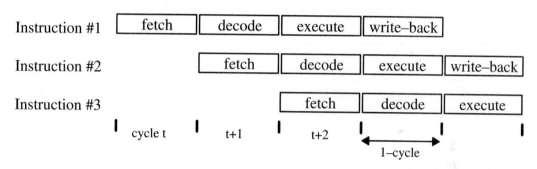

Figure 1-1. RISC Pipeline

With a 4–stage pipeline an instruction takes four cycles to complete, assuming the pipeline stages are clocked at each processor cycle. However, the processor is able to start a new instruction at each new processor cycle, and the average processing time for an instruction is reduced to 1–cycle. Instructions which execute in 1–cycle have only 1–cycle latency as their results are available to the next instruction.

The 4–stage pipeline of the 29K processor family supports a simplified execute stage. This is made possible by simplifying instruction formats, limiting instruction complexity and operating on data help in registers. The simplified execute stage means that only a single processor cycle is required to complete execute–stage processing and the cycle time is also minimized.

CISC processors support a complex execution–stage which require several processor cycles to complete. When an instruction is ready for execution it is broken down into a sequence of microinstructions (see Figure 1-2). These simplified instructions are supplied by the on–chip microprogram memory. Each microinstruction must be decoded and executed separately before the instruction execution–stage

---

is complete. Depending on the amount of microcode needed to implement a CISC instruction, the number of cycles required to complete instruction processing varies from instruction to instruction.

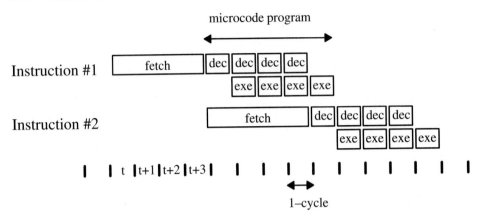

Figure 1-2. CISC Pipeline

Because the hardware used by the execute–stage of a CISC processor is utilized for a number of processor cycles, the other stages of the pipeline have available additional cycles for their own operation. For example, if an execute–stage requires four processors cycles, the overlapping fetch–stage of the next instruction has four cycles to complete. If the fetch–stage takes four or less cycles, then no stalling of the pipeline due to execute–stage starvation shall occur. Starvation or pipeline stalling occurs when a previous stage has not completed its processing and can not pass its results to the input of the next pipeline stage.

During the evolution of microprocessors, earlier designs operated with slower memories than are available today. Both processor and memory speeds have seen great improvements in recent years. However, the low cost of high performance memory devices now readily available has shifted microprocessor design. When memory was slow it made sense overlapping multicycle instruction fetch stages with multicycle execute stages. Once an instruction had been fetched it was worthwhile getting as much execute–value as possible since the cost of fetching the instruction was high. This approach drove processor development and lead to the name Complex Instruction Set Computer.

Faster memory means that instruction processing times are no longer fetch–stage dominated. With a reduction in the number of cycles required by the fetch–stage, the execute–stage becomes the dominant factor in determining processor performance. Consequently attention turned to the effectiveness of the microcode sequences used to perform CISC instruction execution. Careful analysis of CISC instruction usage revealed that the simpler instructions were much more frequently used than the complex ones which required long microcode sequences. The conclusion drawn was that microcode rarely provides the exact sequence of operations required to support a high level language instruction.

The variable instruction execution times of CISC instructions results in complex pipeline management. It is also more difficult for a compiler to work out the execution times for different combinations of CISC instructions. For that matter it is harder for the assembly level programmer to estimate the execution times of, say, an interrupt handler code sequence compared to the equivalent RISC code sequence. More importantly, streamlining pipeline operations enables reduced processor cycle times and greater control by a compiler of the processor's operation. Given that the execute–stage dominates performance, the RISC *approach* is to fetch more instructions which can be simply executed. Although a RISC program may contain 20% more instructions than a program for a CISC, the total number of cycles required to perform a task is reduced.

A number of processor characteristics have been proposed in the press as indicative of RISC or CISC. Many of these proposals are made by marketing departments which wish to control markets by using RISC and CISC labels as marketing rather than engineering expressions. I consider a processor to be RISC if it is microcode free and has a simple instruction execute–stage which can complete in a single cycle.

1.2 FAMILY MEMBER FEATURES

Although this book is about Programming the 29K RISC Family, the following sections are not restricted to only describing features which can be utilized by software. They also briefly describe key hardware features which affect a processor's performance and hence its selection.

All members of the family have User mode binary code compatibility. This greatly simplifies the task of porting application code from one processor to another. Some system–mode code may need to be changed due to differences in such things as field assignments of registers in special register space.

Given the variation between family members such as the 3–bus Am29050 floating–point processor and the Am29205 microcontroller it is remarkable that there is so much software compatibility. The number of family members is expected to continue to grow; but already there is a wide selection enabling systems of ranging performance and cost to be constructed (see Figure 1-3). If AMD continues to grow the family at "both ends of the performance spectrum", we might expect to see new microcontroller family members as well as superscaler microprocessors [Johnson 1991]. AMD has stated that future microprocessors will be pin compatible with the current 2–bus family members.

I think one of the key features of 29K family members are their ability to operate with varying memory system configurations. It is possible to build very high per-

---

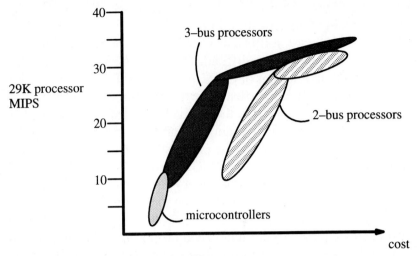

Figure 1-3.   Processor Price–Performance Summary

formance Harvard type architectures, or low cost — high access latency — DRAM based systems. Two types of instruction memory caching are supported. Branch Target Cache (BTC) memory is used in 3–bus family members to hide memory access latencies. The 2–bus family members make use of more conventional *bandwidth improving* instruction cache memory.

A second key feature of processors in the 29K family is that the programmer must supply the interrupt handler save and restore mechanism. Typically a CISC type processor will save the processor context, when an exception occurs, in accordance with the on–chip microcode. The 29K family is free of microcode, making the user free to tailor the interrupt and exception processing mechanism to suit the system. This often leads to new and more efficient interrupt handling techniques. The fast interrupt response time, and large interrupt handling capacity made possible by the flexible architecture, has been sited as one of the key reasons for selecting a 29K processor design.

All members of the 29K family make some use of burst–mode memory interfaces. Burst–mode memory accesses provide a simplified transfer mechanism for high bandwidth memory systems. Burst–mode addressing only applies to consecutive access sequences, it is used for all instruction fetches and for load–multiple and store–multiple data accesses.

The 3–bus microprocessors are dependent on burst–mode addressing to free–up the address bus after a new instruction fetch sequence has been established. The memory system is required to supply instructions at sequential addresses without the processor supplying any further address information; at least until a jump or call type instruction is executed. This makes the address bus free for use in data memory access.

The non 3–bus processors can not simultaneously support instruction fetching and data access from external memory. Consequently the address bus continually supplies address information for the instruction or data access currently being supported by the external memory. However, burst–mode access signals are still supplied by the processor. Indicating that the processor will require another access at the next sequential address, after the current access is complete, is an aid in achieving maximum memory access bandwidth. There are also a number of memory devices available which are internally organized to give highest performance when accessed in burst–mode.

1.3   THE Am29000 3–BUS MICROPROCESSOR

The Am29000™ processor is pin compatible with other 3–bus members of the family (see Table 1-1) [AMD 1989][Johnson 1987]. It was the first member of the family, introduced in 1987. It is the core processor for many later designs, such as the current 2–bus processor product line. Much of this book describes the operation of the Am29000 processor as the framework for understanding the rest of the family.

Table 1-1. Pin Compatible 3–bus 29K Family Processors

Processor	Am29000	Am29050	Am29005
instruction Cache	BTC 32x4 words	BTC 64x4 or 128x2 words	No
Cache Associativity	2 Way	2 Way	N/A
On–Chip Floating–Point	No	Yes	No
On–Chip MMU	Yes	Yes	No
Half Speed External Bus	No	No	No
Programmable bus Sizing	No	No	No
On–Chip Interrupt Controller Inputes	Yes 6	Yes 6	Yes 6
Clock Speeds (MHz)	16,20,25,33	20,25,33,40	16

The processor can be connected to separate Instruction and data memory systems, thus exploiting the Harvard architectural advantages (See Figure 1-4). Alternatively, a simplified 2–bus system can be constructed by connecting the data and address busses together; this enables a single memory system to be constructed.

When the full potential of the 3–bus architecture is utilized, it is usually necessary to include in the memory system a *bridge* to enable instruction memory to be accessed. The processor does not support any on–chip means to transfer information on the instruction bus to the data bus.

The load and store instructions, used for all external memory access, have an option field (OPT2–0) which is presented to device pins during the data transfer operation. Option field value OPT=2 is defined to indicate the bridge should permit ROM space to be read as if it were data. Instructions can be located in two separate spaces: Instruction space and ROM space. Often these spaces become the same, as the IREQT pin (instruction request type) is not decoded so as to enable distinction between the two spaces. When ROM and Instruction spaces are not common, a range of data memory space can be set aside for accessing Instruction space via the bridge. It is best to avoid overlapping external address spaces if high level code is to access any memory located in the overlapping regions (see section 1.7.4).

All processors in the 29K family support byte and half–word size read and write access to data memory. The original Am29000 (pre rev–D, 1990) only supported word sized data access. This resulted in read–modify–write cycles to modify sub–word sized objects. The processor supports insert– and extract–byte and half–word instructions to assist with sub–word operations. These instructions are little used to-day.

The processor has a Branch Target Cache (BTC) memory which is used to supply the first four instructions of previously taken branches. Successful branches are 20% of a typical instruction mix. Using burst–mode and interleaf techniques, memory systems can sustain the high bandwidths required to keep the instruction hungry RISC fed. However, when a branch occurs, memory systems can present considerable latency before supplying the first instruction of the branch target. For example, consider an instruction memory system which has a 3–cycle first access latency but can sustain 1–cycle access in burst–mode. Typically every 5th instruction is a branch and for the example the branch instruction would take effectively 5–cycles to complete its execution (the pipeline would be stalled for 4–cycles (see section 1.10)). If all other instructions were executed in a single–cycle the average cycle time per instruction would be 1.8 (i.e. 9/5); not the desired sustained single–cycle operation. The BTC can hide all 3–cycles of memory access latency, and enable the branch instruction to execute in a single–cycle.

The programmer has little control over BTC operation; it is maintained internally by processor hardware. There are 32 cache entries (known as cache blocks) of four instructions each. They are configured in a 2–way set associative arrangement. Entries are tagged to distinguish between accesses made in User mode and Supervisor mode; they are also tagged to differentiate between virtual addresses and physical addresses. Because the address in the program counter is presented to the BTC at the same time it is presented to the MMU, the BTC does not operate with physical

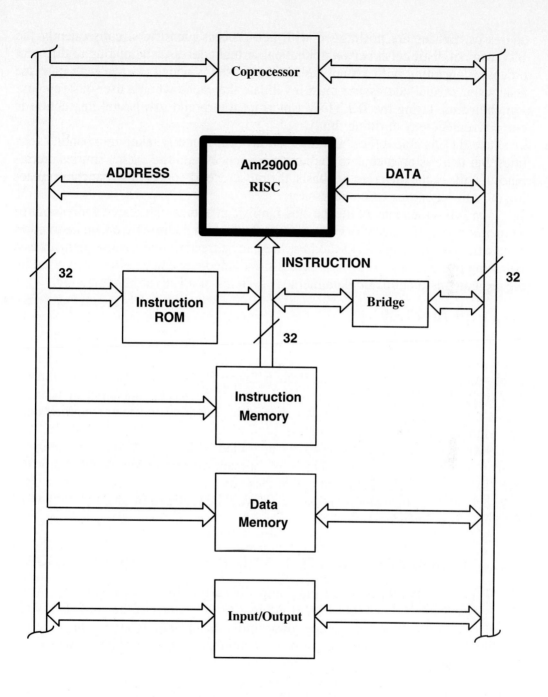

Figure 1-4. Am29000 Processor 3–bus Harvard Memory System

addresses. Entries are not tagged with per–process identifiers; consequently the BTC can not distinguish between identical virtual addresses belonging to different processes operating with virtual addressing. Systems which operate with multiple tasks using virtual addressing must invalidate the cache when a user–task context switch occurs. Using the IRETINV (interrupt return and invalidate) instruction is one convenient way of doing this.

The BTC is able to hold the instructions of frequently taken trap handler routines, but there is no means to lock code sequences into the cache. Entries are replaced in the cache on a random basis, the most recently occurring branches replacing the current entries when necessary.

The 3–bus members of the the 29K family can operate the shared address bus in a pipeline mode. If a memory system is able to latch an address before an instruction or data transfer is complete, the address bus can be freed to start a subsequent access. Allowing two accesses to be in progress simultaneously can be effectively used by the separate instruction and data memory systems of a Harvard architecture.

1.3.1 The Am29005

The Am29005™ is pin compatible with other 3–bus members of the family (see Table 1-1). It is an inexpensive version of the Am29000 processor. The Translation Look–Aside Buffer (TLB) and the Branch Target Cache (BTC) have been omitted. It is available at a lower clock speed, and only in the less expensive plastic packaging. It is a good choice for systems which are price sensitive and do not require Memory Management Unit support or the performance advantages of the BTC. An Am29005 design can always be easily upgraded with an Am29000 replacement later. In fact the superior debugging environment offered by the Am29000 or the Am29050™ may make the use of one of these processor a good choice during software debugging. The faster processor can always be replaced by an Am29005 when production commences.

1.4   THE Am29050 3–BUS FLOATING–POINT MICROPROCESSOR

The Am29050 processor is pin compatible with other 3–bus members of the family (see Table 1-1) [AMD 1991a]. Many of the features of the Am29050 were already described in the section describing its closely related relative, the Am29000. The Am29050 processor offers a number of additional performance and system support features when compared with the Am29000. The most notable is the direct execution of double–precision (64–bit) and single–precision (32–bit) floating–point arithmetic on–chip. The Am29000 has to rely on software emulation or the Am29027™ floating–point coprocessor to perform floating–point operations. The introduction of the Am29050 eliminated the need to design the Am29027 coprocessor into floating–point intensive systems.

The processor contains a Branch Target Cache (BTC) memory system like the Am29000; but this time it is twice as big, with 32 entries in each of the two sets rather than the Am29000's 16 entries per set. BTC entries are not restricted to four instructions per entry; there is an option (bit CO in the CFG register) to arrange the BTC as 64 entries per set, with each entry containing two instructions rather than four. The smaller entry size is more useful with lower latency memory systems. For example, if a memory system has a 2–cycle first–access start–up latency it is more efficient to have a larger number of 2–instruction entries. After all, for this example system, the third and fourth instructions in a four per entry arrangement could just as efficiently be fetched from the external memory.

The Am29050 also incorporates an Instruction Forwarding path which additionally helps to reduce the effects of instruction memory access latency. When a new instruction fetch sequence commences, and the target of the sequence is not found in the BTC, an external memory access is performed to start filling the Instruction Prefetch Buffer (IPB). With the Am29000 processor the fetch stage of the processor pipeline is fed from the IPB, but the Am29050 can by–pass the fetch stage and feed the first instruction directly into the decode pipeline stage using the instruction forwarding technique. By–passing also enables up to four cycles of external memory latency to be hidden when a BTC hit occurs (see section 1.10).

The Am29050 incorporates a Translation Look–Aside Buffer (TLB) for Memory Management Unit support, just like the Am29000 processor. However it also has two region mapping registers. These permit large areas of memory to be mapped without using up the *smaller* TLB entries. They are very useful for mapping large data memory regions, and their use reduces the TLB software management overhead.

The processor can also speed up data memory accesses by making the access address available a cycle earlier than the Am29000. The method is used to reduce memory load operations which have a greater influence on pipeline stalling than store operations. Normally the address of a load appears on the address bus at the start of the cycle following the execution of the load instruction. If virtual addressing is in use, then the TLB registers are used to perform address translation during the second half of the load execute–cycle. To save a cycle, the Am29050 must make the physical address of the load available at the start of the load instruction execution. It has two ways of doing this.

The access address of a load instruction is specified by the RB field of the instruction (see Figure 1–13, page 41). A 4–entry Physical Address Cache (PAC) memory is used to store most recent load addresses. The cache entries are tagged with RB field register numbers. When a load instruction enters the decode stage of the pipeline, the RB field is compared with one of the PAC entries, using a direct mapping technique, with the lower 2–bits of the register number being used to select the PAC entry. When a match occurs the PAC supplies the address of the load, thus avoiding the delay of reading the register file to obtain the address from the register selected by the RB field of the LOAD instruction. If a PAC miss occurs, the new physical address is written to the appropriate PAC entry. The user has no means of controlling the PAC; its operation is completely determined by the processor hardware.

The second method used by the Am29050 processor to reduce the effect of pipeline stalling occurring as a result of memory load latency is the Early Address Generator (EAG). Load addresses are frequently formed by preceding the load with CONST, CONSTH and ADD type instructions. These instructions prepare a general purpose register with the address about to be used during the load. The EAG circuitry continually generates addresses formed by the use of the above instructions in the hope that a load instruction will immediately follow and use the address newly formed by the preceding instructions. The EAG must make use of the TLB address translation hardware in order to make the physical address available at the start of the load instruction. This happens when, fortunately, the RB field of the load instruction matches with the destination register of the previous address computation instructions.

Software debugging is better supported on the Am29050 processor than on any other current 29K family member. All 29K processors have a trace facility which enables single stepping of processor instructions. However, prior to the Am29050 processor, tracing did not apply to the processor operation while the DA bit (disable all traps and interrupts) was set in the current processor status (CPS) register. The DA bit is typically set while the processor is operating in Freeze mode (FZ bit set in the CPS register). Freeze mode code is used during the entry and exit of interrupt and trap handlers, as well as other critical system support code. The introduction of Monitor mode operation with the Am29050 enables tracing to be extended to Freeze mode code debugging. The processor enters Monitor mode when a synchronous trap occurs while the DA bit is set. The processor is equipped with a second set of PC buffer registers, known as the shadow PC registers, which record the PC–bus activity while the processor is operating in Monitor mode. The first set of PC buffer registers have their values frozen when Freeze mode is entered.

The addition of two hardware breakpoint registers aids the Am29050 debug support. As instructions move into the execute stage of the processor pipeline, the instruction address is compared with the break address values. The processor takes a trap when a match occurs. Software debug tools, such as monitors like Mini-MON29K, used with other 29K family members, typically use illegal instructions to implement breakpoints. The use of breakpoint registers has a number of advantages over this technique. Breakpoints can be placed in read–only memories, and break addresses need not be physical but virtual, tagged with the per–process identifier.

1.5   THE Am29030 2–BUS MICROPROCESSOR

The Am29030™ processor is pin compatible with other 2–bus members of the family (see Table 1-2) [AMD 1991b]. It was the first member of the 2–bus family introduced in 1991. Higher device construction densities enable it to offer high performance with a simplified system interface design. From a software point of view the main differences between it and the Am29000 processor occur as a result of replacing the Branch Target Cache (BTC) memory with 8k bytes of instruction cache, and connecting the instruction and data busses together on–chip. However, the system interface busses have gained a number of important new capabilities.

Table 1-2.   Pin Compatible 2–bus 29K Family Processors

Processor	Am29030	Am29035
instruction Cache	8K bytes	4K bytes
Cache Associativity	2 Way	Direct Mapped
On–Chip Floating–Point	No	No
On–Chip MMU	Yes	Yes
Half Speed External Bus	Yes	Yes
Narrow Memory Reads	Yes 8/16 bit	Yes 8/16 bit
Programmable Bus Sizing	No	Yes 16/32 bit
On–Chip Interrupt Controller Input's	Yes 6	Yes 6
Clock Speeds (MHz)	25,33	16

The inclusion of an instruction cache memory reduces off–chip instruction memory access bandwidth requirements. This enables instructions to be fetched via the same device pins used by the data bus. Only when instructions can not be supplied by the cache is there contention for access to external memory. Research [Hill 1987] has shown that with cache sizes above 4k bytes, a conventional instruction cache is more effective than a BTC. At these cache sizes the bandwith requirements are sufficiently reduced as to make a shared instruction/data bus practicable.

Each cache entry (known as a block) contains four consecutive instructions, They are tagged in a similar manner to the BTC mechanism of the Am29000 processor. This allows cache entries to be used for both User mode and Supervisor mode code at the same time, and entries to remain valid during application system calls and system interrupt handlers. However, since entries are not tagged with per–process identifiers, the cache entries must be invalidated when a task context switch occurs. The cache is 2–way set associative. The 4k bytes of instruction cache provided by each set results in 256 entries per set (each entry being four instructions, i.e. 16 bytes).

When a branch instruction is executed and the block containing the target instruction sequence is not found in the cache, the processor fetches the missing block and marks it valid. Complete blocks are always fetched, even if the target instruction lies at the *end* of the block. However, the cache forwards instructions to the decoder without waiting for the block to be reloaded. If the cache is not disabled and the block to be replaced in the cache is not valid and locked, then the fetched block is placed in the cache. The 2–way cache associativity provides two possible cache blocks for storing any selected memory block. When a cache miss occurs, and both associated blocks are valid but not locked, a block is chosen at random for replacement.

Locking valid blocks into the cache is not provided for on a per–block basis but in terms of the complete cache or one set of the two sets. When a set is locked, valid blocks are not replaced; invalid blocks will be replaced and marked valid and locked. Cache locking can be used to preload the cache with instruction sequences critical to performance. However, it is often difficult to use cache locking in a way that can out–perform the supported random replacement algorithm.

The processor supports Scalable Clocking which enables the processor to operate at the same or twice the speed of the off–chip memory system. A 33MHz processor could be built around a 20MHz memory system, and depending on cache utilization there may be little drop–off in performance compared to having constructed a 33MHz memory system. This provides for higher system performance without increasing memory system costs or design complexity. Additionally, a performance upgrade path is provided for systems which were originally built to operate at lower speeds. The processor need merely be replaced by a pin–compatible higher frequency device (at higher cost) to realize improved system performance.

Memory system design is further simplified by enforcing a 2–cycle minimum access time for data and instruction accesses. Even if 1–cycle burst–mode is supported by a memory system, the first access in the burst is hardwired by the processor to take 2–cycles. This is effective in relaxing memory system timing constraints and generally appreciated by memory system designers. The high frequency operation of the Am29030 processor can easily result in electrical noise [AMD1992c]. Enforcing 2–cycle minimum access times ensures that the address bus has more time to settle before the data bus is driven. This reduces system noise compared with the data bus changing state during the same cycle as the address bus.

At high processor clock rates, it is likely that an interleafed memory system will be required to obtain bandwidths able to sustain 1–cycle burst mode access. Interleafing requires the construction of two, four or more memory systems (known as banks), which are used in sequence. When accessed in burst–mode, each bank is given more time to provide access to its next storage location. The processor provides an input pin, EARLYA (early address), by which a memory system can request early address generation by the processor. This can be used to simplify the implementation of interleaved memory systems. When requested, the processor provides early the address of even–addressed banks, allowing the memory system to begin early accesses to both even– and odd–addressed banks.

The processor can operate with memory devices which are not the full 32–bit width of the data bus. This is achieved using the Narrow Read capability. Memory systems which are only 8–bit or 16–bit wide are connected to the upper bits of the data/instruction bus. They assert the RDN (read narrow) input pin along with the RDY (ready) pin when responding to access requests. When this occurs the processor will automatically perform the necessary sequences of accesses to assemble instructions or data which are bigger than the memory system width.

The Narrow Read ability can not be used for data writing. However, it is very useful for interfacing to ROM which contains system boot–up code. Only a single 8–bit ROM may be required to contain all the necessary system initialization code. This can greatly simplify system design, board space, and cost. The ROM can be used to initialize system RAM memory which, due to its 32–bit width, will permit faster execution.

1.5.1 Am29030 Evaluation.

AMD provides a low cost evaluation board for the Am29030 at 25MHz, known as the EZ030 (pronounced easy–030). Like the microcontroller evaluation board, it is a standalone, requiring an external 5v power supply and connection to a remote computer via an RS–232 connection. The board is very small, measuring about 4 inches by 4 inches (10x10 cm).

It contains 128k bytes of EPROM, which is accessed via 8–bit narrow bus protocol. There is also 1M byte of DRAM arranged as 256kx32 bits. The DRAM is expandable to 4M bytes. The EPROM is preprogrammed with the MiniMON29K debug monitor and the OS–boot operating system described in Chapter 7.

1.5.2 The Am29035

The Am29035™ processor is pin compatible with other 2–bus members of the family (see Table 1-2). As would be expected, given the AMD product number, its operation is very similar to the Am29030 processor. It is only available at lower clock frequencies, compared with its close relative. And with half the amount of instruction cache memory, it contains one set of the two sets provided by the

Am29030. That is, it has 4k bytes of instruction memory cache which is directly mapped. Consequently it can be expected to operate with reduced overall performance.

In all other aspects it is the same as the Am29030 processor, except it has Programmable Bus Sizing which the Am29030 processor does not. Programmable Bus Sizing provides for lower cost system designs. The processor can be dynamically programmed (via the configuration register) to operate with a 16–bit instruction/data bus, performing both read and write operations. When the option is selected, 32–bit data is accessed by the processor hardware automatically performing two consecutive accesses. The ability to operate with 16–bit and 32–bit memory systems makes the 2–bus 29K family members well suited to scalable system designs, in terms of cost and performance.

1.6 THE Am29200 MICROCONTROLLER

The Am29200™ was the first of the 29K family microcontrollers (see Table 1-3) [AMD 1992b]. To date the Am29205™ is the only other microcontroller added to the family. Being microcontrollers, many of the device pins are assigned I/O and other dedicated support tasks which reduce system glue logic requirements. For this reason none of the devices are pin compatible. The system support facilities, included within the Am29200 package, make it ideal for many highly integrated and low cost systems.

The processor supports a 32–bit address space which is divided into a number of dedicated regions (see Figure 1-5). This means that ROM, for example, can only be located in the region preallocated for ROM access. When an address value is generated, the associated control–logic for the region is activated and used to control data or instruction access for the region.

There is a 32–bit data bus and a separate 24–bit address bus. The rest of the 140 pins used by the device are mainly for I/O and external peripheral control tasks associated with each of the separate address regions.

By incorporating memory interface logic within the chip, the processor enables lower system costs and simplified designs. In fact, DRAM devices can be wired directly to the microcontroller without the need for any additional circuitry.

At the core of the microcontroller is an Am29000 processor. The additional I/O devices and region control mechanisms supported by the chip are operated by programmable *registers* located in the *control register region* of memory space.

Accessing memory or peripherals located in each address region is achieved with a dedicated region controller. While initializing the control registers for each region it is possible to specify the access times and, say, the DRAM refresh requirements for memory devices located in the associated region.

Other peripheral devices incorporated in the microcontroller, such as the UART, are accessed by specific control registers. The inclusion of popular peripher-

Table 1-3. *Micorcontroller Members of 29K Processor Family*

Processor	Am29200	Am29205
instruction Cache	No	No
Cache Associativity	N/A	N/A
On–Chip Floating–Point	No	No
On–Chip MMU	No	No
Half Speed External Bus	No	No
Data/Instruction Bus Width	32 bit	16 bit
Programmable I/O	16 pins	8 pins
ROM width DRAM width	8/16/32 bit 16/32 bit	16 bit 16 bit
On–Chip Interrupt Controller Inputs	Yes 14	Yes 10
Clock Speeds (MHz)	16.7	16.7

al devices and the associated *glue* logic for peripheral and memory interfaces within a single RISC chip, enables higher performance at lower costs than existing systems (see Figure 1-6). Let's take a quick look at each of the region controllers and specialized on–chip peripherals in turn.

1.6.1 ROM Region

First thing to realize is that ROM space is really intended for all types of ROM and SRAM devices. Controlling access to these types of memories is very similar. The region is divided into four *banks*. Each bank is individually configurable in width and timing characteristics. A bank can be associated with 8–bit, 16–bit or 32–bit memory and can contain as much as 16M bytes of memory (enabling a 64M bytes ROM region).

Bank 0, the first bank, is normally attached to ROM memory as code execution after processor reset starts at address 0. The SA29200 evaluation board contains an 8–bit EPROM at bank 0. Other banks may contain, say, 32–bit SRAM with different wait state requirements. It is possible to arrange banks to form a contiguous address range.

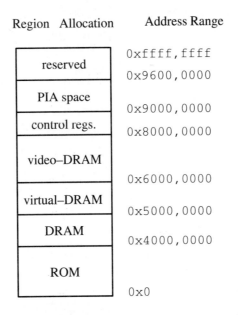

Region   Allocation   Address Range

Region	Address Range
reserved	0xffff,ffff
	0x9600,0000
PIA space	0x9000,0000
control regs.	0x8000,0000
video–DRAM	0x6000,0000
virtual–DRAM	0x5000,0000
DRAM	0x4000,0000
ROM	0x0

Figure 1-5.   Am29200 Microcontroller Address Space Regions

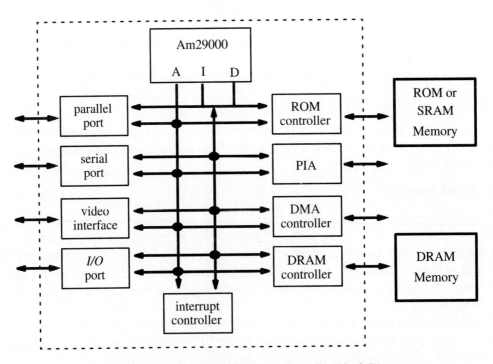

Figure 1-6.   Am29200 Microcontroller Block Diagram

Whenever memory in the ROM address range is accessed, the controller for the region is activated and the required memory chip control signals such as CE (chip enable), R/W, OE (output enable) and others are generated by the microcontroller. Thus SRAM and EPROM devices are wired directly to pins on the microcontrol chip.

1.6.2 DRAM Region

In a way similar to the ROM region, there is a dedicated controller for DRAM devices which are restricted to being located in the DRAM address region. Once again the region is divided into four banks which may each contain as much as 16M bytes of off–chip memory. The DRAM region controller supports 16–bit or 32–bit wide memory banks which may be arranged to appear as contiguous in address range.

DRAM, unlike ROM, is assumed to have 4–cycle access times. However, if page–mode DRAM is used it is possible to achieve 2–cycle rather than 4–cycle burst–mode accesses. Burst–mode is used when consecutive memory addresses are being accessed, such as during instruction fetching between program branches.

The control register associated with each DRAM bank, maintains a field for DRAM refresh support. This field indicates the number of processor cycles between DRAM refresh. If refresh is not disabled, "CAS before RAS" cycles are performed when required. Refresh is overlapped in the background with non–DRAM access when possible.

If a DRAM bank contains video–DRAM rather than conventional DRAM, then it is possible to perform data transfer to the VDRAM shift register via accesses in the VDRAM address range. The VDRAM is aliased over the DRAM region. Accessing the memory as VDRAM only changes the timing of memory control signals such as to indicate a video shift register transfer is to take place rather than a CPU memory access.

1.6.3 Virtual DRAM Region

A 16–Mbyte (24 address bit) virtual address space is supported via four mapping registers. The virtually addressed memory is divided into 64K byte (16 address bits) memory pages which are mapped into physical DRAM. Each mapping register has two 8–bit fields specifying the upper address bits of the mapped memory pages. When memory is accessed in the virtual address space range, and one of the four mapping registers contains a match for the virtually address page being accessed, then the access is redirected to the physical DRAM page indicated by the mapping register.

When no mapping register contains a currently valid address translation for the required virtual address, a processor trap occurs. In this case memory management support software normally updates one of the mapping registers with a valid mapping and normal program execution is restarted.

Only DRAM can be mapped into the virtual address space. The address region supports functions such as image compression and decompression that yield lower overall memory requirements and, thus, lower system costs. Images can be stored in virtually addressed space in a compressed form, and only uncompressed into physically accessed memory when required for image manipulation or output video imaging.

1.6.4 PIA Region

The Peripheral Interface Adapter (PIA) region is divided into six banks, each of 24–bit address space. Each bank can be directly attached to a peripheral device. The control registers associated with the region give extra flexibility in specifying the timing for signal pins connecting the microcontroller and PIA peripherals. The PIA device–enable and control signals are again provided on–chip rather than in external support circuitry.

When *external* DMA is utilized, transfer of data is always between DRAM and PIA space. More on DMA follows.

1.6.5 DMA Controller

When an off–chip device wishes to gain access to the microcontroller DRAM, it makes use of the Direct Memory Access (DMA) Controller. On–chip peripherals can also perform DMA transfers; this is referred to as internal DMA. DMA is initiated by an external or internally generated peripheral DMA request.

The only internal peripherals which can generate DMA requests are the parallel port, the serial port and the video interface. These three devices are described shortly. There are two external DMA request pins, one for each of the two on–chip DMA control units. Internal peripherals have a control register field which specifies which DMA controller their DMA request relates to.

The DMA controllers must be initialized by software before data transfer from, or to, DRAM takes place. The associated control registers specify the DRAM start address and the number of transfers to take place. Once the DMA control registers have been prepared, a DMA transfer will commence immediately upon request with–out any further CPU intervention. Once the DMA transfer is complete the DMA controller may generate an interrupt. The processor may then refresh the DMA control unit parameters for the next expected DMA transfer.

One of the DMA control units has the special feature of having a duplicate set of DMA parameter registers. At the end of a DMA transfer, when the primary set of DMA parameter registers have been exhausted, the duplicate set is immediately copied into the primary set. This means the DMA unit is instantly refreshed and prepared for a further DMA request. Ordinarily the DMA unit is not ready for further use until the support software has executed, usually via an end of DMA interrupt request. Just such an interrupt may be generated but it will now be concerned with preparing parameters for the duplicate control registers for the one–after–next DMA request. This DMA queue technique is very useful when DMA transfers are occurring to the video controller. In such case DMA can not be postponed as video imaging requirements mean data must be available if image distortion is to be avoided.

External DMA can only occur between DRAM and two of the six PIA address space banks. DMA only supports an 8–bit address field within a PIA address bank.

One further note on DMA, the microcontroller does support an external DMA controller; enabling random access by the external DMA device to DRAM and ROM. The external DMA unit must activate the associated control pins and place the address on the microcontroller address bus. In conjunction with the microcontroller, the external DMA unit must complete the single 32–bit data access.

1.6.6 16–bit I/O Port

The I/O port supports bit programmable access to 16 input or output pins. These pins can also be used to generate level sensitive or edge sensitive interrupts. When used as outputs, they can be actively driven or used in open collector mode.

1.6.7 Parallel Port

The parallel port is intended for connecting the microcontroller chip to a host processor, where the controller acts as an intelligent high performance control unit. Data can be transferred in both directions, either via software controlled 8–bit or 32–bit data words, or via DMA unit control. Once again the associated control registers give the programmer flexibility in specifying the timing requirements for connecting the parallel port directly to the host processor.

1.6.8 Serial Port

The on–chip serial port supports high speed full duplex, bi–directional data transfer using the RS–232 protocol. The serial port can be used in an polled or interrupted driven mode. Alternatively, it may request DMA access. The lightweight interrupt structure of the Am29000 processor core, coupled with the smart on–chip peripherals, presents the software engineer with a wide range of options for controlling the serial port.

1.6.9 I/O Video Interface

The video interface provides direct connection to a number of laser–beam marking engines. It may also be used to receive data from a raster input device such as a scanner or to serialize/deserialize a data stream. It is possible with external circuitry support that a noninterleaved composite TV video signal could be generated.

The video shift register clock must be supplied on an asynchronous input pin, which may be tied to the processor clock. (Note, a video image is built by serially clocking the data in the shift register out to the imaging hardware. When the shift register is empty it must be quickly refilled before the next shift clock occurs.) The imaged page may be synchronized to an external page–sync signal. Horizontal and vertical image margins as well as image scan rates are all programmable via the now familiar on–chip control register method.

The video shift registers are duplicated, much like some of the DMA control registers. This reduces the need for rapped software response to maintain video shift register update. When building an image, the shift register is updated from the duplicate support register. Software, possibly activated via a video–register–empty interrupt, must fill the duplicate shift register before it becomes used–up. Alternatively, the video data register can be maintained by the DMA controller without the need for frequent CPU intervention.

1.6.10 The SA29200 Evaluation Board

The SA29200 is an inexpensive software development board utilizing the Am29200 microcontroller. Only a 5v supply and a serial cable connection to a host computer are required to enable board operation. Included on the board is an 8–bit wide EPROM (128Kx8) which contains the MiniMON29K debug monitor and the OS–boot operating system. There is also 1M byte of 32–bit DRAM (256Kx32) into which programs can be loaded via the on–chip UART. The processor clock rate is 16M Hz and the DRAM operates with 4–cycle initial access and 2–cycle subsequent burst accesses. So, although the performance is good, it is not as high as other members of the 29K family.

The SA29200 board measures about 3 by 3.5 inches (10x9 cm) and has connections along both sides which enable attachment to an optional hardware prototyping board (see following section). This extension board has additional I/O interface devices and a small wire–wrap area for inclusion of application specific hardware.

1.6.11 The Prototype Board

The prototying board is inexpensive because it contains mainly sockets, which can support additional memory devices, and a predrilled wire–wrap area. The RISC microcontroller signals are made available on the prototyping board pins. Some of these signals are routed to the empty memory sockets so as to enable simple memory expansions for 8–bit, 16–bit or 32–bit EPROM or SRAM. There is also space for up to 16M bytes of 32–bit DRAM.

Using the wire–wrap area the microcontroller I/O signals can be connected to devices supporting specific application tasks, such as A/D conversion or peripheral control. This make the board ideal for a student project. Additionally, the access times for memory devices are programmable, thus enabling the effects of memory performance on overall system operation to be evaluated.

1.6.12 Am29200 Evaluation

The Combination of the GNU tool chain and the low cost SA29200 evaluation board, and associated prototping board, makes available an evaluation environment for the industry's leading embedded RISC. The cost of getting started with embedded RISC is very low and additional high performance products can be selectively purchased from specialized tool builders. The evaluation package should be of particular interest to university undergraduate and post–graduate courses studying RISC.

1.6.13 The Am29205 Microcontroller

The Am29205 is a microcontroller member of the 29K family (see Table 1-3). It is functionally very similar to the Am29200 microcontroller. It differs as a result of reduced system interface specifications. This reduction enables a lower device pin–count and packaging cost. The Am29205 is available in a 100–lead Plastic Quad Flat Pack (PQFP) package. It is suitable for use in price sensitive systems which can operate with the somewhat reduced on–chip support circuitry.

The reduction in pin count results in a 16–bit data/instruction bus. The processor generates two consecutive memory requests to access instructions and data larger than 16–bits. The memory system interface has also been simplified in other ways. Only 16–bit transfers to memory are provided for; no 8–bit ROM banks are supported. The parallel port, DMA controller, and PIA, also now support transfers limited to the 16–bit data width.

Generally the number of service support pins such as: programmable Input/Output pins (now 8, 16 for the Am29200 processor); serial communication handshake signals DTR, DSR; DMA request signals; interrupt request pins; and number of decoded PIA and memory banks, have all been reduced. The signal pins supporting video–DRAM and burst–mode ROM access have also been omitted. These omissions do not greatly restrict the suitability of the Am29205 microcontroller for many projects. The need to make two memory accesses to fetch instructions, which are not supported by an on–chip cache memory, will result in reduced performance. However, many embedded systems do not require the full speed performance of a 32–bit RISC processor.

AMD provides a low cost evaluation board known as the SA29205. The board is standalone and very like the SA29200 evaluation board; in fact, it will fit with the same prototype expansion board used by the SA29200. It is provided with a 256k byte EPROM, organized as 128kx16 bits. The EPROM memory is socket upgradable to 1M byte. There is 512K byte of 16–bit wide DRAM. For debugging purposes, it can use the MiniMON29K debug monitor utilizing the on–chip serial port.

1.7   REGISTER AND MEMORY SPACE

Most of the 29K instructions operate on information held in various processor registers. Load and store type instructions are available for moving data between external memory and processor registers. Members of the 29K family generally support registers in three independent register regions which make up the 29K register space. These regions are the General Purpose registers, Translation Look–Aside (TLB) registers, and Special Purpose registers. Members of the 29K family which do not support Memory Management Unit operation, do not have TLB registers implemented.

There are currently two *core* processors within the 29K family, the Am29000 and the Am29050. Other processors are generally derived from one of these core processors. For example, the Am29030 has an Am29000 at its core, with additional silicon area being used to implement instruction cache memory and a 2–bus processor interface. The differences between the core processors and their derivatives is reflected in expansions to the special register space.

However, the special register space does appear uniform through out the 29K family. Generally only those concerned with generating operating system support code are concerned with the details of the special register space. AMD has specified a subset of special registers which are supported on all 29K family processors. This aids in the development and porting of Supervisor mode code.

The core processors support a 3–bus Harvard Architecture, with instructions and data being held in separate external memory systems. There is one 32–bit bus each for the two memory systems and a shared 32–bit address bus. Other RISC chips have a 4–bus system, where there is an address bus for each of the two memory systems. This avoids the contention for use of a shared address bus. Unfortunately, it also results in increased pin–count and, consequently, processor cost. The 29K 3–bus processors avoid conflicts for the address bus by supporting burst mode addressing and a large number of on–chip registers. It has been estimated that the Am29000 processor losses only 5% performance as a result of the shared address bus.

All instruction fetches are directed to instruction memory; data accesses are directed to data memory. These two externally accessible spaces constitute two of the four external access spaces. The other two are the ROM space and the coprocessor space. The ROM space is accessed via the instruction bus. Like the instruction space it covers a 2^{32} range.

1.7.1 General Purpose Registers

All members of the family have general purpose registers which are made up from 128 *local* registers and more than 64 *global* registers (see Figure 1-7). These registers are the primary source and destination for most 29K instructions. Instructions have three 8–bit operand fields which are used to supply the addresses of general registers. All User mode executable instructions and code produced by high level language compilers, are restricted to only directly assessing general purpose registers. The fact that these registers are all 32–bit and that there is a large number of them, vis–a–vis CISC, reduces the need to access data held in external memory.

General purpose registers are implemented by a multiport register file. This file has a minimum of three access ports, the Am29050 processor has an additional port for writing–back floating–point results. Two of the three ports provide simultaneous read access to the register file; the third port is for updating a register value. Instructions generally specify two general purpose register operands which are to be operated on. After these operands have been presented to the execution unit, the result of the operation is made available in the following cycle. This allows the result of an integer operation to be written back to the selected general purpose register in the cycle following its execution. At any instant, the current cycle is used to write–back the result of the previous computation.

The Am29050 can execute floating–point operations in parallel with integer operations. The latency of floating–point instructions can be more than the 1–cycle achieved by the integer operation unit. Floating–point results are written back, when the operation is complete, via their own write–back port, without disrupting the integer units ability to write results into the general purpose register file.

Global Registers

The 8–bit operand addressing fields enable only the lowcr 128 of the possible 256 address values to be used for *direct* general purpose register addressing. This is because the most significant address bit is used to select a register base–plus–offset addressing mode. When the most significant bit is zero, the accessed registers are known as Global Registers. Only the upper 64 of the global registers are implemented in the register file. These registers are known as *gr64–gr127*. Some of the lower address–value global registers are assigned special support tasks and are not really general purpose registers.

The Am29050 processor supports a condition code accumulator with global registers *gr2* and *gr3*. The accumulator can be used to concatenate the result of several Boolean comparison operations into a single condition code. Later the accumulated condition can be quickly tested. These registers are little used and on the whole other, more efficient, techniques can be found in preference to their use.

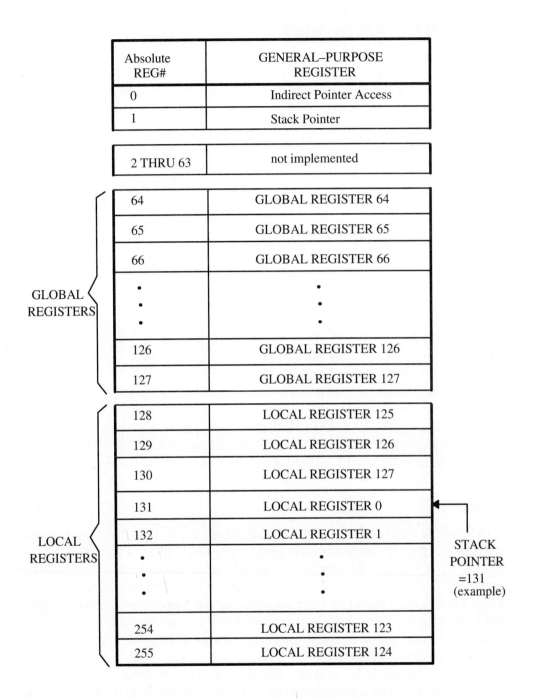

Absolute REG#	GENERAL–PURPOSE REGISTER
0	Indirect Pointer Access
1	Stack Pointer

2 THRU 63	not implemented

GLOBAL REGISTERS

64	GLOBAL REGISTER 64
65	GLOBAL REGISTER 65
66	GLOBAL REGISTER 66
• • •	• • •
126	GLOBAL REGISTER 126
127	GLOBAL REGISTER 127

LOCAL REGISTERS

128	LOCAL REGISTER 125
129	LOCAL REGISTER 126
130	LOCAL REGISTER 127
131	LOCAL REGISTER 0
132	LOCAL REGISTER 1
• • •	• • •
254	LOCAL REGISTER 123
255	LOCAL REGISTER 124

STACK POINTER =131 (example)

Figure 1-7. General Purpose Register Space

Local Registers

When the most significant address bit is set, the upper 128 registers in the general purpose register file are accessed. The lower 7–bits of the address are used as an offset to a base register which *points* into the 128 registers. These general purpose registers are known as the Local Registers. The base register is located at the global register address *gr1*. If the addition of the 7–bit operand address value and the register base value produces a results too big to be contained in the 7–bit local register address space, the result is rounded modulo–128. When producing a general purpose register address from a local register address, the most significant bit of the general purpose register address value is always set.

The local register base address can be read by accessing global register *gr1*. However, the base register is actually a register which shadows global register *gr1*. The shadow support circuitry requires that the base be written via an ALU operation producing a result destined for *gr1*. This also requires that a one cycle delay follow the setting of the base register and any reference to local registers.

Global register address *gr0* also has a special meaning. Each of the three operand fields has an indirect pointer register located in the special register space. When address *gr0* is used in an operand field, the indirect pointer is used to access a general purpose register for the associated operand. Each of the three indirect pointers has an 8–bit field and can point anywhere in the general purpose register space. When indirect pointers are used, there is no distinction made between global and local registers.

All of the general purpose registers are accessible to the processor while executing in User mode unless register bank protection is applied. General purpose registers starting with *gr64* are divided into groups of 16 registers. Each group can have access restricted to the processor operating in Supervisor mode only. The AMD high level language calling convention specifies that global registers *gr64–gr95* be reserved for operating system support tasks. For this reason it is normal to see the special register used to support register banking set to disable User mode access to global registers *gr64–gr95*.

1.7.2 Special Purpose Registers

Special purpose register space is used to contain registers which are not accessed directly by high level languages. Registers such as the program counter and the interrupt vector table base pointer are located in special register space. Normally these registers are accessed by operating system code or assembly language *helper* routines. Special registers can only be accessed by move–to and move–from type instructions; except for the move–to–immediate case. This requires the use of a general purpose register when communicating with special register space. It is worth noting that move–to special register instructions are among a small group of instructions which cause processor serialization. That is, all outstanding operations, such as

---

overlapping load or store instructions, are completed before the serializing instruction commences.

Special register space is divided into two regions (see Figure 1-8). Those registers whose address is below *sr128* can only be accessed by the processor operating in Supervisor mode. Different members of the 29K family have extensions to the global registers shown in Figure 1-8. However, special registers *sr0–sr14* are a subset which appear in all family members. Certain, generally lower cost, family members such as the Am29005 processor, which have no memory management unit, do not have the relevant MMU support registers (*sr13* and *sr14*). I shall first describe the restricted access, or protected, special registers. I shall not go into the exact bit–field operations in detail, for an expansion of field meanings see later chapters or the relevant processor User's Manual. The objective here is to provide a framework for better understanding the special register space.

Special registers are not generally known by their special register number. For example, the program counter buffer register PC1 is known as PC1 by assembly language programming tools rather than *sr11*.

Vector Area Base

Special register *sr0*, better known as VAB, is a pointer to the base of a table of address values. Each interrupt or trap is assigned a unique vector number. When an interrupt or trap exception is taken, the vector number is used to index the table of address values. The identified address value is read and used as the start address of the exception handling routine. Alternatively with 3–bus members of the 29K family, the vector table can contain 256 blocks of instructions. The VF bit (vector fetch) in the processor Configuration register (CFG) is used to select the vector table configuration. Each block is limited to 64 instructions, but via this method the interrupt handler can be reached faster as the start of, say, an interrupt handler need not be preceded by a fetch of the address of the handler. In practice the table of vectors to handlers, rather than handlers themself, is predominantly used due to the more efficient use of memory. For this reason the two later 2–bus members of the 29K family only support the table of vectors method; and the VF bit in the CFG register is reserved and effectively set.

The original Am29000 processor had a VAB register which required the base of the vector table to be aligned to a 64K byte address boundary. This could be inconvenient and lead to memory wastage. More recent family members provide for a 1k byte boundary. Because the 3–bus family members support instructions being located in Instruction space and ROM space (memory space is described in section 1.7.4), it is possible with these processors to specify that handler routines are in ROM space by setting the RV bit (ROM vector area) in the CFG register when the VF bit is zero. Or, when the more typical table of vectors method is being used by, setting bit–1 of the handler address. Since handler routines all start on 4–byte instruction boundaries, bits 0 and 1 of the vector address are not required to hold address infor-

Mnemonic

Protected Registers	
Vector Area Base Address	VAB
Old Processor Status	OPS
Current Processor Status	CPS
Configuration	CFG
Channel Address	CHA
Channel Data	CHD
Channel Control	CHC
Register Bank Protect	RBP
Timer Counter	TMC
Timer Reload	TMR
Program Counter 0	PC0
Program Counter 1	PC1
Program Counter 2	PC2
MMU Configuration	MMU
LRU Recommendation	LRU

Reg. No.: 0, 1, 2, 3, 4, 5, 6, 7, 8, 9, 10, 11, 12, 13, 14

Unprotected Registers	
Indirect Pointer C	IPC
Indirect Pointer A	IPA
Indirect Pointer B	IPB
Q	Q
ALU Status	ALU
Byte pointer	BP
Funnel Shift Count	FC
Load/Store Count Remaining	CR

Reg. No.: 128, 129, 130, 131, 132, 133, 134, 135

Floating–Point Environment	FPE
Integer Environment	INTE
Floating–Point Status	FPS

Reg. No.: 160, 161, 162

Figure 1-8. Special Purpose Register Space for the Am29000 Mircoprocessor

mation. The 2–bus and microcontroller members of the 29K family do not support ROM space and RV bit in the CFG registers is reserved.

Processor Status

Two special registers, *sr1* and *sr2*, are provide for processor status reporting and control. The two registers OPS (old processor status) and CPS (current processor status) have the same bit–field format. Each bit position has been assigned a unique task. Some bit positions are not effective with particular family members. For example, the Am29030 processor does not use bit position 15 (CA). This bit is used to indicate coprocessor activity. Only the 3–bus family members support coprocessor operation in this way.

The CPS register reports and controls current processor operation. Supervisor mode code is often involved with manipulating this register as it controls the enabling and disabling of interrupts and address translation. When a program execution exception is taken, or an external event such as an interrupt occurs, the CPS register value is copied to the OPS register and the processor modifies the CPS register to enter Supervisor mode before execution continues in the selected exception handling routine. When returning from the handler routine, the interrupted program is restarted with an IRET type instruction. Execution of an IRET instruction causes the OPS register to be copied back to the CPS register, helping to restore the interrupted program context. Supervisor mode code often prepares OPS register contents before executing an IRET and starting User mode code execution.

Configuration

Special register *sr3*, known as the configuration control register (CFG), establishes the selected processor operation. Such options as big or little endian byte order, cache enabling, coprocessor enabling, and more are selected by the CFG setting. Normally this register value is established at processor boot–up time and is infrequently modified.

The original Am29000 (rev C and later) only used the first six bits of the CFG register for processor configuration. Later members of the family offer the selection of additional processor options, such as instruction memory cache and early address generation. Additional options are supported by extensions to the CFG bit–field assignment. Because there is no overlap with CFG bit–field assignment across the 29K family, and family members offer a matrix of functionality, there are often reserved bit–fields in the CFG register for any particular 29K processor.

The upper 8–bits of the CFG register are used for processor version and revision identification. The upper 3–bits of this field, known as the PRL (processor revision level) identify the processor. The Am29000 processor is identified by processor number 0, the Am29050 is processor number 1, and so on. The lower 5–bits of the PRL give the the revision level; a value of 3 indicates revision 'D'. The PRL field is read–only.

Data Access Channel

Three special registers, *sr4–sr6*, known as CHA (channel address), CHD (channel data) and CHC (channel control), are used to control and record all access to external data memory. Processors in the 29K family can perform data memory access in parallel with instruction execution. This offers a considerable performance boost, particularly where there is high data memory access latency. Parallel operation can only occur if the instruction pipeline can be kept *fed* from the: instruction prefetch buffer (IPB), instruction memory cache, or via separate paths to data and instruction memory (Harvard style 3–bus processors). It is an important task of a high level language compiler to schedule load and store instructions such that they can be successfully overlapped with other nondependent instructions.

When data memory access runs in parallel, its completion will occur some time after the instruction originally making the data access. In fact it could be several cycles after the original request, and it may not be possible to determine the original instruction. On many processors, keeping track of the original instruction is required in case the load or store operation does not complete for some reason. The original instruction is restarted after the interrupting complication has been dealt with. However, with the 29K family the original instruction is not restarted. All access to external memory is via the processor Data Channel. The three channel support registers are used to restart any interrupted load or store operation. Should an exception occur during data memory access, such as an address translation fault, memory access violation, or external interrupt, the channel registers are updated by the processor reporting the state of the in–progress memory access.

The channel control register (CHC) contains a number of bit–fields. The contents–valid bit (CV) indicates that the channel support registers currently describe a valid data access. The CV bit is normally seen set when a channel operation is interrupted. The ML bit indicates a load– or store–multiple operation is in progress. LOADM and STOREM instructions set this bit when commencing and clear it when complete. It is important to note that non–multiple LOAD and STORE instructions do not set or clear the ML bit. When a load– or store–multiple operation is interrupted and nested interrupt processing is supported, it is not sufficient to just clear the CV bit to temporary cancel the channel operation. If the ML bit was left set a subsequent load or store operation would become confused with a multiple type operation. The ML bit should be cleared along with the CV bit; this is best done by writing zero into the CHC register.

Integer operations complete in a single cycle, enabling the result of the previous integer operation to be written back to the general purpose register file in the current cycle. Because external memory reads are likely to take several cycles to complete, and pipeline stalling is to be avoided, the accessed data value is not written back to the global register file during the following instruction (the write–back cycle). This results in the load data being held by the processor until access to the write–back port is available. This is certain to occur during the execution of any future load or store instruction which itself can not make use of its *own* write–back cycle. The processor makes available via *load forwarding* circuitry the load data which awaits write–back to the register file.

Register Access Protection

Special register *sr7*, known as RBP (register bank protect), provides a means to restrict the access of general purpose register by programs executing in User mode. General purpose registers starting with *gr64* are divided into groups of 16 registers. When the corresponding bit in the RBP register is set, the associated bank of 16 registers is protected from User mode access. The RBP register is typically used to prevent User mode programs accessing Supervisor maintained information held in global registers *gr64–gr95*. These registers are reserved by the AMD high level language calling convention for system level information.

On–Chip Timer Control

Special registers *sr8* and *sr9*, known as TMC (timer counter) and TMR (timer reload value), support a 24–bit real–time clock. The TMC register decrements at the rate of the processor clock. When it reaches zero it will generate an interrupt if enabled. In conjunction with support software these two registers can be used to implement many of the functions often supported by off–chip timer circuitry.

Program Counter

A 29K processor contains a master and slave PC (program counter) address register. The master PC register contains the address of the instruction currently being fetched. The slave contains the next sequential instruction. Once an instruction flows into the execution unit, unless interrupted, the following instruction, currently in decode, will always flow into the execution unit. This is true for all instructions except for instructions such as IRET. Even if the instruction in execute is a jump–type, the following instruction known as the delay–slot instruction is executed before the jump is taken. This is known as delayed branching and can be very useful in hiding memory access latencies, as the processor pipeline can be kept busy executing the delay–slot instruction while the new instruction sequence is fetched. It is an important activity of high level language compilers to find useful instructions to place in delay–slot locations.

The master PC value flows along the PC–bus and the bus activity is recorded by the PC buffer registers, see Figure 1-9. There are three buffer registers arranged in sequence. These buffer registers are accessible within special registers space as *sr10–sr12*, better known as PC0, PC1 and PC2. The PC0 register contains the address of the instruction currently in decode; register PC1 contains the address of the instruction currently in execute; and PC2 the instruction now in write–back.

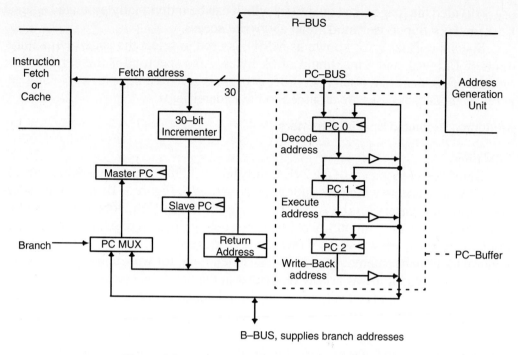

Figure 1-9. Am29000 Processor Program Counter

When a program exception occurs the PC–buffer registers become *frozen*. This is signified by the FZ bit in the current processor status register being set. When frozen, the PC–buffer registers accumulate no new PC–bus information. The frozen PC information can be used later to restart program execution. An IRET instruction causes the PC1 and PC0 register information to be copied to the master and slave PC registers and instruction fetching to commence. For this reason it is important to maintain both PC1 and PC0 values when dealing with such system level activities as nestcd interrupt servicing. Since the PC2 register records the address of a now executed instruction, maintenance of its value is less important; but it can play an important role in debugging

MMU control

The last of the generally available special registers are concerned with memory management unit (MMU) operation. Processors which have the Translation Look–Aside Buffer registers omitted will not have these two special registers. The operation of the MMU is quite complex, and Chapter 6 is fully dedicated to the description of its operation. Many computer professionals working in real–time projects may be unfamiliar with MMU operation. The MMU enables virtual addresses generated by the processor to be translated into physical memory addresses. Additionally, mem-

---

ory is divided into page sized quantities which can be individually protected against User mode or Supervisor mode read and write access.

Special register *sr13*, known as MMU, is used to select the page size; a minimum of 1k bytes, and a maximum of 8k bytes. Also specified is the current User mode process identifier. Each User mode process is given a unique identifier and Supervisor mode processes are assumed to have identifier 0.

Additional Protected Special Registers

Am29050

Some newer members of the 29K family have additional Supervisor only accessible special registers which are addressed above *sr14*. Figure 1-10 shows the additional special registers for the Am29050 processor. In the Am29050 case, the additional special registers support two functions: debugging and region mapping. Special register *sr15*, known as RSN (reason vector), records the trap number causing Monitor mode to be entered. Monitor mode extends the software debugging capability of the Am29050; it was briefly described in the previous section describing the processor features, and is dealt with in detail in later chapters. The shadow Program Counter registers constituted a second set of PC–buffer registers. They record the PC–bus activity and are used to support Monitor mode debugging The final extension to special register space, for debug purposes, is the inclusion of the breakpoint support registers. They facilitate the control of instruction access breakpoints.

Four special registers in the range *sr16–sr19* extend the virtual address mapping capabilities of the TLB registers. They support the mapping of two regions which are of programmable size. Their use reduces the demand placed on TLB registers to supply all of a systems address mapping and memory access protection requirements.

Am29030

Figure 1-11 shows the additional special registers for the Am29030 processor. There are only two additional registers, *sr29* and *sr30*, compared with the set of special registers supported by the Am29000. Note, these registers are located just above the additional special registers incorporated into the Am29050 processor. Both registers are used for communicating with the instruction memory cache supported by the Am29030 and Am29035 processors. Supervisor mode support code controls cache operation via the processor configuration register (CFG), and is not likely to make use of the cache interface registers. These registers may be used by debuggers and monitors to preload and examine cache memory contents.

User Mode Accessible Special Registers

Figure 1-8 showed the special register space with its two regions. The region addressed above *sr128* is always accessible; and below *sr128*, registers are only accessible to the processor when operating in Supervisor mode.

Special Purpose
Reg. No.   **Protected Registers**   Mnemonic

Reg. No.	Protected Registers	Mnemonic
15	Reason Vector	RSN
16	Region Mapping Address 0	RMA0
17	Region Mapping Control 0	RMC0
18	Region Mapping Address 1	RMA1
19	region Mapping Control 1	RMC1
20	Shadow Program Counter 0	SPC0
21	Shadow Program Counter 1	SPC1
22	Shadow Program Counter 2	SPC2
23	Instruction Breakpoint Address 0	IBA0
24	Instruction Breakpoint Control 0	IBC0
25	Instruction Breakpoint Address 0	IPA1
26	Instruction Breakpoint Control 0	IBC1

Figure 1-10. Additional Special Purpose Registers for the Am29050 Microprocessor

Special Purpose
Reg. No.   **Protected Registers**   Mnemonic

Reg. No.	Protected Registers	Mnemonic
29	Cache Interface Register	CIR
30	Cache Data Register	CDR

Figure 1-11. Additional Special Purpose Registers for the Am29030 Microprocessor

The original Am29000 processor defined a subset of User mode accessible registers, in fact those shown in Figure 1-8. Every 29K processor supports the use of these special registers, but, only the Am29050 has the full complement implemented.

Registers in the range *sr128–sr135* are always present. However, the three registers *sr160–sr162* are used to support floating–point and integer operations which are only directly supported on Am29050 processor hardware. All other 29K family members virtualize these three registers. When not available, an attempt to access

---

them causes a protection violation trap. The trap handler identifies the attempted operation and redirects the access to shadow copies of the *missing* registers. The accessor is unaware that the virtualization has occurred, accept for the delay in completing the requested operation. In practice, floating–point supporting special registers are not frequently accessed; except for the case of floating–point intensive systems which tend to be constructed around an Am29050 processor.

Indirect Pointers

Special registers *sr128–sr130*, better known as IPA, IPB and IPC, are the indirect pointers used to access the general purpose register file. For instructions which make use of the three operand fields, RA, RB and RC, to address general purpose registers, the indirect pointer can be used as an alternative operand address source. For example, the RA operand field supplies the register number for the source operand–A; if global register address *gr0* is used in the RA instruction field, then the operand register number is provided by the IPA register.

The IPA, IPB and IPC registers are pointers into the global register file. They are generally used to point to parameters passed to User mode helper routines. They are also used to support instruction emulation, where trap handler routines perform in software the *missing* instruction. The operands for the emulated instruction are passed to the trap handler via the indirect pointers.

ALU Support

Special registers *sr131–sr134* support arithmetic unit operation. Register *sr131*, better known as Q, is used during floating–point and integer multiply and divide steps. Only the Am29050 processor can perform floating–point operations directly, that is, without coprocessor or software emulation help. It is also the only processor which directly supports integer multiply. All other current members of the 29K family perform these operations in a sequence of steps which make use of the Q register.

The result of a comparison instruction is placed in a general purpose register, as well as in the condition field of the ALU status register (special register *sr132*). However, the ALU status register is not conveniently tested by such instructions as conditional branch. Branch decisions are made on the basis of True or False values held in general purpose registers. This makes a lot of sense, as contention for use of a single resource such as the ALU status register would lead to a resource conflict which would likely result in unwanted pipeline stalling.

The ALU status register controls and reports the operation of the processor integer operation unit. It is divided into a number of specialized fields which, in some cases, can be more conveniently accessed via special registers *sr134* and *sr135*. The *short hand* access provided by these additional registers avoids the read, shift and mask operations normally required before writing to bit–fields in the ALU register.

Data Access Channel

The three channel control registers, CHA, CHD and CHC, were previously described in the protected special registers section. However, User mode programs have a need to establish load– and store–multiple operations which are controlled by the channel support registers. Special register *sr135*, known as CR, provides a means for a User mode program to set the Count Remaining field of the protected CHC register. This field specifies the number of consecutive words transferred by the multiple data move operation. Should the operation be interrupted for any reason, the CR field reports the number of transfers yet to be completed. Channel operation is typically restarted (if enabled) when an IRET type instruction is issued.

Instruction Environment Registers

Special registers *sr160* and *sr162*, known as FPE and FPS, are the floating–point environment and status registers. The environment register is used by User mode programs to establish the required floating–point operations, such as, double– or single–precision, IEEE specification conformance, and exception trap enabling. The status register reports the outcome of floating–point operations. It is typically examined as a result of a floating–point operation exception occurring.

The integer environment is established by setting special register *sr161*, known as INTE. There are two control bits which separately enable integer and multiplication overflow exceptions. If exception detection is enabled, the processor will take an Out–of–Range trap when an overflow occurs.

Additional User Mode Special Registers

Am29050

The Am29050 has an additional special register, shown in Figure 1-12. Register *sr164*, known as EXOP, reports the instruction operation code causing a trap. It is used by floating–point instruction exceptions. Unlike other 29K processors the Am29050 directly executes all floating–point instructions. Exception traps can occur during these operations. When instruction emulation techniques are being used, it is an easy matter to determine the instruction being emulated at the time of the trap. However, with direct execution things are not as simple. The processor could examine the memory at the address indicated by the PC–buffer registers to determine the relevant instruction opcode. But the Am29050 supports a Harvard memory architecture and there is no path within the processor to access the instruction memory as if it were data. The EXOP register solves this problem. Whenever an exception trap is taken, the EXOP register reports the opcode of the instruction causing the exception.

Users of other 3–bus Harvard type processors such as the Am29000 and Am29005 should take note; virtualizing the unprotected special registers *sr160–162* requires that the instruction space be readable by the processor. This can only be achieved by connecting the instruction and data busses together (disabling the Har-

---

Special Purpose
Reg. No.

Unprotected Registers

Mnemonic

164	Exception Opcode

EXOP

Figure 1-12. Additional Special Purpose Register for the Am29050 Microprocessor

vard architecture advantages by creating a 2–bus system) or providing an off–chip bridge. This bridge must enable the address space to be reached from within some range of data memory space, at least for word–size read accesses, and, all be it, with additional access time penalties.

The Am29050 processor has an additional group of registers known as the floating–point accumulators. There are four 64–bit accumulators ACC3–0 which can be used with certain floating–point operations. They can hold double– or single–precision numbers. They are not special registers in the sense they lie in special register space. They are located in their own register space, giving the Am29050 one more register space than the normal three register spaces of the other 29K family members. However, like special registers, they can only be accessed by move–to and move–from accumulator type instructions.

Double–precision numbers (64–bit) can be moved between accumulators and general registers in a single cycle. Global registers are used in pairs for this operation. This is possible because the Am29050 processor is equipped with an additional 64–bit right–back port for floating point data, and the register file is implemented with a width of 64–bits.

1.7.3 Translation Look–Aside Registers

Although some 29K family members are equipped with region mapping registers, a Translation Look–Aside Buffer (TLB) technique is generally used to provide virtual to physical address translation. The TLB is two–way set associative and a total of 64 translations are cached in the TLB support registers.

The TLB registers form the basis for implementing a Memory Management Unit. The scheme for reloading TLB registers is not dictated by processor micorcode, but left to the programmer to organize. This enables a number of performance boosting schemes to be implemented with low overhead costs. However, it does place the burden of creating a TLB maintenance scheme on the user. Those used to having to work around a processor's microcode imposed scheme will appreciate the freedom.

TLB registers can only be accessed by move–to TLB and move–from TLB instructions executed by the processor operating in Supervisor mode. Each of the 64 translation entries requires a pair of TLB registers to fully describe the address translation and access permissions for the mapped page. Pages are programmable in size from 1k bytes to 8k bytes, and separate read, write and execute permissions can by enabled for User mode and Supervisor mode access to the mapped page.

There is only a single 32–bit virtual address space supported. This space is mapped to real instruction, data or I/O memory. Address translation is performed in a single cycle which is overlapped with other processor operations. This results in the use of an MMU not imposing any run–time performance penalties, except where TLB misses occur and the TLB cache has to be refilled. Each TLB entry is tagged with a per–process identifier, avoiding the need to flush TLB contents when a user–task context switch occurs. Chapter 6 fully describes the operation of the TLB.

1.7.4 External Address Space

The 3–bus members of the 29K family support five external 32–bit address spaces. They are:

- Data Memory — accessed via the data bus.

- Input/Output — also accessed via the data bus.

- Instruction — accessed via the instruction bus, normally read–only.

- ROM — also accessed via the instruction bus, normally read–only.

- Coprocessor — accessed via both data and address busses. Note, the address bus is only used for stores to coprocessor space. This enables 64–bit transfers during stores and 32–bit during loads.

The address bus is used for address information when accessing all address spaces except the coprocessor space. During load and store operations to coprocessor space, address information can be supplied in a limited way by the OPT2–0 field of the load and store instructions. Of course, with off–chip address decoding support, access to coprocessor space could always be made available via a region of I/O or data space. Coprocessors support off–chip extensions to a processor's execution unit(s). AMD has supplied only one coprocessor, which was for floating–point support, the Am29027. It is possible that a user could construct their own coprocessor for some specialized support task.

Earlier sections discussed the read–only nature of the instruction bus of 3–bus processors. Instructions are fetched along the instruction bus from either the ROM space or the Instruction space. Access to the two 32–bit spaces is distinguished by the IREQT processor pin. The state of this pin is determined by the RE (ROM enable) bit of the current processor status register (CPS). This bit can be set by software or via programmed event actions, such as trap processing. ROM space is intended for system level support code. Typically systems do not decode this pin and the two spaces are combined into one.

The Input/Output (I/O) space can be reached by setting the AS (address space) bit in load and store instructions. Transfers to I/O space, like coprocessor space and data space transfers, are indicated by the appropriate value appearing on the DREQT1–0 (data request type) processor pins. I/O space access is only convenient for assembly level routines. There is typically no convenient way for a high level language to indicate an access is to be performed to I/O space rather than data space. For this reason use of I/O space is often best avoided, unless it is restricted to accessing some Supervisor maintained peripheral which is best handled via assembly language code.

The 2–bus 29K family processors support a reduced number of off–chip address spaces. In fact, only two: Input/Output space, and a combined Instruction/Data memory space. Accessing both instructions and data via a shared instruction/data bus simplifies the memory system design. It can also simplify the software; for example, instruction space and data space can no longer overlap. Consider a 3–bus system which has physical memory located at address 0x10000 in instruction space and also different memory located at address 0x10000 in data space. Software errors can occur regarding accessing the correct memory for address 0x10000. It can also complicate system tasks such as virtual memory management, where separate free–page lists would have to be kept for the different types of memory.

The Translation Look–Aside buffer (TLB), used to support virtual memory addressing, supports separate enabling of data and instruction access via the R/W/X (read/write/execute) enable bits. However, permission checking is only performed after address translation is performed. It is not possible to have two valid virtual–to–physical address translations present in the TLB at the same time for the same virtual address, even if one physical address is for data space and the other instruction space. This complicates accessing overlapping address spaces via a single 32–bit virtual space.

Accessing virtual memory has similar characteristics to accessing memory via a high level language. For example, C normally supports a single address space. It is difficult and nonportable to have C code which can reach different address spaces. Except for instruction fetching, all off–chip memory accesses are via load and store type instructions. The OPT2–0 field for these instructions specifies the size of the data being transferred: byte, half–word or 32–bit. The compiler assigns OPT field values for all load and store instructions it generates. Unless via C language extensions or assembly code post–processing, there is no way to set the load and store instruction address–space–selecting options. Software is simplified by locating all external peripherals and memory in a single address space; or when a Harvard architecture is used, by not overlapping the regions of data and instruction memory spaces used.

1.8 INSTRUCTION FORMAT

All instructions for the Am29000 processor are 32 bits in length, and are divided into four fields, as shown in Figure 1-13. These fields have several alternative definitions, as discussed below. In certain instructions, one or more fields are not used, and are reserved for future use. Even though they have no effect on processor operation, bits in reserved fields should be 0 to insure compatibility with future processor versions.

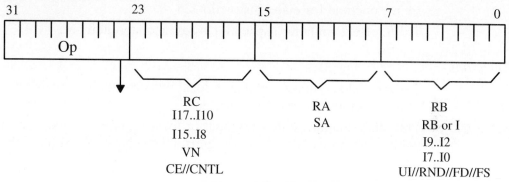

Figure 1-13. Instruction Format

The instruction fields are defined as follows:

BITS 31–24

Op   This field contains an operation code, defining the operation to be performed. In some instructions, the least–significant bit of the operation code selects between two possible operands. For this reason, the least–significant bit is sometimes labeled "A" or "M", with the following interpretations:

A   (Absolute) : The A bit is used to differentiate between Program–Counter relative (A = 0) and absolute (A = 1) instruction addresses, when these addresses appear within instructions.

M   (IMmediate) : The M bit selects between a register operand (M = 0) and an immediate operand (M = 1), when the alternative is allowed by an instruction.

BITS 23–16

RC   The RC field contains a global or local register–number, which is the destination operand for many instructions.

I17..I10   This field contains the most–significant 8 bits of a 16–bit instruction address. This is a word address, and may be Program–Counter relative or absolute, depending on the A bit of the operation code.

I15..I8	This field contains the most–significant 8 bits of a 16–bit instruction constant.
VN	This field contains an 8–bit trap vector number.
CE//CNTL	This field controls a load or store access.

BITS 15–8

RA	The RA field contains a global or local register–number, which is a source operand for many instructions.
SA	The SA field contains a special–purpose register–number.

BITS 7–0

RB	The RB field contains a global or local register–number, which is a source operand for many instructions.
RB or I	This field contains either a global or local register–number, or an 8–bit instruction constant, depending on the value of the M bit of the operation code.
I9..I2	This field contains the least–significant 8 bits of a 16–bit instruction address. This is a word address, and may be Program–Counter relative, or absolute, depending on the A bit of the operation code.
I7..I0	This field contains the least–significant 8 bits of a 16–bit instruction constant.

UI//RND//FD//FS

This field controls the operation of the CONVERT instruction.

The fields described above may appear in many combinations. However, certain combinations which appear frequently are shown in Figure 1-14.

1.9 KEEPING THE RISC PIPELINE BUSY

If the external interface of a microprocessor can not support an instructon fetch rate of one instruction per cycle, execution rates of one per cycle can not be sustained. As described in detail in Chapter 6, a 4–1 DRAM (4–cycle first access, 1–cycle subsaquent burst–mode access) memory system used with a 3–bus Am29000 processor, can sustain an average processing time per instruction of typically two cycles, not the desired 1–cycle per instruction. However, a 2–1 SRAM based system comes very close to this target. From these example systems it can be seen that even if a memory system can support 1–cycle burst–mode access, there are other factors which prevent the processor from sustaining single–cycle execution rates.

It is important to keep the processor pipeline busy doing usefull work. Pipeline stalling is a major source of lost processor performance. Stalling occurs as a result of:

Three operands, with possible 8–bit constant :

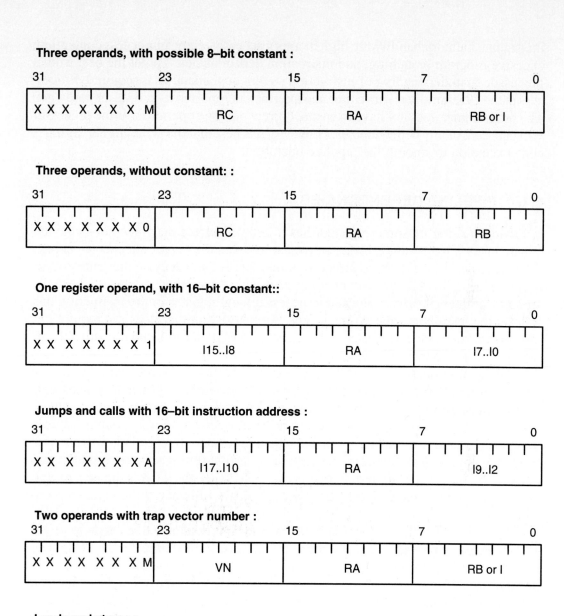

31	23	15	7	0
X X X X X X X M	RC	RA	RB or I

Three operands, without constant: :

31	23	15	7	0
X X X X X X X 0	RC	RA	RB

One register operand, with 16–bit constant::

31	23	15	7	0
X X X X X X X 1	I15..I8	RA	I7..I0

Jumps and calls with 16–bit instruction address :

31	23	15	7	0
X X X X X X X A	I17..I10	RA	I9..I2

Two operands with trap vector number :

31	23	15	7	0
X X X X X X X M	VN	RA	RB or I

Loads and stores :

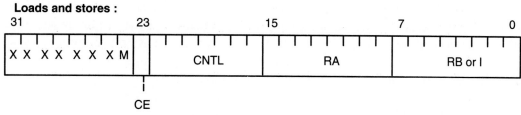

31	23	15	7	0
X X X X X X X M	CNTL	RA	RB or I

CE

Figure 1-14. Frequently Occurring Instruction–Field Uses

inadaquate memory bandwidth, high memory access latency, bus access contention, excesive program branching, and instruction dependancies. To get the best from a processor an understanding of instruction stream dependancies is required. Processors in the 29K familiy all have pipeline interlocks supported by processor hardware. The programmer does not have to ensure correct pipeline operation, as the processor will take care of any dependancies. However, it is best that the programmer arranges code execution to smooth the pipeline operation.

1.10   PIPELINE DEPENDENCIES

Modification of some registers has a delayed effect on processor behavior. When developing assembly code, care must be taken to prevent unexpected behavior. The easiest of the delayed effects to remember is the one cycle that must follow the use of an indirect pointer after having set it. This occurs most often with the register stack pointer. It cannot be used to access a local register in the instruction that follows the instruction that writes to *gr1*. An instruction that does not require *gr1* (and that means all local registers referenced via *gr1*) can be placed immediately after the instruction that updates *gr1*.

Direct modification of the Current Processor Status (CPS) register must also be done carefully. Particularly where the Freeze (FZ) bit is reset. When the processor is frozen, the special-purpose registers are not updated during instruction execution. This means that the PC1 register does not reflect the actual program counter value at the current execution address, but rather at the point where freeze mode was entered. When the processor is unfrozen, either by an interrupt return or direct modification of the CPS, two cycles are required before the PC1 register reflects the new execution address. Unless the CPS register is being modified directly, this creates no problem.

Consider the following examples. If the FZ bit is reset and trace enable (TE) is set at the same time, the next instruction should cause a trace trap, but the PC–buffer registers frozen by the trap will not have had time to catch up with the current execution address. Within the trap code the processor will have appeared to have stopped at some random address, held in PC1. If interrupts and traps are enabled at the same time as the FZ bit is cleared, then the next instruction may suffer an external interrupt or an illegal instruction trap. Once again, the PC–buffer register will not reflect the true execution address. An interrupt return would cause execution to commence at a random address. The above problems can be avoided by resetting FZ two cycles before enabling the processor to once again enter freeze mode.

Instruction Memory Latency

The Branch Target Cache (BTC), or the Instruction Memory Cache, can be used to remove the pipeline stalling that normally occurs when the processor executes a branch instruction. For the purpose of illustrating memory access latency, the effects of the BTC shall be illustrated. The address of a branch target appears on the address pins at the start of the write-back stage. Figure 1-15 shows the instruction flow through the pipeline stages, assuming the external instruction memory returns the target of a jump during the same cycle in which it was requested. This makes the Target instruction available at the fetch stage while the Delay instruction has to be stalled before it can enter the execute stage. In this case, execution is stalled for two cycles when the BTC is not used to supply the target instruction.

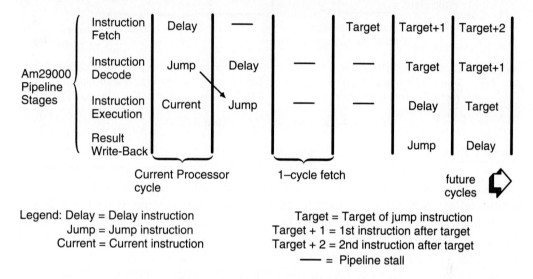

Figure 1-15. Pipeline Stages for BTC Miss

The address of the fetch is presented to the BTC hardware during the execute stage of the jump instruction, the same time the address is presented to the memory management unit. When a hit occurs, the target instruction is presented to the decode stage at the next cycle. This means no pipeline stalling occurs. The external instruction memory has up to three cycles to return the instruction four words past the target address. That is, if single-cycle burst–mode can be established in three cycles (four cycles for the Am29050 processor) or less, then continuous execution can be achieved. The BTC supplies the target instructions and the following three instructions, assuming another jump is not taken. Figure 1-16 shows the flow of instructions through the pipeline stages.

Data Dependencies

Instructions that require the result of a load should not be placed immediately after the load instruction. The Am29000 processor can overlap load instructions with other instructions that do not depend on the result of the load. If 4-cycle data memory

---

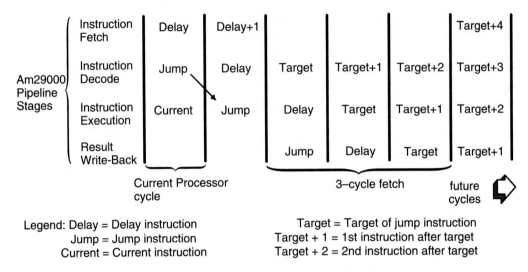

Figure 1-16. Pipeline Stages for a BTC Hit

is in use, then external data loads should (if possible) have four instructions (4-cycles) between the load instructions and the first use of the data. Instructions that depend on data whose loads have not yet completed, cause a pipeline stall. The stall is minimized by forwarding the data to the execution unit as soon as it is available.

Consider the example of an instruction sequence shown in Figure 1-17 . The instruction at *Load+1* is dependent on the data loaded at *Load*. The address of load data appears on the address pins at the start of the write-back stage. At this point, instruction *Load+1* has reached the execution stage and is stalled until the data is forwarded at the start of the next cycle, assuming the external data memory can return data within one cycle.

If the instruction were not dependent on the result of the load, it would have executed without delay. Because of data forwarding and a 1-cycle data memory, the load data would be available for instruction *Load+2* without causing a pipeline stall.

1.11   ARCHITECTURAL SIMULATION, sim29

AMD has for a long time made available a 29K simulator which accurately models the processor operation. This simulator, known as the Architectural Simulator, can be configured to incorporate memory system characteristics. Since memory system performance can greatly influence overall system performance, the use of the simulator before making design decisions is highly recommended.

Simulation of all the 29K family members is supported, making the simulator useful in determining processor choice [AMD 1991c][AMD 1993c]. For example, does a floating–point intensive application require an Am29050 or will an Am29000

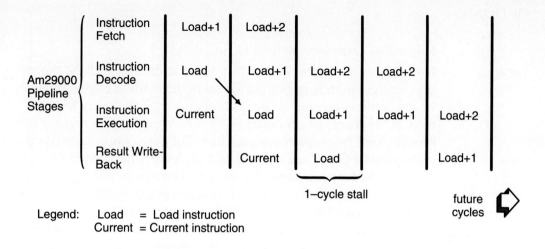

Figure 1-17. Data Forwarding and Bad–Load Scheduling

suffice? Alternatively, the performance penalties of connecting the data and instruction busses together on a 3–bus Harvard Architecture processor can be determined.

Because the simulator models detailed processor operation, such as, pipeline stages, cache memory, instruction prefetch, channel operation and much more, the simulation run–times are longer than if the Instruction Set Simulator (ISS) were used. Consequently, the Architectural Simulator is seldom used for program debugging. The ISS simulator is described in Chapter 7 (*Software Debugging*). This is one of the reasons that the Architectural simulator does not utilize the Universal Debugger Interface (see section 7.5). Without a UDI interface, the simulator can not support interactive debugging. Simulation results are directed to a log file. Interpretating their meaning and dealing with log file format takes a little practice; more on this later.

When used with a HIF conforming operating system, the standard input and output for the simulated program use the standard input and output for the executable simulator. Additionally, the 29K program standard output is also written to the simulation log file. AMD does not supply the simulator in source form; it is available in binary for UNIX type hosts and 386 based PCs. The simulator driver, **sim29**, supports several command line options, as shown below for version 1.1–8:

```
sim29   [-29000 | -29005 | -29030 | -29035 | -29050 | -29200 | -29205]
        [-cfg=xx] [-d] [-e eventfile] [-f freq] [-h heapsize] [-L] [-n]
        [-o outputfile] [-p from-to] [-r osboot] [-t max_sys_calls] [-u]
        [-v] [-x[codes]]
        execfile [... optional args for executable]
```

OPTIONS

-29000|29005|29030|29035|29050|29200|29205
Select 29K processor, default is Am29000.

-cfg=xx
Normally the simulator starts execution at address 0, with the processor Configuration Register (CFG) set to the hardware default value. Its the application code or the *osboot* code responsibility to modify the CFG registers as necessary. Alternatively, the CFG register can be initialized from the command–line. The *–cfg* option specifies the setting for CFG, where *xx* is a 1 to 5 digit HEX number. If the *–cfg* option is used, no run–time change to CFG will take effect, unless an Am292xx processor is in use. The *–cfg* option is seldom used; it should be used where an *osboot* file is not supplied with the *–r* option. Alternatively it can be used to override the cache enable/disable operation of *osboot* code. This can enable the effects of cache to be determined without the need to built a new *osboot* file.

-d
This option instructs the simulator to report the contents of processor registers in the *logfile* at end of simulation.

-e eventfile
An event file is almost always used. It enables memory system characteristics to be defined and the simulation to be controlled (see section 1.11.1).

-f frequency
Specify CPU frequency in MHz; the default for the Am292xx and Am29035 is 16 MHz; the Am2900x default is 25 MHz; and the default frequency for the Am29030 and Am29050 is 40 MHz.

-h heapsize
This option specifies the amount of resource memory available to the simulated 29K system. This memory is used for the register stack and memory stack support as well as the run–time heap. The default size is 32 K bytes; a *heapsize* value of 32.

-L
This option is similar in nature to the *–cfg* option. It can be used to select the large memory model for the Am292xx memory banks. Normally this selection is performed in the *osboot* file. However, the *–L* option can be used to override the *osboot* settings, without having to build a new *osboot* file.

-n
Normally the simulator will allow access to the two words following the end of a data section, without generating an access violation. Some of the support library routines, such as strcpy(), used by 29K application code, use a read–ahead technique to improve performance. If the read–ahead option is not supported, then the *–n* option should be used.

-o outputfile
The simulator normally presents simulation results in file *sim.out*. However an alternative result file can be selected with this option.

-p from-to	The simulator normally produces results of a general nature, such as average number of instructions per second. It is possible, using this option to examine the operation of specific code sequences within address range *from* to *to*.
-r osboot	The simulator can load two 29K executable programs via command–line direction: *osboot* and *program*. It is normal to load an operating system to deal with application support services; this is accomplished with *osboot*. It is sometimes referred to as the *romfile*, because when used with 29K family members which support separate ROM and Instruction spaces, *osboot* is loaded into ROM space. AMD supplies a HIF conforming operating system called OS–boot which is generally used with the *–r* option. Your simulation tool installation should have a 29K executable file called *osboot, romboot* or even *pumaboot* which contains the OS–boot code. Care should be taken to identify and use the correct file.

-t max_sys_calls

Specify maximum number of system call types that will be used during simulation This switch controls the internal management of the simulator; it is seldom used and has a default value of 256.

-u	The Am292xx microcontroller family members have built–in ROM and DRAM memory controllers. Programmable registers are used to configure the ROM and DRAM region controllers. If the *–u* option is used, application code in file *program* can modify the controller settings, otherwise only code in *osboot* can effect changes. This protects application code from accidentally changing the memory region configuration.
-v	The OS–boot operating system, normally used to implement the *osboot* file, can modify its warm–start operation depending on the value in register *gr104* (see section 7.4). The *–v* switch causes *gr104* to be initialized to 0. When OS–boot is configured to operate with or without MMU support, a run–time *gr104* value of 0 will turn off MMU use.
-x[code]	If a 29K error condition occurs during simulation, execution is not stopped. The *–x* option can be used to cause execution to stop under a selected range of error conditions. Each error condition is given a code letter. If *–x* is used with no selected codes, then all the available codes are assumed active. Supported code are:

A	Address error; data or instruction address out of bounds.
K	Kernel error; illegal operation in Supervisor mode.
O	Illegal opcode encountered.

F   Floating–point exception occurred; such as divide by zero.

P   A protection violation occurred in User mode

S   An event file error detected.

execfile   Name of the executable program to be loaded into memory; followed by any command–line arguments for the 29K executable. It is important that the program be correctly linked for the intended memory system. This is particularly true for systems based nf Am292xx processors. They have ROM and DRAM regions which can have very different memory access performance. If SRAM devices are to be used in the ROM region, it is important that the application be linked for the ROM region use rather than the DRAM.

It is best to run **sim29** with the –*r osboot* option. This is sometimes called cold–start operation. The *osboot* program must perform processor initialization, bringing the processor into what is known as the warm–start condition. At this point, *execution* of the loaded program commences. It is possible to run the simulator without the use of an *osboot* file; this is known as warm–start simulation. When this is done the simulator initializes the processor special registers CFG and CPS to a predefined warm–start condition. AMD documentation explains the chosen settings; they are different for each processor. Basically, the processor is prepared to run in User mode with traps and interrupts enabled and cache in use.

To support *osboot* operation, the simulator prepares processor registers before *osboot* operation starts (see Figure 1-18).

gr105	address of end of physical memory
gr104	Operating system control info.
gr103	start of command line args (argv)
gr102	register stack size
g101	memory stack size
gr100	first instruction of User loaded code
gr99	end address of program data
gr98	start address of program data
gr97	end address of program text
gr96	start address of program text
lr3	argument pointer, argv
lr2	argument count, argc

Figure 1-18. Register Initialization Performed by **sim29**

The initial register information is extracted from the *program* file. Via the register data, the *osboot* code obtains the start address of the *program* code. If *osboot* code is not used (no –*r* command–line switch), the 29K Program Counter is initialized to the start address of *program* code, rather than address 0. To support direct entry into warm–start code, the program argument information is duplicated in *lr2* and *lr3*. Normally this information is obtained by *osboot* using the data structure pointed to by *gr103*.

The simulator *intercepts* a number of HIF service calls (see section 2.2). These services mainly relate to operating system functions which are not simulated, but dealt with directly by the simulator. All HIF services with identification numbers below 256 are intercepted. Additionally service 305, for queering the CPU frequency, is intercepted. Operating services which are not intercepted, must be dealt with by the *osboot* code. The simulator will intercept a number of traps if the –*x[codes]* command line option is used; otherwise all traps are directed to *osboot* support code, or any other trapware installed during 29K run–time.

1.11.1 The Simulation Event File

Simulation is driven by modeling the 29K processor pipeline operation. Instructions are fetched from memory, and make their way through the decode, execute and write–back stages of the four–stage pipeline. Accurate modeling of processor internals enables the simulator to faithfully represent the operation of real hardware.

The simulator can also be driven from an event file. This file contains commands which are to be performed at specified time values. All times are given in processor cycles, with simulation starting at cycle 0. The simulator examines the event file and performs the requested command at the indicated cycle time.

The syntax of the command file is very simple; each command is entered on a single line preceded with a integer cycle–time value. There are 13 different commands; most of them enable extra information to be placed in the simulation results file. Information such as recording register value changes, displaying cache memory contents, monitoring floating–point unit operation, and much more. A second group of commands are mainly used with microcontroller 29K family members. They enable the on–chip peripheral devices to be incorporated in the simulation. For example, the Am29200 parallel port can *receive* and *transmit* data from files representing off–chip hardware.

In practice, most of these commands are little used; with one exception, the SET command. Most users of **sim29** simply wish to determine how a code sequence, representative of their application code, will perform on different 29K family members with varying memory system configurations. The SET command is used to configure simulation parameters and define the characteristics of system memory and buss arrangements. I will only describe the parameters used with the MEM option to the SET command. The cycle–time value used with the commands of interest is zero, as the memory system characteristics are established before simulation commences.

One other option to the SET command of interest is SHARED_ID_BUS; when used, it indicates the Instruction and Data buses are connected together. This option only makes sense with 3–bus members of the 29K family. All the 2–bus members already share a single bus for data and instructions, the second bus being used for address values. The syntax for the commands of interest is show below:

0   SET_SHARED_ID_BUS
0   SET MEM *access* TO *value*

Am29000 and Am29050

Note, when the Instruction bus and Data busses are tied together with 3–bus processors, the ROM space is still decoded separately from the Instruction space. Tying the busses together will reduce system performance, because instructions can no longer be fetched from Instruction space, or ROM space, while the Data bus is being used.

Considering only the most popular event file commands simplifies the presentation of **sim29** operation; and encourages its use. Those wishing to know more about event file command options should contact AMD. They readily distribute the **sim29** executable software for popular platforms and with relevant documentation.

Table 1-4 shows the allowed *access* and *value* parameters for 3–bus members of the 29K family, that is the Am29000 and Am29050 processors. Off–chip memory can exist in three separately addressed spaces: Instruction, ROM , and Data. Memory address–decode and access times (in cycles) must be entered for each address space which will be accessed by the processor; default values are provided.

*Table 1-4. **3–bus** Processor Memory Modeling Parameters for **sim29***

Instruction	ROM	Data	value	default	Operation
IDECODE	RDECODE	DDECODE	0–n	0	Decode address
IACCESS	RACCESS	DRCCESS	1–n	1	First read
		DWACCESS	1–n	1	First write
IBURST	RBURST	DBURST	T|F	false	Burst–mode supported
IBACCESS	RBACCESS	DBRACCESS	1–n	1	Burst read
		DBWACCESS	1–n	1	Burst write

If a memory system supports burst mode, the appropriate *BURST access parameter must be set to value TRUE. The example below sets Instruction memory accesses to two cycles; subsequent burst mode accesses are single–cycle. The example commands only affect Instruction memory; additional commands are required to establish Data memory access characteristics. Many users of the simulator only require memory modeling parameters from Table 1-4, even if DRAM is in use.

```
0       SET MEM IACCESS TO 2
0       SET MEM IBURST TO true
0       SET MEM IBACCESS TO 1
```

If DRAM memory devices are used, there are several additional *access* parameters which can be used to support memory system modeling (see Table 1-5). DRAM devices are indicated by the *PAGEMODE parameter being set. The 29K family internally operates with a page size of 256 words, external DRAM memory always operates with integer multiples of this value. For this reason, there is never any need to change the *PGSIZE parameter setting from its default value. The first read access to DRAM memory takes *PFACCESS cycles; second and subsequent read accesses take *PSACCESS cycles. However, if the memory system supports burst mode, subsequent read accesses take *PBACCESS cycles rather than *PSACCESS.

Table 1-5. *3–bus* Processor DRAM Modeling Parameters for **sim29** (continued)

Instruction	ROM	Data	value	default	Operation
IPAGEMODE	PAGEMODE	DPAGEMODE	T|F	false	Memory is paged
IPGSIZE	RPGSIZE	DPGSIZE	1–n	256	Page size in words
IPFACCESS	RPFACCESS	DPFRACCESS	1–n	1	First read in page mode
		DPFWACCESS	1–n	1	First write in page mode
IPSACCESS	RPSACCESS	DPSRACCESS	1–n	1	Secondary read within page
		DPSWACCESS	1–n	1	Secondary write within page
IPBACCESS	RPBACCESS	DPBRACCESS	1–n	1	Burst read within page
		DPBWACCESS	1–n	1	Burst write within page

If static column DRAM memories are used, then memory devices do not require *CAS* signals between same–page accesses. Static column memory use is indicated by the *STATCOL parameter. Initial page accesses suffer the additional *PRECHARGE access penalties, subsequent accesses all have same access latencies. Note, burst mode access can also apply to static column DRAM memory. Table 1-6 shows memory modeling parameters for static column memories.

Table 1-6. *3–bus* Processor Static Column Modeling Parameters for **sim29** (continued)

Instruction	ROM	Data	value	default	Operation
ISTATCOL	RSTATCOL	DSTATCOL	T|F	false	Static column memory used
ISMASK	RSMASK	DSMASK	0xfffffff0	0	Column address mask, 64–words
IPRECHARGE	RPRECH..	DPRECHARGE	0–n	0	Precharge on page crossing
ISACCESS	RSACCESS	DSRACCESS	1–n	1	Read access within static column
		DSWACCESS	1–n	1	Write access within static column

Separate regions of an address space may contain more than one type of memory device and control mechanism. To support this, memory *banking* is provided for in the simulator (see Table 1-7). The [I|R|D]BANKSTART parameter is used to specify the start address of a memory bank; a bank is a contiguous region of memory of selectable size, within an indicated address space. Once the *BANKSTART command has been used, all following commands relate to the *current* bank, until a new bank is selected. This type of command is more frequently used with microcontroller members of the 29K family.

*Table 1-7. **3–bus** Processor Memory Modeling Parameters for **sim29** (continued)*

Instruction	ROM	Data	value	default	Operation
IBANKSTART	RBANK..	DBANKSTART	0–n	–	Start address of memory region
IBANKSIZE	BBAKSIZE	DBANKSIZE	1–n	1	Size in bytes of memory region

Am29030 and Am29035

The parameters used with the SET command, when simulating 2–bus 29K family members are a little different from 3–bus parameters (see Table 1-8). There is no longer a ROM space, and although instructions and data can be mixed in the same memory devices, separate modeling parameters are provided for instruction and data accesses.

Consider accessing memory for instructions; IACCESS gives the access time, unless DRAM is used, in such case, access time is given by IPACCESS. The use of DRAM is indicated by the *PRECHARGE parameter value being non zero. First accesses to DRAM pages suffer an addition access delay of *PRECHARGE. If burst mode is supported, with all memory device types, the access times for instruction memory, other than the first access, is given by IBACCESS.

Both the current 2–bus 29K family members support scalable clocking, enabling a half speed external memory system. They also support narrow, 8–bit or 16–bit, memory reads. The Am29035 processor also supports dynamic bus sizing. All external memory accesses can be 16–bit or 32–bit; processor hardware takes care of multiple memory accesses when operating on 32–bit data. As with the 3–bus 29K family members, the simulator provides for memory banking. This enables different memory devices to be modeled within specified address ranges.

Table 1-8. **2–bus** *Processor Memory Modeling Parameters for* **sim29**

Instruction	Data	value	default	Operation
IACCESS	DRACCESS	2–n	2	First read from SRAM
	DWACCESS	2–n	2	First write from SRAM
IBURST	DBURST	T|F	true	Burst–mode supported
IBACCESS	DBRACCESS	1–n	1	Burst read within page
	DBWACCESS	1–n	1	Burst write within page
IWIDTH	DWIDTH	8,16,32	32	Memory width
IPRECHARGE	DPRECHARGE	0–n	0	Precharge on page crossing
IPACCESS	DPRACCESS	2–n	2	First access in page mode
	DPWACCESS	2–n	2	First write in page mode
IBANKSTART	DBANKSTART	0–n	–	Start address of memory region
IBANKSIZE	DBANKSIZE	1–n	1	Size in bytes of memory region
HALFSPEED	HALFSPEED	T|F	false	Memory system is 1/2 CPU speed

Am29200 and Am29205

The simulator does not maintain different memory access parameters for instruction and data access when modeling microcontroller members of the 29K family. However, it does support separate memory modeling parameters for DRAM and ROM address regions (see Table 1-9). Each of these two memory regions has its own memory controller supporting up to four banks. A bank is a contiguous range of memory within the address range accessed via the region controller. The DRAM region controller is a little more complicated than the ROM region controller.

The DRAM access is fixed at four cycles (1 for precharge + 3 for latency), it can not be programmed. Subsequent accesses to the same page take four cycles unless pagemode memories are supported. Note the first access is only three cycles rather than four, as the *RAS* will already have met the precharge time. Basically, to precharge the *RAS* bit lines, all *RAS* lines need to be taken high in between each change of the row addresses. A separate cycle is needed for precharge when back–to–back DRAM accesses occurs. Use of pagemode memories is indicated by the PAGEMODE parameter being set; when used, the processor need not supply *RAS* memory strobe signals before page *CAS* strobes for same page accesses. This reduces subsequent page access latency to three cycles. Additionally, when pagemode is used and a data burst is attempted within a page, access latency is twocycles. The DRAM memory width can be set to 16 or 32–bits. Of course when an Am29205 is used, all data memory accesses are restricted by the 16–bit width of the processor data bus.

To explain further, access times to DRAM for none pagemode memories follow the sequence:

X,3,4,4,4,X,3,4,4,4,X,X,3,X,3,...

Where X is a non–DRAM access, say to ROM or PIA space. For DRAM systems supporting pagemode the sequence would be:

X,3,2,2,2,<boundary crossing>,4,2,2,<boundary crossing>,X,3,2,2,2

Memory devices located in ROM space can be modeled with a wider range of parameter values. Both SRAM and ROM devices can be modeled in ROM space. Using the RBANKNUM parameter, the characteristics of each bank can be selectively described. Burst–mode addressing is only supported for instruction or data reading. When the burst option is used (RBURST set to TRUE), read accesses, other than the first for a new burst, take RBACCESS cycles rather than the standard RRACCESS cycles. Memory device widths can be 8, 16 or 32–bits. If an Am29205 microcontroller is being modeled, memory accesses wider than the 16–bit bus width always require the processor to perform multiple memory transfers to access the required memory location.

Table 1-9. **Microcontroller** *Memory Modeling Parameters for* **sim29**

ROM	value	default	DRAM	value	default	Operation
					1	Precharge on page crossing
RRACCESS	1–n	1			3	First read
RWACCESS	2–n	2			3	First write
RBURST	T|F	false				Burst address in ROM region
RBACCESS	1–n	1			2	Burst read within page
					2	Burst write within page
ROMWIDTH	8,16,32	32	DRAMWIDTH	16,32	32	Width of memory
			PAGEMODE	T|F	false	Page mode supported
RBANKNUM	0–3	–	DBANKNUM	0–3	–	Select which memory bank

Preparing **sim29** for modeling an Am29200 system is not difficult. The following commands configure the first two ROM banks to access non–burst–mode memories which are 32–bits wide, and have a 1–cycle read access, and a 2–cycle write access.

```
0       COM ROM bank 0 parameters
0       SET  MEM  rbanknum  to 0
0       SET  MEM  rraccess  to  1
0       SET  MEM  rwaccess  to  2

0       COM ROM bank 1 parameters
0       SET  MEM  rbanknum  to 1
0       SET  MEM  rraccess  to  1
0       SET  MEM  rwaccess  to  2
```

The following DRAM parameters, like the ROM parameters above, are correct for modeling an SA29200 evaluation board. The first DRAM bank is configured to support pagemode DRAM access, giving access latencies of 4:3:2 (4 for first, 3 for same–page subsequent, unless they are bursts which suffer only 2–cycle latency).

```
0       COM DRAM bank 0 parameters
0       SET  MEM  dbanknum  to 0
0       SET   MEM  dpagemode  to  true
```

1.11.2 Analyzing the Simulation Log File

Running the architectural simulator is simple but rather slow. The inclusion of detail about the processor pipeline results in slow simulation speeds. For this reason, users typically select a portion of their application code for simulation. This portion is either representative of the overall code or subsections whose operation is critical to overall system performance.

For demonstration purposes I have merely simulated the "hello world" program running on an Am29000 processor. The C source file was compiled with the High C 29K compiler using the default compiler options; object file *hello* was produced by the compile/link process. The memory model was the simulator default, single–cycle operation. Given the selection of default memory parameter, there is no need for an *eventfile* establishing memory parameters. However, I did use an *eventfile* with the following contents:

```
0       log on channel
```

This option has not previously been described; it enables the simulator to produce an additional log file of channel activity. This can occasionally be useful when studying memory system operation in detail. The simulator was started with the command:

```
sim29 -29000 -r /gnu/29k/src/osboot/sim/osboot -e eventfile   hello
```

Two simulation result files were produced; the most important of which, the default simulation output file, *sim.out*, we shall briefly examine. The *channel.out* file reports all instruction and data memory access activity. The contents of the *sim.out* file are shown below exactly as produced by the simulator:

```
AMD ARCHITECTURAL SIMULATOR, V# 1.0-17PC
### T=3267 Am29000 Simulation of "hello" complete -- successful termination.
--------------------------------------------------------
       <<<<< S U M M A R Y   S T A T I S T I C S >>>>>

       CPU Frequency = 25.00MHz

              Nops:50
                         total instructions = 2992

       User Mode:            291 cycles (0.00001164 seconds)
       Supervisor Mode:     2977 cycles (0.00011908 seconds)
       Total:               3268 cycles (0.00013072 seconds)

       Simulation speed:     22.89 MIPS (1.09 cycles per instruction)

       ---------- Pipeline ----------
         8.45% idle pipeline:
                    6.46% Instruction Fetch Wait
                    0.46% Data Transaction Wait
                    0.18% Page Boundary Crossing Fetch Wait
                    0.00% Unfilled BTCache Fetch Wait
                    0.49% Load/Store Multiple Executing
                    0.03% Load/Load Transaction Wait
                    0.83% Pipeline Latency

       Total Wait:                 276 cycles  (0.00001104 seconds)

       ---------- Branch Target Cache ----------
       Partial hits:                   0
       Branch btcache access:        2418
       Branch btcache hits:          2143
       Branch btcache hit ratio:            88.63%
       ---------- Translation Lookaside Buffer ----------
       TLB access:                    0
       TLB hits:                      0
       TLB hit ratio:           0.00%
       ---------- Bus Utilization ----------
       Inst Bus Utilization:                70.01%
                  2288 Instruction Fetches

       Data Bus Utilization:        10.86%
                  20 Loads
                 335 Stores
```

```
---------- Register File Spilling/Filling ----------
                 0 Spills,          0 Fills
Opcode Histogram
  ILLEGAL:       CONSTN:6        CONSTH:68        CONST:121
  MTSRIM:5       CONSTHZ:          LOADL:          LOADL:
    CLZ:            CLZ:          EXBYTE:         EXBYTE:
. . .


System Call Count Histogram
    EXIT     1:1         GETARGS   260:1        SETVEC   289:2
. . .


------ M E M O R Y   S U M M A R Y ------
  Memory Parameters for Non-banked Regions
    I_SPEED: Idecode=0 Iaccess=1 Ibaccess=1
. . .
```

The simulator reports the total number of processor cycles simulated. Because our example is brief, there are few User mode cycles. Most cycles are utilized by the *osboot* operating system. The operating system runs in Supervisor mode and initializes the processor to run the "hello world" program in User mode. The fast memory system has enabled the processor pipeline to be kept busy, an 8.45% idle pipeline is reported. A breakdown of the activities contributing to pipeline stalling is shown.

Next reported is the Branch Target Cache (BTC) activity. If a processor incorporating an Instruction Cache Memory rather than a BTC had been simulated, the corresponding results would replace the BTC results shown. There were 2418 BTC accesses, of which 2143 found valid entries. This gives a hit ratio of 88.63%. Partial hits refer to the number of BTC entries which were not fully used. This occurs when one of the early entries in the four–entry cache block contains a jump.

If the operating system had arranged for Translation Look–Aside Buffer (TLB) use then the next section reports its activity. In the example, the application ran with physical addressing which does not require TLB support. Next reported is bus activity. The large number of processor registers results in little off–chip data memory access, and hence Data Bus utilization. The Instruction Bus is used to fill the Instruction Prefetch Buffer and BTC, and shows much higher utilization. Typically, programs are more sensitive to instruction memory performance than data memory.

The simulator then produces a histogram of instruction and system call usage. The listing above only shows an extract of this information, as it is rather large. Examining this data can reveal useful information, such as extensive floating–point instruction use.

Finally reported is a summary of the memory modeling parameters used during simulation. This information should match with the default parameters or any parameters established by the *eventfile*. It is useful to have this information recorded along with the simulation results.

Chapter 2

Applications Programming

Application programming refers to the process of developing task specific software. Typical 29K tasks are controlling a real–time process, processing communications data, real–time digital signal processing, and manipulating video images. There are many more types of applications, such as word processing which the 29K is suited for, but the 29K is better known in the embedded engineering community which typically deals with real–time processing.

This chapter deals with aspects of application programming which the Software Engineer is required to know. Generally, computer professionals spend more time developing application code, compared to other software development projects such as operating systems. Additionally, applications are increasingly developed in a high level language. Since C is the dominant language for this task, I shall present code examples in terms of C. Assembly level programming is dealt with in a separate chapter.

The first part of this chapter deals with the mechanism by which one C procedure calls another, and how they agree to communicate data and make use of processor resources [Mann et al. 1991b]. This is termed the *Calling Convention*. It is possible that different tool developers could construct their own calling mechanism, but this may lead to incompatibilities in mixing routines compiled by different vendor tools. AMD avoided this problem by devising a calling convention which was adopted by all tool developers. Detailed knowledge, of say, individual register support tasks for the calling convention is not presented, except for the register and memory stacks which play an important role in the 29K calling mechanism. In practice, C language developers typically do not need to be concerned about individual register assignments, as it is taken care of by the compiler [Mann 1991c]. Chapter 3 expands on register assignment, and it is of concern here only in terms of understanding the calling convention concepts and run–time efficiencies.

Operating system support services (HIF services) are then dealt with. The transition form operating system to the application main() routine is described. Operating system services along with other support routines are normally accessed through code libraries. These libraries are described for the predominant tool–chains. Using the available libraries and HIF services, it is an easy task to arrange for interrupts to be processed by C language handler routines; the mechanism is described. Finally, utility programs for operations such as PROM preparation are listed and their capabilities presented.

2.1 C LANGUAGE PROGRAMMING

Making a subroutine call on a processor with general-purpose registers is "expensive" in terms of time and resources. Because functions must compete for register use, registers must be saved and restored through register-to-memory and memory-to-register operations. For example, a C function call on the MC68000 processor [Motorola 1985] might use the statements:

```
char  bits8;
short bits16;
printf ("char= %c short=%d", bits8, bits16);
```

After they are compiled, the above statements would generate the assembly-level code shown below:

```
L15:    .ascii   "char= %c short=%d\0"

        MOVE.W   -4[A6],D         ;copy bits16 variable
        EXT.L    D0               ; to register
        MOVE.L   D0,-[A7]         ;now push on stack
        MOVE.B   -1[A6],D0        ;copy bits8 variable
        EXTB.L   D0               ; to register
        MOVE.L   D0,-[A7]         ;now push on stack
        PEA      L15              ;stack text string pointer
        JSR      _printf
        LEA      12[A7],A7        ;repair stack pointer
```

The assembly listing above shows how parameters pass via the memory stack to the function being called. The LINK instruction copies the stack pointer *A7* to the local frame pointer *A6* upon entry to a routine. Within the printf() routine, the parameters passed and local variables in memory are referenced relative to register *A6*.

To reduce future access delays, the printf() routine will normally copy data to general-purpose registers before using them. For instance, using a memory-to-memory operation when moving data from the local frame of the function call stack

---

would reduce the number of instructions executed. However, these are *CISC* instructions that require several machine cycles before completion.

In the example, the C function call passes two variables, *bits8* and *bits16,* to the library function printf(). The following assembly code shows part of the printf() function for the MC68020.

```
_printf:
        LINK    A6,#-32             ;local variable space
        LEA     8[A6],A0            ;unstack string pointer
        . . .
        UNLK    A6
        RTS                         ;return
```

Several multi–cycle instructions (like LINK and UNLK) are required to pass the parameters and establish the function context. Unlike the variable instruction format in the MC68020, the 29K processor family has a fixed 32–bit instruction format (see section 1.8). The same C statements compiled for the Am29000 processor generate the following assembly code for passing the parameters and establishing the function context:

```
L1:     .ascii  "bits8=%c bits16=%d\0"
        const   lr2,L1
        consth  lr2,L1
        add     lr3,lr6,0           ;move bits8 and bits16
        add     lr4,lr8,0           ;to bottom of the
                                    ;activation record
        call    lr0,printf          ;return address in lr0
```

The number of instructions required is certainly less, and they are all simple single–cycle RISC instructions. However, to better understand just how parameters are passed during a function call, explanation of the procedure activation records and their use of the local register file is first required.

2.1.1 Register Stack

A register stack is assigned an area of memory used to pass parameters and allocate working registers to each procedure. The register cache replaces the top of the register stack, as shown in Figure 2-1. All 29K processors have a 128–word local register file; these registers are used to implement the cache for the top of the register stack.

The global registers *rab* (*gr126*) and *rfb* (*gr127*) point to the top and the bottom of the register cache. Global register *rsp* (also known as *gr1*) points to the top of the register stack. The register cache, or stack window, moves up and down the register stack as the stack grows and shrinks. Use of the register cache, rather than the memory portion of the register stack, allows data to be accessed through local registers at

---

high speed. On–chip triple–porting of the register file (two read ports and one write port for most 29K family members), enables the register stack to perform better than a data memory cache, which cannot support read and write operations in the same cycle.

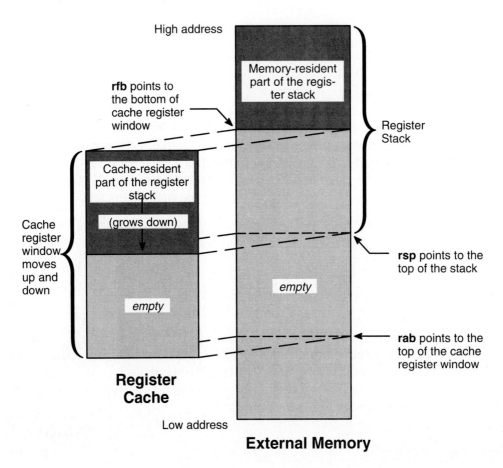

Figure 2-1. Cache Window

2.1.2 Activation Records

A 29K processor does not apply *push* or *pop* instructions to external memory when passing procedure parameters. Instead each function is allocated an activation record in the register cache at compile time. Activation records hold any local variables and parameters passed to functions.

The caller stores its outgoing arguments at the bottom of the activation record.The called function establishes a new activation record below the caller's record. The top of the new record overlaps the bottom of the old record, so that the outgoing parameters of the calling function are visible within the called functions activation record.

Although the activation record can be any size within the limits of the physical cache, the compiler will not allocate more than 16 registers to the parameter-passing part of the activation record. Functions that cannot pass all of their outgoing parameters in registers must use a memory stack for additional parameters; global register *msp (gr125)* points to the top of the memory stack. This happens infrequently, but is required for parameters that have their address taken. Data parameters at known addresses cannot be supported in register address space because data addresses always refer to memory, not to registers.

The following code shows part of the printf() function for the 29K family:

```
printf:
        sub     gr1,gr1,16          ;function prologue
        asgeu   V_SPILL,gr1,rab     ;compare with top of window
        add     lr1,gr1,36          ;rab is gr126
        . . .
        jmpi    lr0                 ;return
         asleu  V_FILL,lr1,rfb      ;compare with bottom
                                    ;of window gr127
```

The register stack pointer, *rsp,* points to the bottom of the current activation record. All local registers are referenced relative to *rsp*. Four new registers are required to support the function call shown, so *rsp* is decremented 16 bytes. Register *rsp* performs a role similar to the MC68000's *A7* and *A6* registers, except that it points to data in high-speed registers, not data in external memory.

The compiler reserves local registers *lr0* and *lr1* for special duties within each activation record. The *lr0* contains the execution staring address when it returns to the caller's activation record. The *lr1* points to the top of the caller's activation record, the new frame allocates local registers *lr2* and *lr3* to hold printf() function local variables.

As Figure 2-2 shows, the positions of five registers overlap. The three printf() parameters enter from *lr2, lr3* and *lr4* of the caller's activation record and appear as *lr6, lr7* and *lr8* of the printf() function activation record.

2.1.3 Spilling And Filling

If not enough registers are available in the cache when it moves down the register stack, then a V_SPILL trap is taken, and the registers spill out of the cache into memory. Only procedure calls that require more registers than currently are available in the cache suffer this overhead.

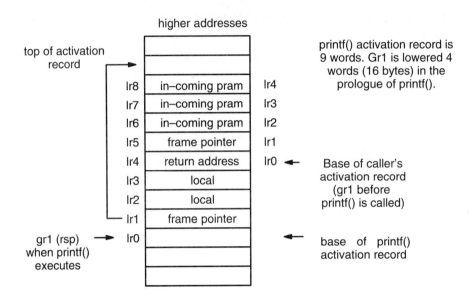

Figure 2-2. Overlapping Activation Record Registers

Once a spill occurs, a fill (V_FILL trap) can be expected at a later time. The fill does not happen when the function call causing the spill returns, but rather when some earlier function that requires data held in a previous activation record (just below the cache window) returns. Just before a function returns, the *lr1* register, which points to the top of the caller's activation record, is compared with the pointer to the bottom of the cache window(*rfb*). If the activation record is not stored completely in the cache, then a fill overhead occurs.

The register stack improves the performance of call operations because most calls and returns proceed without any memory access. The register cache contains 128 registers, so very few function calls or returns require register spilling or filling.

Because most of the data required by a function resides in local registers, there is no need for elaborate memory addressing modes, which increase access latency. The function-call overhead in the 29K family consists of a small number of single-cycle instructions; the overhead in the MC68020 requires a greater number of multi-cycle instructions.

2.1.4 Global Registers

In the discussion of activation records (section 2.1.2), it was stated that functions can use activation space (local registers) to hold procedure variables. This is true, but procedures can also use processor global registers to hold variables. Each

29K processor has a group of registers (global registers) which are located in the register file, but are not part of the register cache. Global registers *gr96–gr127* are used by application programs. When developing software in C, there is no need to know just how the compiler makes use of these global registers; the Assembly Level Programming chapter, section 3.3, discusses register allocation in detail.

Data held in global registers, unlike procedure activation records, do not survive procedure calls. The compiler has 25 global registers available for holding temporary variables. These registers perform a role very similar to the eight–data and eight–address general purpose registers of the MC68020. The first 16 of the global registers, *gr96–gr111,* are used for procedure return value passing. Return objects larger than 16 words, must use the memory stack to return data (see section 3.3).

An extension to some C compilers has been made (High C® 29K™ compiler for one), enabling a calling procedure to assume that some global registers will survive a procedure call. If the called function is defined before calls are made to it, the compiler can determine its register usage. This enables the global register usage of the calling function to be restricted to available registers, and the calling function need only save in local registers those global registers it knows are used by the by the callee.

2.1.5 Memory Stack

Because the register cache is limited in size, a separate memory stack is used to hold large local variables (structs or arrays), as well as any incoming parameters beyond the 16th parameter. (Note, small structs can still be passed in local registers as procedure parameters). Register *msp* is the memory stack pointer. (Note, having two stacks generally requires several operating system support mechanisms not required by a single stack CISC based system.)

2.2   RUN–TIME HIF ENVIRONMENT

Application programs need to interact with peripheral devices which support communication and other control functions. Traditionally embedded program developers have not been well served by the tools available to tackle the related software development. For example, performing the popular C library service printf(), using a peripheral UART device, may involve developing the printf() library code and then underlying operating system code which controls the communications UART. One solution to the problem is to purchase a real–time operating system. They are normally supplied with libraries which support printf() and other popular library services. In addition, operating systems contain code to perform task context switching and interrupt handling.

Typically each operating system vendor has their own operating system interface specification. This means that library code, like printf(), which ultimately makes operating system service requests, is not easily ported between different operating systems. In addition, compiler vendors which typically develop library code for the target processor for sale along with the compiler, can not be assured of a standard interface to the available operating system services.

AMD wished to relieve this problem and allow library code to be used on any target 29K platform. In addition AMD wished to ensure a number of services would be available. These operating system services were considered necessary to enable performance benchmarking of application code (for example the *cycles* service returns a 56–bit elapsed processor cycle count). The result was the Host Interface specification, known as HIF. It specifies a number of operating system services which must always be present. The list is very small, but it enables library producers to be assured that their code will run on any 29K platform. The HIF specification states how a system call will be made, how parameters will be passed to the operating system, and how results will be returned. Operating system vendors need not support HIF conforming services if they wish; they could just continue to use their own operating system interface and related library routines. But to make use of the popular library routines from the Metaware High C 29K compiler company, the operating system company must virtualize the HIF services on top of the underlying operating system services.

The original specification grew into what is now known as HIF 2.0. The specification includes services for signal handling (see following sections on C language interrupt handlers), memory management support, run–time environment initialization and other processor configuration options. Much of this development was a result of AMD developing a small collection of routines known as OS–boot (see section 7.4). This code can take control of the processor from RESET, prepare the run–time environment for a HIF conforming application program, and support any HIF request made by the application. OS–boot effectively implements a single application–task operating system. It is adequate for many user requirements, which may be merely to benchmark 29K applications. With small additions and changes it is adequate for many embedded products. However, some of the HIF 2.0 services, requested by the community who saw OS–boot as an adequate operating system, were of such a nature that they often cannot be implemented in an operating system vendor's product. For example the *settrap* service enables an entry to be placed directly into the processor's interrupt vector table; some operating systems, for example UNIX, will not permit this to occur as it is a security risk and, if improperly used, an effective way to crash the system.

There are standard memory, register and other initializations that must be performed by a HIF-conforming operating system before entry into a user program. In C language programs, this is usually performed by the module **crt0.s**. This module receives control when an application program is invoked, and executes prior to invocation of the user's main() function. Other high-level languages have similar modules.

The following three sections describe: What a HIF conforming operating system must perform before code in **crt0.s** starts executing; what is typically achieved in **crt0.s** code; and finally, what run–time services are specified in HIF 2.0.

2.2.1 OS Preparations before Calling start In crt0

According to the HIF specification, operating system initialization procedures must establish appropriate values for the general registers mentioned below before execution of a user's application code commences. Linked application code normally commences at address label **start** in module **crt0.s**. This module is automatically linked with application code modules and libraries when the compiler is used to produce the final application executable. In addition, file descriptors for the standard input and output devices must be opened, and any Am29027 floating–point coprocessor support as well as other trapware support must be initialized.

Register Stack Pointer (*gr1*)

Register *gr1* points to the top of the register stack. It contains the main memory address in which the local register *lr0* will be saved, should it be spilled, and from which it will be restored. The processor can also use the *gr1* register as the base in base–plus–offset addressing of the local register file. The content of *rsp* is compared to the content of *rab* to determine when it is necessary to spill part of the local register stack to memory. On startup, the values in *rab, rsp*, and *rfb* should be initialized to prevent a spill trap from occurring on entry to the **crt0** code, as shown by the following relations:

$$(64*4) + rab \le rsp < rfb$$
$$rfb = rab + 512$$

This provides the **crt0** code with at least 64 registers on entry, which should be a sufficient number to accomplish its purpose. Note, *rab* and *rfb* are normally set to be a window distance apart, 128 words (512 bytes), but this is not the only valid settings, see section 4.3.1.

Register Free Bound (*gr127*)

The register stack free–bound pointer, *rfb*, contains the register stack address of the lowest-addressed word not contained within the register file. Register *rfb* is referenced in the epilog of most user program functions to determine whether a register fill operation is necessary to restore previously spilled registers needed by the function's caller. The *rfb* register should be initialized to point to the highest address of the memory region allocated for register stack use. It is recommended that this memory region not be less than 6k bytes.

Register Allocate Bound (gr126)

The register stack allocate–bound pointer, *rab*, contains the register stack address of the lowest-addressed word contained within the register file. Register *rab* is referenced in the prolog of most user program functions to determine whether a register spill operation is necessary to accommodate the local register requirements of the called function. Register *rab* is normally initialized to be a window distance (512 bytes) below the *rfb* register value

Memory Stack Pointer (*gr125*)

The memory stack pointer (*msp*) register points to the top of the memory stack, which is the lowest-addressed entry on the memory stack. Register *msp* should be initialized to point to the highest address in the memory region allocated for memory stack use. It is recommended that this region not be less than 2k bytes.

Am29027 Floating–Point Coprocessor Support

The Am29027 floating–point coprocessor has a *mode* register which has a cumbersome access procedure. To avoid accessing the *mode* register a shadow copy is kept by the operating system and accessed in preference when a *mode* register read is required. The operating system shadow mode value is not accessible to User mode code, therefore an application must maintain its own shadow *mode* register value. The floating–point library code which maintains and accesses the shadow mode value, is passed the *mode* setting, initialized by the operating system, when **crt0** code commences. Before entering **crt0**, the Am29027 *mode* register value is copied into global registers *gr96* and *gr97*. Register *gr96* contains the most significant half of the *mode* register value, and *gr97* contains the least significant half.

Open File Descriptors

File descriptor 0 (corresponding to the standard input device) must be opened for text mode input. File descriptors 1 and 2 (corresponding to standard output and standard error devices) must be opened for text mode output prior to entry to the user's program. File descriptors 0, 1, and 2 are expected to be in COOKED mode (see Appendix A, ioctl() service), and file descriptor 0 should also select ECHO mode, so that input from the standard input device (**stdin**) is echoed to the standard output device (**stdout**).

Software Emulation and Trapware Support

A 29K processor may take a trap in support of the procedure call prologue and epilogue mechanism. A HIF conforming operating system supports the associated SPILL and FILL traps by normally maintaining two global registers (in the *gr64–gr95* range) which contain the address of the users spill and fill code. Keeping these addresses available in registers reduces the delay in reaching the typically User mode support code. A HIF conforming operating system also installs the SPILL and FILL trap handler code which *bounces* execution to the maintained handler addresses.

Table 2-1. Trap Handler Vectors

Trap	Description
32	MULTIPLY
33	DIVIDE
34	MULTIPLU
35	DIVID
36	CONVERT
42	FEQ
43	DEQ
44	FGT
45	DGT
46	FGE
47	DGE
48	FADD
49	DADD
50	FSUB
51	DSUB
52	FMUL
53	DMUL
54	FDIV
55	DDIV
64	V_SPILL (Set up by the user's task through a setvec call)
65	V_FILL (Set up by the user's task through a setvec call)
69	HIF System Call

Note: The V_SPILL (64) and V_FILL (65) traps are returned to the user's code to perform the trap handling functions. Application code normally runs in User mode.

Additionally, the trapware code enabling HIF operating system calls is installed, additionally all HIF conforming operating systems provide unaligned memory access trap handlers.

A number of 29K processors do not directly support floating–point instructions in hardware (see section 3.1.7). However the HIF environment requires that all Am29000 User mode accessible instructions be implemented across the entire 29K family. This means that unless an Am29050 processor is being used, trapware must be installed to emulate in software the floating–point instructions not directly supported by the hardware. Table 2-1 lists the traps which an HIF conforming operating system must establish support for before calling **crt0** code.

When a 29K processor is supported by an Am29027 floating–point coprocessor, the operating system may chose to use the coprocessor to support floating–point instruction emulation. For example, the trapware routine used for emulating the MULTIPLY instruction is know as **Emultiply**; however, if the coprocessor is available the **E7multiply** routine is used.

2.2.2 crt0 Preparations before Calling main()

Application code normally begins execution at address **start** in the **crt0.s** module. The previous section described the environment prepared by a HIF conforming operating system before the code in **crt0**.s is executed. The **crt0.s** code makes final preparations before the application main() procedure is called.

The code in **crt0.s** first copies the Am29027 shadow *mode* register value, passed in *gr96* and *gr97*, to memory location __29027Mode. If a system does not have an Am29027 floating–point coprocessor then there is no useful data passed in these registers. However, application code linked with floating–point libraries which make use of the Am29027 coprocessor, will access the shadow memory location to determine the coprocessor operating *mode* value.

The *setvec* system call is then used to supply the operating system with the addresses of the user's SPILL and FILL handler code which is located in **crt0.s**. Because this code normally runs in User mode address space, and the user has the option to tailor the operation of this code, an operating system can not know in advance (pre–**crt0.s**) the required SPILL and FILL handler code operation.

When procedure main() is called, it is passed two parameters; the *argc* parameter indicates the number of elements in *argv*, the second parameter, *argv*, is a pointer to an array of the character strings:

```
        main(argc, argv)
int     argc;
char*   argv[];
```

The *getargs* HIF service is used to get the address of the *argv* array. In many real–time applications there are no parameters passed to main(). However, to support porting of benchmark application programs, many systems arrange for main() parameters to be loaded into a user's data space. The **crt0.s** code walks through the array looking for a NULL terminating string; in so doing, it determines the *argc* value. The register stack pointer was lowered by the start() procedure's prologue code to create a procedure activation record for passing parameters to main().

To aid run–time libraries a memory variable, __LibInit, is defined in uninitialized data memory space (BSS) by the library code. If any library code needs initialization before use, then the __LibInit variable will be assigned to point to a library routine which will perform all necessary initialization. This is accomplished by the linker matching–up the BSS __LibInit variable with an initialized __LibInit variable defined in the library code. The **crt0.s** code checks to see if the __LibInit variable contains a non zero address, if so, the procedure is called.

The application main() procedure is ready to be called by start(). It is not expected that main() wall return. Real–time programs typically never exit. However, benchmark programs do, and this is accomplished by calling the HIF *exit* service. If a main() routine does not explicitly call *exit* then it will return to start(), where *exit* is called should main() return.

2.2.3 Run–Time HIF Services

Table 2-2 lists the HIF system call services, calling parameters, and the returned values. If a column entry is blank, it means the register is not used or is undefined. Table 2-3 describes the parameters given in Table 2-2 . Before invoking a HIF service, the service number and any input parameters passed to the operating system are loaded into assigned global registers. Each HIF service is identified by its associated service number which is placed in global register *gr121*. Parameters are passed , as with procedure calls, in local registers starting with *lr2*. Application programs do not need to issue ASSERT instructions directly when making service calls. They normally use a library of assembly code glue routines. The *write* service glue routine is shown below:

```
__write:        ;HIF assembly glue routine for write service
        const   gr121,21        ;tav is gr121
        asneq   69,gr1,gr1      ;system call trap
        jmpti   gr121,lr0       ;return if sucessful
        const   gr122,_errno    ;pass errror number
        consth  gr122,_errno
        store   0,0,gr121,gr122 ;store errnor number
        jmpi    lr0             ;return if failure
         constn gr96,-1
```

Application programs need merly call the _write() leaf routine to issue the service request. The system call convention states that return values are placed in global registers starting with *gr96*; this makes the transfer of return data by the assembly glue routine very simple and efficient. If a service fails, due to, say, bad input parameters, global register *gr121* is returned with an error number supplied by the operating system. If the service was successful, *gr121* is set to Boolean TRUE (0x80000000). The glue routines check the *gr121* value, and if not TRUE, copy the value to memory location *errno*. This location, unlike *gr121* is directly accessible by a C language application which requested the service.

Run–time HIF services are divided into two groups, they are separated by their service number. Numbers 255 and less require the support of complex operating system services such as file system management. Service numbers 256 and higher relate to simpler service tasks. Note, AMD reserves service numbers 0–127 and 256–383 for HIF use. Users are free to extend operating system services using the unreserved service numbers. Operating systems which implement HIF, OS–boot for example,

---

Table 2-2. HIF Service Calls

Service	Calling Parameters				Returned Values		
Title	gr121	lr2	lr3	lr4	gr96	gr97	gr121
exit	1	exitcode			Service does not return		
open	17	pathname	mode	pflag	fileno		errcode
close	18	fileno			retval		errcod
read	19	fileno	buffptr	nbytes	count		errcode
write	20	fileno	buffptr	nbytes	count		errcode
lseek	21	fileno	offset	orig	where		errcode
remove	22	pathname			retval		errcode
rename	23	oldfile	newfile		retval		errcode
ioctl	24	fileno	mode				errcode
iowait	25	fileno	mode		count		errcode
iostat	26	fileno			iostat		errcode
tmpnam	33	addrptr			filename		errcode
time	49				secs		errcode
getenv	65	name			addrptr		errcode
gettz	67				zonecode	dstcode	errcode
sysalloc	257	nbytes			addrptr		errcode
sysfree	258	addrptr	nbytes		retval		errcode
getpsize	259				pagesize		errcode
getargs	260				baseaddr		errcode
clock	273				msecs		errcode
cycles	274				LSBs cycles	MSBs cycles	errcode
setvec	289	trapno	funaddr		trapaddr		errcode
settrap	290	trapno	trapaddr		trapaddr		errcode
setim	291	mask	di		mask		errcode
query	305	capcode			hifvers		errcode
		capcode			cpuvers		errcode
		capcode			027vers		errcode
		capcode			clkfreq		errcode
		capcode			memenv		errcode
signal	321	newsig			oldsig		errcode
sigdfl	322	[gr125 points to HIF signal frame]			Service does not return		
sigret	323	[gr125 points to HIF signal frame]			Service does not return		
sigrep	324	[gr125 points to HIF signal frame]			Service does not return		
sigskp	325	[gr125 points to HIF signal frame]			Service does not return		
sendsig	326	sig					errcode

do not always directly support services 255 and lower. These HIF services are often translated into native operating system calls which are virtualising HIF services. For example, when a HIF conforming application program is running on a UNIX based system, the HIF services are translated into the underlying UNIX services. OS–boot supports the more complex services by making use of the MiniMON29K message system to communicate the service request to a debug support host processor (see Chapter 7). For this reason, services 255 and lower are not always available. Services with numbers 256 and higher do not require the support of a remote host processor. These services are implemented directly by OS–boot. If an underlying operating system, such as UNIX, is being used, then some of these services may not be available as they may violate the underlying operating systems security.

When application benchmark programs use HIF services, care should be taken. If a program requests a service such as *time* (service 49) it will suffer the delays of communicating the service request to a remote host if the OS–boot operating system is used. This can greatly effect the performance of a program, as execution will be delayed until the remote host responds to the service request. It is better to use services such as *cycles* (service 274) or *clock* (service 273) which are executed by the 29K processor and do not suffer the delays of remote host communication.

The assembly level glue routines for HIF services 255 and lower are rarely requested directly by an application program. They are more frequently called upon by library routines. For example, use of the library printf() routine is the typical way of generating a *write* HIF service request. The mapping between library routines and HIF services may not be always direct. The printf() routine, when used with a device operating in COOKED mode, may only request *write* services when flushing buffers supporting device communication. Appendix A contains a detailed description of each HIF service in terms of input and output parameters, as well as error codes.

2.2.4 Switching to Supervisor Mode

Operating systems which conform to HIF normally run application code in User mode. However, many real–time applications require access to resources which are restricted to Supervisor mode. If the HIF *setrap* service is supported, it is easy to install a trap handler which causes application code to commence execution in Supervisor mode. The example code sequence below uses the settrap() HIF library routine to install a trap handler for trap number 70. The trap is then asserted using assembly language glue routine assert_70().

```
extern int super_mode();      /* Here in User mode */
_settrap(70,&super_mode);     /* install trap handler */
assert_70();                  /* routine to assert trap */
. . .                         /* Here in Supervisor mode */
```

The trap handler is shown below. Its operation is very simple, it sets the Supervisor mode bit in the old processors status registers (OPS) before issuing a trap return instruction (IRET). Other application status information is not affected. For example, if the application was running with address translation turned on, then it will continue to run with address translation on, but now in Supervisor mode.

In fact the example relies on application code running with physical addressing; or if the Memory Management Unit is used to perform address translation, then vir-

---

tual addresses are mapped directly to physical addresses. This is because the Freeze mode handler, super_mode(), runs in Supervisor mode with address translation turned off. But the *settrap* system call, which installs the super_mode() handler address, runs in User mode and thus operate with User mode address values.

```
        .global _super_mode
_super_mode:                        ;gr64 is an OS temporary
        mfsr    gr64,ops            ;read the OPS register
        or      gr64,gr64,0x10      ;set SM bit in OPS
        mtsr    ops,gr64            ;iret back to Supervisor mode
        iret
```

The super_mode() and assert_70() routines have to be written in assembly language. The IRET instruction in super_mode() starts execution of the JMPI instruction in the assert_70() routine shown below. The method, shown of forcing a trap can be used to test a systems interrupt and trap support software.

```
        .global _assert_70
_assert_70:                         ;leaf routine
        asneq   70,gr96,gr96        ;force trap 70
        jmpi    lr0                 ;return
        nop
```

Table 2-3. HIF Service Call Parameters

Parameter	Description
027vers	The version number of the installed Am29027 arithmetic accelerator chip (if any)
addrptr	A pointer to an allocated memory area, a command-line-argument array, a pathname buffer, or a NULL-terminated environment variable name string.
baseaddr	The base address of the command-line-argument vector returned by the **getargs** service.
buffptr	A pointer to the buffer area where data is to be read from or written to during the execution of I/O services, or the buffer area referenced by the **wait** service.
capcode	The capabilities request code passed to the **query** service. Code values are: 0 (request HIF version), 1 (request CPU version), 2 (request Am29027 arithmetic accelerator version), 3 (request CPU clock frequency), and 4 (request memory environment).
clkfreq	The CPU clock frequency (in Hertz) returned by the **query** service.
count	The number of bytes actually read from file or written to a file.
cpuvers	The CPU family and version number returned by the **query** service.
cycles	The number of processor cycles (returned value).
di	The disable interrupts parameter to the **setim** service.
dstcode	The daylight savings time in effect flag returned by the **gettz** service.
errcode	The error code returned by the service. These are usually the same as the codes returned in the UNIX *errno* variable.
exitcode	The exit code of the application program.

(continued)

Table 2-4. *HIF Service Call Parameters (Concluded)*

(continued)

Parameter	Description
filename	A pointer to a NULL-terminated ASCII string that contains the directory path of a temporary filename.
fileno	The file descriptor which is a small integer number. File descriptors 0, 1, and 2 are guaranteed to exist and correspond to open files on program entry (0 refers to the UNIX equivalent of **stdin** and is opened for input; 1 refers to the UNIX **stdout**, and is opened for output; 2 refers to the UNIX **stderr**, and is opened for output).
funaddr	A pointer to the address of a spill or fill handler passed to the **setvec** service.
hifvers	The version of the current HIF implementation returned by the **query** service.
iostat	The input/output status returned by the **iostat** service.
mask	The interrupt mask value passed to and returned by the **setim** service.
memenv	The memory environment returned by the **query** service.
mode	A series of option flags whose values represent the operation to be performed. Used in the **open, ioctl,** and **wait** services to specify the operating mode.
msecs	Milliseconds returned by the **clock** service.
name	A pointer to a NULL-terminated ASCII string that contains an environment variable name.
nbytes	The number of data bytes requested to be read from or written to a file, or the number of bytes to allocate or deallocate from the heap.
newfile	A pointer to a NULL-terminated ASCII string that contains the directory path of a new filename.
newsig	The address of the new user signal handler passed to the **signal** service.
offset	The number of bytes from a specified position (*orig*) in a file, passed to the **lseek** service.
oldfile	A pointer to NULL-terminated ASCII string that contains the directory path of the old filename.
oldsig	The address of the previous user signal handler returned by the **signal** service.
orig	A value of 0, 1, or 2 that refers to the beginning, the current position, or the position of the end of a file.
pagesize	The memory page size in bytes returned by the **getpsize** service.
pathname	A pointer to a NULL-terminated ASCII string that contains the directory path of a filename.
pflag	The UNIX file access permission codes passed to the **open** service.
retval	The return value that indicates success or failure.
secs	The seconds count returned by the **time** service.
sig	A signal number passed to the **sendsig** service.
trapaddr	The trap address returned by the **setvec** and **settrap** services. A trap address passed to and returned by the **settrap** service.
trapno	The trap number passed to the **setvec** and **settrap** services.
where	The current position in a specified file returned by the **lseek** service.
zonecode	The time zone minutes correction value returned by the **gettz** service.

2.3   COMPILER FEATURES

I know of six C language compilers producing code for the 29K family. The most widely used of these are: the High C 29K compiler developed by Metaware Inc; and GNU supported by the Free Software Foundation. Developers of 29K software normally operate in a cross development environment, editing and compiling code on one machine which is intended to run on 29K target hardware. The High C 29K compiler is sold by a number of companies, including AMD, and packaged along with other vendor tools. High C 29K can produce code for both big– and little–endian 29K operation. The GNU compiler, **gcc**, currently (version 2.1) produces big–endian code. This does not present a problem as the 29K is used predominantly in big–endian.

The compilers make use of a number of code optimization techniques which it is difficult for the assembly language programmer to consistently make use of. Some of these techniques are briefly described below. For example:

```
...
c=a+b;
...
d=a+b;   /* sub-expression used again */
...
```

The expression a+b is a common sub-expression, it does not need to be evaluated twice. A more efficient compiler would store the result of the first evaluation in a local or global register and reuse the value in the second expression.Temporary variables used during interim calculations are optimized by the compiler. These compiler-generated temporaries are allocated to register cache locations.

Both compilers perform "strength reduction," replacing expensive instructions with less expensive ones. For example, they replace multiplies by factors of two with more efficient shift instructions. Also, reduction of code within loops is applied. The amount of code required to support each loop iteration is minimal, and loop invariant code is moved outside loops.

The compilers perform "delay slot filling" (see section 3.1.8). Delay slots occur whenever a 29K processor experiences a disruption in consecutive instruction execution. The processor always executes the instruction in the decode pipeline stage, even if the execute stage contains a jump instruction. Delay slot is the term given to the instruction following the jump or conditional branch instruction. Effectively, the branch instruction is delayed one cycle. Unlike assembly language programmers, the compiler easily finds useful instructions to insert after branching instructions. These instructions, which are executed regardless of the branch condition, are effectively achieved at no cost. Typically, an instruction that is invariant to the branch outcome is moved into the delay slot just after the branch or jump instruction.

The 29K allows load and store instructions to be overlapped with other instructions that do not depend on the load or store data. Ordinarily, a processor will load data into a register before it makes use of it in the subsequent instruction. To enable overlapping of the external memory access, the load instruction must be executed at an earlier stage, before it is required. Best results are obtained if code motion techniques are used to push the load instruction back by as many instructions as there are memory access delay cycles (another name for this technique is instruction pre-scheduling). This will prevent processor pipeline stalling caused by an operand value not being available. Once again, code motion is best left to the compiler to worry about.

2.3.1 Metaware High C 29K Compiler

The Metaware Inc. compiler, invoked with the **hc29** driver, has held the position as the top performing 29K compiler for a number of years. It generally produces the fastest code, which is of the smallest size. It is available on SUN and HP workstation platforms as well as IBM PC–AT machines. It may be made available on other platforms depending on customer demand. A number of companies resell the compiler along with other tools, such as debuggers and emulators.

2.3.2 Free Software Foundation, GCC

The GNU compiler, **gcc**, can be obtained from any existing user who is in a position, and has the time, to duplicate their copy. Alternatively, the Free Software Foundation can be contacted. For a small fee, Cygnus Support Inc. will ship you a copy along with their documentation. The GNU compiler is available in source form, and currently runs on UNIX type host machines as well as 386 based IBM PCs and compatibles.

Considering the Stanford University benchmark suite, the **gcc** compiler (version 2.1) produces code which is on average 15–20% slower in execution compared to **hc29**. The GNU compiler also used considerably more memory to contain the compiled code. Of course your application program may experience somewhat different results.

2.3.3 C++ Compiler Options

Programmers first started developing C++ code for the 29K in 1988; they used the AT&T preprocessor, *cfront*, along with the High C 29K compiler. A number of support utilities where developed at that time to enable the use of *cfront*: nm29, munch29, and szal29, which gave the size and alignment of 29K data objects (required for cross development environments).

Because the GNU tool chains can support C++ code development directly with the the GCC compiler there is little use being made of the AT&T *cfront* preprocessor. Additionally, MRI and Metaware are expected to shortly have commercial C++ compilers available. (C++ makes extensive use of dynamic memory resources, see section 2.4.1.)

2.3.4 Linking Compiled Code

After application code modules have been compiled or assembled, they must be linked together to form an executable file. There are three widely used linker tools: Microtec Research Inc. developed **ld29**; Information Processing Corp. developed **ld29i**; and the GNU tool chain offers **gld**. Sometimes these tools are repackaged by vendors and made available under different names. They all operate on AMD COFF formatted files. However, they each have different command line options and link command–file formats. A further limitation when mixing the use of these tools is that **ld29** operates with a different library format compared to the others. It uses an MRI format which is maintained by the **lib29** tool. The others use a UNIX System V format supported by the well known **ar** librarian tool.

It is best to *drive* the linker from the compiler command line, rather than invoking the linker directly. The compiler driver program, **gcc** or **hc29** for example, can build the necessary link command file and include the necessary libraries. This is the ideal way to link programs, even if assembly language modules are to be named on the compiler command line. Note, the default link command files frequently used align text and data sections to 8k (8192) byte boundaries. This is because the OS–boot operating system (see Chapter 7) normally operates with address translation turned on. The maximum page size of 8k bytes is used to reduce run–time Memory Management Unit support overheads.

When developing software for embedded applications there is always the problem of what to do with initialized data variables. The problem arises because variables must be located in RAM, but embedded programs are typically not *loaded* by an operating system which prepares the data memory locations with initialized values. Embedded programs are stored in ROM; this means there is no problem with program instructions unless a program wishes to modify its own code at run–time.

Embedded system support tools typically provide a means of locating initialized data in ROM; and transferring the ROM contents to RAM locations before program execution starts. The High C 29K linker, **ld29**, provides the INITDATA command for this purpose. Programs must be linked such that all references to writeable data occur to RAM addresses. The INITDATA scans a list of sections and transfers the data variables found into a new **.initdat** section. The list contains the names of sections containing initialized data. The linker is then directed to locate the new **.initdata** section in ROM.The start address of the new section is marked with symbol **initdat**.

Developers are provided with the source to a program called **initcopy()** which must be included in the application program. This program accesses the data in ROM

---

starting at label **initdat** and transfers the data to RAM locations. The format of the data located in the **.initdat** section is understood by the **initcopy()** routine. This routine must be run before the application main() program. A user could place a call to the initialization routine inside **crt0.s**.

Note, because **initcopy()** must be able to read the appropriate ROM devices, these devices must be placed in an accessible address space. This is not a problem for 2–bus members of the 29K family, but 3–bus members can have a problem if the **.initdat** section is located in a ROM device along with program code. Processors with 3–bus architectures, such as the Am29000, have separately addressed Instruction and ROM spaces which are used for all instruction accesses. The Am29000 processor has no means of reading these two spaces to access data unless an external bridge is provided. If program code and initialized data are located in the same ROM device, the **initcopy()** program can only be used if an external *bridge* is provided. This bridge connects the Am29000 processor data memory bus to the instruction memory bus. If a 3–bus system does not have a bridge the **romcoff** utility can be used to initialize data memory.

The **romcoff** utility can be used when the **ld29** linker is not available and the INITDATA linker command option is not provided. Besides being able to work with 3–bus architectures which have no bridge, it can be used to process program sections other than just initialized data. Sections which ultimately must reside in RAM can be initialized from code located in ROM.

Fully linked executables are processed by **romcoff** to produce a new linkable COFF file. This new module has a section called **RI_text** which contains a routine called **RAMInit()**. When invoked, this routine initializes the processed sections,during preparation of the relevant RAM regions. The new COFF file produced by **romcoff()** must be relinked with the originally linked modules. Additionally, a call to **RAMInit()** must be placed in **crt0.s** or in the processor boot–up code (cold–start code) if the linked executable is intended to control the processor during the processor RESET code sequence.

When **romcoff** is not used with the "–r" option, it assumes that the ROM memory is not readable. This results in a **RAMInit()** function which uses CONST and CONSTH instructions to produce the data values to be initialized in RAM. This results in extra ROM memory requirements to contain the very much larger **RAMInit()** routine, but ensures that 3–bus architectures which do not incorporate a bridge can initialize their RAM memory.

2.4 LIBRARY SUPPORT

2.4.1 Memory Allocation

The HIF specification requires that conforming operating systems maintain a memory heap. An application program can acquire memory during execution by using the malloc() library routine. This routine makes use of the underlying *sysalloc* HIF service. The malloc() call is passed the number of consecutive memory bytes required; it returns a pointer to the start of the memory allocated from the heap.

Calls to malloc() should be matched with calls to library routine free(). This routine is passed the start address of the previously allocated memory along with the number of bytes acquired. The free() routine is supported by the *sysfree* HIF service. The HIF specification states "no dynamic memory allocation structure is implied by this service". This means the *sysfree* may do nothing; in fact, this service with OS–boot (version 0.5) simply returns. Continually using memory without ever releasing it and thus making it reusable, will be a serious problem for some application programs, in particular C++ which frequently constructs and destructs objects in heap memory.

For this reason the library routines which interface to the HIF services perform their own heap management. The first call to malloc() results in a *sysalloc* HIF request for 8k bytes, even in the malloc() was for only a few bytes. Further malloc() calls do not result in a *sysalloc* request until the 8k byte pool is used up. Calls to free() enable previously allocated memory to be returned to the pool maintained by the library.

The alloca() library routine provides a means of acquiring memory from the memory stack rather than the heap. A pointer to the memory region within the calling procedure's memory stack frame, is returned by alloca(). The advantage of this method is that there is no need to call a corresponding *free* routine. The temporary memory space is automatically freed when the calling procedure returns. Users of the alloca() service must be careful to remember the limited lifetime of data objects maintained on the memory stack. After returning from the procedure calling alloca(), all related data variables cease to exist and should not be referenced.

2.4.2 Setjmp and Longjmp

The setjmp() and longjmp() library routines provide a means to jump from the current procedure environment to a previous procedure environment. The setjmp() routine is used to mark the position which a longjmp() will return to. A call to setjmp() is made by a procedure, passing it a pointer to an environment buffer, as shown below:

```
int     setjmp(env)
jmp_buf env;
```

The buffer definition is shown below. It records the value of register stack and memory stack support registers in use at the time of the setjmp() call. The setjmp() call returns a value zero.

```
typedef struct jmp_buf_str
{       int*    gr1;
        int*    msp;
        int*    lr0;
        int*    lr1;
} *jmp_buf;
```

The setjmp() routine is very simple. It is listed below to assist with the understanding of the longjmp() routine. It is important to be aware that setjmp(), longjmp(), SPILL and FILL handlers, along with the signal trampoline code (see section 2.5.2) form a matched set of routines. Their operation is interdependent. Any change to one may require changes to the others to ensure proper system operation.

```
_setjmp:                              ;lr2 points to buffer
        store   0,0,gr1,lr2           ;copy gr1 to buffer
        add     lr2,lr2,4
        store   0,0,msp,lr2           ;copy msp
        add     lr2,lr2,4
        store   0,0,lr0,lr2           ;copy lr0
        add     lr2,lr2,4
        store   0,0,lr1,lr2           ;copy lr1
        jmpi    lr0                   ;return
        const   gr96,0
```

When longjmp() is called it is passed a pointer to an environment buffer which was initialized with a previous setjmp() call. The longjmp() call does not return directly. It does return, but as the corresponding setjmp() establishing the buffer data. The longjmp() return–as–setjmp() can be distinguished from a setjmp() return as itself, because the longjmp() appears as a setjmp() return with a non–zero value. In fact the *value* parameter passed to longjmp() becomes the setjmp() return value. A C language outline for the longjmp() routine is shown below:

```
void    longjmp(env, value)
jmp_buf env;
int     value)
{
        gr1 = env->gr1;
        lr2addr = env->gr1 + 8;
        msp = env->msp;

        /* saved lr1 is invalid if saved lr2address > rfb */
        if (lr2addr > rfb) {
```

```
                /*
                 * None of the registers are useful.
                 * Set rfb to lr2address-512 & rab to rfb-512
                 * the FILL assert will take care of filling
                 */
                lr1 = env->lr1;
                rab = lr2addr - windowsize;
                rfb = lr2addr;
        }
        lr0 = env->lr0;
        if (rfb < lr1)
                raise V_FILL;
        return value;
}
```

The actual longjmp() routine code, shown below, is written in assembly language. This is because the sequence of modifying the register stack support registers is very important. An interrupt could occur during the longjmp() operation. That interrupt may require a C language interrupt handler to run. The signal trampoline code is required to understand all the possible register stack conditions, and fix–up the stack support registers to enable further C procedure call to be made.

```
_longjmp:
        load    0,0,tav,lr2      ;gr1 = env->gr1
        add     gr97,lr2,4       ;gr97 now points to msp
        cpeq    gr96,lr3,0       ;test return "value", it must
        srl     gr96,gr96,31     ; be non zero
        or      gr96,lr3,gr96    ;gr96 has return value
        add     gr1,tav,0        ; gr1 = env->gr1;
        add     tav,tav,8        ;lr2address =env->gr1+8
        load    0,0,msp,gr97     ;msp = env->msp
        cpleu   gr99,tav,rfb     ;if (lr2address > rfb)
        jmpt    gr99,$1
;{
        add     gr97,gr97,4      ;gr97 points to lr0
        add     gr98,gr97,4      ;gr98 points to lr1
        load    0,0,lr1,gr98     ;lr1 = value from jmpbuf
        sub     gr99,rfb,rab     ;gr99 has windowsize
        sub     rab,tav,gr99     ;rab = lr2address-windowsize
        add     rfb,tav,0        ;rfb = lr2address
$1: ;}
        load    0,0,lr0,gr97     ;lr0 = env->lr0
        jmpi    lr0              ;return
        asgeu   V_FILL,rfb,lr1   ;if (rfb < lr1) raise V_FILL;
                                 ; may fill from rfb to lr1
```

2.4.3 Support Libraries

The GNU tool chain is supported with a single library, libc.a. However the High C 29K tool chain is supported with a range of library options. It is best to use the compiler driver, **hc29**, to select the appropriate library. This avoids having to master the library naming rules and build linker command files.

The GNU libraries do not support word–sized–access–only memory systems. Originally, the Am29000 processor could not support byte–sized accesses and all memory accesses were performed on word sized objects. This required read–mod-ify–write access sequences to manipulate byte sized objects located in memory. Be-cause all current 29K processors support byte–size access directly, there is no need to have specialized libraries for accessing bytes. However, the High C 29K tool chain still ships the *old* libraries to support existing (pre–Rev D, 1990) Am29000 processors.

The **hc29** driver normally links with three libraries: the ANSI standard C sup-port library (libs*.lib), the IEEE floating–point routine library (libieee.lib), and the HIF system call interface library (libos.lib). There are actually eight ANSI libraries. The driver selects the appropriate library depending on the selected switches. The reason for so many libraries is due to: the support of the old word–only memory sys-tems, the option to talk with an Am29027 coprocessor directly, and finally, the op-tion to select Am29050 processor optimized code.

The ANSI library includes transcendental routines (sin(), cos(), etc.) which were developed by Kulus Inc. These routines are generally faster than the transcen-dental routines developed by QTC Inc., which were at one time shipped with High C 29K. The QTC transcendentals are still supplied as the libq*.lib libraries, and must now be explicitly linked. The Kulus transcendentals also have the advantage in that they support double and single floating–point precision. The routines are named slightly differently, and the compiler automatically selects the correct routine de-pending on parameter type. The GNU libraries (version 2.1) include the QTC tran-scendental routines.

Most 29K processors do not support floating–point instructions directly (see section 3.1.7). When a non–implemented floating–point instruction is encountered, the processor takes a trap, and operating system routines emulate the operation in trapware code. If a system has an Am29027 floating–point coprocessor available, then the trapware can make use of the coprocessor to achieve faster instruction emu-lation. This is generally five times faster than software based emulation. Keeping the presence of the Am29027 coprocessor hidden in operating system support trapware, enables application programs to be easily moved between systems with and without a coprocessor.

However, an additional (about two times) speed–up can be achieved by appli-cation programs talking to the Am29027 coprocessor directly, rather than via trap-ware. When the High C 29K compiler is used with the "–29027" or "–f027" switches, inline code is produced for floating–point operations which directly access the coprocessor. Unfortunately the compiled code can not be run on a system which has no coprocessor. The ANSI standard C support libraries also support inline

Am29027 coprocessor access with the libs*7.lib library. When instructed to produce direct coprocessor access code, the compiler also instructs the linker to use this library in place of the standard library, libs*0.lib.

The Am29050 processor supports integer multiply directly in hardware rather than via trapware. It also supports integer divide via converting operands to floating–point before dividing and converting back to integer. The High C 29K compiler performs integer multiply and divide by using transparent helper routines (see section 3.6); this is faster than the trapware method used by the GNU compiler. When the High C 29K compiler is used with the "–29050" switch, and the GNU compiler with the "–m29050" switch, code optimized for the use for an Am29050 processor is used. This code may not run on other 29K family members, as the Am29050 processor has some additional instructions (see sections 3.1.6 and 3.1.7).

2.5   C LANGUAGE INTERRUPT HANDLERS

Embedded application code developers typically have to deal with interrupts from peripheral devices requiring attention. As with general code development there is a desire to deal with interrupts using C language code rather than assembly language code. Compared to CISC type processors, which generally do not have a register stack, this is a little more difficult to achieve with the 29K family. In addition, 29K processors do not have microcode to automatically save their interrupted context. The interrupt architecture of a 29K processor is very flexible and is dealt with in detail in Chapter 4. This section presents two useful techniques enabling C language code to be used for interrupts supported by a HIF conforming operating system.

The characteristics of the C handler function are important in determining the steps which must be taken before the handler can execute. It is desirable that the C handler run in Freeze mode because this will reduce the overhead costs. These costs are incurred because interrupts may occur at times when the processor is operating in a condition not suitable for immediately commencing interrupt processing. Most of these overheads are concerned with register stack support and are described in detail in section 4.4. This section deals with establishing an interrupt handler which can run in Freeze mode. The following section 2.5.2 deals with all other types of C language interrupt handlers.

A C language interrupt handler qualifies for Freeze mode execution if it meets with a number of criteria:

■   It is a small leaf routine which does not attempt to lower the register stack pointer. This means that, should the interrupt have occurred during a critical stage in register stack management, the stack need not be brought to a valid condition.

- Floating–point instructions not directly supported by the processor are not used. Many members of the 29K family emulate floating–point instructions in software (see Chapter 3).

- Instructions which may result in a trap are not used. All interrupts and traps are disabled while in Freeze mode. This means the Memory Management Unit cannot be used for memory access protection and address translation.

- The handlers execution is short. Because the handler is to be run in Freeze mode its execution time will add to the system interrupt latency.

- Transparent procedure calls are not used. They typically require the support of indirect pointer which are not temporarily saved by the code presented in this section.

The methods shown in this and the following section rely on application code running with physical addressing; or if the Memory Management Unit is used to perform address translation, then virtual addresses are mapped directly to physical addresses. This is because the macros used to install the Freeze Mode trap handlers are used to generate code in User mode and thus operate with User mode address values. However, Freeze mode code runs in Supervisor mode with address translation turned off.

The Metaware High C 29K and GCC compilers currently have no C language extension to aid with interrupt handling. There have been investigations into adding the key word *Interrupt* to the compiler; this would result in additional tag data (see section 3.5) being added to interrupt handler routines. As yet this has not occurred. The only way to identify if a handler routine qualifies for the above Freeze mode handler status, is to compile it with the "–S" option and examine the assembly language code. Alternatively, handler routines which make function calls can be immediately eliminated as unsuitable for operation in Freeze mode. Examining the assembly language code would enable the *nregs* value used in the following code to be determined. Small leaf routincs operate with global registers only. Starting with *gr96*, *nregs* is the number of global registers used by a C leaf handler routine.

The **interrupt_handler** macro defined below can be used to install a C level interrupt handler which is called upon when the appropriate trap or interrupt occurs. The code is written in assembly language because it must use a carefully crafted instruction sequence; the first part of which uses the HIF *settrap* service to install, in the processor vector table, the address ($1) which will be vectored to when the interrupt occurs. The necessary code is written as a macro rather than a procedure call because the second part of the macro contains the start of the actual interrupt handler code. This code, starting at address $1, is unique to each interrupt and can not be shared. Note, the code makes use of *push* and *pop* macro instructions to transfer data between registers and the memory stack. These assembly macros are described in section 3.3.1.

```
        .reg    it0,gr64                    ;freeze mode interrupt
        .reg    it1,gr65                    ;temporary registers

        .macro interrupt_handler, trap_number, C_handler, nregs

                sub     gr1,gr1,4*4         ;get lr0-lr3 space
                asgeu   V_SPILL,gr1,rab     ;check for stack spill
                add     lr1,gr121,0         ;save gr121
                add     lr0,gr96,0          ;save gr96
                const   gr121,290           ;HIF 2.0 SETTRAP service
                const   lr2,trap_number     ;trap number, macro parameter
                const   lr3,$1              ;trap handler address
                consth  lr3,$1
                asneq   69,gr1,gr1          ;HIF service request
                add     gr121,lr1,0         ;restore gr121
                add     gr96,lr0,0          ;restore gr96
                add     gr1,gr1,4*4         ;restore stack
                jmp     $2                  ;macro code finished
                 asleu  V_FILL,lr1,rfb      ;check for stack fill    <---

        $1:     push    msp,lr0             ;start of Interrupt handler
                pushsr  msp,it1,ipa         ;save special reg. ipa
                const   it0,nregs-2         ;number or regs. to save
                const   it1,96<<2           ;starting with gr96
        $3:     mtsr    ipa,it1
                add     it1,it1,1<<2        ;increment ipa
                sub     msp,msp,4           ;decrement stack pointer
                jmpfdec it0,$3
                 store  0,0,gr0,msp         ;save global registers
        ;
                const   lr0,C_handler
                consth  lr0,C_handler
                calli   lr0,lr0             ;call C level handler
                 nop
        ;
                const   it0,nregs-2         ;number of global registers
                const   it1,(96+nregs-1)<<2
        $4:     mtsr    ipa,it1
                load    0,0,gr0,msp         ;restore global register
                sub     it1,it1,1<<2        ;decrement ipa
                jmpfdec it0,$4
                 add    msp,msp,4           ;increment stack pointer
                popsr   ipa,it0,msp         ;restore ipa
                pop     lr0,msp             ;restore lr0
                iret
        $2:
          .endm
```

Because the C level handler is intended to run in Freeze mode, there is very little code before the required handler, *C_handler*, is called. Registers *lr0* and IPA are saved on the memory stack before they are temporarily used. Then the required number of global registers (*nregs*) starting with *gr96* are also saved on the stack. The programmer must determine the *nregs* value by examining the handler routine assembly code.

The **interrupt_handler** macro must be used in an assembly language module unless the Metaware High C 29K compiler is being used. The compiler supports an extension to C which enables assembly code to be directly inserted into C code modules. This enables a C macro to be defined which will call upon the assembly language macro code. The example code below shows the C macro definition.

```
#define interrupt_handler(tap_number, C_handler, nregs) \
/*int  trap_number; \
 void  (*C_handler)(); \
 int   nregs; */ \
 _ASM(" interrupt_handler "#trap_number","#C_handler","#nregs);
```

Alternatively the C macro could contain the assembly macro code directly. Using the technique shown, C modules which use the macro must be first compiled with the "–S" option; this results in an assembly language output file. The assembly language file (.s file) is then assembled with an include file which contains the macro definition. Note, C modules which use the macro must use the "_ASM" C extension to include the assembly language macro file (shown below) for its later use by the assembler.

```
_ASM(" .include \"interrupt_macros.h\"");
         /* int2_handler uses 8 regs. and is called
           when hardware trap number 18 occurs */
interrupt_handler(18,int2_handler,8);
```

2.5.1 Using an Interrupt Context Cache

The **interrupt_handler** macro code, described in the previous section, prepares the processor to handle a C language interrupt handler which can operate within the processor Freeze mode restrictions. The code saves the interrupted processor context onto the current memory stack position before calling the C handler.

The **interrupt_cache** macro shown below can be used in place of the previously described macro. Its use is also restricted to preparing the processor to handle a C level handler which meets the Freeze mode execution criteria. However, its operation is considerably faster due to the use of an Interrupt Context Cache. Section 4.3.9 describes context caching in more detail. A cache is used here only to save sufficient context to enable a non–interruptable C level handler to execute.

The cache is implemented using operating system registers *gr64–gr80*. These global registers are considered operating system temporaries, at least *gr64–gr79* are (also known as *it0–it3* and *kt0–kt11*). Processors which do not directly support floating–point operations contain instruction emulation software (trapware) which normally uses registers in the *gr64–gr79* range to support instruction emulation. Given application code can perform a floating–point operation at any time, an operating system can not consider these registers contents remain static after application code has run. For this reason and additionally floating–point trapware normally runs with interrupts turned off, it is convenient to use these registers for interrupted context caching.

The **interrupt_handler** macro uses a loop to preserve the global registers used by the Freeze mode interrupt handler. The **interrupt_cache** macro *unrolls* the loop and uses register–to–register operations rather than register–to–memory. In place of traversing the loop *nregs* times, the *nregs* value is used to determine the required entry point to the unrolled code. These techniques reduce interrupt preparation times and interrupt latency.

```
        .macro interrupt_cache, trap_number, C_handler, nregs

        sub     gr1,gr1,4*4      ;get lr0-lr3 space
        asgeu   V_SPILL,gr1,rab  ;check for stack spill
        add     lr1,gr121,0      ;save gr121
        add     lr0,gr96,0       ;save gr96
        const   gr121,290        ;HIF 2.0 SETTRAP service
        const   lr2,trap_number  ;trap number, macro parameter
        const   lr3,$1-(nregs*4) ;trap handler address
        consth  lr3,$1-(nregs*4)
        asneq   69,gr1,gr1       ;HIF service request
        add     gr121,lr1,0      ;restore gr121
        add     gr96,lr0,0       ;restore gr96
        add     gr1,gr1,4*4      ;restore stack
        jmp     $2               ;macro code finished
         asleu  V_FILL,lr1,rfb   ;check for stack fill         ←

        add     gr80,gr111,0     ;save gr111 to interrupt
        add     gr79,gr110,0     ; context cache
        add     gr78,gr109,0
        add     gr77,gr108,0     ;the interrupt handler starts
        add     gr76,gr107,0     ;somewhere in this code range
        add     gr75,gr106,0     ;depending on the register
        add     gr74,gr105,0     ;usage of the C level code
        add     gr73,gr104,0
        add     gr72,gr103,0
        add     gr71,gr102,0
        add     gr70,gr101,0
        add     gr69,gr100,0
        add     gr68,gr99,0
        add     gr67,gr98,0
        add     gr66,gr97,0      ;save gr97
        add     gr64,lr0,0       ;save lr0
$1:
        const   lr0,C_handler
        consth  lr0,C_handler
        calli   lr0,lr0          ;call C level handler
         add    gr65,gr96,0      ;save gr96
```

```
        ;
                jmp     $2-4-(nregs*4)  ;determine registers used
                 add    lr0,gr64,0      ;restore lr0
                add     gr111,gr80,0    ;restore gr111 from interrupt
                add     gr110,gr79,0    ; context cache
                add     gr109,gr78,0
                add     gr108,gr77,0
                add     gr107,gr76,0
                add     gr106,gr75,0
                add     gr105,gr74,0
                add     gr104,gr73,0
                add     gr103,gr72,0
                add     gr102,gr71,0
                add     gr101,gr70,0
                add     gr100,gr69,0
                add     gr99,gr68,0
                add     gr98,gr67,0
                add     gr67,gr66,0
                add     gr96,gr65,0     ;retsore gr96
                iret
        $2:
          .endm
```

2.5.2 Using Signals to Deal with Interrupts

Some C language interrupt handlers will not be able to run in Freeze mode. Because (as described in section 2.5) they are unsuitable leaf routines, or are not leaf routines and thus require use of the register stack. In this case the signal trampoline code described in section 4.4 and Appendix B must be used. The trampoline code is called by the Freeze mode interrupt handler after critical registers have been saved on the memory stack. The C language handler is called by the trampoline code after the register stack is prepared for further use. Note, interrupts can occur at times when the register stack condition is not immediately usable by a C language handler.

The signal mechanism works by *registering* a signal handler function address for use when a particular signal number occurs. This is done with the library routine signal(). Signals are normally generated by abnormal events and the signal() routine allows the operating system to call a user supplied routine which will be called to deal with the event. The signal() function uses the *signal* HIF service to supply the address of a library routine (*sigcode*) which will be called for all signals generated. The library routine is then responsible for calling the appropriate C handler from a table of handlers indexed by the signal number. When signal() is used a table entry is constructed for the indicated signal.

```
                signal(sig_number, func)
        int     sig_number;
        void    (*func)(sig_number);
```

A signal can only be generated for an interrupt if the code vectored to by the interrupt calls the shared library routine known as the *trampoline* code. It is known as the trampoline code because signals *bounce* from this code to the registered signal handler. To ensure that the trampoline code is called when an interrupt occurs, the Freeze mode code vectored to by the interrupt must pass execution to the trampoline code, indicating the signal which has occurred. The **signal_associate** macro shown below can be used to install the Freeze Mode code and associate a signal number with the interrupt or trap hardware number.

```
.reg    it0,gr64                    ;freeze mode interrupt
.reg    it1,gr65                    ;temporary registers

.macro signal_associate, trap_number, sig_number

        sub     gr1,gr1,4*4         ;get lr0-lr3 space
        asgeu   V_SPILL,gr1,rab     ;check for stack spill
        add     lr1,gr121,0         ;save gr121
        add     lr0,gr96,0          ;save gr96
        const   gr121,290           ;HIF 2.0 SETTRAP service
        const   lr2,trap_number     ;trap number, macro parameter
        const   lr3,$1              ;trap handler address
        consth  lr3,$1
        asneq   69,gr1,gr1          ;HIF service request
        add     gr121,lr1,0         ;restore gr121
        add     gr96,lr0,0          ;restore gr96
        add     gr1,gr1,4*4         ;restore stack
        jmp     $2                  ;macro code finished
         asleu  V_FILL,lr1,rfb      ;check for stack fill          ←

$1:     const   it0,sig_number      ;start of Interrupt handler
        push    msp,it0             ;push sig_number on
        push    msp,gr1             ; interrupt context frame.
        push    msp,rab             ;use push macro,
        const   it0,512             ; see section 3.3.1
        sub     rab,rfb,it0         ;set rab = rfb-512
;
        pushsr  msp,it0,pc0         ;push special registers
        pushsr  msp,it0,pc1
        pushsr  msp,it0,pc2
        pushsr  msp,it0,cha
        pushsr  msp,it0,chd
        pushsr  msp,it0,chc
        pushsr  msp,it0,alu
        pushsr  msp,it0,ops
;
        push    msp,tav             ;push tav (gr121)
        mfsr    it0,ops             ;set DI in OPS
        or      it0,it0,0x2         ;this disables interrupts
        mtsr    ops,it0             ; in signal trampoline code
;
        mtsrim  chc,0               ;the trampoline code is
        const   it1,RegSigHand      ; described in section 4.4.1
        consth  it1,RegSigHand      ;RegSigHand is a library
```

```
        load    0,0,it1,it1       ; variable
        cpeq    it0,it1,0         ;test for no handler
        jmpt    it0,SigDfl        ;jmup if no handler(s)
        add     it0,it1,4         ;it1 has trampoline address
        mtsr    pc1,it1           ;IRET to signal
        mtsr    pc0,it0           ; trampoline code
        iret
$2:                               ;end of macro
    .endm
```

The above macro code does not disable the interrupt from the requesting device. This is necessary for external interrupts, as if interrupts are reenabled the interrupt shall immediately be taken again. The code sets the the DI–bit in the OPS special register; this means interrupts will remain disabled in the trampoline code. It will be the responsibility of the C language handler to clear the interrupt request, this may require accessing an off–chip peripheral device. An alternative is to clear the interrupt request in the above Freeze mode code and not set the DI–bit in the OPS. This would enable the trampoline and C language handler code to execute with interrupts enabled. This would lead to the possibility of nested signal events; however, the signal trampoline code is able to deal with such complex events.

With the example **signal_associate** macro the trampoline code and the C handler run in the processor mode at the time the interrupt occurred. They can be forced to run in Supervisor mode by setting the Supervisor mode bit (SM–bit) when OR–ing the DI–bit in the OPS register. Supervisor mode may be required to enable accessing of the interrupting device when disabling the interrupt request. The address translation bits (PA and PD) may also be set at this time to turn off virtual addressing during interrupt processing. To make these changes to the above example code, the value 0x72 should be OR–ed with the OPS register rather than the 0x2 value shown.

As described in the previous section, a C language macro can be used to access the assembly level macro instruction, when the High C 29K compiler is being used. The definition of the C macro is shown below.

```
#define signal_associate(tap_number, sig_number) \
/*int  trap_number; \
 int  sig_number; */ \
 _ASM(" signal_associate "#trap_number","#sig_number);
```

When the macro is used to associate a signal number with a processor trap number, it is also necessary to supply the address of the C language signal handler called when the signal occurs. The following example associates trap number 18 (floating–point exception) with signal number 8. This signal is known to UNIX and HIF users as SIGFPE; when it occurs the C handler **sigfpe_handler** is called.

```
_ASM(" .include \"interrupt_macros.h\"");
signal_associate(18,8);    /* trap 18, F–P */
signal(8,sigfpe_handler);  /* signal 8 handler */'
```

C language signal handlers are free of many of the restrictions which apply to Freeze mode interrupt handlers. However, the HIF specification still restricts their operation to some extent. Signal handlers can only use HIF services with service numbers greater than 256. This means that printf() cannot be used. The reason for this is HIF services below 256 are not reentrant, and a signal may occur while just such a HIF service request was being processed. Return from the signal handler must be via one of the signal return services: sigdft, sigret, sigrep or sigskp. If the signal handler simply returns, the trampoline code will issue a sigdfl service request on behalf of the signal handler.

A single C level signal routine can be used to dispatch several C language interrupt handlers. Section 4.3.12 describes an interrupt queuing method, where interrupt handlers run in Freeze mode and build an interrupt descriptor (bead). Each descriptor is placed in a list (string of beads) and a *Dispatcher* routine is used to process desriptors. The signal handling method described above can be used to register a C level Dispatcher routine. This results in C level context being prepared only once, and the Dispatcher routine calling the appropriate C handler.

2.6 SUPPORT UTILITY PROGRAMS

There are a number of important utility programs available to the software developer. These tools are generally available on all development platforms and are shared by different tool vendors. Most of the programs operate on object files produced by the assembler or linker. All linkable object files and executable files are maintained in AMD Common Object File Format (COFF). This standard is very closely based on the AT&T standard used with UNIX System V. Readers wishing to know more about the details of the format may consult the High C 29K documentation or the AT&T Programmer's Guide for UNIX System V. The *coff.h* include file found on most tool distributions, describes the C language data structures used by the COFF standard — often described as the COFF wrappers.

2.6.1 Examining Object Files (Type .o And a.Out)

nm29

The **nm29** utility program is used to examine the symbol table contained in a binary COFF file produced by the compiler, assembler or linker. The format is very much like the UNIX *nm* utility. Originally **nm29** was written to supply symbol table information to the **munch29** utility in support of the AT&T C++ *cfront* program. A number of command line options have been added to enable additional information to be printed, such as symbol type and section type.

One useful way to use **nm29** is to pipe the output to the *sort* utility, for example: "nm29 a.out I sort I more"; each symbol is printed preceded by its value. The *sort* utility arranges for symbol table entries to be presented in ascending value. Since most symbols are associated with address labels, this is a useful way to locate an address relative to its nearest address labels.

munch29

This utility is used with the AT&T C++ preprocessor. This program is known as *cfront* and converts C++ programs into C. After the C++ program has been converted and linked with other modules and libraries, it is examined with **nm29** to determine the names of any static constructor and destructor functions. The C++ translator builds these functions as necessary and tags their names with predefined character sequences. The output from **nm29** is passed to **munch29** which looks for constructor and destructor names. If found, **munch29** builds C procedures which call all the identified object constructors and destructors. Because the constructor functions must execute before the application main() program, the original program is relinked with the constructor procedures being called before main(). The main() entry is replaced with _main(). This also enables the call to destructor procedures to be made in _main() when main() returns.

Because G++ is now available for C++ code development (note, G++ is incorporated into the GCC compiler), there is little use being made of the AT&T *cfront* preprocessor. Additionally, MRI and Metaware are expected to shortly have commercial C++ compilers available.

rdcoff

The **rdcoff** utility is only available to purchasers of the High C 29K product. This utility prints the contents of a COFF conforming object file. Each COFF file section is presented in an appropriate format. For example, text sections are disassembled. If the symbol table has not been striped from the COFF file, then symbol values are shown. The utility is useful for examining COFF header information, such as the text and data region start addresses. Those using GNU tools can use the **coff** and **objdump** utilities to obtain this information

coff This utility is a shorthand way of examining COFF files. It reports a summary of COFF header information, followed by similar reports for each of the sections found in the object file. The utility is useful for quickly checking the link mapping of a.out type files; especially when a project is using a number of different 29K target systems which have different memory system layouts, requiring different program linkage.

objdump

This utility is supplied with the GNU tool chain. It can be used to examine selected parts of object files. It has an array of command line options which are compatible with the UNIX System V utility of the same name. In a similar way

---

to the **rdcoff** utility it attempts to format selected information in a meaningful way.

2.6.2 Modifying Object Files

cvcoff

The COFF specification states that object file information is maintained in the endian of the host processor. This need not be the endian of the target 29K processor. As described in Chapter 1, 29K processors can run in big– or little–endian but are almost exclusively used in big–endian format. Endian refers to which byte position in a word is considered the byte of lowest address. With big–endian, bytes further left have lower addresses. Machines such as VAXs and IBM–PCs operate with little–endian; and machines from SUN and HP tend to operate with big–endian.

What this means to the 29K software developer is that COFF files on, say, a PC will have little–endian COFF wrappers. And COFF files on, say, a SUN machine will have big–endian wrapers, regardless of the endianness of the 29K target code. When object files or libraries containing object files are moved between host machines of different endianness, the **cvcoff** utility must be used to convert the endianness of the COFF wraper information. The **cvcoff** utility can also be used to check the endianess of an object file. Most utility programs and software development tools expect to operate on object files which are in host endian; however, there are a few tools which can operate on COFF files of either host endianness. In practice this reduces the need to use the **cvcoff** utility.

strpcoff

This utility can be used to remove unnecessary information from a COFF file. When programs are compiled with the "–g" option, additional symbol information is added to the COFF file. The **strpcoff** utility can be used to remove this information and any other details such as relocation data and line–number pointers. Typically linkers have an option to automatically strip this information after linking. (**ld29** has the "–s" option.) The COFF file header information needed for loading a program is not stripped.

2.6.3 Getting a Program into ROM

After a program has been finally linked, and possibly adjusted to deal with any data initialization problems (see section 2.3.4), it must be transferred into ROM devices. This is part of the typical software development cycle for embedded processor products. A number of manufacturers make equipment for programming PROM de-

---

vices. They normally operate with data files which must be appropriately formatted. Tektronix Hex format and Motorola S3 Records are two of the commonly used file formats. The **coff2hex** utility can be used to convert the COFF formatted executable file produced by the linker, into a new file which is correctly formatted for the selected PROM programmer. If more than one PROM is to required to store the program, **coff2hex** can be instructed to divide the COFF data into a set of appropriate files. Alternatively, this task can be left to more sophisticated programming equipment. The utility has a number of command line options; the width and size of PROM devices can be chosen, alternatively specific products can be selected by manufacture part number.

Chapter 3

Assembly Language Programming

Most developers of software for the 29K family will use a high level language, such as C, for the majority of code development. This makes sense for a number of reasons: Using a high level language enables a different processor to be selected at some future date. The code, if written in a portable way, need only be recompiled for the new target processor. The ever increasing size of embedded software projects makes the higher productivity achievable with a high level language attractive. And additionally, the 29K family has a RISC instruction set which can be efficiently used by a high level language compiler [Mann et al 1991b].

However, the software developer must resort to the use of assembly code programming in a number of special cases. Because of the relentless efficiency of the current C language compilers for the 29K, it is difficult for a programmer to out–perform the code generating abilities of a compiler for any reasonably sized program. For this reason it is best to limit the use of assembly code as much as possible. Some of the support tasks which do require assembly coding are:

- Low–level support routines for interrupts and traps (see Chapter 4).

- Operating system support services such as system calls and application–task context switching (see Chapter 5). Also, taking control of the processor during the power–up and initialization sequence.

- Memory Management Unit trapware (see Chapter 6).

- Floating–point and complex integer operation trapware, where the 29K family member does not support the operation directly in hardware.

- High performance versions of critical routines. In some cases it may be possible to enhance a routines performance by implementing assembly code short–cuts not identified by a compiler.

This chapter deals with aspects of assembly level programming. There are some differences between 29K family members, particularly in the area of on–chip peripherals for microcontrollers. The chapter does not go into details peculiar to individual family members; for that it is best to study the processor User's Manual. The material covered is relevant to all 29K family members.

3.1   INSTRUCTION SET

The Am29000 microprocessor implements 112 instructions. All hardware implemented instructions execute in a single–cycle, except for IRET, IRETINV, LOADM and STOREM. Instruction format was discussed in section 1.8. All instructions have a fixed 32–bit format, with an 8–bit opcode field and 3, 8–bit, operand fields. Field–C specifies the result operand register (DEST), field–A and field–B supply the source operands (SRCA and SRCB). Most instructions operate on data held in global or local registers, and there are no complex addressing modes supported. Field–B, or field–B and field–A combined, can be used to provide 8–bit or 16–bit immediate data for instructions. Access to external memory can only be performed with the LOAD[M] and STORE[M] instructions. There are a number of instructions, mostly used by operating system code, for accessing the processor special registers.

The following sections deal with the different instruction classes. Some of the instructions described are not supported by all members of the 29K family. In particular, many of the floating–point instructions are only directly executed by the Am29050 processor. If an instruction is not directly supported by the processor hardware, then a trap is generated during instruction execution. In this case, the operating system uses *trapware* to implement the instruction's operation in software. Emulating nonimplemented instructions in software means some instruction execution speeds are reduced, but the instruction set is compatible across all family members.

3.1.1 Integer Arithmetic

The Integer Arithmetic instructions perform add, subtract, multiply, and divide operations on word–length (32–bit) integers. All instructions in this class set the ALU Status Register. The integer arithmetic instructions are shown Tables 3–1 and 3–2.

The MULTIPLU, MULTIPLY, DIVIDE, and DIVIDU instructions are not implemented directly on most 29K family members, but are supported by traps. To determine if your processor directly supports these instructions, check with the processor User's Manual or the tables in Chapter 1. The Am29050 microprocessor supports the multiply instructions directly but not the divide instructions.

Table 3-1. *Integer Arithmetic Instructions*

Mnemonic	Operation Description
ADD	DEST <– SRCA + SRCB
ADDS	DEST <– SRCA + SRCB IF signed overflow THEN Trap (Out Of Range)
ADDU	DEST <– SRCA + SRCB IF unsigned overflow THEN Trap (Out Of Range)
ADDC	DEST <– SRCA + SRCB + C (from ALU)
ADDCS	DEST <– SRCA + SRCB + C (from ALU) IF signed overflow THEN Trap (Out Of Range)
ADDCU	DEST <– SRCA + SRCB + C (from ALU) IF unsigned overflow THEN Trap (Out Of Range)
SUB	DEST <– SRCA – SRCB
SUBS	DEST <– SRCA – SRCB IF signed overflow THEN Trap (Out Of Range)
SUBU	DEST <– SRCA – SRCB IF unsigned underflow THEN Trap (Out Of Range)
SUBC	DEST <– SRCA – SRCB – 1 + C (from ALU)
SUBCS	DEST <– SRCA – SRCB – 1 + C (from ALU) IF signed overflow THEN Trap (Out Of Range)
SUBCU	DEST <– SRCA – SRCB – 1 + C (from ALU) IF unsigned underflow THEN Trap (Out Of Range)
SUBR	DEST <– SRCB – SRCA
SUBRS	DEST <– SRCB – SRCA IF signed overflow THEN Trap (Out Of Range)
SUBRU	DEST <– SRCB – SRCA IF unsigned underflow THEN Trap (Out Of Range)
SUBRC	DEST <– SRCB – SRCA – 1 + C (from ALU)

(continued)

Table 3-2. Integer Arithmetic Instructions (Concluded)

(continued)

Mnemonic	Operation Description
SUBRCS	DEST <- SRCB - SRCA - 1 + C (from ALU) IF signed overflow THEN Trap (Out Of Range)
SUBRCU	DEST <- SRCB - SRCA - 1 + C (from ALU) IF unsigned underflow THEN Trap (Out Of Range)
MULTIPLU	Q//DEST <- SRCA * SRCB (unsigned)
MULTIPLY	Q//DEST <- SRCA * SRCB (signed)
MUL	Perform one–bit step of a multiply operation (signed)
MULL	Complete a sequence of multiply steps
MULU	Perform one–bit step of a multiply operation (unsigned)
DIVIDE	DEST <- (Q//SRCA)/SRCB (signed) Q <- Remainder
DIVIDU	DEST <- (Q//SRCA)/SRCB (unsigned) Q <- Remainder
DIV0	Intitialize for a sequence of divide steps (unsigned)
DIV	Perform one–bit step of a divide operation (unsigned)
DIVL	Complete a sequence of divide steps (unsigned)
DIVREM	Generate remainder for divide operation (unsigned)

3.1.2 Compare

The Compare instructions test for various relationships between two values. For all Compare instructions except the CPBYTE instruction, the comparisons are performed on word–length signed or unsigned integers. There are two types of compare instruction. The first writes a Boolean value into the result register (selected by the instruction DEST operand) depending on the result of the comparison. A Boolean TRUE value is represented by a 1 in the most significant bit position. A Boolean FALSE is defined as a 0 in the most significant bit. The 29K uses a global or local register to contain the comparison result rather than the ALU status register. This offers a performance advantage as there is less conflict over access to a single shared resource. Compare instructions are frequently followed by conditional Jump or Call instructions which depend on the contents of the compare result register.

The second type of compare instruction incorporates a conditional test in the same instruction cycle accomplishing the comparison. These type of instructions, known as Assert instructions, allow instruction execution to continue only if the result of the comparison is TRUE. Otherwise a trap to operating system code is taken. The trap number is supplied in the field–C (DEST) operand position of the instruction. Assert instructions are used in procedure prologue and epilogue routines to perform register stack bounds checking (see Chapter 2). Their fast operation makes them ideal for reducing the overhead of register stack support. They are also used as a means of requesting an operating system support service (system call). In this case a condition known to be FALSE is asserted, and the trap number for the system call is supplied in instruction field–C. The Compare instructions are shown in Tables 3–3 and 3–4.

The CPBYTE performs four comparisons simultaneously. The four bytes in the SRCA operand are compared with the SRCB operand and if any of them match then Boolean TRUE is placed in the DEST register. The instruction can be very efficiently used when scanning character strings. In particular, the C programming language marks the end of character strings with a 0 value. Using the CPBYTE instruction with SRCB supplying an immediate value 0, the string length can be quickly determined.

3.1.3 Logical

The Logical instructions perform a set of bit–by–bit Boolean functions on word–length bit strings. All instructions in this class set the ALU Status Register. These instructions are shown in Table 3-5.

3.1.4 Shift

The Shift instructions (Table 3-6) perform arithmetic and logical shifts on global and local register data. The one exception is the EXTRACT instruction which operates on doube–word data. When EXTRACT is used, SRCA and SRCB operand registers are concatenated to form a 64–bit data value. This value is then shifted by the *funnel shifter* by the amount specified by the Funnel Shift Count register (FC). The high order 32–bits of the shifted result are placed in the DEST register. The funnel shifter can be used to perform barrel shift and rotate operations in a single cycle. Note, when the SRCA and SRCB operands are the same register, the 32–bit operand is effectively rotated. The result may be written back to the same register or placed in a different global or local register (see Figure 3-1). The funnel shifter is useful for *fixing–up* unaligned memory accesses. The two memory words holding the unaligned data can be loaded into global registers, and then aligned by the EXTRACT

Table 3-3. Compare Instructions

Mnemonic	Operation Description
CPEQ	IF SRCA = SRCB THEN DEST <– TRUE ELSE DEST <– FALSE
CPNEQ	IF SRCA <> SRCB THEN DEST <– TRUE ELSE DEST <– FALSE
CPLT	IF SRCA < SRCB THEN DEST <– TRUE ELSE DEST <– FALSE
CPLTU	IF SRCA < SRCB (unsigned) THEN DEST <– TRUE ELSE DEST <– FALSE
CPLE	IF SRCA <= SRCB THEN DEST <– TRUE ELSE DEST <– FALSE
CPLEU	IF SRCA <= SRCB (unsigned) THEN DEST <– TRUE ELSE DEST <– FALSE
CPGT	IF SRCA > SRCB THEN DEST <– TRUE ELSE DEST <– FALSE
CPGTU	IF SRCA > SRCB (unsigned) THEN DEST <– TRUE ELSE DEST <– FALSE

(continued)

instruction into the destination register. A code example showing the rotate operation of the funnel shifter is given below:

```
mtsrim  fc,8              ;rotate 8-bits left
extract gr96,gr97,gr97    ;source in gr97
```

Table 3-4. Compare Instructions (Concluded)

(continued)

Mnemonic	Operation Description
CPGE	IF SRCA >= SRCB THEN DEST <– TRUE ELSE DEST <– FALSE
CPGEU	IF SRCA >= SRCB (unsigned) THEN DEST <– TRUE ELSE DEST <– FALSE
CPBYTE	IF (SRCA.BYTE0 = SRCB.BYTE0) OR (SRCA.BYTE1 = SRCB.BYTE1) OR (SRCA.BYTE2 = SRCB.BYTE2) OR (SRCA.BYTE3 = SRCB.BYTE3)THEN DEST <– TRUE ELSE DEST <– FALSE
ASEQ	IF SRCA = SRCB THEN Continue ELSE Trap (Vector Number – in field–C)
ASNEQ	IF SRCA <> SRCB THEN Continue ELSE Trap (Vector Number – in field–C)
ASLT	IF SRCA < SRCB THEN Continue ELSE Trap (Vector Number – in field–C)
ASLTU	IF SRCA < SRCB (unsigned) THEN Continue ELSE Trap (Vector Number – in field–C)
ASLE	IF SRCA <= SRCB THEN Continue ELSE Trap (Vector Number – in field–C)
ASLEU	IF SRCA <= SRCB (unsigned) THEN Continue ELSE Trap (Vector Number – in field–C)
ASGT	IF SRCA > SRCB THEN Continue ELSE Trap (Vector Number – in field–C)
ASGTU	IF SRCA > SRCB (unsigned) THEN Continue ELSE Trap (Vector Number – in field–C)
ASGE	IF SRCA >= SRCB THEN Continue ELSE Trap (Vector Number – in field–C)
ASGEU	IF SRCA >= SRCB (unsigned) THEN Continue ELSE Trap (Vector Number – in field–C)

Table 3-5. Logical Instructions

Mnemonic	Operation Description
AND	DEST <- SRCA & SRCB
ANDN	DEST <- SRCA & ~ SRCB
NAND	DEST <- ~ (SRCA & SRCB)
OR	DEST <- SRCA I SRCB
NOR	DEST <- ~ (SRCA I SRCB)
XOR	DEST <- SRCA ^ SRCB
XNOR	DEST <- ~ (SRCA ^ SRCB)

Table 3-6. Shift Instructions

Mnemonic	Operation Description
SLL	DEST <- SRCA << SRCB (zero fill)
SRL	DEST <- SRCA >> SRCB (zero fill)
SRA	DEST <- SRCA >> SRCB (sign fill)
EXTRACT	DEST <- high-order word of (SRCA//SRCB << FC)

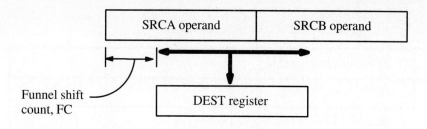

Figure 3-1. The EXTRACT Instruction uses the Funnel Shifter

3.1.5 Data Movement

The Data Movement instructions (Tables 3–7 and 3–8) move bytes, half–words, and words between processor registers. In addition, the LOAD[M] and STORE[M] instructions move data between general–purpose registers and external devices, memories or coprocessor. The Am29050 processor has two additional instructions not shown in Table 3-7. They are MFACC and MTACC; and are used to access the four double–word floating point accumulators (see section 3.3.5).

The LOAD and STORE instructions are most interesting (see Figure 3-2 for the instruction format). Instruction field–C is assigned a number of bit–field tasks which control the external access operation. Bit CE, when set, indicates that the data transfer is to coprocessor space. AMD makes a floating–point coprocessor, Am29027, which was frequently used with the Am29000 processor before the Am29050 processor became available. Because the Am29050 directly supports floating–point instructions there are no new designs making use of the Am29027 coprocessor.

Bit field AS when set is used to indicate that the access is to Input/Output (I/O) space. I/O space is little used as there is no convenient means of accessing it from a high level language such as C. For this reason peripheral devices are typically mapped into external data memory space rather than I/O space.

The PA and UA bits are used by Supervisor mode code; PA is used by operating systems which run with address translation turned on, but need to to access an external memory physical address. When bit PA is set, address translation is turned off for the LOAD or STORE data access. This is useful when accessing peripheral devices. When operating system code wishes to access a User's code space, it sets the UA bit. This causes the data transfer operation to execute with User rather than Supervisor permission. If the User mode program was running with address translation on then, the PID field of the MMU register is used when checking TLB access permissions. Normally Supervisor mode code operates with a fixed PID value of zero.

Table 3-7. Data Move Instructions

Mnemonic	Operation Description
LOAD	DEST <– EXTERNAL WORD [SRCB]
LOADL	DEST <– EXTERNAL WORD [SRCB] assert *LOCK output during access
LOADSET	DEST <– EXTERNAL WORD [SRCB] EXTERNAL WORD [SRCB] <– h'FFFFFFFF', assert *LOCK output during access
LOADM	DEST.. DEST + COUNT <– EXTERNAL WORD [SRCB] .. EXTERNAL WORD [SRCB + COUNT * 4]
STORE	EXTERNAL WORD [SRCB] <– SRCA
STOREL	EXTERNAL WORD [SRCB] <– SRCA assert *LOCK output during access
STOREM	EXTERNAL WORD [SRCB] .. EXTERNAL WORD [SRCB + COUNT * 4] <– SRCA .. SRCA + COUNT
EXBYTE	DEST <– SRCB, with low–order byte replaced by byte in SRCA selected by BP
EXHW	DEST <– SRCB, with low–order half–word replaced by half–word in SRCA selected by BP
EXHWS	DEST <– half–word in SRCA selected by BP, sign–extended to 32 bits
INBYTE	DEST <– SRCA, with byte selected by BP replaced by low–order byte of SRCB
INHW	DEST <– SRCA, with half–word selected by BP replaced by low–order half–word of SRCB
MFSR	DEST <– SPECIAL
MFTLB	DEST <– TLB [SRCA]
MTSR	SPDEST <– SRCB

(continued)

Programming the 29K RISC Family

Table 3-8. Data Move Instructions (Concluded)
(continued)

Mnemonic	Operation Description
MTSRIM	SPDEST <- 0I16 (16–bit date formed with SRCA and SCRB fields
MTTLB	TLB [SRCA] <- SRCB

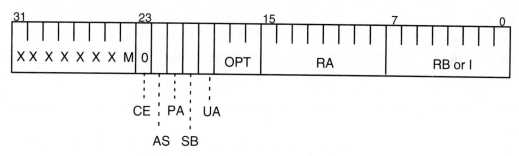

Figure 3-2. LOAD and STORE Instruction Format

The original versions of the Am29000 processor (rev–A to rev–C) did not support byte sized access to external memory. For this reason bytes and half–words had to be extracted from words after they had been read from memory; the Extract Byte (EXBYTE) and Extract half–word (EXHW) instructions are supported by the processor for just this purpose. Additionally, when data objects smaller than a word were written to external memory, a read–modify–write process had to be used. The Insert Byte (INBYTE) and Insert half–word (INHW) instructions supported the process.

Rev–D and later versions of the Am29000 processor and all other 29K family members directly support byte and half–word accesses to memory. The instructions described above need no longer be used. To enable current versions of the Am29000 processor to be compatible with the original processor, the DW bit was added to the processor configuration register (CFG). When the DW bit is clear the processor performs rev–A type memory accesses. All new designs operate with the DW bit set; and other 29K family members operate with an implied DW bit set.

The OPT field bits specify the size of the data object being moved. They are also used to indicate a word sized access to Instruction ROM space is requested. External logic must be incorporated in a memory system design if this option is to be supported. The OPT field appears on the OPT(2:0) output pins during the memory access. It is important that the object size is consistent with the address boundaries defined by the lower bits of the memory address. For example, if a word sized access

(OPT filed value is 0) is attempted with lower address bits aligned to a byte boundary (A[1:0] not equal 0) then an unaligned access trap may occur. The Unaligned Access (UA) bit of the Current Processor Status (CPS) register must be set for the trap to be taken. Additionally, alignment checking is only performed for instruction and data memory, not for I/O or coprocessor space accesses.

The SB bit is used when reading bytes or half–words from external memory. Sub–word sized accesses are determined by the OPT field; the processor right–justifies the accessed data within the destination register. The SB bit when set causes the remainder of the destination to be sign extended with the sign of the loaded data object. When SB is clear, the destination register value is zero–extended. The SB bit has no effect during external memory writes. During write operations, the data object is replicated in all positions of the data bus. For example, a byte write would result in the stored byte appearing in all four positions of the stored word. It is the responsibility of external memory to decode the OPT field and lower address bits when determining which byte position should be written. Note, the micorcontroller members of the 29K family implement the memory *glue* logic on–chip.

Instruction field–B (SRCB) supplies the external memory address for LOAD and STORE instructions. Typically a CONST, or CONST and CONSTH, instruction sequences precedes the LOAD or STORE instruction and establishes the access address for memory. However, the first 256 bytes of memory can be accessed with immediate addressing, where the 8–bit SRCB value contains the address. Some systems may be able to make use of this feature where performance is critical and the use of CONST type instructions is to be avoided.

As described in Chapter 1, the use of LOAD and STORE instructions can effect the processor pipeline utilization. Members of the 29K family which support a Harvard memory architecture, or contain on–chip instruction memory cache, can perform LOAD and STORE operations in parallel with other instructions. This prevents pipeline stalling, as the instruction execution sequence can continue in parallel with the external memory access. However, if the instruction following a LOAD operates on the accessed data then pipeline stalling will still occur. For this reason LOAD instructions should be positioned early in the instruction sequence, enabling the data memory access latency to be hidden. Pipeline stalling will also occur if LOAD and store type instructions arc placcd back–to–back, as this can result in channel access conflicts. For this reason, LOAD and Store instructions should be separated with other instructions as much as possible

3.1.6 Constant

The Constant instructions (Table 3-9) provide the ability to place half–word and word constants into registers. Most instructions in the instruction set allow an 8–bit constant as an operand. The Constant instructions allow the construction of larger constants. The Am29050 processor has an additional instruction, CONSTHZ, not supported in other 29K family members. It places a 16–bit constant in the upper half–word position while the lower 16–bits are zero filled.

Table 3-9. Constant Instructions

Mnemonic	Operation Description
CONST	DEST <– 0I16 (16–bit date formed with SRCA and SCRB fields
CONSTH	Replace high–order half–word of SRCA by I16
CONSTN	DEST <– 1I16

3.1.7 Floating–point

The Floating–Point instructions (Tables 3–10 and 3–11) provide operations on single–precision (32–bit) or double–precision (64–bit) floating–point data. In addition, they provide conversions between single–precision, double–precision, and integer number representations. In most 29K family members, these instructions cause traps to routines which perform the floating–point operations in software. The Am29050 processor supports all floating–point instructions directly in hardware. It also has four additional instructions not shown in Tables 3–10 and 3–11. They are MFAC ,DMAC and FMSM, DMSM; and are used to to perform single and double–precision multiply–and–accumulate type instructions (see section 3.3.5).

3.1.8 Branch

The Branch instructions (Table 3-12) control the execution flow of instructions. Branch target addresses may be absolute, relative to the Program Counter (with the offset given by a signed instruction constant), or contained in a general–purpose register (indirect addressing). For conditional jumps, the outcome of the jump is based on a Boolean value in a general–purpose register. Only the most significant bit in the specified condition register is tested, Boolean TRUE is defined as bit–31 being set. Procedure calls are unconditional, and save the return address in a general–purpose register. All branches have a delayed effect; the instruction following the branch is executed regardless of the outcome of the branch.

Table 3-10. Floating–Point Instructions

Mnemonic	Operation Description
FADD	DEST (single–precision) <– SRCA (single–precision) + SRCB (single–precision)
DADD	DEST (double–precision) <– SRCA (double–precision) + SRCB (double–precision)
FSUB	DEST (single–precision) <– SRCA (single–precision) – SRCB (single–precision)
DSUB	DEST (double–precision) <– SRCA (double–precision) – SRCB (double–precision)
FMUL	DEST (single–precision) <– SRCA (single–precision) * SRCB (single–precision)
DMUL	DEST (double–precision) <– SRCA (double–precision) * SRCB (double–precision)
FDIV	DEST (single–precision) <– SRCA (single–precision)/ SRCB (single–precision)
DDIV	DEST (double–precision) <– SRCA (double–precision)/ SRCB (double–precision)
FEQ	IF SRCA (single–precision) = SRCB (single–precision) THEN DEST <– TRUE ELSE DEST <– FALSE
DEQ	IF SRCA (double–precision) = SRCB (double–precision) THEN DEST <– TRUE ELSE DEST <– FALSE
FGE	IF SRCA (single–precision) >= SRCB (single–precision) THEN DEST <– TRUE ELSE DEST <– FALSE
DGE	IF SRCA (double–precision) >= SRCB (double–precision) THEN DEST <– TRUE ELSE DEST <– FALSE
FGT	IF SRCA (single–precision) > SRCB (single–precision) THEN DEST <– TRUE ELSE DEST <– FALSE

(continued)

Table 3-11. Floating–Point Instructions (Concluded)

(continued)

Mnemonic	Operation Description
DGT	IF SRCA (double–precision) = SRCB (double–precision) THEN DEST <– TRUE ELSE DEST <– FALSE
SQRT	DEST (single–precision, double–precision, extended–precision) <–SQRT[SRCA (single–precision, double–precision, extended–precision)
CONVERT	DEST (integer,single–precision, double–precision) <–SRCA (integer, single–precision, double–precision)
CLASS	DEST (single–precision, double–precision, extended–precision) <–CLASS[SRCA (single–precision, double–precision, extended–precision)]

The instruction following the branch instruction is referred to as the *delay slot* instruction. Assembly level programmers may have some difficulty in always finding a useful instruction to put in the delay slot. It is best to find an operation required regardless of the outcome of the branch. As a last resort a NOP instruction can be used, but this makes no effective use of the processor pipeline. When programming in a high level language the compiler is responsible for making effective use of delay slots. Programmers not familiar with delayed branching often forget the delay slot is always executed, with unfortunate consequences. For this reason, the example code throughout this book shows delay slot instructions indented one space compared to other instructions. This has proven to be a useful reminder.

The delay slots of unconditional branches are easier to fill than conditional branches. The instruction at the target of the branch can be moved to, or duplicated at, the delay slot; and the jump address can be changed to the instruction following the original target instruction.

The JMPFDEC instruction is very useful for implementing control loops based on a decrementing loop. The counter register (SRCA) is first tested to determine if the value is FALSE, then it is decremented. The jump is then taken if a FALSE value was detected. The code example below shows how *count* words of external memory can be written with zero. Note how the address pointer is incremented in the delay slot of the jump instruction. Additionally, the SRCA register must be initialized to *count–2*; this is because the loop is taken when the count value is 0 and –1, because the count decrement is performed after the condition test. In practice, memory sys-

---

Table 3-12. Branch Instructions

Mnemonic	Operation Description
CALL	DEST <- PC//00 + 8 PC <- TARGET Execute delay instruction
CALLI	DEST <- PC//00 + 8 PC <- SRCB Execute delay instruction
JMP	PC <- TARGET Execute delay instruction
JMPI	PC <- SRCB Execute delay instruction
JMPT	IF SRCA = TRUE THEN PC <- TARGET Execute delay instruction
JMPTI	IF SRCA = TRUE THEN PC <- SRCB Execute delay instruction
JMPF	IF SRCA = FALSE THEN PC <- TARGET Execute delay instruction
JMPFI	IF SRCA = FALSE THEN PC <- SRCB Execute delay instruction

JMPFDEC	IF SRCA = FALSE THEN
	    SRCA <- SRCA - 1
	    PC <- TARGET
	ELSE
	    SRCA <- SRCA - 1
	Execute delay instruction

tems supporting burst–mode accesses would use a STOREM instruction to more efficiently clear data memory.

```
        const   gr97,count-2    ;establish loop count
        const   gr98,0
        const   gr96,address    ;establish memory address
        consth  gr96,address
 clear: store   0,0,gr98,gr96   ;write zero to memory
        jmpfdec gr97,clear      ;test and decrement count
        add     gr96,gr96,4     ;advance pointer
;arrive here when loop finished, gr97=-2
```

3.1.9 Miscellaneous Instructions

The Miscellaneous instructions (Table 3-13) perform various operations which cannot be grouped into other instruction classes. In certain cases, these are control functions available only to Supervisor–mode programs.

The Count Leading Zeros instruction can be very useful to assembly level programmers. It determines the position of the most–significant one bit in the SRCB operand. If all bits are zero, then 32 is returned. The instruction is useful when determining priorities for, say, queues of interrupt requests, where each interrupt may set a bit in the register operated on. The highest priority interrupt in the queue can be quickly determined by the CLZ instruction.

Table 3-13. Miscellaneous Instructions

Mnemonic	Operation Description
CLZ	Determine number of leading zeros in a word
SETIP	Set IPA, IPB, and IPC with operand register–numbers
EMULATE	Load IPA and IPB with operand register–numbers, and Trap Vector Number in field–C
INV	Reset all Valid bits in Branch Target Cache to zeros
IRET	Perform an interrupt return sequence
IRETINV	Perform an interrupt return sequence, and reset all Valid bits in Branch Target Cache to zeros
HALT	Enter Halt mode on next cycle

3.1.10 Reserved Instructions

The remaining operation codes are reserved for instruction emulation. These instructions cause traps, much like the unimplemented floating–point instructions, but currently have no specified interpretation. The relevant operation codes, and the corresponding trap vectors are given in the processor User's Manual.

These instructions are intended for future processor enhancements, and users desiring compatibility with future processor versions should not use them for any purpose.

The software developer should be aware of the trap taken with the reserved instruction opcode 0xff. When execution is attempted with this opcode a trap 63 is taken. This can occur when a program goes out–of–control and attempts to fetch instructions from nonexistent memory.

3.2   CODE OPTIMIZATION TECHNIQUES

When a high level programming language is used for software development, code optimization is left to the compiler. With assembly language programming, care must be taken to avoid code sequences which impact upon the processor's performance. Section 3.1.5 described how LOAD and STORE instruction must be carefully positioned if pipeline stalling is to be avoided. Section 3.1.8 discussed the delay slot of branch instructions, and the importance of finding a useful instruction for delay slot filling. This section describes a few more useful coding techniques which can improve code execution performance.

Common Subexpression Elimination is a technique where a frequently occurring code sequence is eliminated to only one occurrence. This usually requires the result of the code sequence to be held in register space for frequent and fast access. The trade–off between expression reevaluation and consuming additional register resources is easily made with the 29K family because of the large number of general purpose registers available. Code subexpressions need not be large. They may be as short as an address calculation using a pair of CONST – CONSTH instructions. The calculation can be done once and the address kept around in a register for reuse.

Moving code out of loops is another technique frequently used to improve performance. However, the typically small number of registers in a CISC processor can often mean loop invariant code results have to be held in external memory. This can lead to trade–offs between adding code within a loop or suffering the external memory access penalties. Again, the large number of general purpose registers in the 29K assist the programmer to achieve improved code.

Branch instructions are to be avoided as their use impacts badly on performance. Processors supporting burst–mode addressing operate most efficiently when instruction bursting is not disrupted with a branch instruction. This is particularly true for memory systems which have a high first–access latency. The Branch Target Cache incorporated in some 29K family members can help hide the effects of branching, but as the number of branch instructions is increased the chance of a hit occurring in the cache is reduced.

Loop Inversion is a useful technique at reducing the use of branch instructions. Often programmers will construct loops which have the loop condition test at the *top* of the loop. This requires a branch be used at the bottom of the loop. If the conditional branch is moved to the bottom of the loop then the number of branch instructions is reduced

3.3 AVAILABLE REGISTERS

In essence, global registers *gr64–gr95* are reserved for interrupt handlers and the operating system use. The remaining 32 global registers (*gr96–gr127*) are reserved for holding User mode program context. The high level language calling convention described in Chapter 2 established this convention. Figure 3-3 illustrates the partitioning of the global registers among the operating system and user program tasks. General purpose registers *gr128–gr255* are better known as local registers, and accessed via the registers stack pointer, *gr1*, rather than directly addressed as global registers.

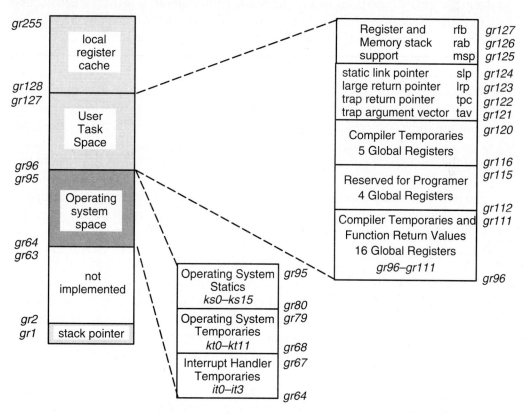

Figure 3-3.   General Purpose Register Usage

The calling convention goes further than just dividing the register space into two groups. The user space registers are assigned particular high level language support tasks. All but four registers (*gr112–gr115*) in user task space will be accessed and modified by compiler generated code at various times. Most of the registers are used as compiler temporaries; three registers are used to support memory and register stacks; and the remaining four registers support the high level language procedure call mechanism and system calls. Global registers in the range *gr121–gr127* are known to the programmer by special synonym; however the registers themselves operate no differently from other global registers.

In particular *gr121* (*tav*) and *gr122* (*tpc*) are used to pass arguments to trap routines invoked with Assert type instructions. This occurs during procedure prologue and epilogue as well as operating system service calls.

Register *gr123* (*lrp*) is known as the Large Return Pointer. It is used when a procedure is required to return an object which is larger than 16 words and therefore cannot fit in the normal return space (*gr96–gr111*). The caller must assign *lrp* to point to memory which will hold the 17th and higher words of return data.

Register *gr124* (*slp*) is known as the Static Link Pointer. It is used when accessing data variables defined in a parent procedure. This occurs in some languages, Pascal for example, where nested procedure declarations are permitted.

A called procedure can locate its dynamic parent and the variables of the dynamic parent because of the the caller–callee activation record linkage (see section 3.5). However, the linkage is not adequate to locate variables of the static parent which may be referenced in the procedure. If such references appear in a procedure, the procedure must be provided with a local register which forms part of the static link pointer chain. Since there can be a hierarchy of static parents, the *slp* points to the *slp* of the immediate parent, which in turn points to the *slp* of its immediate parent.

The memory–stack support register *gr125* (*msp*) and the register–stack support registers *gr126* (*rab*), *gr127* (*rfb*) and *gr1* (*rsp*), were discussed in detail in Chapter 2. They maintain the current positions of the stack resources.

The calling convention does not assign any particular task to the registers in the operating system (OS) group (*gr64–gr95*). However, over time a convention has evolved among 29K processor users.The subdivision of the OS registers shown in Figure 3-3 is widely adhered to. The subgroups are known as: the interrupt freeze mode temporaries (given synonyms *it0–it3*); the operating system temporaries (*kt0–kt11*); and the operating system statics support registers (*ks0–ks15*).

When developing a new assembly language procedure a useful technique is to construct a C language routine which receives any passed parameters and implements the appropriate task. With the AMD High C 29K compiler, the procedure can be compiled to produce an assembly language output file with the "–S –Hanno" compiler switches. The Assembly level code can then be directly modified into the required code sequence.

3.3.1 Useful Macro–Instructions

The code examples shown in later chapters make use of a number macros for pushing and popping special registers to an external memory stack. A macro instruction is composed of a sequence of simpler instructions. Effectively, a macro is an in–line procedure call. Using macros is faster than making an actual procedure call but consumes more instruction memory space.The macro definitions are presented below:

```
.macro pushsr,sp,reg,srcg    ;macro name and parameters
      mfsr    reg,sreg        ;copy from special
      sub     sp,sp,4         ;decrement pointer
      store   0,0,reg,sp      ;store on stack
.endm
;
.macro popsr,sreg,reg,sp      ;macro name and parameters
      load    0,0,reg,sp      ;get from stack
      add     sp,sp,4         ;increment pointer
      mtsr    sreg,reg        ;move to special
.endm
```

Note how the LOAD instruction is used first when *poping*. This enables the ADD and MTSR instruction to overlap the LOAD execution and thus reduce pipeline stalling. This is particularly useful when *popsr* macro instructions are used back–to–back in sequence. Such sequences are useful when a memory system does not support burst mode addressing. If bust mode is supported then it can be more efficient to use a LOADM instruction and then transfer the global register date into the special registers. However, LOADM and STOREM cannot be used in Freeze mode code which frequently require *popsr* and *pushsr* instruction sequences. Similar macros are used to push and pop global registers:

```
.macro push,sp,reg           ;macro name and parameters
      sub     sp,sp,4         ;decrement pointer
      store   0,0,reg,sp      ;store on stack
.endm
;
.macro pop,reg,sp            ;macro name and parameters
      load    0,0,reg,sp      ;get from stack
      add     sp,sp,4         ;increment pointer
.endm
```

3.3.2 Using Indirect Pointers and gr0

Three of the 29K special registers are known as indirect pointers: IPA, IPB, and IPC. These registers are used to point into general purpose register space, and support indirect register access. They hold the absolute register number of the general purpose register being accessed, and are used in instructions by referencing the pseudo–register *gr0*. When an indirect pointer is to be used to identify an instruction operand, gr0 is placed in the appropriate instruction operand field. Indirect pointer IPA is used with the SRCA operand field. Similarly, IPB and IPC apply with the SRCB operand and DEST instruction fields.

The indirect pointer registers are set with the SETIP and EMULATE instructions. Additionally, they are set when a trap is taken as a result of executing an instruction which is not directly supported by the 29K processor. With some family members this occurs with floating–point operations and integer multiply and divide. The example code below shows how the *gr0* register is used to select indirect pointer use. Note, indirect pointers can not be accessed in the cycle following the one in which they are set; this explains the NOP instruction.

```
setip   gr98,lr2,gr96    ;set indirect pointers
nop                      ;delay
add     gr0,gr97,gr0     ;gr98 = gr97+gr96
```

The main use of indirect pointers is to support transparent routines (see section 3.6) and instruction emulation. With most 29K family members the integer multiply instruction (MULTIPLY) is not directly supported.

```
multiply lr4,gr98,lr10  ;integer multiply, lr4 = gr98*lr10
```

On entering the trapware support routine for the vector assigned to the MULTIPLY instruction (vector number 32) the indirect pointers are set to IPC=*lr4*, IPA=*gr98* and IPB=*lr10* for the above example. This enables the trap handler to easily and efficiently access the register operands for the instruction without having to examine the actual instruction in memory.

When using a MTSRIM instruction to set an indirect pointer register value, it is important to remember that the most significant bit (bit position 9) must be set if local registers are to be accessed. This is because indirect pointers operate with absolute register numbers. See the following section discussing the use of *gr1* for more details on register addressing.

3.3.3 Using *gr1*

Global register *gr1* performs the special task of supporting indirect access of the 128 local registers. When an instruction operand, say SRCA, has its top most bit set then base–plus–offset addressing is used to access the operand. This means only general purpose registers in the range *gr1–gr127* can be addressed via their absolute register number given the supported instruction operand decoding. (Indirect pointers enable all general purpose registers to be accessed via absolute address numbers.) The lower 7–bits of the operand supply the offset which is shifted left 2–bits then added with the local register base held in register *gr1*. Register *gr1* is a 32–bit register, and bits 8–2 contain the local register base (see Figure 3-4).

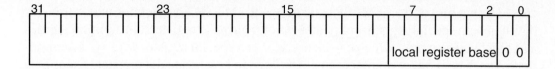

Figure 3-4. Global Register gr1 Fields

The base offset calculation is performed modulo–128. The most significant address bit is assumed set when forming the absolute address for all local register accesses.

29K processors use a shadow copy of the *gr1* register when performing local register addressing. The shadow copy can only be modified by an arithmetic or logical instruction; a load into *gr1* will not update the shadow copy. Because of the shadow register technique, there must be a delay of one cycle before the register file can be accessed after *gr1* has been modified.

3.3.4 Accessing Special Register Space

The special registers control the operation of the processor. They are divided into two groups: those that can be accessed only in Supervisor mode and those which have unrestricted access. Access of special registers *sr128* and above do not generate a protection violation when accessed in User mode. Special register space was described in section 1.7.2. Not all 29K family members have fully implemented special register spaces. In the Supervisor–only accessible space there are a number of differences due to differences in on–chip resources such as cache memory and hardware breakpoint registers. Because these are not accessible to application code they do not effect application code portability.

However, some members of the 29K family do not implement, in hardware, all of the special registers accessible by User mode programs. In particular the floating point support registers (*sr160–sr162*) are only implemented on processors which directly support floating–point instructions in hardware. All other family members virtulize these registers. An attempted access to unimplemented special registers causes a Protection Violation trap to occur. The trapware code implements the access and returns the result. Unfortunately the trapware code does not use the indirect pointer as they are not set by a protection violation trap. This means the trapware must read the instruction space to determine the special register being accessed. This leads to the consequence that the special floating point support registers can not be virtualized with Harvard memory architectures which do not provide a memory bridge to enable instruction memory to be accessed as data. The emulation technique also requires the support of three operating system registers. The trapware is typically configured to use global registers *ks13–ks15* (*gr93–gr95*) for this task.

Special registers are located in their own register space. They can only be accessed by the move–from (MFSR) and move–to (MTSR) instructions which transfer data between special register space and general purpose registers. In addition there is a MTSRIM instruction which can be used to set a special register with 16–bit immediate data. The indirect pointers can not be used to access special register space. This imposes some restriction in accessing special registers but in practice is acceptable. However, where the address of a special register to be accessed is contained in a general purpose register, the technique shown below can be used. In the example, *lr2* contains the address of the special register to be read with a MFSR instruction. The example assumes instruction memory can be written to; the required instruction is built in *gr97* and stored in memory at an address given by *gr98*. The instruction is then *visited* with a JMPI instruction. A jump instructions target address is *visited* when the jump instruction contains a further jump in its delay slot. The second jump is in the decode stage of the processor pipeline when the first jump is in execute. This means the second jump must be taken, and only the first instruction of the new instruction stream is started before execution continues at label **continue**.

```
           const    gr98,I_memory    ;establish instruction address
           consth   gr98,I_memory
           const    gr97,0xC6600000  ;MFSR, DEST=gr96, SRCA=0
           consth   gr97,0xC6600000
           sll      lr2,lr2,8        ;lr2 has special register number
           or       lr2,lr2,gr97     ;instruction now constructed
           store    0,0,lr2,gr98     ;store target instruction
           jmpi     gr98             ;visit the target instruction
            jmp     continue         ;must execute the delay slot
continue:
```

The constructed MFSR instruction places the result in register *gr96*. The *lr2* source address value had to be shifted left 8–bits into the SRCA field position of the MFSR instruction.

3.3.5 Floating–point Accumulators

The Am29050 processor is currently the only member of the 29K family which directly supports in hardware floating–point arithmetic operations. In addition to supporting floating–point operations without using trapware emulation, functions involving multiply–and–accumulate operations are supported by four additional hardware instructions not implemented in other 29K family members. Sum–of–product type operations are frequently required by many floating–point intensive applications, such as matrix multiplication. Implementing this operation efficiently in hardware makes the Am29050 processor suitable for use in graphics and signal processing applications.

The FMAC and DMAC instructions can be used to multiply two general purpose register values together and sum the product with one of the four floating–point accumulators. The DMAC instruction operates on double–precision operand data and the FMAC operates on single–precision. Double–precision operands can be accessed from the register file in a single cycle as the register file is implemented as 64–bits wide, and there is 64–bit wide ports supplying data to the floating–point execution unit components. Double–precision operands must be aligned on double–register address boundaries.

The FMSM and DMSM instructions support single and double–precision floating–point multiply–and–sum. One operand for the multiplication is a general purpose register, the second is accumulator 0; the product is summed with the second instruction operand and the result placed back in the register file. These two instructions can be used when the multiplier is a fixed value such as with SAXPY (single–precision A times X plus Y).

The Floating–Point Unit on the Am29050 processor is constructed from a number of specialized operation pipelines; one for addition/subtraction, one for multiplication , and one for division/square root. The functional units used by the pipelines all operate separately. This enables multiple floating–point instructions to be in execute at the same time. Additionally floating–point operations can commence in parallel with operations carried out by the processor's integer pipeline. The operation of some of the pipeline functional units can be multicycle and contention for resources can result if simultaneous floating–point operations are being performed. However, all floating–point operations are fully interlocked, and operations requiring the result of a previous functional unit operation are prevented from proceeding until that result is available. The programmer never has to become involved in the pipeline stage details to ensure the success of an operation.

To sustain efficient use of the floating–point pipelines, four floating–point accumulator registers are provided. The programmer must multiplex their use during heavily pipelined code sequences to reduce resource contention. The Am29050 processor can issue a new floating–point instruction every cycle but many of the operations have multicycle latency. Thus to avoid pipeline stalling, the results should not be used until a sufficient number of delay cycles has passed (see Am29050 processor User's Manual). The processor has an additional 64–bit write port on the general purpose register file for use by the floating–point unit. This enables floating–point results to be written back at the same time as integer pipeline results.

The floating–point accumulators can be accessed by the MTACC (move–to) and MFACC (move–from) instructions which are available to User mode code. Only 29K family members which directly support floating–point operations implement these instructions.

3.4   DELAYED EFFECTS OF INSTRUCTIONS

Modification of some registers has a delayed effect on processor behavior. When developing assembly code, care must be taken to prevent unexpected behavior. The easiest of the delayed effects to remember is the one cycle that must follow the use of an indirect pointer after having set it. This occurs most often with the register stack pointer. It cannot be used to access a local register in the instruction that follows the instruction that writes to *gr1*. An instruction that does not require *gr1* (and that means all local registers referenced via *gr1*) can be placed immediately after the instruction that updates *gr1*.

Direct modification of the CPS register must also be done carefully. Particularly where the freeze (FZ) bit is cleared. When the processor is frozen, the special-purpose registers are not updated during instruction execution. This means that the *PC1* register does not reflect the actual program counter value at the current execution address, but rather at the point where freeze mode was entered. When the processor is unfrozen, either by an interrupt return or direct modification of the CPS, two cycles are required before the PC1 buffer register reflects the new execution address. Unless the CPS register is being modified directly, this creates no problem.

Consider the following examples. If the FZ bit is cleared and trace enable (TE) is set at the same time, the next instruction should cause a trace trap, but the PC buffer registers frozen by the trap will not have had time to catch up with the current execution address. Within the trap code the processor will have appeared to have stopped at some random address, held in PC1. If interrupts and traps are enabled at the same time the FZ bit is cleared, then the next instruction could suffer an external interrupt or an illegal instruction trap. Once again, the PC buffer register will not reflect the true execution address. An interrupt return would cause execution to commence at a random address. The above problems can be avoided by clearing FZ two cycles before enabling the processor to once again enter freeze mode.

3.5   TRACE–BACK TAGS

When the compiler generates the code for a procedure, it places a one or two word tag before the first instruction of the procedure. The tag information is used by debuggers to determine the sequence of procedure calls and the value of program variables at a given point in program execution. The trace–back tag describes the memory frame size and the number of local registers used by the associated procedure. A one word tag is used unless the memory stack usage is greater than 2k words, in which case a two–word tag is used. Figure 3-5 shows the format of the tag data.

Most of the tag data fields are self explanatory. The *M* bit–field is set if the the procedure uses the memory stack. In such case, *msize* is the memory stack frame size in double words. The *argcount* is the number of in–coming arguments in registers plus two. The *T* bit–field, when set, indicates the routine is transparent (see section 3.6).

When procedures are built in assembly language rather than, say C, the programmer is responsible for building the appropriate tag data word[s] ahead of the

---

first instruction. Figure 3-6 shows an example register stack history for three levels of procedure calls. In the example, the *current* procedure is a small leave procedure. Small leaves differ from large leave procedures in that they do not lower the register stack and allocate new local registers to the procedure.

Looking at the parent of the current procedure it can be seen the stack was lowered by six words (*rsize*) during the parent procedure prologue. The top of the activation record is identified by the procedure *lr1* register value. In principal the start of the grandparent procedure activation record can be found by subtracting the *argcount* value from the address identified by the parent *lr1*. In this way the *rsize* for the parent procedure can be determined; adding *rsize* to the parent's *gr1* value enables the grandparent *gr1* value to be obtained. Repeating the mechanism with the grandparent *lr1* value allows all previous activation records to be identified until the first procedure call is found. The first procedure is identified by a tag value of zero, and is normally the **start** procedure in file **crt0.s**.

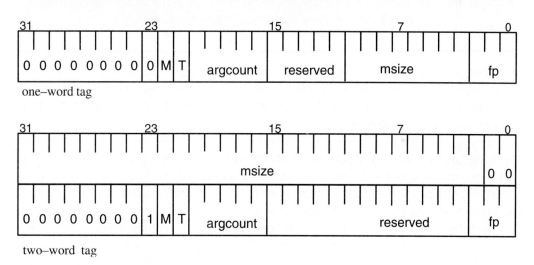

Figure 3-5. *Trace–Back Tag Format*

However, there is a problem with this scheme as shown in Figure 3-6. Small leave procedures do not have *lr1* values for their own activation record; they share the *lr1* value of their parent. Additionally, large leave procedures have a new *lr1* register assigned, but because leaves do not call other procedures, the *lr1* register is not assigned to point to the top of the activation record. For this reason, the *lr1* value can not be initially used as a mechanism for walking back through procedure call register allocation.

In practice, most debuggers walk back through instruction memory till they find the current procedure tag value, then they look at the immediately following

---

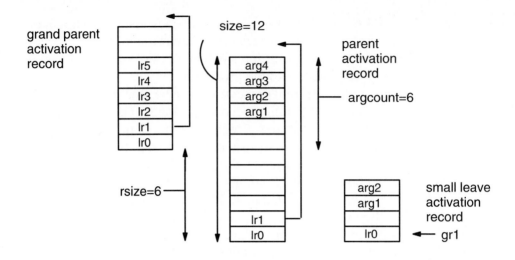

Figure 3-6. Walking Back Through Activation Records

prologue code. The first prologue instruction is normally a "SUB *gr1*, *gr1*, *rsize**4*".
If the *rsize* is bigger than 64, then it is a CONST followed by a SUB. In any case the
rsize value is determined by this method rather than computing it from an
lr1–argcount based calculation.

Before the Am29050 processor became available, floating–point intensive applications were normally supported with an Am29027 coprocessor. The procedure
call mechanism specified that coprocessor float registers 0–2 are allowed to be
modified by the callee and are not saved across calls. Float registers 3–7 may also be
modified by the callee but are preserved across procedure calls. Thus the caller must
first save them before making a call, and restore them upon callee return. A region of
the procedure activation record is assigned for saving the coprocessor registers. Additionally, the *fp* field in the tag word is used to indicate the the number of registers
saved.

When using an Am29050 processor the *fp* field value is always zero. The four
double–word accumulator registers are not preserved across a procedure call. If a
procedure uses the accumulators and wishes to preserve their contents it must first
save them before making a procedure call. This may involve temporary modifying
the special floating–point environment registers. Because the floating–point accumulators are normally accessed by assembly language leaf routines, caller saving of
the accumulators results in a reduced overhead compared to callee saving.

3.6   TRANSPARENT ROUTINES

Transparent routines are used to support small highly efficient procedure calls. They are like small leave procedures in that they do not lower the register stack and allocate a new activation record. They are unlike leaves in that the only global registers which the caller does not expect to survive the call are *tav* (*gr121*) and *tpc* (*gr122*). They are normally used to support compiler specific support routines such as integer multiply (where the 29K hardware does not directly support this operation).

Parameters are passed to transparent routines using *tav* and the indirect pointer registers. Return values are via *tpc* and possibly the modified register identified by indirect pointer *ipc*. Leaf procedures can call transparent routines without changing their status as leaf routines.

3.7   INITIALIZING THE PROCESSOR

Reset mode is entered when the processor's *RESET pin is activated. This causes the Current Processor Status (CPS) register to be set to the Reset mode values; the processor operates in Supervisor mode with all data and instruction addresses being physical (no address translation); all traps and interrupts are disabled and the processor Freeze mode bit is set. (See the Initialization section of the processor User's Manual for the exact CPS register setting.) Individual 29K family members have additional Reset mode conditions established, such as disabling cache memory where appropriate.

Instruction execution begins at address 0. For processors supporting both Instruction memory space and read–only memory (ROM) space, ROM space is used when fetching instructions from external memory. However, many Am29000 processor systems apply no distinction when decoding instruction and ROM memory space.

The programmer must establish control of the processor and available resources. Section 7.4 discusses how this is achieved with the OS–boot operating system. OS–boot is made available by AMD, and is used to implement a single–task application environment which supports HIF (see Chapter 2) system call services. Because OS–boot is so freely available to the 29K community, it is convenient to use the included processor start–up code sequence for any new designs.

3.8   ASSEMBLER SYNTAX

Assembly language, like all languages, has a character set and a set of grammar rules. Purchasers of the ASM29K™ assembly language tool package from AMD or other tool company, shall obtain a copy of the assembly language syntax specifica-

---

tion. There are a number of assembler tools available and all of them comply (but not always fully) with the AMD defined syntax for assembly level programming.

Many of the assemblers have options which are unique, but it has been my experience that assemblers will generally accept code which is produced by any of the available compilers.

3.8.1 The AMD Assembler

The AMD assembly language tool package, ASM29K, was used to develop all of the assembly language examples shown in this book. The assembler, linker and librarian tools included in the package were developed by Microrec Research Inc. (MRI) for AMD. The tools are available on a number of platforms; the most popular being SUN and HP workstations and IBM PCs and compatibles. This section does not cover the details of the AMD assembler (as29) and its options as they are well documented in the literature supplied with each purchased tool package.

During the introduction of the Am29000 processor, AMD had a second assembly level tool package developed by Information Processing Techniques Corp. (IPT). This second tool chain forms the basis of a number of elaborate tool packages made available by third party tool suppliers. All of the tool suppliers are listed in the AMD Fusion29K^{sm} Catalogue [AMD 1992a][AMD 1993b]. Both assemblers fully comply with the AMD assembler syntax for 29K code. However, the librarian tools supplied with the different tool packages maintain library code in different formats. This means libraries cannot be shared unless reformatting is applied.

3.8.2 Free Software Foundation (GNU), Assembler

The Free Software Foundation Inc. is an organization based in Cambridge MA, USA, which helps develop and distribute software development tools for a range of processors. Anyone can contribute programs to the the foundation and users of foundation supplied tools have the freedom to distribute copies of tools freely (or can charge for this service if they wish). The foundation tools (often known as GNU tools) include a complete tool chain for software development for the 29K family. The GNU assembler is known as GAS, and is available in source form from AMD and from the Cygnus Support company.

GAS is primarily intended to assemble the output from the GNU C language compiler, GCC (see Chapter 2). It does accept code complying with the AMD assembly language syntax; however, there are a number of differences. Most notably, it does not support macro instructions. Developers may wish to use a UNIX utility such as M4 to support macros with the GAS tool.

A number of developers have compiled GAS for use in a cross–development environment where the target processor is a 29K, but the development platform is a SUN or HP workstation or an IBM 386–PC. These tools are available among the 29K GNU community, many of which are university engineering departments. AMD has a University Support Program which helps universities wishing to include the 29K in educational programs, to obtain hardware and software development tools as well as other class materials. There may be a university near you which will supply you with a copy of the compiled GNU tools for a small tape handling charge.

If you get a copy of GAS from AMD or Cygnus or other Fusion29K partner, then it is likely that the documentation supporting the tool was supplied. After installing the tools on a UNIX machine and updating the MANPATH variable to include the GNU manual pages, it should be possible to just type "man gas" and obtain a display of the GAS program options. Alternatively look in the GAS source directories for a file called 29k/src/gas/doc/gas.1 or as.1 to obtain the necessary documentation. Below is a extract from the GAS manual pages which indicates some of the capabilities of the tool.

```
gas [-a | -al | -as] [-f] [-I path] [-K] [-L] [-o objfile] [-R] [-v] [-W]
    files...
```

OPTIONS

`-a | al | as`
Turn on assembly listing; *–al*, listing only; *–as,* symbols, *–a*, everything.

`-f`   *Fast* —skip preprocessing (assume source is compiler output).

`-I path`
Add *path* to search list for .include directives.

`-K`   Issue warning when difference tables altered for long displacements

`-L`   Keep (in symbol table) local symbols starting with *L*.

`-o objfile`
Name the object–file output for GAS.

`-R`   Fold data sections into text sections.

`-v`   Announce GAS version.

`-W`   Suppress warning messages.

Chapter 4

Interrupts and Traps

This chapter describes techniques for writing interrupt and trap handlers for 29K processor-based systems. It also describes the interrupt hardware for the 29K Processor Family, and the software environment within which interrupt handlers execute.

Handler descriptions are separated into two major sections. The first discusses Supervisor mode handlers and the second covers User mode handlers. The descriptions apply equally well to interrupts and traps. For the purposes of this chapter, User mode handlers refer to interrupt and trap handlers written in a high-order language. However, it is possible to enter User mode without first establishing high-order language support. Additionally, for our purposes we shall call machine level handlers Supervisor mode handlers.

Although interrupts are largely asynchronous events, traps most often occur synchronously with instruction execution; however, both share common logic in the 29K Processor Family and are often handled entirely in Supervisor mode, with interrupts disabled and Freeze mode (described later) in effect. However, interrupt and trap handlers may execute in one or more of the stages shown in Figure 4-1. Each stage implies an increased level of complexity, and may execute a return from interrupt (IRET instruction) if the process is complete. However, in the case where User mode has been entered, the handler must first reenter Supervisor mode before executing an IRET instruction.

The first stage is entered when an interrupt occurs. In this stage the processor is running in Supervisor mode, with Freeze mode enabled and interrupts disabled. In the second stage Freeze mode is turned off (disabled), but the processor remains in Supervisor mode with interrupts disabled. The third stage execution takes place with

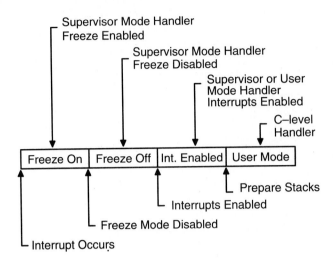

Figure 4-1.   Interrupt Handler Execution Stages

interrupts enabled, but with the processor still operating in Supervisor mode. In the fourth stage, execution continues in User mode. Each stage is discussed in the following sections of this chapter.

Before entering into a discussion of Supervisor mode interrupts and traps, it is necessary to first understand the way interrupts are handled by the 29K family hardware.

4.1   29K PROCESSOR FAMILY INTERRUPT SEQUENCE

When an interrupt or trap occurs and is recognized, the processor initiates the following sequence of steps.

- Instruction execution is suspended.

- Instruction fetching is suspended.

- Any in-progress load or store operation, which was not the cause of a trap, is completed. In the case of load- and store-multiple, any additional operations are suspended.

- The contents of the Current Processor Status (CPS) register are copied into the Old Processor Status (OPS) register.

- The CPS register is modified as shown below (the letter "u" means unaffected, and "r" indicates that this bit depends on the value of the RV bit in the CFG register, or the R bit in the fetched interrupt vector).

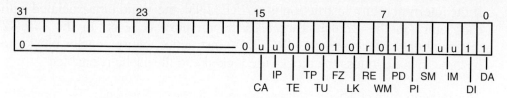

Figure 4-2. The Format of Special Registers CPS and OPS

- The setting of the Freeze (FZ) bit freezes the Channel Address (CHA), Channel Data (CHD), Channel Control (CHC), Program Counters (PC0–PC2), and ALU Status registers.

- The address of the first instruction of the interrupt or trap handler is determined. If the VF bit of the Configuration register is 1, the address is obtained by accessing a vector from data memory. The access is performed by using the physical address obtained from the Vector Area Base Address register and the vector number. If the VF bit is 0, the instruction address is directly given by the Vector Area Base Address register and the vector number.

  If the VF bit is 1, the R bit in the vector fetched above is copied into the RE bit of the CPS register. If the VF bit is 0, the RV bit of the Configuration register is copied into the RE bit. This determines whether or not the first instruction of the interrupt handler is an instruction-ROM-space or instruction-space.

- An instruction fetch is initiated using the instruction address determined above. At this point, normal instruction execution resumes.

  No registers (beyond the interrupted program's CPS) are saved when an interrupt occurs. Any registers whose contents are essential to restarting the interrupted program must be deliberately saved if they are going to be modified by the interrupt handler.

4.2   29K PROCESSOR FAMILY INTERRUPT RETURN

After the handler has processed the interrupt, and control is given back to the interrupted task, execution of an IRET or IRETINV instruction is used to cause the Am29000 processor to initiate the following steps.

- Any in-progress LOAD or STORE operation is completed. If a load-multiple or store-multiple sequence has been suspended, the interrupt return is not completed until that operation is finished.

- Interrupts and traps are disabled, regardless of the settings of the DA, DI, and IM fields of the CPS register.

- If the interrupt return instruction is an IRETINV, the Valid bit associated with each entry in the Branch Target Cache memory is reset. In the case of the Am29030 processor, the IRETINV instruction causes cache blocks to become invalid, unless the blocks are locked and the cache is enabled.

- The contents of the OPS register are copied into the CPS register. This normally resets the FZ bit, allowing the Program Counters (PC0–PC2) and the CHA, CHD, CHC, and ALU Status registers to update normally. The Interrupt Pending bit (IP) of the CPS register is always updated by the processor. The copy operation is irrelevant for this bit.

- The address in Program Counter 1 (PC1) is used to fetch an instruction. The CPS register conditions the fetch. This step is treated as a branch, in the sense that the processor searches the Branch Target Cache memory for the target of the fetch.

- The fetched instruction above enters the decode stage of the pipeline.

- The address in PC0 is used to fetch an instruction. The CPS register conditions the fetch. This step is treated as a branch, in the sense that the processor searches the Branch Target Cache memory for the target of the fetch.

- The first fetched instruction enters the execute stage of the pipeline, and the second instruction fetched enters the decode stage.

- If the Contents Valid (CV) bit of the CHC register is 1, and the Not Needed (NN) and Multiple Operation (ML) bits are both 0, an external access is restarted. If the PC1 register points to an interrupted load- or store-multiple instruction, and the ML bit is one, then an interrupted load- or store-multiple operation is restarted. The external memory access is continued based on the contents of the CHA, CHD, and CHC registers. The interrupt return is not completed until this operation is finished.

- Interrupts and traps are enabled per the appropriate bits in the CPS register.

- The processor resumes normal operation.

It is important to remember that once an interrupt or trap occurs, the processor is immediately vectored to the appropriate handler, with interrupts disabled, Freeze mode enabled, and Supervisor mode execution. The next section discusses Supervisor mode interrupt handlers. The final section describes User mode interrupt handlers. Both sections include 29K Processor Family assembly language source code examples.

4.3 SUPERVISOR MODE HANDLERS

4.3.1 The Interrupt Environment

After an interrupt or trap occurs, and the event is recognized by the processor, the 29K family hardware interrupt sequence, described earlier, is initiated. Interrupt handler code begins execution at this point.

The amount of code necessary to handle an interrupt or trap depends on the nature of the interruption, and the degree to which a given operating system supports interrupts and traps. For robust systems, interrupt and trap handlers must be sure to return to an environment guaranteed to be intact when their processing is complete. Some systems may elect to terminate a program if certain interrupts and traps occur, while others may ignore these entirely. The operating system will also set some standards for register availability in interrupt routines. As stated in the section describing the calling convention (Chapter 2), AMD recommends that the 29K processor's global registers $gr95$ and below be reserved for non User-mode code. Additionally section 3.3, of Assembly Language Programming, goes further, and suggests an allocation scheme for operating system, reserved registers. (See Table 4-1.)

Table 4-1. Global Register Allocations

Registers	Name	Description
$gr1$	rsp	Local register stack pointer
$gr64$–67	$it0$–$it3$	Interrupt handler temporaries
$gr68$–79	$kt0$–$kt11$	Temporaries for use by operating system
$gr80$–92	$ks0$–$ks12$	Operating system statics
$gr93$–95	$ks13$–$ks15$	Floating-point trap handler statics
$gr96$–127	various	Reserved by Am29000 processor calling conventions

In essence, global registers ($gr64$–$gr95$) are reserved for interrupt handlers and the operating system. The remaining 32 global registers ($gr96$–$gr127$) are reserved for holding the interrupted program's context.

Existing floating-point trap handlers use $gr64$–$gr78$ as temporary registers, with interrupts disabled. In addition, registers $gr93$–$gr95$ are used to hold static variables for these routines. The register assignments in these routines can easily be changed, but fifteen temporary global registers and three static global registers must be allocated. Note, with the Am29050 processor, only the integer divide instructions are not directly supported by the processor hardware and require trapware support. This requires six temporary global registers and no static global registers.

If all of the local registers are given over to User-mode code use, then interrupt and trap handlers must also assume that the local registers are being used and may not be arbitrarily rewritten, unless the values they contain are saved upon entry, and are restored prior to exit. If a cache window size (*rfb–rab*) less than the physical register file size is used, then a number of non-static temporary local registers can be made available for handler use.

Fortunately, most interrupt handlers can operate very efficiently using only a few temporary registers. Global registers *gr64–gr67* (*it0–it3*) have been allocated for this purpose. However, additional temporary registers *kt0–kt3* may be used for interrupt handlers if these registers are not used by the operating system.

4.3.2 Interrupt Latency

The determination of the number of cycles required to reach the first instruction of an interrupt or trap handler is a little complicated. First consider the case for the non-vector fetch, table of handlers method.

An external interrupt line may have to be held active for one cycle before the processor internally recognizes it. Once recognized, one cycle is required to internally synchronize the processor. Now any in-progress load or store must be completed (*Dc* cycles, where $0 \leq Dc \leq Dw$, note *Dw* is the number of cycles required to complete a data memory write and is often greater than *Dr*, the number of cycles required to complete a data memory read). One cycle is then required to calculate the vector. The first instruction can then be fetched (*Ir* cycles) and presented to the instruction fetch unit. One cycle is required by the fetch unit and a further cycle by the decode unit before the instruction reaches execute. If the first instruction is found in the cache, then the Branch Target Cache memory forwards the instruction directly to the decode unit. The total latency (minimum of five cycles for the hit case) is given by the equation below.

```
delay(miss) = 1 + 1 + DC + 1 + Ir + 1 + 1


delay(hit) = 1 + 1 + DC + 1 + 1 + 1
```

Now let's consider the case for a table of vectors, that is the VF bit in the CFG register is set (always the case for an Am29030 processor). The vector must still be calculated and any in-progress load or store completed before the vector can be fetched from data memory. The number of cycles required to read the data memory is represented by *Dr*. Once the address of the handler has been fetched it must be routed to the processor PC, this takes one cycle. A further cycle occurs before the address reaches the Address Pins. Delays involved in fetching the first instruction are then the same as described above. Once again, if the first instruction is found in the cache, the Branch Target Cache memory forwards the instruction directly to the decode unit. The total latency (minimum of seven cycles for the hit case) is given by the equation below.

```
delay(miss) = 1 + 1 + Dc + 1 + Dr + 1 + 1 + Ir + 1 + 1

delay(hit) = 1 + 1 + Dc + 1 + Dr + 1 + 1 + 1
```

The Am29050 processor supports instruction forwarding. This enables instructions to be forwarded directly to the decode unit, bypassing the fetch unit and saving one cycle. The minimum latency for the Am29050 processor for the vector fetch and non-vector fetch methods is six cycles and four cycles, respectively.

4.3.3 Simple Freeze-mode Handlers

The simplest interrupt or trap handler will execute in its entirety in Supervisor mode, with interrupts disabled, and with the FZ bit set in the CPS register. This corresponds to the first stage depicted in Figure 4-1.

The FZ bit in the Current Processor Status register is responsible for locking the values in the Program Counters (PC0–PC2), the Channel registers (CHA, CHD and CHC), and the ALU status. As long as the FZ bit remains set, these registers will not be updated. Note, the PC0–PC2 registers are not the actual Program counter, but a three-stage buffer store that records the stages of program execution.

If the intention is to ignore the interrupt and return control to the interrupted process, the entire handler can consist of little more than an IRET instruction. After the interrupt request has been cleared, execution of this instruction will cause the processor to perform the interrupt return sequence described above, resuming execution of the interrupted program at the point of interruption.

4.3.4 Operating in Freeze mode

Interrupt or trap handlers executing only a small number of instructions before returning will benefit from the very short latency of the interrupt sequence performed by the 29K processor. This is because the 29K processor offers superior performance when compared with conventional processors that save a great deal of context whenever an interrupt or trap occurs.

Because the executing program's context is often not disturbed by the interrupt or trap handling code, both the reaction time (latency) and processing time of the interrupt handler are minimized.

In this context, no registers (except the CPS) have been saved when an interrupt or trap handler is given control by the processor. In addition, if the Program Counter registers (PC0 and PC1) are left undisturbed, the 29K processor's instruction pipeline is more quickly restarted when the handler returns.

But, because Freeze mode has frozen the contents of several important registers, there are some instructions that should not be used in this context, or whose use is restricted. These instructions are:

- Instructions that can generate traps. These should not be used because traps are disabled in Freeze mode. These include ASSERT, emulated floating-point operations (e.g., FADD), and certain integer operations whose execution could cause a trap to occur. Note, the Am29050 processor executes all floating point operations directly and thus these instructions can be used with the Am29050 processor as they will not generate a trap.

If a trap generating instruction is executed it will have the same affect as a NOP instruction. An exception trap is caused by bad memory accesses. These traps are always taken, even if they occur in Freeze-mode code. Because the processor registers were already frozen at the time of the *nested* trap, it can be difficult to determine the cause of the trap or issue an IRET instruction.

However, if an Am29050 processor is being used and a trap occurs when the DA bit is set in the CPS register, Monitor mode is entered. Monitor mode (section 4.3.5) can be used by monitors to debug kernel Freeze-mode code.

- Instructions that use special registers—these instructions may be used; however, any modified registers may have to be saved and restored before the interrupt handler returns. The EXTRACT and INSERT instructions are in this category.

- Instructions that modify special registers— because of the normal sideeffect of their operation, these instructions must be used with caution. There are three subgroups within this group:

—Arithmetic and logical instructions that set the Z, N, V, and C status bits in the ALU Status register. These instructions can be used in Freeze mode if the ALU status bits are not used. Because Freeze mode disables updating the ALU Status register, extended precision arithmetic instructions, such as ADDC or SUBC, will not execute properly.

—Load-Multiple and Store Multiple. These instructions cannot be used in Freeze mode, because the Channel registers (CHA, CHD, and CHC) upon which their execution depends are frozen.

—LOAD and STORE instructions with the set BP option enabled, if the Data Width Enable (DW bit) is 0. In this case, if BP must be set, it will have to be done explicitly by using a Move-To-Special Register (MTSR) instruction. Therefore, LOAD and STORE instructions with word-aligned addresses (i.e., those whose least significant 2 bits are 0) may be used without additional effort; however, if byte or half-word instructions are needed, the BP register must be explicitly set prior to execution of a non-word-aligned LOAD, STORE, INSERT, or EXTRACT instruction.

All other instructions may be used without restriction, keeping in mind the inherent implications of Freeze mode. (Note: Other restrictions apply to Am29000 processors manufactured prior to revision C.)

4.3.5 Monitor mode

Monitor mode only applies to the Am29050 processor. If a trap occurs when the DA bit in the CPS register is a 1, the processor starts executing at address 16 in instruction ROM space. Monitor mode is not entered as a result of asynchronous events such as timer interrupts or activation of the TRAP(1–0) or INTR(3–0) lines.

On taking a Monitor mode trap the Reason Vector register (RSN) is set to indicate the cause of the trap. Additionally, the MM bit in the CPS register is set to 1. When the MM bit is set, the shadow program counters (SPC0, SPC1, and SPC2) are frozen, in a similar way to the FZ bit freezing the PC0–PC2 registers. Because the shadow program counters continue to record PC-bus activity when the FZ bit is set, they can be used to restart Freeze mode execution. This is achieved by an IRET or IRETINV instruction being executed while in Monitor mode.

Because Monitor mode traps are used by monitors in the debugging of trap and interrupt handlers and are not intended for operating system use, they are dealt with further in Chapter 7 (*Software Debugging*).

4.3.6 Freeze-mode Clock Interrupt Handler

The code shown in this example illustrates one way to program a clock that keeps the current time. One important aspect of this routine is the need to minimize overhead in the function, taking as little time as possible to update the clock when an interrupt occurs. Allocating two Operating System Static registers to contain millisecond and second values reduces the need to access data memory inside the handler.

```
; freeze mode clock interrupt handler
;
        .equ    IN,0x0200000     IN-bit of TMR reg

        .reg    CLOCK,ks0        ;1 ms increments
        .reg    SECS,ks1         ;time in seconds

        .equ    CPUCLK,25        ;CPU clock in MHz
        .equ    RATE,1000        ;ints per second

intr14:
        const   it0,IN           ;IN-bit in TMR
        consth  it0,IN
        mfsr    it1,tmr
        andn    it1,it1,it0      ;clear IN-bit
```

```
        mtsr    tmr,it1
        const   it0,RATE
        cplt    it0,CLOCK,it0   ;check if 1 sec
        jmpf    it0,carry       ;jump if CLOCK > RATE
         add    CLOCK,CLOCK,1   ;increment CLOCK
        iret
carry:
        const   CLOCK,0
        add     SECS,SECS,1     ;increment seconds
        iret
```

This handler executes once each time an interrupt from the on-board timer occurs. In the preceding code, timer interrupts are assumed to occur once each millisecond, therefore the value in the *CLOCK* register will increment 1000 times in one second. When the 1000th interrupt occurs, the *CLOCK* register is set to 0, and the *SECS* variable is incremented.

The 29K processor Timer Counter register includes a 24-bit Timer Count Value (TCV) field that is automatically decremented on every processor cycle. When the TCV field decrements to 0, it is written with the Timer Reload Value (TRV) field of the Timer Reload (TMR) register on the next cycle. The Interrupt (IN) bit of the TMR register is set at the same time. The following code illustrates a technique to initialize the timer for this purpose.

```
; freeze mode clock interrupt initialization
;
        .equ    TICKS, (CPUCLK*1000000/RATE)
        .equ    IE,0x1000000    ;IE-bit in TMR reg

clkinit:
        const   it0,TICKS       ;i.e., 25,000
        consth  it0,TICKS
        mtsr    tmc,it0         ;set counter value
        const   it0,(IE|TICKS)  ;value+int.-enable
        consth  it0,(IE|TICKS)
        mtsr    tmr,it0         ;set reload value
        const   SECS,0          ;set seconds=0
        jmpi    lr0
         const  CLOCK,0         ;set clock=0
```

Assuming the processor is running at 25 MHz, setting the timer reload and count values to 25000 causes the count to decrement to 0 once each millisecond. This will accumulate 1000 counts during one second of CPU execution. If two Operating System Static registers can not be spared for this purpose, the *SECS* variable should be located in main memory. The modified code for incrementing the seconds counter in memory is shown below.

```
SECS:   .word   0

carry:
        const   it0,SECS
```

```
consth    it0,SECS
load      0,0,it1,it0
add       it1,it1,1
const     CLOCK,0
store     0,0,it1,it0
iret
```

Because the *SECS* variable is only referenced once per second, the performance degradation due to this change would be minimal. The initialization code would also need to be modified to set the memory location for *SECS* to 0 in this case.

4.3.7 Removing Freeze mode

Some interrupt handlers will benefit from removing Freeze mode, without enabling interrupts, in order to use the load-multiple and store-multiple instructions. A less common, reason for removing Freeze mode is the ability to use ALU Status bits: V, N, Z, and C. In either case, several registers must be saved before the Freeze-mode bit in the CPS register can be cleared.

The removal of Freeze mode represents entry into the second stage of interrupt handling, as shown in Figure 4-1.

The frozen Program Counters (PC0 and PC1) must be saved so that the handler will be able to resume execution of the interrupted program. If external data memory is to be accessed, the CHA, CHD and CHC Channel registers must be saved so that their contents can be restored after a load- or store-multiple instruction has been executed. Saving the channel registers also saves the Count Remaining register, which is contained within the CHC register. Additionally, before any ALU/Logical operations are performed, the ALU register must be saved.

After the Program Counters have been saved and before any Channel or ALU operation is executed, Freeze mode can be removed by clearing the Freeze (FZ) bit of the CPS register. This immediately removes the freeze condition, and all registers, including the Program Counters, will update normally. The PC0 register shall reflect the PC-BUS activity on the cycle following the clearing of Freeze mode. One cycle later, the PC1 register shall begin to reflect the PC-BUS activity for the current execution stream. Other registers will only be updated when the relevant instructions are performed (as described above).

The primary benefit of leaving Freeze mode is the ability to use the load- and store-multiple instructions. After Freeze mode has been exited, the DA bit in the CPS register is still set and instructions causing traps should not be used. Thus, many of the restrictions listed in the section titled Operating in Freeze mode (section 4.3.4) will still apply, with the additional requirement that several of the interrupt temporary global registers will be needed to hold the saved registers.

An example of code that implements removing Freeze mode is shown below.

```
; Removing Freeze mode example code
;
        .equ    FZ,0x00000400   FZ-bit in CPS
        .equ    SM,0x00000010   SM-bit in CPS
        .equ    PD,0x00000040   PD-bit in CPS
        .equ    PI,0x00000020   PI-bit in CPS
        .equ    DI,0x00000002   DI-bit in CPS
        .equ    DA,0x00000001   DA-bit in CPS
        .equ    REMOVE,(SM|PD|PI|DI|DA)
        .equ    FREEZE,(REMOVE|FZ)

intr0:  ;interrupt vector points here
        mfsr    it0,pc0         ;save PC0
        mfsr    it1,pc1         ;save PC1
        mtsrim  cps,REMOVE      ;remove Freeze mode
        mfsr    it3,alu         ;save ALU
        mfsr    kt0,cha         ;save CHA
        mfsr    kt1,chd         ;save CHD
        mfsr    kt2,chc         ;save CHC
;
; The interrupt handler code goes here
;
        mtsr    chc,kt2         ;restore CHC
        mtsr    chd,kt1         ;restore CHD
        mtsr    cha,kt0         ;restore CHA
        mtsr    alu,it3         ;restore ALU
        mtsrim  cps,FREEZE      ;set Freeze mode
        mtsr    pc1,it1         ;restore PC1
        mtsr    pc0,it0         ;restore PC0
        iret
```

The example code begins by saving the Program Counters (PC0 and PC1), using MFSR instructions to move the values from special registers to temporary global registers *it0* and *it1*.

Freeze mode is then disabled by clearing the FZ bit in the CPS register. (Note the bits set by the MTSRIM instruction are system implementation dependent; the RE bit may be required.) Once Freeze mode is turned off, the ALU register will be modified by any ALU/Logical operation. Thus, it is important that the ALU register be saved now. (Note that two processor cycles are needed, after Freeze mode is removed, to allow the program state to properly update the program counters.)

If interrupts are not to be re-enabled and the kernel does not require the use of global registers (*kt0–kt2*), then these registers can be used to extend the number of available interrupt temporary registers.

The ALU register is saved in temporary kernel register *it3*. The Channel registers (CHA, CHD and CHC) are then saved in operating system temporary registers *kt0–kt2*.

The interrupt handler is still executing with interrupts disabled at this point in the program, but load- and store-multiple instructions can be freely used, as long as they do not cause another interrupt or trap to occur. Note, even with the DA bit in the CPS register set, certain traps such as a Data Access Exception can still be taken. When the handler is finished, it must reverse the process by restoring all the saved registers. No particular order of instructions is necessary, as long as Freeze mode is entered before PC1 and PC0 are restored. Additionally, instructions affecting the ALU register must not be used after the saved value has been restored. By restoring the ALU unit after Freeze mode is entered, instructions are prevented from affecting the ALU register.

When the IRET instruction is executed, the restored Program Counters (PC0–PC1) are used to resume the interrupted program. The restored CPS (saved in OPS by the CPU) and Channel register contents are used to restart any unfinished operations.

If enough global registers are not available for saving the Program Counters and Channel registers, memory could be used for this purpose. In this case, six words of memory are needed. Example code for saving and restoring the registers in the user's memory stack is shown below. Note, the *pushsr* and *popsr* macro instructions first introduced in section 3.3.1 (page 119), are used in the example code and are presented again below:

```
        .macro  pushsr,sp,reg,sreg
        mfsr    reg,sreg
        sub     sp,sp,4
        store   0,0,reg,sp
        .endm

;       .macro  popsr,sreg,reg,sp
        load    0,0,reg,sp
        add     sp,sp,4
        mtsr    sreg,reg
        .endm

; save registers on memory stack
;
        pushsr  msp,it0,pc0     ;save  PC0
        pushsr  msp,it0,pc1     ;save  PC1
        pushsr  msp,it0,alu     ;save  ALU
        pushsr  msp,it0,cha     ;save  CHA
        pushsr  msp,it0,chd     ;save  CHD
        pushsr  msp,it0,chc     ;save  CHC
;
        const   it3,FZ
        mfsr    it2,cps
        andn    it2,it2,it3
        mtsr    cps,it2         ;remove Freeze mode
;
; The interrupt handler code goes here
;
        const   it3,FZ
        mfsr    it2,cps
```

```
        or      it2,it2,it3
        mtsr    cps,it2          ;set Freeze mode
;
        popsr   chc,it0,msp      ;restore CHC
        popsr   chd,it0,msp      ;restore CHD
        popsr   cha,it0,msp      ;restore CHA
        popsr   alu,it0,msp      ;restore ALU
        popsr   pc1,it0,msp      ;restore PC1
        popsr   pc0,it0,msp      ;restore PC0
        iret
```

The previous code can be made more efficient by saving more registers at a time, at the expense of using a greater number of global registers. Using store-multiple instructions to save the registers' contents takes advantage of Burst mode in the processor memory system.

4.3.8 Handling Nested Interrupts

Handling Nested Interrupts is a complex topic, and the method presented in this section discusses multiple levels of interrupt nesting [Mann 1992b]. Two methods are presented. The first method results in an interrupt mechanism similar to the interrupt scheme used by some CISC microprocessors. The second method takes advantage of the 29K family RISC architecture, and offers better performance. The following section, titled *An Interrupt Queuing Model* (section 4.3.10), provides an alternative solution to the problem that offers better interrupt processing throughput.

For any interrupt handler taking a significant amount of time to execute, it is usually important to permit interrupts of a higher priority to occur. This keeps the latency of higher priority interrupts within acceptable limits. Whenever an interrupt is allowed to preempt the execution of another interrupt handler, the interrupts are said to be "nested." That is, execution of the lower priority handler is interrupted, and the higher priority handler begins execution immediately.

To allow for nested interrupts, it is only necessary to save the registers or temporary variables that could be overwritten by a new interrupt handler's context. As in the previous example, the program counters (PC0 and PC1) and channel registers (CHA,CHD, and CHC) need to be saved. In addition, because more than one execution thread may need to be restarted, the Old Processor Status (OPS) and ALU registers must be saved.

Because an interrupt may occur immediately after being enabled, it is important that the PC0 and PC1 registers reflect the activity of the current execution PC-BUS. As already described in the *Removing Freeze Mode* section, a two cycle delay occurs before the PC1 register starts updating. Thus Freeze mode must be removed two cycles before interrupts are enabled.

If the interrupt handler intends to use integer multiply or divide instructions or emulated floating point instructions, the contents of the Indirect Pointers (IPA, IPB and IPC) and the Q register should also be saved. Before interrupts are enabled, it is also important to clear the CHC register, so that incomplete load- or store-multiple instructions are not restarted when the first interrupt return (IRET) instruction is executed. Figure 4-3 illustrates the context in which this could lead to unfortunate results.

In Figure 4-3, execution of a load-multiple instruction in the main program is in progress when an external interrupt occurs. This results in control being given to a first-level interrupt handler. The handler enables interrupts, and another interrupt occurs (e.g., a Timer Interrupt). When this happens, the second-level interrupt handler is given control.

After completing its processing, execution of an IRET instruction causes the processor to use the information in its CHC register to resume the interrupted load-multiple instruction; but this is in the context of the first-level interrupt handler, rather than in the main program where it was interrupted.

This CHC discussion is merely an explanation to stress that the CHC register should not only be saved and restored in each interrupt level, but that CHC should also be cleared before interrupts are enabled. This will ensure that only when the proper copy of the CHC is restored will execution of an IRET instruction restart the interrupted load- or store-multiple operation.

Additionally, when a trap occurs as a result of a Data Exception Error (DERR) the TF bit in the CHC will become set. It is important that the CHC register be cleared rather than be restored for the context containing the violating data access. Otherwise an interrupt handler loop will result.

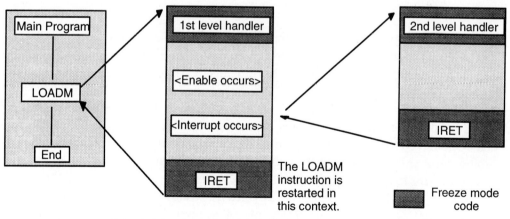

Figure 4-3. Interrupted Load Multiple Instruction

4.3.9 Saving Registers

The following code illustrates saving the necessary registers, turning off Freeze mode, and enabling interrupts.

```
;multi-level nested interrupt handler
;example code
;

intr0:          ;save registers
        pushsr  msp,it0,pc0     ;save PC0
        pushsr  msp,it0,pc1     ;save PC1
        pushsr  msp,it0,alu     ;save ALU
        pushsr  msp,it0,cha     ;save CHA
        pushsr  msp,it0,chd     ;save CHD
        pushsr  msp,it0,chc     ;save CHC
        pushsr  msp,it0,ops     ;save OPS
;
;come off freeze - could use mtsrim
        const   it1,FZ
        mfsr    it0,cps         ;get CPS
        andn    it0,it0,it1
        mtsr    cps,it1         ;remove Freeze mode
;
;save more regs while PC0,1 get in step
        pushsr  msp,it0,ipa     ;save IPA
        pushsr  msp,it0,ipb     ;save IPB
        pushsr  msp,it0,ipc     ;save IPC
        pushsr  msp,it0,q       ;save Q
;
        mtsrim  CHC,0           ;clear CHC
        andn    it0,it1,(DI|DA)
        mtsr    cps,it1         ;enable interrupts
dispatch:
;
; Interrupt handler code starts here.
; Dispatch to appropriate service routine.
```

Saving the Indirect Pointers and Q register is a user preference, but their contents are modified by several 29K processor instructions. It is important to bear this in mind when writing interrupt handlers. The safest approach is to always save the contents of these registers.

The above code uses a stack to save the register contents, similar to the way a CISC processor's microcode saves processor state. However, better performance can be achieved by use of the large number of processor registers to cache the interrupted context before having to resort to an interrupt context stack. The following code performs much the same task as the previous code, but it can reach the interrupt dispatcher (label **dispatch**:) in twelve cycles less for the first interrupt and costs only an additional two cycles for interrupts at greater levels of nesting (assuming MTSRIM is used to update the CPS register).

This code implements a first level interrupt context cache in global registers *kt4–kt10*. Global register *kt11* is used to keep a record of the current level of interrupt nesting; and should be initialized to −1, that is cache empty. Considering the speed of the 29K family, it is likely the first-level interrupt processing will be complete before a further interrupt occurs, thus avoiding the need to save context on a memory stack. The use of registers rather than memory to save context also results in reduced latency between the time the interrupt occurred and the appropriate service routine starts executing.

The example code below does not store the indirect pointer registers (IPA, IPB, IPC, and Q). These registers do not need to be saved except by interrupt handlers which either make use of the indirect pointers, use emulated arithmetic instructions, or use integer multiply or divide. Best performance is achieved by postponing the saving of these registers to the specific handler routine which expects to use them. Correspondingly, a handler which uses them is also responsible for restoring them.

```
        .equ     Kmode,(PD|PI|SM|IM)

    not_1st:                        ;save on stack
        pushsr   msp,it0,pc0        ;save PC0
        pushsr   msp,it0,pc1        ;save PC1
        pushsr   msp,it0,alu        ;save ALU
        pushsr   msp,it0,cha        ;save CHA
        pushsr   msp,it0,chd        ;save CHD
        pushsr   msp,it0,chc        ;save CHC
        pushsr   msp,it0,ops        ;save OPS
        jmp      dispatch-8
         mtsrim  cps,REMOVE         ;remove Freeze mode

    intr0:                          ;save registers
        jmpf     kt11,not_1st       ;test cache in use
         add     kt11,kt11,1        ;level count
    ;
    cache:            ;save in cache
        mfsr     kt4,pc0            ;save PC0
        mfsr     kt5,pc1            ;save PC1
        mtsrim   cps,REMOVE         ;remove Freeze mode
        mfsr     kt6,alu            ;save ALU
        mfsr     kt7,cha            ;save CHA
        mfsr     kt8,chd            ;save CHD
        mfsr     kt9,chc            ;save CHC
        mfsr     kt10,ops           ;save OPS
    ;
        mtsrim   chc,0              ;clear CHC
        mtsrim   cps,Kmode          ;enable interrupts
    ;
    dispatch:
    ;
    ; Interrupt handler code starts here.
    ; Dispatch to appropriate handler.
```

4.3.10 Enabling Interrupts

Interrupts are enabled by clearing the DI and DA bits of the CPS. If an unmasked interrupt is pending at this point (the IP bit of the CPS register is set to 1), the processor will immediately process the interrupt and execute the handler at the new vector address.

In the previous code example, when interrupts are enabled, and if an interrupt occurs, the succeeding register saves will not be performed; however, the recently invoked interrupt handler will save these registers if it intends to enable interrupts during its execution. The contents of the Indirect Pointers and Q register will be preserved, or not touched, depending on the nature of the nested interrupt handler.

When clearing the DI and DA bits of the CPS register, the state of the other bits must be saved. The first example code illustrates this by using an ANDN instruction to AND the current contents of the register, with a complement bit pattern of the DA and DI bits in that register (i.e., 1111 1111 1111 1100).

Figure 4-4 shows the interrupt enable logic of the Am29000 processor. Notice that interrupts generated by the on-chip timer are controlled by the DA bit in the CPS register. This indicates it is impossible to enable traps for use by ASSERT and other instructions, without also permitting asynchronous interrupts from the timer to occur (unless the on-chip timer is not being used). If it is necessary to avoid timer interrupts, the IE bit in the TMR register can be saved, then cleared to disable timer interrupts.

The interrupt inputs to the Prioritizer logic (as shown in Figure 4-4) are not latched, and must be continuously asserted by an interrupting external device until the interrupt has been recognized. Recognition of the interrupt is usually accomplished by executing an instruction that accesses the interrupting device. This removes the interrupt request, which must be done before interrupts are enabled; otherwise, the same interrupt will recur immediately when interrupts are enabled.

The Interrupt Mask (IM) field of the CPS register can be used to disable recognition of interrupt requests on the INTR inputs. The mask bits implement a simplified interrupt priority scheme that can be set up to recognize only higher-priority interrupts, while another handler is in execution.

The two-bit IM field allows four priority levels to be established. An IM field value of zero (IM=00) enables only the interrupts occurring at the INTR0 input. When IM = 01, both INTR0 and INTR1 are enabled; if IM = 10, then INTR0, INTR1, and INTR2 are enabled; and if IM = 11, then INTR0, INTR1, INTR2, and INTR3 are enabled. The only way to disable the INTR0 input is to set the DI (Disable Interrupts) bit to 1 in the CPS register.

An example code fragment that sets the IM bits for a handler, according to its priority, is shown below.

```
; set interrupt mask according to priority
;
        .equ    MYLEVEL,2
        .equ    IM,0b1100

setim:
```

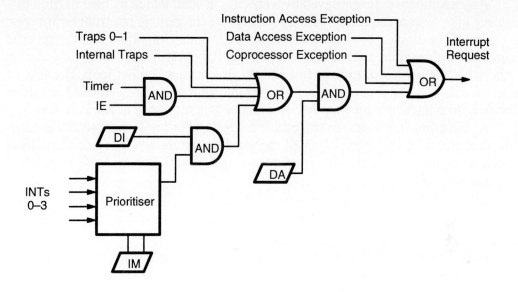

Figure 4-4. Am29000 Processor Interrupt Enable Logic

```
mfsr    it0,cps
andn    it0,it0,(IM|DI|DA)
or      it0,it0,((MYLEVEL-1)<<2)
mtsr    cps,it0
```

In the above example, after the CPS has been moved to a global register, the bits corresponding to the IM field, the DI bit, and the DA bit are cleared by ANDing them with a complement mask. Next, the bits defined by the MYLEVEL definition (decreased by 1) are ORed into the proper position in the IM field, and the result is stored back into the CPS. With the values shown, the IM field is set to the value 01, which enables interrupts on INTR0 and INTR1.

In the main part of the handler, any Am29000 processor instructions can be executed; however, because most of the global registers have not been saved, the handler may not have any extra working space. Depending on the number of registers needed to carry out the handler's task, a few additional global registers may have to be saved, then restored.

4.3.11 Restoring Saved Registers

The final act of an interrupt or trap handler, before executing the IRET instruction, is to restore the contents of all saved registers so the complete environment of the interrupted task is restored before execution is resumed. The proper approach to restoring the saved registers is to reverse the steps taken to save them.

Any additional registers saved by a specific handler called by the interrupt dispatcher must restore the additional registers before the generic interrupt return code is executed. In the case of an external interrupt, it is also important that the specific handler has cleared the external device causing the interrupt line to be held active. Otherwise, the processor may be forced into an interrupt handler loop. Because of internal delays in the processor, the external interrupt must be cleared at least three cycles before interrupts are enabled. In practice this requirement is easily met.

At this point, interrupts are still enabled. The last portion of the restoration process must run with interrupts disabled, because important processor configuration data is being reloaded, and an interrupt occurring during this phase could hopelessly confuse the process.

The final code fragment is shown below:

```
;  code to disable interrupts and complete
;  the restoration of registers prior to
;  issuing an IRET instruction.
;
        popsr    msp,it0,q         ;save Q
        popsr    msp,it0,ipc       ;save IPC
        popsr    msp,it0,ipb       ;save IPB
        popsr    msp,it0,ipa       ;save IPA
;
        const    it3,(FZ|DI|DA)
        mfsr     it2,cps           ;disable interrupts
        or       it2,it2,it3       ;and
        mtsr     cps,it2           ;set Freeze mode
;
        popsr    ops,it0,msp       ;restore OPS
        popsr    chc,it0,msp       ;restore CHC
        popsr    chd,it0,msp       ;restore CHD
        popsr    cha,it0,msp       ;restore CHA
        popsr    alu,it0,msp       ;restore ALU
        popsr    pc1,it0,msp       ;restore PC1
        popsr    pc0,it0,msp       ;restore PC0
        iret
```

The interrupt context restore code for the first-level context cache method is shown below. Restoring the context from registers is much faster than accessing an external memory stack.

```
        .equ    DISABLE,(PD|PI|SM|DI|DA)
        .equ    FREEZE,(DISABLE|FZ)
;
        sub     kt11,kt11,1       ;decrement
        jmpf    kt11,not_1st      ;level counter
         mtsrim cps,FREEZE        ;disable and Freeze
;
                                  ;restore from cache
        mtsr    ops,kt10          ;restore OPS
```

```
            mtsr      chc,kt9            ;restore CHC
            mtsr      chd,kt8            ;restore CHD
            mtsr      chc,kt7            ;restore CHA
            mtsr      alu,kt6            ;restore ALU
            mtsr      pc1,kt5            ;restore PC1
            mtsr      pc0,kt4            ;restore PC0
            iret
    ;
    not_1st:                             ;restore from stack
            popsr     ops,it0,msp        ;restore OPS
            popsr     chc,it0,msp        ;restore CHC
            popsr     chd,it0,msp        ;restore CHD
            popsr     cha,it0,msp        ;restore CHA
            popsr     alu,it0,msp        ;restore ALU
            popsr     pc1,it0,msp        ;restore PC1
            popsr     pc0,it0,msp        ;restore PC0
            iret
```

4.3.12   An Interrupt Queuing model

One approach to solving the latency demands of a high-performance system is to simply queue interrupts in a linked list when they occur, and process them in a higher-level context. Figure 4-5 illustrates the structure and linkages of individual entries in the example queue. This method results in a greater interrupt processing throughput. Less time is spent executing Freeze mode context stacking and unstacking when compared with the previously described nested interrupt handling method.

In the example program, only a few global registers are allocated—because placing an entry into a global queue is a simple operation.

The example code in this section applies to handling receive data interrupts from a UART port, but several types of interrupts can easily share the same queue. For simplicity, queue entries consist of three words plus an optional data block.

- Pointer to the next entry in the queue (forward link).

- Received data count / active flag.

- Pointer to the handler for this entry.

- An optional data block.

Once an I/O operation has begun (in this case, reception of data from a UART), an interrupt occurs for the UART device and the handler is called to place a new entry into the global queue.

As each byte arrives, the first section of the handler continues the I/O process, often by simply reading the data from the UART and indicating that the data has been accepted. This causes the UART to remove the interrupt input and prepare to receive new data.

Only one receive operation for a given interrupt can be in progress at a time. This allows the queue entry to contain three things: a static entry descriptor that holds

---

a pointer to the next entry in the queue, the byte count, and a pointer to the high-level handler function.

The example shown below uses four global (interrupt temporary) registers for its queue building processes. Because interrupts are disabled during this entire part of the process, handlers for other interrupts can use these same registers.

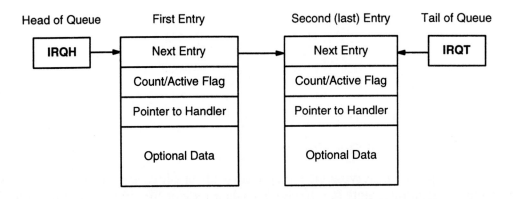

Figure 4-5.   Interrupt Queue Entry Chaining

After the first byte has been stored in the static buffer, the handler must determine if the queue is empty or if it already contains one or more entries. If empty, the handler can immediately invoke a routine to process the entry. If the queue contains one or more entries, the current entry is linked into the queue. The code is shown below.

```
; UART receive interrupt handler (intr0)
;
        .reg    irqh,gr80       ;queue head pointer
        .reg    irqt,gr81       ;queue tail pointer

        .data
entry:
        .word   0,0,receive     ;entry descriptor
        .block  256             ; and data block

intr0:
        const   it1,entry+4     ;address of entry
        consth  it1,entry+4
        load    0,0,it0,it1     ;get count
        add     it3,it1,8       ;address of data
        add     it3,it3,it0     ;add count
        add     it0,it0,4       ;increment count
        store   0,0,it0,it1     ;count->entry+4
        const   it2,uart_rcv    ;UART data address
```

```
          consth    it2,uart_rcv
          load      0,1,it2,it2        ;get data from UART
          store     0,1,it2,it3        ;save in buffer

          cpeq      it0,it0,4          ;first byte?
          jmpt      it0,startup        ;yes, start daemon
           nop
          iret                         ;no, return

  startup:                 ;go daemon if not already running
          cpeq      it2,irqh,0         ;is queue empty
          jmpf      it2,add            ;no, link this entry
           sub      it1,it1,4          ;point to entry
          jmp       daemon             ;yes, go daemon
           add      irqh,it1,0         ;init queue header

  add:
          store     0,0,it1,irqt       ;tail->entry
          add       irqt,it1,0         ;entry->tail
          iret                         ;return
```

When interrupts occur for the second and succeeding bytes, they are stored in the local data block, following the static descriptor entry.

After each byte has been stored, the handler can immediately return because a routine has been invoked to process the entire queue. In UNIX systems, this routine is often called a *daemon*. Once invoked, it continues to process entries until the queue is empty, at which point it terminates its own execution. The title *Dispatcher* shall be used to describe the routine invoked to process queue entries (see Figure 4-6). A dispatcher routine may operate in User mode; in such case it's operation is very similar to a signal handler (described in section 4.4).

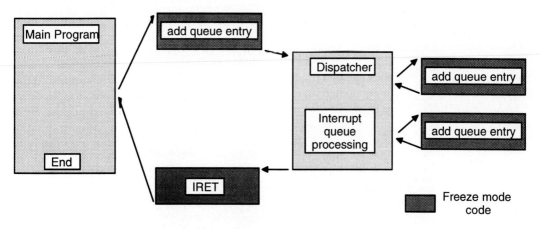

Figure 4-6.   An Interrupt Queuing Approach

The queue processing Dispatcher for this example must run with interrupts enabled; otherwise, new data bytes could not be received from the UART, and other interrupt driven processes could not execute. Before interrupts are enabled, a number of processor registers must be saved, as indicated earlier. Nine kernel temporary registers are allocated for this purpose (*kt3–kt11*). Because the Dispatcher is used to process all queued interrupts, it will not be necessary to push these temporary registers onto the memory stack. The example queue processing code is shown below.

```
; queue processing Dispatcher
;
          .equ    DISABLE,(PD|PI|SM|DI|DA)
          .equ    Kmode,(PD|PI|SM|IM)
          .equ    FREEZE,(DISABLE|FZ)
;
Dispatcher:
          mfsr    kt3,PC0             ;save PC0
          mfsr    kt4,PC1             ;save PC1
          mfsr    kt5,PC2             ;save PC2
          mfsr    kt6,CHA             ;save CHA
          mfsr    kt7,CHD             ;save CHD
          mfsr    kt8,CHC             ;save CHC
          mfsr    kt9,ALU             ;save ALU
          mfsr    kt10,OPS            ;save OPS
          mtsrim  CPS,DISABLE         ;remove Freeze mode
          mtsrim  CHC,0               ;clear CHC
          add     irqt,irqh,0         ;set tail = head

   loop:
          mtsrim  CPS,Kmode           ;enable interrupts
          add     kt11,irqh,8         ;point to handler
          load    0,0,kt11,kt11       ;get address
          calli   kt11,kt11           ;call handler
          nop
          mtsrim  CPS,DISABLE         ;disable interrupts

          cpeq    kt11,irqt,irqh      ;queue empty?
          jmpt    kt11,finish         ;yes, wrapup
          nop
          load    0,0,kt11,irqh       ;no, get next entry
          jmp     loop                ;and loop back
          add     irqh,kt11,0         ;with head<-next

   finish:
          mtsrim  cps,FREEZE          ;enable freeze mode
          const   irqh,0              ;make queue empty
          mtsr    PC0,kt3             ;restore PC0
          mtsr    PC1,kt4             ;restore PC1
          mtsr    PC2,kt5             ;restore PC2
          mtsr    CHA,kt6             ;restore CHA
          mtsr    CHD,kt7             ;restore CHD
          mtsr    CHC,kt8             ;restore CHC
          mtsr    ALU,kt9             ;restore ALU
```

```
mtsr      OPS,kt10          ;restore OPS
iret                        ;terminate execution
```

Note that the example code does not save the Indirect Pointers (IPA–IPC) or the Q register. If any of the individual high-level handlers will disturb the contents of these registers, they must also be saved. If high-level handlers are written carefully, it will not be necessary to save.

The queue processor is responsible for removing entries from the queue and calling the handler associated with each entry. In the above example, a pointer to the high level handler is contained in the third word of the entry descriptor (in this case, receive).

The handler is called after Freeze mode has been disabled, and interrupts are enabled. When the handler receives control, the IRQH register points to the queue entry.

The high-level handler is responsible for removing the data associated with a queue entry, and it must do this with interrupts disabled; however, interrupts need only be disabled while the data is being removed and when the queue entry data count is reset to zero. Any other portions of the handler not relevant to these tasks can run with interrupts enabled.

After the handler has disposed of the data, it returns control to the Dispatcher, which disables interrupts, enables Freeze mode, and attempts to process the next entry in the queue. If no entries remain, it restores the saved registers from kernel temporary registers *kt3–kt10*, and executes an IRET instruction to return control to the interrupted task.

In cases where a transaction with an external device takes a long time, compared with the execution time of the high-level handler, the data is moved in chunks. An execution profile of this process might include the following threads.

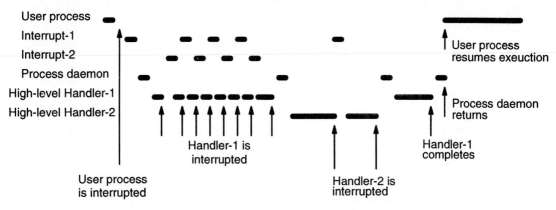

Figure 4-7. Queued Interrupt Execution Flow

■   Interrupt function stores several bytes of data into the data block.

- Process Dispatcher executes the high-level handler, which empties the bytes, zeros the count in the queue entry.

- Another handler might execute for another active interrupt task.

- Interrupt function creates new queue entry for the next series of received data bytes.

- High-level handler gets called to remove the bytes after the process Dispatcher has finished with the current queue entry.

Figure 4-7 illustrates this process. The occurrence of Interrupt-1 causes the on-going User process to be interrupted, and initiates execution of its interrupt handler. The process builds the first queue entry and initiates execution of the Process Dispatcher. The Dispatcher passes control to High-level Handler-1, which begins execution.

This handler is interrupted by the occurrence of Interrupt-2 and Interrupt-1 events as it executes between these interruptions. When Handler-1 completes, it returns control to the Process Dispatcher, which selects the next queue entry and turns control over to high-level Handler-2.

During this execution, one more Interrupt-1 event occurs, which results in the creation of another queue entry. This entry is processed when high-level Handler-2 finishes its execution and the Process Dispatcher again receives control.

High-level Handler-1 processes the remaining data and returns control to the Process Dispatcher which, upon finding no more queue entries, returns to the interrupted user process.

Each execution of the interrupt processes Interrupt-1 or Interrupt-2, as well as the Process Dispatcher and high-level Handler-1 and high-level Handler-2 code segments, is quite short; however, with the short execution approach, individual interrupt priorities are not taken into account. If priority handling of interrupts is important, a different approach is needed. For example, entries could be linked into a single queue, with their position in the queue determined by their priority. In this case, more sophisticated queue handling procedures would have to be implemented; however, a given high-level handler would still execute to completion before another handler is given control.

To handle fully-nested priority-oriented interrupts, that is the ability of a higher priority interrupt to preempt the execution of a lower priority handler, requires an interrupt stack (possibly with the support of a interrupt context cache). It is questionable whether the responsiveness of the nested interrupt technique would override the increased overhead of saving and restoring many sets of registers.

In the approach shown in the previous code only nine global registers are required. These serve for all interrupt handlers in the system. During the execution of the Freeze-mode interrupt handler only four interrupt temporary registers are used ($it0$–$it3$).

Programming the 29K RISC Family

4.3.13 Making Timer Interrupts Synchronous

The 29K on–chip timer can be configured to generate an interrupt when the Timer Counter Register (TCR) decrements to zero; more accurately, when the 24–bit TCV field of the TCV register reaches zero. The TCV field is decremented with each processor cycle; when it reaches zero, it is loaded with the Timer Reload Value field (TRV) in the Timer Reload register (TR).

When the Interrupt Enable bit (IE) of the TR register is set and the TCV reaches zero, the processor will take a timer interrupt unless the DA bit is set in the Configuration Register (CFG). Two–bus and microcontroller members of the 29K family can additionally disable timer interrupts by setting the TD bits in the CPS register. Timer interrupts are not disabled by setting the DI bit in the CFG. This means timer interrupts can not be simply disabled along with other external asynchronous interrupts by setting DI.

It is often desirable to disable timer interrupts during critical code stages, because timer interrupts often lead to such tasks as context switching. However, timer interrupts may be required to support a real–time clock, and to maintain accuracy, a timer interrupt can not be missed. The timer interrupt must be taken but processing the event can be postponed till later, when it can be dealt with. To do this efficiently, the Freeze mode interrupt handler for the timer should set register *ast* to true. This register is a kernel space support register chosen from the range *ks0–ks15* (*gr80–gr95*). It indicates an Asynchronous Software Trap (AST) is ready for processing. The *ast* register can be quickly tested with an ASSERT type instruction, as shown below:

```
mfsr     it0,ops        ;get OPS register, DA alreay clear
andn     it0,it0,1      ;clear DI bit
mtsrim   ops,it0        ;enable interrupts
asneq    V_AST,ast,0    ;trap if ast != 0, timer 'event'
iret                    ;otherwise iret
```

Clearing the DI bit reenables asynchronous interrupts, but we must check to see if an AST is pending (timer event). The *high level* timer processing is performed before the IRET instruction is executed, via trapware supporting the V_AST trap.

4.4   USER-MODE INTERRUPT HANDLERS

Many present day operating systems allow interrupt handlers to be written in high-order languages. User mode routines for 29K Processor Family based systems are no different. When providing this facility, the operating system designer must be aware of the following concerns.

- User mode programs are often written by programmers who lack specific knowledge of the operating system and it's allocation of global registers.

- The User mode handler, when written in a high-level language, such as C, will require access to the local register stack, as well as global registers defined for its management.

A good approach for addressing these concerns is to perform all necessary register saving, with interrupts disabled, while in Supervisor mode; remove the cause of the interrupt, then enable interrupts and enter User mode to execute the user's interrupt handler code. This allows interrupt (signal) handlers to be compatible with AMD's *Host Interface (HIF) v2.0 Specification* (see section 2.2), which includes the definition of operating system services . These services install and invoke user-supplied interrupt handlers for floating-point exceptions and keyboard interrupt (SIGFPE and SIGINT) events. It also allows the operating system to perform its own register preservation and restoration processes, without burdening the user with technical operating system details. Complete listings of the code contained in this section are provided in Appendix B and also by AMD in their library source code. Users who intend to modify any of this code should bear in mind that the **SPILL**, **FILL**, **setjmp**, **longjmp**, and **Signal Trampoline** code are highly interdependent.

The code uses an expanded interface definition that uses a set of global registers to hold the important local register stack support values emitted by compiler generated code in User mode programs. The registers defined for this environment are shown in Table 4-2, and were discussed in detail in section 3.3 (page 117).

Table 4-2. Expanded Register Usage

Names	Registers	Usage Description
tav	gr121	Trap Argument Vector
tpc	gr122	Trap Return Pointer
lrp	gr123	Large Return Pointer
slp	gr124	Static Link Pointer
msp	gr125	Memory Stack Pointer
rab	gr126	Register Allocate Bound
rfb	gr127	Register Free Bound

In order to prepare for execution of a User mode handler, the HIF specification indicates that the Supervisor mode portion of the handler must save important registers in the user's memory stack, as shown in Figure 4-8. In the figure, the stack pointer *(msp)* is shown decremented by 48 bytes (12 registers times 4 bytes each), and positioned to point to the saved value of register *tav*.

Other registers may need to be saved to allow complete freedom in executing 29K processor instructions (such as multiply or divide trap routines) in the User-mode handler code. Candidates for saving are the Indirect Pointers (IPA–IPC), the Q register, the stack frame pointer, *fp* (*lr1*), and the local register stack bounds in *rfb*. In addition, because high-level languages use many of the global registers as temporaries, these (*gr96–gr124*) may also have to be saved.

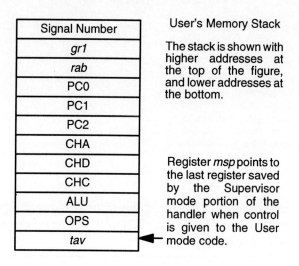

Figure 4-8. Saved Registers

4.4.1 Supervisor mode Code

When an interrupt occurs, the supervisor portion of the interrupt handler is executed. This code is responsible for saving important processor registers, as shown in Figure 4-8. The assembler macro instructions, used earlier in this chapter (*push, pop, pushsr* and *popsr*), and described in detail in section 3.3.1 (page 119), are used in the following code examples to aid in pushing special registers onto the memory stack.

The code to save the registers is executed in Supervisor mode, with Freeze mode enabled, as indicated in prior section 4.3.7. This ensures that a higher priority interrupt does not disrupt this critical section of code. The code is shown below.

```
; supervisor portion of interrupt handler
;
sigint:
        jmp interrupt
          const   it0,2           ;SIGINT
;
sigfpe:
        const   it0,8             ;SIGFPE
;
interrupt:
        sub     msp,msp,4
        store   0,0,it0,msp       ;save signal number
```

```
        sub        msp,msp,4
        store      0,0,gr1,msp        ;push gr1
        sub        msp,msp,4
        store      0,0,rab,msp        ;push rab
        const      it0,512
        sub        rab,rfb,it0        ;set rab = rfb-512
;
        pushsr     msp,it0,PC0
        pushsr     msp,it0,PC1
        pushsr     msp,it0,PC2
        pushsr     msp,it0,CHA
        pushsr     msp,it0,CHD
        pushsr     msp,it0,CHC
        pushsr     msp,it0,ALU
        pushsr     msp,it0,OPS
;
        sub        msp,msp,4
        store      0,0,tav,4          ;push tav
```

At this point in the code, with all of the critical registers saved, the memory stack will appear as shown in Figure 4-8. When the User mode interrupt handler is complete, these registers will be restored.

Special provisions have been made to anticipate the following situation: If a **FILL** operation is interrupted, and the **trampoline** code has not yet realigned the *rab* register to *rfb*-**WindowSize**, another interrupt occurring at that point could again activate the **trampoline** code. This interrupt could cause the trampoline code to assume that a **FILL** operation was in progress, thereby causing it to "reposition" the value in PC1 to recommence the (assumed) **FILL** operation.

```
; Now come off freeze, and go to user-mode code.
; ensure load/store does not restart
;
trampoline:                           ;ensure load/store
        mtsrim     chc,0              ; does not restart
        const      it1,RegSigHand
        consth     it1,RegSigHand
        load       0,0,it1,it1
        cpeq       it0,it1,0
        jmpt       it0,SigDfl         ;jump if no handler(s)
        add        it0,it1,4
        mtsr       pc1,it1
        mtsr       pc0,it0
        iret
```

Two types of interrupts are handled by this code: keyboard interrupts and floating-point exceptions. It is assumed that the interrupt vectors were previously set to vector to either **sigint** or **sigfpe**, depending on the type of interrupt. Interrupt temporary (*it0*) is used to contain the type of interrupt (signal), when entering the common code at label **interrupt**.

Once the memory stack is set up as indicated, the User mode portion of the handler (beginning at label **sigcode**) is placed into execution by loading Program Count-

---

ers (PC0 and PC1) with the address of the handler. Then while still in Freeze mode with interrupts disabled, an IRET instruction is executed to begin execution of the handler.

The HIF specification indicates that User mode signal handlers must call one of the specified signal return services to return control to the user's code at the appropriate point. When one of these services (**sigret**, **sigrep**, **sigdfl**, or **sigskp**) is called via an ASSERT instruction, *msp* will point to the same location shown in Figure 4-8, so the supervisor portion of the handler can properly restore the interrupted task's environment.

The following code fragment illustrates how one of the return services restores all of the registers. It is invoked by the HIF Service Trap (69) with interrupts disabled and Freeze mode enabled—as is the case with any interrupt or trap.

```
; Signal return service, restore registers
;
sigret:
; assume msp points to tav
        load    0,0,tav,msp      ;restore tav
        add     msp,msp,4
;
        popsr OPS,it0,msp         ;pop specials
        popsr ALU,it0,msp
        popsr CHC,it0,msp
        popsr CHD,it0,msp
        popsr CHA,it0,msp
        popsr PC2,it0,msp
        popsr PC1,it0,msp
        popsr PC0,it0,msp
        load    0,0,rab,msp       ;pop rab
        add     msp,msp,4
        load    0,0,it0,msp       ;pop rsp
        add     gr1,it0,0
        add     msp,msp,8         ;discount signal
        iret                      ;   number
```

As indicated in the HIF Specification, User mode interrupt handlers must save a number of additional registers, to prepare for executing high-level language code. The following section discusses some of the necessary preparations.

4.4.2 Register Stack Operation

The 29K Processor Family contains 128 general registers that can be configured as a register stack. In this case, global register (*gr1*) is used to point to the first register in this group that belongs to the current process. This first register is addressed as *lr0* (local register 0).

Several additional global registers provide other information describing the register stack bounds. These are all shown in Figure 4-9, which illustrates the implementation of the local register file as a shadow copy of the memory-based register stack cache.

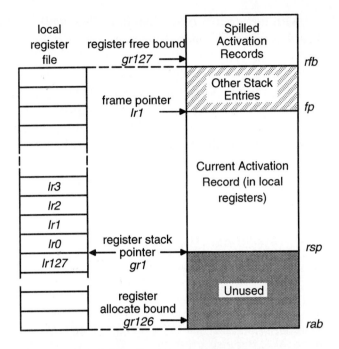

Figure 4-9. Register and Stack Cache

The *rab, rsp, lr1,* and *rfb* registers (shown in Figure 4-9) contain the bounds of the current memory stack cache in the form of addresses.

The *rsp* (register stack pointer) shown in Figure 4-9 is assigned to global register *gr1*, whose low-order 9 bits (bits 0 and 1 are not used for register addressing) are used to address the local register file whenever a local register number is encountered in a 29K processor instruction. Therefore, local register *lr2* is actually referenced by the CPU, by adding 8 (2 words) to the value held in register *gr1*.

Other important details of the register stack and local register file are discussed in Chapter 7 (*Operating System Issues*).

The important concern in writing interrupt handlers that use local registers is that the local register file bounds and contents at the time of an interrupt reflect the current state of the interrupted program.

For example, looking at Figure 4-9, when an application calls a function, the activation record for the new function is allocated immediately below the current *rsp;* occupying part of the register file whose corresponding section is indicated as "unused." If the new activation record is larger than the currently unused space (i.e., *rsp* is decremented to point below the current value in the *rab* register), the stack is said to have overflowed. When this overflow occurs, some of the existing registers in the local register file must be "spilled" to make room for the new activation record.

Programming the 29K RISC Family

The number of registers involved in the "spill" must be sufficient to allow the entire new activation record to be wholly contained in the local register stack.

A similar situation occurs when a called function is about to return to its caller and the entire activation record of the caller is not currently contained in the local register file. In this case, the portion of the caller's activation record not located in the register file must be "filled" from the memory stack cache. Management of the local register file requires the use of User mode functions that perform **SPILL** and **FILL** operations, in concert with a Supervisor mode trap handler when the **SPILL** or **FILL** operation is needed.

4.4.3 SPILL and FILL Trampoline

High-level language compilers automatically generate code that tests for a required **SPILL** upon entry to a called function, and for a required **FILL** operation just before a called function exits. In either case, the **SPILL** or **FILL** is initiated by an ASSERT instruction whose assertion fails. This causes the **SPILL** or **FILL** trap handler to begin its execution in Supervisor mode with special registers frozen.

The Supervisor mode code must initiate execution of the appropriate handler by leaving Supervisor mode, and doing its processing in User mode. Several benefits are obtained from operating **SPILL** or **FILL** handlers in User mode. First, the overhead of leaving Freeze mode is avoided, handlers must leave Freeze mode because they require the use of load- and store-multiple instructions. Additionally, **FILL** and **SPILL** handlers may require several machine cycles to complete, if they were to operate with DA set, a potential interrupt latency problem would result.

The following entry points, **SpillTrap** and **FillTrap** are directly invoked by their corresponding hardware vectors when the associated ASSERT instruction is executed. The operands **SpillAddrReg** and **FillAddrReg** are aliased to kernel static registers (two of *ks0–ks15*), which hold the addresses of the User mode **SPILL** and **FILL** handlers.

Because the processor's execution jumps from Supervisor mode to User mode in this fashion, the **SpillTrap** and **FillTrap** code is called a **trampoline**. The **SpillTrap** and **FillTrap trampoline** code is shown below.

```
SpillTrap:
;
; Preserve the return address in the
; designated register
        mfsr    tpc,PC1
;
; Fixup PC0 and PC1 to point at the user
; designated spill handler
        mtsr    PC1,SpillAddrReg
        add     tav,SpillAddrReg,4
        mtsr    PC0,tav
```

```
        ;
        ; And return to that handler
                iret


        FillTrap:
        ;
        ; Preserve the return address in the
        ; designated register
                mfsr    tpc,PC1
        ;
        ; Fixup PC0 and PC1 to point at the user
        ; designated fill handler
                mtsr    PC1,FillAddrReg
                add     tav,FillAddrReg,4
                mtsr    PC0,tav
        ;
        ; And return to that handler
                iret
```

The **SpillTrap** and **FillTrap** routines both turn control over to the User mode sections of their respective handlers by modifying the addresses held in the processor's frozen PC0 and PC1 registers. This happens after the current address in PC1 has been temporarily saved in register *tpc (gr122)*.

When the IRET instruction is executed, the processor reenters User mode, with the same interrupt enable state as when the trap occurred, and begins execution at the address loaded into PC1.

4.4.4 SPILL Handler

The **FILL** and **SPILL** handlers are executed in User mode to ensure the greatest processor performance for these operations. The handlers are invoked by the Supervisor mode trap handler, usually with interrupts enabled. This permits **SPILL** and **FILL** operations to be interrupted, and to use load- and store-multiple operations to accomplish their task.

An example User mode **SPILL** handler is shown below.

```
        ; spill handler
        ;
        ; spill registers from (*gr1-*rab)
        ; and move rab down to where gr1 points.
        ;
        ; On entry: rfb - rab = windowsize,
        ;               gr1 < rab.
        ;
        ; Near the end: rfb - rab > windowsize,
        ;               gr1 == rab
        ;
        ; On exit: rfb - rab = windowsize,
        ;               gr1 == rab
```

```
;
        .global  spill_handler

spill_handler:
        sub      tav,rab,gr1      ;bytes to spill
        srl      tav,tav,2        ;bytes to words
        sub      tav,tav,1        ;make zero based
        mtsr     CR,tav           ;set CR register
        sub      tav,rab,gr1
        sub      tav,rfb,tav      ;dec. rfb by tav
        add      rab,gr1,0        ;put rsp into rab
        storem   0,0,lr0,tav      ;store lr0..lr(tav)
        jmpi     tpc              ;return...
        add      rfb,tav,0
```

In the above code, that the condition for entry is that global register *gr1* (*rsp*) has already been decremented to a value less than the current value in *rab*. This lower value is what signals the need to spill some registers. The order in which the management registers are changed by the **SPILL** handler is very important, particularly if an interrupt were to occur during the **SPILL** operation. In this case, register *rab* must be changed before *rfb*.

The value in register *rab* is maintained for convenience, and performance gain; it is a cache of the *rfb*-**WindowSize** value. The *rfb* register is the *anchor* point for local register file (cache) and memory resident register-stack crossover.

4.4.5 FILL Handler

The **FILL** handler is similar to the **SPILL** handler, except that bytes are moved from the memory stack to the local register file. This handler is initiated when the value in *lr1* is larger than the current value in the *rfb* register.

```
; fill registers from [*rfb..*lr1)
; and move rfb upto where lr1 points.
;
; On entry: rfb - rab = windowsize,
;               lr1 > rfb
; Near the end: rfb - rab < windowsize,
;               lr1 == rab + windowsize
; On exit: rfb - rab = windowsize,
;               lr1 == rfb
;
        .global  fill_handler
fill_handler:
        const    tav,(0x80<<2)
        or       tav,tav,rfb      ;tav=[rfb]<<2
        mtsr     IPA,tav          ;ipa = [rfb]<<2
        sub      tav,lr1,rfb      ;tav = byte count
        add      rab,rab,tav      ;push up rab
        srl      tav,tav,2        ;word count
        sub      tav,tav,1        ;zero based
        mtsr     CR,tav           ;set CR register
```

```
loadm    0,0,gr0,rfb     ;load registers
jmpi     tpc             ;return...
 add     rfb,lr1,0       ;...pushing up rfb
```

In the case of a fill condition, the *rfb* register must be changed only after the **FILL** operation is complete; however, the *rab* register is modified prior to execution of the LOADM instruction. That is, the *anchor* point indicated by register *rfb* must be updated only after the data transfer has been accomplished.

4.4.6 Register File Inconsistencies

The discussion of **SPILL** and **FILL** User mode handlers is important when writing interrupt routines because a **SPILL** or **FILL** may be incomplete at the time the interrupt occurs. Depending on whether a **SPILL** or **FILL** is in progress, the interrupt handler must prepare the register stack support registers before attempting to pass control to a User mode handler that makes use of the local register file.

Figure 4-10 illustrates a global view of the register stack, as it might appear both in the local registers and in the memory stack cache at the time of an interrupt. In this case, the interrupt occurred during execution of a **SPILL** operation, probably during execution of the STOREM instruction. Therefore, the address in register *gr1* has already been decremented in anticipation that the proposed activation record will fit in the local registers. In addition, because a **SPILL** operation was necessary, the *rab* register has also been set equal to *gr1* in the **SPILL** handler.

The interrupt handler must recognize this condition because it must prepare the register stack for entry into a C language user interrupt function. This will require the stack management registers to be consistent. Repairing stack inconsistencies depends on the interrupt handler being able to recognize each unique situation where such an inconsistency could occur. In the case of the C language environment, there are three situations that must be detected.

- The interrupt occurred when a **SPILL** was in progress, in which case the distance between the values in the *rfb* and *rab* registers exceeds the size of the local register file (referred to as the **WindowSize**).

- The interrupt occurred when a **FILL** operation was in progress, in which case the distance between the values in the *rfb* and *rab* registers is less than the size of the local register file.

- The interrupt occurred during a far-**longjmp** operation (see Figure 4-12a), in which case the value $(gr1 + 8)$ — which is the address of local register *lr2* on the register memory stack — is greater than the value in *the rfb* register.

The following code fragment illustrates a method of recognizing these inconsistent stack conditions.

The Supervisor mode portion of the interrupt handler has saved the important processor registers as shown in Figure 4-8. Because the User mode portion of the

---

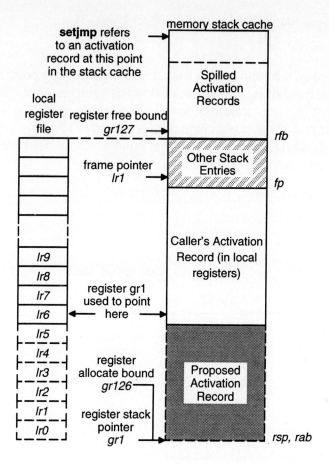

Figure 4-10. Stack Upon Interrupt

handler is intended to execute a C language function, additional registers will need to be saved. The register stack support registers, indirect pointers (IPA–IPC), as well as global registers (*gr96–gr124*) are pushed onto the memory stack just below the signal context frame.

```
sigcode:
        push    msp,lr1         ;push R-stack
        push    msp,rfb         ; support
        push    msp,msp         ;M-stack support
        sub     msp,msp,3*4     ;Floating Point
;
        pushsr  msp,tav,IPA     ;User mode specials
        pushsr  msp,tav,IPB
        pushsr  msp,tav,IPC
        pushsr  msp,tav,Q
```

```
     ;
          sub     msp,msp,29*4      ;push gr96-gr124
          mtsrim  cr,29-1
          storem 0,0,gr96,msp
```

Additional space on the memory stack is allocated for floating point registers. If the C language signal handler is to make use of floating point resources then the necessary critical support registers should be saved. Further discussion of these and an explanation of the format of the saved context information can be found in Chapter 5 (*Operating System Issues*). After the additional context status has been saved the register stack condition can then be examined.

```
     ;Recognize inconsistent stack conditions

          const   gr96,WindowSize;get cache size
          consth  gr96,WindowSize
          load    0,0,gr96,gr96
          add     gr98,msp,SIGCTX_RAB
          load    0,0,gr98,gr98    ;interrupted rab
          sub     gr97,rfb,gr98    ;rfb-rab <= WS
          cpgeu   gr97,gr97,gr96
          jmpt    gr97,nfill       ;jmp if spill
           add    gr97,gr1,8       ;or normal stack
          cpgtu   gr97,gr97,rfb    ;longjmp test
          jmpt    gr97,nfill       ;yes, longjmp case
           nop                     ;jmp if gr1+8 > rfb
     ;
     ;Fixup registers to re-start FILL operation

     ifill:
          add     gr96,msp,SIGCTX_RAB+4
          push    gr96,rab         ;resave rab=rfb-512
          const   gr98,fill_handler+4
          consth  gr98,fill_handler+4
          push    gr96,gr98        ;resave PC0
          sub     gr98,gr98,4
          push    gr96,gr98        ;resave PC1
          const   gr98,0
          sub     gr96,gr96,3*4    ;point to CHC
          push    gr96,gr98        ;resave CHC=0
```

The variable **WindowSize** is initialized to the size of the local register stack, in bytes, when the library signal function is first called. Referring to Figure 4-10, and to the code fragment shown above, it is clear that the result of subtracting the saved *rab* from *rfb* will be larger than the local register stack size. Therefore, the program will handle the spill (and normal interrupt) cases by jumping to label **nfill**. The **longjmp** case, once detected, is also sent to the **nfill** label, where the code discriminates between the conditions.

```
     ;discriminate between SPILL, longjmp and
     ; normal interrupts
```

```
nfill:
        cpgtu    gr96,gr1,rfb      ;if gr1 > rfb
        jmpt     gr96,lower        ;then gr1 = rfb
        cpltu    gr96,gr1,rab      ;if gr1 < rab
        jmpt     gr96,raise        ;then gr1 = rab
        nop
sendsig:
```

In the interrupted **FILL** case, the saved *rab* value is over-written with the re-aligned *rab* value. The send-signal code (section 4.4.1) subtracted the **WindowSize** from the value in *rfb* to determine the aligned *rab* value. This was done before issuing an IRET to **sigcode**.

Essentially, this restores *rab* to where it pointed immediately before executing the function call that caused the **FILL** operation. Note that this recomputation is also valid for a normal case, where the management registers are consistent.

The two comparisons shown below determine which method, if any, should be used to repair the value in register *gr1*. The method depends on whether a **longjmp**, **SPILL**, or normal interrupt occurred. This is required to align *gr1* to a valid cache position where **longjmp** or **SPILL** is interrupted. The following code fragment shows the code associated with the **lower** and **raise** labels.

```
;lower or raise value in gr1

lower:
        jmp      sendsig
        sll      gr1,rfb,0         ;set gr1 = rfb
raise:
        jmp      sendsig
        sll      gr1,rab,0         ;set gr1 = rab
```

According to the situation depicted in Figure 4-10, when a **SPILL** operation is interrupted, code at the **raise** label is exccuted; however, the code resumes at the label **sendsig**.

The code fragment titled "fix–up registers to restart FILL operation", shown above, is entered if the interrupt occurred during a **FILL** operation. If so, it is necessary to change the saved values for the Program Counters, PC0 and PC1, and clear the value saved in the CHC register. These registers are assumed to have been saved in the order shown in Figure 4-8. This is required in addition to realigning the register stack support register, *rab*.

The identifiers called SIGCTX_RAB, and SIGCTX_SIG are defined as numeric offsets (to be added) to the memory stack address held in register *msp*. Making these changes will effectively restart the **FILL** operation from its beginning. This code also falls into the code beginning at label **nfill**, but in the case of an interrupted **FILL** operation, the value in register *gr1* will not be adjusted.

4.4.7 Preparing the C Environment

After stack repairs have been made to the (possibly inconsistent) management registers, it is necessary to prepare for C language interrupt handler code execution. These preparations consist mainly of setting up a new stack frame from which the user's handler can execute. At this point in the process, the register stack and memory cache appear as shown in Figure 4-11.

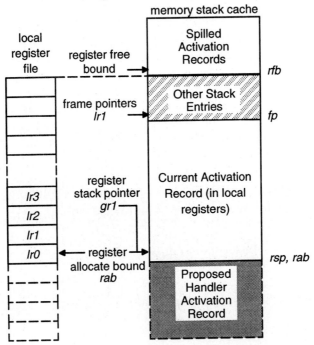

Figure 4-11. Stack After Fix–up

The following code fragment picks up at the label **sendsig**, which is repeated for clarity. The handler is almost ready to pass control to the user's C language handler code, but first it must set up a stack frame that looks as though the user's function was called in a normal fashion (rather than being invoked as part of an interrupt handler). This is accomplished in the same way a normal C language function allocates its stack frame upon entry.

```
        ; Create an activation record on the stack
        ; for our handler, so the user code will
        ; operate as though it has been "called"
        ;
        .equ    RALLOC,4*4      ;space for function
sendsig:
        sub     gr1,gr1,RALLOC
        asgeu   V_SPILL,gr1,rab
        add     lr1,rfb,0       ;set lr1 = rfb
```

```
            add         gr97,msp,SIGCTX_SIG
            load        0,0,lr2,gr97        ;restore sig number
            sub         gr97,lr2,1          ;get handler index
            sll         gr97,gr97,2         ;point to addresses
        ;Handler must not use HIF services other ;than the _sigret() type.
            const       gr96,SigEntry
            consth      gr96,SigEntry
            add         gr96,gr96,gr97
            load        0,0,gr96,gr96       ;registered handler
    cpeq    gr97,gr96,0
            jmpt        gr97,NoHandler
            nop
            calli       lr0,gr96            ;call C-level
            nop                             ;signal handler
    NoHandler:
            jmp         __sigdfl
            nop
```

The user function called by the above code is assumed to be one that has been passed to the signal library function to process either SIGINT or SIGFPE interrupts, or both. The **SigEntry** label in the above code refers to a table of pointers. In the example, one contains the address of a user signal handler for keyboard interrupts (SIGINT) and the other points to the handler for floating-point exceptions (SIGFPE). A pointer to the user handler for each of these is installed in the **SigEntry** table by the signal library function.

4.4.8 Handling Setjmp and Longjmp

Although not strictly related to interrupt handling, many C language libraries contain a **setjmp** routine used to record the values of the register and memory stack support registers, and an additional **longjmp** routine that allows a program to jump to a consistent environment saved by a previous call to the **setjmp** routine.

Figure 4-12 illustrates the location in the stack and memory cache to which the saved information from a previously executed **setjmp** call might refer. The saved information (stored in a special record specified in the call to **setjmp**), contains the values of *gr1, msp, lr0,* and *lr1,* as they appear when the call to **setjmp** was made.

Interrupt handler code must make provisions for a User mode handler to call the **longjmp** function from within the code. During the course of executing the **longjmp**, the values stored in the marker record are loaded into their respective registers. The processor is executing in User mode, with interrupts enabled, so this process might be interrupted at any point. The interrupt handler code that recognizes stack inconsistencies (presented earlier) handles this case by fixing up the management registers, to establish a consistent stack. When the interrupt handler returns, the **longjmp** will be properly completed.

Not all User mode signal handlers will have to contend with the complexities introduced by **setjmp** and **longjmp** function calls. In this case, the code presented earlier can be somewhat simplified; however, because the amount of code devoted to this potential situation is very small, it is recommended that users provide the additional checks and compensating code.

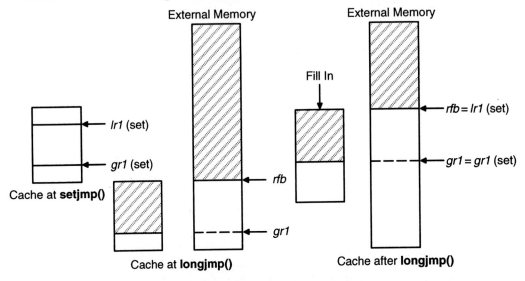

(a) Long–Jump to a far Setjm

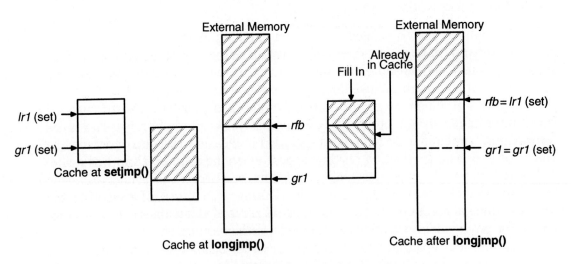

(b) Long–Jump to a near Setjmp

Figure 4-12. Long–Jump to Setjmp

Chapter 5

Operating System Issues

Because application programs make use of operating system services, the overhead costs associated with typically requested services is of great interest. With the performance levels offered by the best RISC implementations, these overhead costs have become very low. However, the often increased complexity of RISC operating systems has lead to some confusion about the efficiency of operating system implementations.

This chapter discusses in detail the various forms of context switching which occur between operating system and application code. This particular task is one of the more complex functions supported by a typical operating system. Also discussed are general issues related to context switching. The large number of registers available to application programs may initially suggest that the 29K is not ideal at performing application context switching. However, there are a number of optimizations which, when applied, greatly reduce context save and restore times [Mann 1992a].

The code examples shown makes use of a number macros for pushing and popping special registers to an external memory stack. These macros were presented in section 3.3.1, *Assembly Programming*.

Within this chapter, context information will be frequently stored and reloaded from a per–task data region known as the Process Control Block (PCB). An operating system register in the range of *ks0–ks12* is assumed to point within the PCB stack. The example code assumes that the relevant register known as *pcb* has already been assigned the correct memory address value by operating system specific code. The example code also uses constants of the form CTX_CHC. These are offsets from the top of the PCB stack (lower address) to the relevant address containing the desired register information (the CHC register in the example). When a memory stack is used to save the context in place of the PCB data structure, the CTX_ offset constants may still be used.

5.1 REGISTER CONTEXT

Part of the increased performance of the 29K family comes from using 128 internal registers as a register stack cache. The cache holds the top of the run–time stack. Each procedure obtains its necessary register allocation by claiming a region of the register stack. The register cache does not have to be flushed (spilled) until there is insufficient unallocated register space. This happens infrequently. The register stack offers greater performance benefits over a data memory cache, due to register cache triple porting on–chip (two read ports and one write port). Note, the Am29050 has an additional write port which can be used to simultaneously write–back a result from the floating–point unit. Chapter 2 explains in detail the procedure calling mechanism's use of the cache.

However, when a context switch is required from one user task to another user task, it is necessary to copy all internal registers currently allocated to the current user task to a data memory save region. This makes the registers available for use by the "in–coming" task.

In performing a context switch, a clear understanding is required of processor register usage. The AMD C Language register usage convention (see section 2.1) makes 33 of the 65 global registers (*gr1*, *gr96–gr127*) available for User data storage. Global registers *gr128–gr255*, used to implement the local register stack, are also used by the compiler generated code. (See section 3.3 (page 117) of Chapter 3, *Assembly Language Programming*, for global register assignment.)

Processor global registers *gr64–gr95* are not accessed by C generated code. These registers are normally used by the Supervisor to store operating system information or implement interrupt handler temporary working space. Particular Supervisor implementations may store data in registers *gr64–gr95*. This data is relevant to the task currently executing, and includes such information as pointers to memory resident data structures containing system support information. This data may also have to be copied–out to memory when a task switch is required.

The C procedure calling convention specifies that global registers *gr96–gr111* are used for return value passing. For a procedure returning a 32–bit integer, only register *gr96* is required to store return value information. The compiler generally uses these global registers for temporary working space before the return value data is determined. The compiler has nine more temporary registers in the *gr112–gr127* range which can also be used for temporary data storage. Other registers in this range are used to implement register stack support functions.

When more registers are required by a procedure for data storage, the local register stack can be used. This reduces the need to use external data memory to store procedure data.

The prologue of each procedure lowers the register stack pointer (*gr1*) by the amount necessary to allocate space for a procedure's in–coming and out–going parameters. The prologue code is generated by the compiler, and can thus lower the stack pointer by an additional amount to make temporary registers available to the procedure. The compiler is more likely to do this when the "–O" optimization switch is used and the procedure has an unusually large register requirement.

Each 29K processor reserves global register *gr1* to implement a register stack

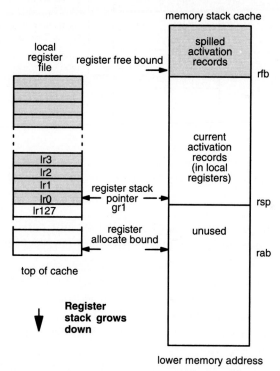

Figure 5-1. A Consistent Register Stack Cache

pointer, which points to the base of the current procedure register allocation (activation record) (see Figure 5-1). Register *gr1* points to the first "local" register allocated to the procedure, known as *lr0*. Local register *lr1*, located in the register cache at location [*gr1*]+4, is the second local register available to the procedure. The C calling convention rules state that this register is reserved for pointing to the top of the procedure activation record. The *lr1* register, known as the *frame pointer,* points to the first register above the register group allocated to the current procedure (see Figure 5-2). The frame pointer is used during register stack filling (cache filling)

---

when it must be determined if the registers allocated to the current procedure are located in the register stack and not spilled–out (flushed out) to external data memory.

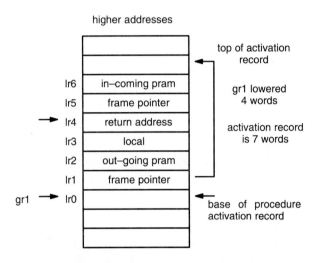

Figure 5-2. Current Procedures Activation Record

A leaf procedure is defined as one that does not call any other procedure. Because leaf procedures have no out–going parameters (data passed to called functions), they do not have to lower the register stack pointer and create an activation record. It is likely they have sufficient temporary working space in the 25 global registers available to each procedure. Of course, when one procedure calls another it must assume the called procedure will use available global registers, and thus store critical data to local register locations or external data memory. However, a particularly large leaf procedure may allocate an activation record to gain access to additional local register storage. Leaf procedures which do this obtain a new *lr1* register that need not be used to point to the top of the activation record (because leaves do not call other procedures). In this case, a leaf procedure is free to use local register *lr1* as additional temporary storage.

It is interesting to note, a performance gain is achieved by some C compilers by breaking a previously listed rule. That is, a calling procedure need not always assume the called procedure will use all 25 global registers. If the called procedure is defined before calls are made to it, the compiler can determine its register usage. This enables the compiler to only issue code to save the global registers effected by the callee, rather than preserve all global registers which are in use at the time of the call.

5.2 SYNCHRONOUS CONTEXT SWITCH

The discussion in the *Register Context* section is not a complete introduction to the register stack mechanism required to support C procedures executing on a 29K processor (see Chapter 2). However, the information is required to understand the process of a synchronous context switch. In a synchronous context switch, the currently executing user task voluntarily gives up the processor to enable another task to start execution. This is normally done via a system call. Because of the C calling rules, the procedure which makes the system call cannot itself be a leaf function. This means that the *lr1* value, of the procedure making the system call, always contains a valid pointer to the top of the current activation record. If the library routine implementing the system call does not lower the register stack (in practical terms — it is a small leaf procedure), the current *lr1* value is a valid pointer to the top of the activation record.

At first glance it seems the large number of internal registers must result in an expensive context save and restore time penalty. Further study shows that this is not the case.

Much of the time required to complete a context switch is associated with moving data between external memory and internal registers. However, a significant portion of the time is associated with supervisor overhead activities.

When saving the context of the current process all the registers holding data relevant to the current task must have their contents copied to the external data memory save area.

A 29K processor contains a number of special purpose registers. There are eight user task accessible special registers, *sr128–sr135*, used to support certain instruction type execution. Assuming the exiting–task (the one that is being saved) was written in C and the system call library code does not contain any explicit move–to–special–register instructions, there is no need to save the registers as any instructions requiring the support of special registers would have completed by the time of the context switch system call. The AMD C calling convention does not support preservation of these special registers across a procedure call.

Of the 15 supervisor–mode only accessible special registers (*sr0–sr14*), three registers are allocated to controlling access to external data memory (the channel registers). Because at the time of a synchronous context switch there is likely to be no outstanding data memory access activity, these registers also need not be saved. This is only true if an instruction causing a trap is used to issue the system call and there is no outstanding data memory access DERR pending. The Am29000 processor serializes (completes) all channel activity before trap handler code commences. For more detail on the DERR pending issue, see the *Optimization* section which follows.

On entering the system call procedure, the 25 global registers used by the calling procedure no longer contain essential data. This means that they need not be

---

saved. The register stack support registers and the relevant global supervisor registers must be saved.

Additionally four global registers (*gr112–gr115*) reserved for the user (not affected by the compiler) must be saved if any application program uses them. If these registers are not being used on a per–User basis, but shared between all Users and the Supervisor code, then they need not be saved. For example, a real–time system may chose to place peripheral status information in these registers for users to examine. The status information may be updated by Supervisor mode interrupt handlers.

The context information is stored in a per–task data region known as the Process Control Block (PCB). The example task context save code below assume the register pointing to the PCB data region, *pcb,* has already been assigned the correct memory address starting value.

An operating system register in the range *ks0–ks12* is assumed to point to the bottom of the PCB stack. Note, that the CPS register bits set by the MTSRIM instruction are system dependent; the RE bit may be required in some cases and the IM field value is system dependent,

```
        .equ    SIG_SYNC, -1
        .equ    ENABLE,(SM|PD|PI)
        .equ    DISABLE,(ENABLE|DI|DA)
        .equ    FPStat0,gr93    ;floating-point
        .equ    FPStat1,gr94    ;trapware support
        .equ    FPStat2,gr95    ;registers

sync_save:                      ;example synchronous context save
        constn  it0, SIG_SYNC
        push    pcb,it0
        push    pcb,gr1
        push    pcb,rab         ;push rab
        pushsr  pcb,it0,pc0     ;push specials
        pushsr  pcb,it0,pc1
        sub     pcb,pcb,1*4     ;space pc2
        pushsr  pcb,it0         ;push CHA
        pushsr  pcb,it0         ;push CHD
        pushsr  pcb,it0         ;push CHC
        sub     pcb,pcb,1*4     ;space for alu
        pushsr  pcb,ops         ;push OPS
        mtsrim  cps,DISABLE     ;remove freeze
        sub     pcb,pcb,1*4     ;space for tav
        mtsrim  chc,0           ;possible DERR
;
        push    pcb,lr1         ;push R-stack
        push    pcb,rfb         ; support
        push    pcb,msp         ;push M-stack  pnt.
;
        mtsrim  cps,ENABLE      ;enable interrupts
;
        push    pcb,FPStat0     ;floating point
        push    pcb,FPStat1
```

```
            push       pcb,FPStat2
;
            sub        pcb,pcb,4*4      ;space for IPA-Q
;
            sub        pcb,pcb,9*4      ;space gr116-124
            sub        pcb,pcb,4*4      ;push gr112-115
            mtsrim     cr, 4-1
            storem     0,0,gr112,pcb
            sub        pcb,pcb,16*4     ;space for gr96-111
```

Local registers currently in use, those that lie in the region pointed to by *gr1* and *rfb* (*gr127*), require saving. Not all of the local register cache needs saving. The example code below assumes the user was running with address translation on. Thus, to gain access to the user's register stack, the Supervisor must use the UA option bit when storing out the cache contents. If the user had been running in physical address mode, then there is no need for the Supervisor to use the UA option to temporarily obtain User mode access permissions.

The context save code example above, operates with physical addresses in Supervisor mode. This means address translation is not enabled. To enable data address translation when the UA bit is use, the PD bit in the CPS register must be cleared. Some operating system developers may chose to run the Supervisor mode code with address translation turned on; in such cases, the PD bit will already be cleared. Remember, once the PD bit is reset, it is possible to take a TLB miss. With the UA bit set during the cache store operation, the TLB miss will relate to the temporary User mode data memory access.

```
            .equ       UA,0x08          ;UA access
            .equ       PD,0x40          ;PD bit

            mtsrim     cps,ENABLE&~PD   ;virtual data
;
            sub        kt0,rfb,gr1      ;get bytes in cache
            srl        kt0,kt0,2        ;adjust to words
            sub        kt0,kt0,1
            mtsr       cr,kt0
            storem     0,UA,lr0,gr1     ;save lr0-rfb
;
            mtsrim     cps,ENABLE       ;return to physical
```

5.2.1 Optimizations

When an ASSERT instruction is used to enter Supervisor mode, all outstanding data memory access activity is completed before the trap handler gains control. If no data access error (DERR) occurs then the channel registers will contain no valid data and need not be saved. However, when the channel access is serialized and forced to complete, a priority four DERR may have occurred. The DERR trap competes with the priority three system call trap (higher than four), and thus the system call trap

---

handler commences but with the channel still containing information pertaining to the failed data access.

A performance gain can be obtained by not saving the channel registers to external data memory. If the memory system hardware is unable to generate the DERR signal, then the channel registers should not be saved. Additionally, if the software developer knows the previous data memory access has been completed or was to a *known* memory location, there may be no need to save the channel registers. The code shown below is an alternative to the previous system call trap handler entry code, the transaction–fault bit (TF) in the channel control register (CHC) is tested to determine if channel registers need saving.

A further performance gain can be obtained by not saving the PC0 register. When the PC1 register is restored, the PC0 register can be determined by adding 4 to the PC1 address value. To achieve the best performance gains, the code in the subsequent *Restoring Context* section may be optimized to avoid restoring channel registers CHA and CHD if the CHC contents–valid (CV) bit is zero.

```
save_channel:   ;deal with
        pushsr  pcb,it0,cha     ;DERR fault
        pushsr  pcb,it0,chd
        pushsr  pcb,it0,chc
        jmp     channel_saved
         mtsrim chc,0           ;clear TF
sync_save:                      ;example synchronous context save
        constn  it0, SIG_SYNC
        push    pcb,it0
        push    pcb,gr1
        push    pcb,rab         ;push rab
        sub     pcb,pcb,1*4     ;space for pc0
        pushsr  pcb,it0,pc1     ;push pc1
        sub     pcb,pcb,1*4     ;space for pc2
        mfsr    it0,chc         ;test TF bit
        sll     it0,it0,31-10   ; in CHC set
        jmpt    it0,save_channel
         sub    pcb,pcb,2*4     ;space for cha,chd
        const   it0,0
        push    pcb,it0         ;push CHC=0
channel_saved:
        sub     pcb,pcb,1*4     ;space for alu
        pushsr  pcb,ops         ;push OPS
        mtsrim  cps,DISABLE     ;remove freeze
        sub     pcb,pcb,1*4     ;space for tav
```

When restoring the task currently being saved, it is not necessary to reload all 128 local registers, or even the part of the register file in use at context save time ([*gr1*]—[*rfb*]). Only the activation record of the last executing procedure for the task ([*gr1*]—[*lr1*]) (see Figure 5-3). This greatly reduces the time required to restore a task context originally saved by a synchronous context switch. Typically the size of a procedure activation record ([*gr1*]——[*lr1*]) is twelve words. To achieve this

---

optimization, the *push* of *rab* and *rfb,* shown in the previous code fragment, must be changed to the code shown below. This ensures only one activation record is restored.

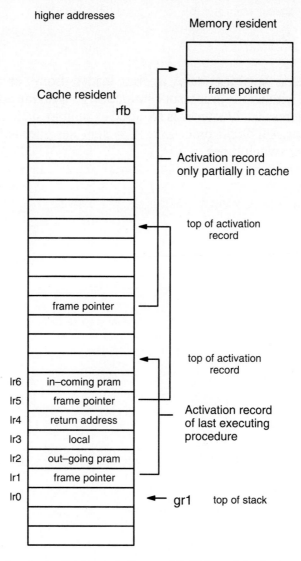

Figure 5-3. Overlapping Activation Records Eventual Spill Out of the Register Stack Cache

```
        .equ    WS,512              ;Window Size

        const   it0,WS              ;replacement for
        sub     rab,lr1,it0         ; push rab
        push    pcb,rab             ;push lr1-512
;
        push    pcb,lr1             ;replacement for
                                    ; push rfb
```

Burst mode enables data to be loaded–from or stored–to memory consecutively, without the processor continuously supplying addresses information. An external address latch/counter is required to support such memory systems with an Am29000 or Am29050 processor. A system designer can use this feature to reduced context switch times.

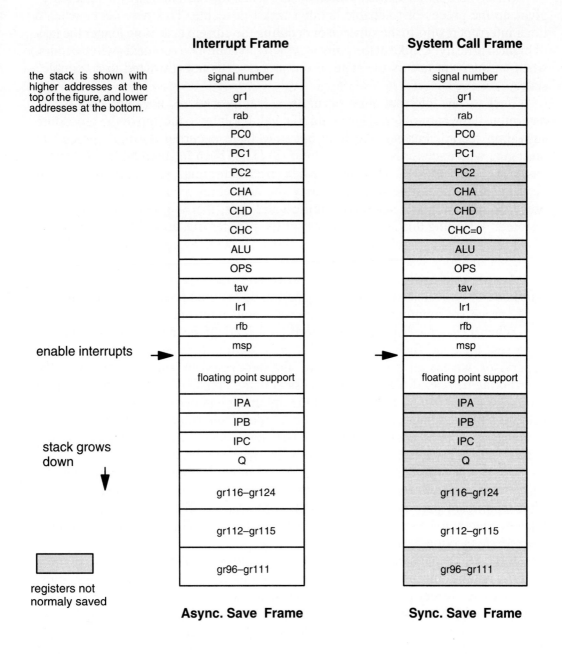

Interrupt Frame

signal number
gr1
rab
PC0
PC1
PC2
CHA
CHD
CHC
ALU
OPS
tav
lr1
rfb
msp
floating point support
IPA
IPB
IPC
Q
gr116–gr124
gr112–gr115
gr96–gr111

Async. Save Frame

System Call Frame

signal number
gr1
rab
PC0
PC1
PC2
CHA
CHD
CHC=0
ALU
OPS
tav
lr1
rfb
msp
floating point support
IPA
IPB
IPC
Q
gr116–gr124
gr112–gr115
gr96–gr111

Sync. Save Frame

the stack is shown with higher addresses at the top of the figure, and lower addresses at the bottom.

enable interrupts ➤

stack grows down ↓

registers not normaly saved

Figure 5-4. Context Save PCB Layout

5.3 ASYNCHRONOUS CONTEXT SWITCH

An asynchronous context switch occurs when the current task "unexpectedly" gives up the processor to enable another task to execute. This may occur when a timer interrupt results in the supervisor deciding the current task is no longer the task of highest priority. Unlike at the point at which a synchronous context switch occurs, when an interrupt occurs the state of the processor is not restricted to a "simple" state.

Because an interrupt may occur in a leaf procedure, it is not possible to determine if the current *lr1* value contains a valid pointer to the top of the procedure activation record. Further, the interrupt may have occurred during a procedure prologue, where the register stack pointer (*gr1*) has been lowered but the *lr1* value has not yet been updated. This means when an asynchronous–saved task is switched back in, it is impossible to restore only the activation record of the interrupted procedure. The register stack containing valid data, that is [*gr1*]—[*rfb*], must be restored. Assuming this amounts to half of the register file, an additional 2.6 micro seconds would be required to restore the task with a single–cycle Am29000 processor memory system at 25MHz.

A task voluntarily giving up the processor via a system call from within a procedure of typical activation record size can be restored faster then a task giving up the processor involuntarily via an asynchronous interrupt.

When a User mode program is interrupted it could mean the current process is to be sent a signal, such as a segmentation violation. It could also mean that the Supervisor wishes to gain control of the processor to support servicing the interrupting device. If the current process is being signaled, the label **user_signal** should be jumped to by Supervisor mode interrupt handler (see the example code below). This is explained in the later section titled *User Mode Signals* (section 5.5). If Supervisor support code is required for peripheral device servicing, then the action to be taken is very much dependent on the interrupting device needs.

Some interrupts can be serviced in Freeze mode, without the need to save the current process context. Use of these so–called *lightweight* interrupt handlers can offer significant performance gains. Other interrupts will require the interrupted process context to be saved. This is described in the following section, *Interrupting User Mode* (section 5.4).

It is possible an interrupt has arrived that requires a signal to be sent to a process which is not the currently executing process. In this case, the operating system must first save the current process context and then restore the context of the signaled process. Once the in–coming process is prepared to run, using the code in the *Restore Context* section (section 5.10), the restored context will have to be then placed on the signal stack as described in the *User Mode Signals* (section 5.5). Thus, execution would begin in the User mode trampoline code of the in–coming process. To follow this in detail, later sections of the chapter shall have to be studied.

```
        .equ      SIGALRM,14        ;alarm signal

time_out:             ;timer interrupt handler
        jmp       interrupt_common
          const   it0,SIGALRM       ;signal number

interrupt_common:

;Depending on required processing,
;jump to user_signal for current process signaling.
;Or, jump to user_interrupt to save the current process context.
```

5.4   INTERRUPTING USER MODE

This section describes how the operating system can prepare the processor to execute a C level interrupt handler, where the handler is to run in Supervisor mode and the interrupt occurred during User mode code execution.

Because the User mode task is being asynchronously interrupted, the complete processor state must be saved. The context information should be stored in the PCB rather than a temporary stack, as a context switch to a new user task may occur after the interrupt has been processed. Storing the state in the PCB saves having to copy the state from the temporary stack to the PCB after the context switch decision has been made. When saving task context, a performance optimization is obtained by only saving the registers which are currently in use. However, such optimizations typically only apply to synchronous–task context saving.

When User mode is interrupted, the special purpose support registers may contain valid data. This means an additional nine special register data values must be copied to external data memory, compared to the synchronous context switch.

Below is a code example of interrupt context saving. Notice the *rab* stack support register is adjusted to a window distance below *rfb* within the interrupt disabled portion of the code. This is to support users who wish to perform the register stack fix–up with User mode code, rather than in the Supervisor code shown. Register *rab* is merely a convenience value for determining *rfb*–WindowSize (WindowSize normally 512) in detecting a **SPILL** condition. However, it is also used to determine **FILL** or **SPILL** interruption. Should the User mode stack fix–up code be interrupted during it's operation, it is important that it does not become confused with the original **SPILL** or **FILL** interrupt. Realigning the *rab* register whilst interrupts are off prevents this confusion.

```
        .equ      WS,512            ;Window Size

user_interrupt:                     ;saving User mode context
        push      pcb,it0           ;stack signal id
        push      pcb,gr1
```

```
          push      pcb,rab              ;stack real rab
          const     it0,WS
          sub       rab,rfb,it0          ;set rab=rfb-512
;
          pushsr    pcb,it0,pc0          ;push specials
          pushsr    pcb,it0,pc1
          pushsr    pcb,it0,pc2
          pushsr    pcb,it0,cha
          pushsr    pcb,it0,chd
          pushsr    pcb,it0,chc
          pushsr    pcb,it0,alu
          pushsr    pcb,it0,ops
          mtsrim    cps,DISABLE          ;remove freeze
          push      pcb,tav
          mtsrim    chc,0                ;clear CHC
;
          push      pcb,lr1              ;push R-stack
          push      pcb,rfb              ; support
          push      pcb,msp              ;M-stack pnt.
;
          mtsrim    cps,ENABLE           ;enable interrupts
;
          push      pcb,FPStat0          ;floating point
          push      pcb,FPStat1
          push      pcb,FPStat2
;
          pushsr    pcb,kt0,ipa          ;more specials
          pushsr    pcb,kt0,ipb
          pushsr    pcb,kt0,ipc
          pushsr    pcb,kt0,q
```

The 25 global registers, known to contain no valid data during a synchronous context switch, must also be considered active, and consequently saved. Because these global registers are located adjacent to the four global registers reserved for the user, a single store–multiple instruction can be used to save the relevant global registers. Considering a single–cycle memory system, two micro seconds should be required to save the additional current task context.

```
          sub       pcb,pcb,29*4         ;push gr96-gr124
          mtsrim    cr,29-1
          storem    0,0,gr96,pcb
```

If the interrupt is expected to result in a context switch then the local registers currently in use require saving. Note, this can be postponed (see the following *optimizations* section). Not all of the local register cache needs to be saved. However, as is explained below, do not simply assume that those that lie in the region pointed to by *gr1* and *rfb* (*gr127*) are the only active cache registers.

When a synchronous context switch occurs the register stack is known to be in a valid condition (see Figure 5-1). With an asynchronous event causing a context switch, the stack may not be in a valid condition. There are three inconsistent situations that must be detected and dealt with.

- The interrupt occurred when a **SPILL** was in progress, in which case the distance between the values in the *rfb* and *rab* registers exceeds the size of the local register file (referred to as the Window Size). All of the local register file must be saved. Some of the cached data may have already been copied out to memory locations just below *rfb*. This data should remain at this location on the memory resident portion of the stack until the task is restarted.

- The interrupt occurred when a **FILL** operation was in progress, in which case the distance between the values in the *rfb* and *rab* registers is less than the size of the local register file. Some data may have been copied in from the top of the memory resident portion of the register stack into local registers just above *rab*. These registers will not be saved during the *normal* cache save (*[gr1]–[rfb]*). To deal with this the **FILL** must be restarted when the context is restored.

- The interrupt occurred during a far–**longjmp** operation. A far–**longjmp** is defined as one in which the future $(gr1 + 8)$ value—which is the address of local register *lr2* on the register memory stack—is greater than the current value in the *rfb* register. In this case the local registers contain no valuable data because a previous activation record (present during **setjmp**) is about to be restored from the memory resident portion of the stack.

```
        .equ    WS,512              ;Window Size

    R_fixup:                        ;register stack fix-up
        add     kt0,pcb,CTX_RAB
        load    0,0,kt2,kt0         ;get rab value
        sub     kt0,rfb,kt2         ;window size
        srl     kt0,kt0,2           ;convert to words
        cpeq    kt1,kt0,WS>>2       ;test for valid
        jmpt    kt1,norm            ; stack condition
        cpltu   kt1,kt0,WS>>2       ;test for FILL
        jmpt    kt1,ifill           ; interrupt
        add     kt1,gr1,8           ;test far-longjmp
        cpgtu   kt1,kt1,rfb         ; interrupt
        jmpt    kt1,illjmp          ;yes, gr1+8 > rfb
        nop
    ;
    ispill:                         ;deal with interrupted SPILL
        const   kt1,WS
        jmp     norm                ;gr1=rfb-512
        sub     gr1,rfb-kt1
    ;
    ifill:                          ;deal wilth interrupted FILL
        add     kt1,pcb,CTX_CHC
        const   kt0,0
        push    kt1,kt0             ;resave CHC=0
        add     kt0,FillAddrReg,4
        add     kt1,pcb,CTX_PC0
        push    kt1,kt0             ;resave PC0,PC1
```

```
        push    kt1,FillAddrReg
        add     kt1,pcb,CTX_RAB
        push    kt1,rab             ;resave rab=rfb-512
;
norm:                               ;deal with consistant stack
        sub     kt1,rfb,gr1         ;bytes in cache
        srl     kt1,kt1,2           ;convert to words
        sub     kt1,kt1,1           ;adjust for storem
        mtsrim  cr,kt1
        mtsrim  cps,ENABLE&~PD      ;virtual data
        storem  0,UA,lr0,gr1        ;copy to stack
        mtsrim  cps,ENABLE          ;physical data
;
illjmp:         ;valid local registers now saved
```

Once the user's User mode register stack has been saved, the interrupt handler continues using the user's Supervisor mode register and memory stacks.

```
        .macro  const32,reg,data
        const   reg,data            ;zero high, set low
        consth  reg,data            ;high 16-bits
        .endm

        const32 msp,SM_STACK        ;Supervisor M-stack
        const32 rab,SR_STACK-WS
        add     gr1,rfb,8           ;prepare Supervisor
        const32 rfb,SR_STACK        ; R-stack support
        add     lr1,rfb             ; registers
;
;call appropriate C-level interrupt handler
```

The current task context has now been saved. After the interrupt has been processed the operating system can select a different task to restore. This operation is described in a subsequent section entitled *Restoring Context (*section 5.10*).* The PCB structure for the out–going task shall not be accessed until the task is again restored as the current executing task.

5.4.1 Optimizations

When User mode is interrupted, processing continues using the user's Supervisor mode stacks. This is necessary because the interrupt may result in the process being *put to sleep* until some time later when it is again able to run. When the process is *put to sleep*, the process state is stored in the Supervisor memory stack, described in the *Interrupting Supervisor Mode* section (section 5.6). If the user's User mode context was saved on a shared interrupt stack rather than the per–process Supervisor stack, then the context would have to be copied from the global interrupt stack to the Supervisor stack before a context switch could proceed.

The code shown above determines the region of cache registers currently in use and stores them out onto the top of the user's User mode register stack. This operation can be postponed. The interrupt handler will use the register cache in conjunction with the Supervisor mode register stack. If the interrupt handler runs to completion and no context switch occurs, then the cache need not be saved. If a context switch does occur then the cache will be saved on the top of the user's Supervisor mode register stack. This means some User mode data contained in the cache may be temporary saved on the the Supervisor stack; however, this is not a problem.

The previous code determines the region of the cache currently in use, it does not bring the stack into a valid condition. The code following the label **R_fixup:** in the *User Mode Signals* section (section 5.5) does bring the stack into a valid condition, and can be used to replace the code shown above. Once the stack support registers are restored to a valid state, the *stack–cut–across* method described in the later *User System Calls* section (section 5.7) can be used to *attach* the cache to the Supervisor mode stack. By this method the storing of cache data can be prevented and any unused portion of the cache is made immediately available to the interrupt service routine.

5.5 USER MODE SIGNALS

Asynchronous context switches often occur because an interrupt has occurred and must be processed by a handler function developed in C. A technique often overlooked in real–time applications is using a signal handler to process the interrupt. This often avoids much of the supervisor overheads associated with a context switch.

It is not necessary to store the contents of the local register file. After signal support code has fixed–up the stack management support registers, the C level handler code can continue to use the register stack as if the interrupted procedure had executed a call to the handler function. In as little as 5.5 micro seconds from the time of receiving the interrupt, the Am29000 can be executing the interrupt handler code which was written in C.

Unlike asynchronous context switching, the interrupted context can not be saved in the PCB. To do so would be convenient if a context switch was possible after the signal handler had finished executing. The PCB structure would be already updated. However, a further interrupt may occur during the C level signal handler execution, which may itself result in an immediate context switch and require the use of the PCB data save area. Additionally, the signal handler may do a **longjmp** to a **setjmp** which occurred in User mode code before the signal handler started executing. For this reason the context information is placed on the User's memory stack pointed to by *msp*.

Users of operating systems complying with the AMD HIF–specification are required to complete signal handler preparation tasks in User mode code supplied in

AMD libraries. HIF compliant operating systems only save the signal–number through the *tav* register portion of the interrupt frame on the user's memory stack. The remaining part of the interrupt frame is saved by the user's code. Any necessary register stack management is performed. The User mode code is shown in Appendix B and described in detail in section 4.4. The following code is for operating systems which save the complete interrupt frame and prepare for a User mode signal while in Supervisor mode

```
        .equ    SIGILL,4           ;illegal operation
        .equ    WS,512             ;Window Size

protect:           ;Protection violation trap handler
        jmp     user_signal        ;send interrupted task a signal
        const   it0,SIGILL         ;signal number
```

If the interrupted User mode code was running with address translation turned on, then the user's memory stack must be accessed by the Supervisor using the UA bit during LOAD and STORE instructions (note, this is also true for the *push* and *pushsr* macros). The following code example shows pushing onto a physically accessible user memory stack. If the user's stack were virtually addressed, then the push instructions would be replaced by move to temporary register instructions. After interrupts were enabled the PD bit in the CPS register would be cleared to enable data address translation, and then the temporary registers would be pushed onto the user's memory stack using the UA bit during the STORE instruction operation. Once the frozen special registers had been saved, via the use of temporary registers, the Supervisor could continue to run with the CPS register bits PD and DA cleared, and store the remaining user state via *push* operations.

```
user_signal:                       ;prepare to process a signal
        push    msp,it0            ;stack signal id
        push    msp,gr1
        const   it0,WS
        sub     rab,rfb,it0        ;set rab=rfb-512
;
        pushsr  msp,it0,pc0        ;push specials
        pushsr  msp,it0,pc1
        pushsr  msp,it0,pc2
        pushsr  msp,it0,cha
        pushsr  msp,it0,chd
        pushsr  msp,it0,chc
        pushsr  msp,it0,alu
        pushsr  msp,it0,ops
        mtsrim  cps,DISABLE        ;remove freeze
        push    msp,tav
        mtsrim  chc,0              ;clear CHC
;
        push    msp,lr1            ;push R-stack
        push    msp,rfb            ; support
        push    msp,msp            ;M-stack support
```

```
;
        mtsrim  cps,ENABLE          ;enable interrupts
;
        push    msp,FPStat0         ;floating point
        push    msp,FPStat1
        push    msp,FPStat2
;
        pushsr  msp,kt0,ipa         ;more specials
        pushsr  msp,kt0,ipb
        pushsr  msp,kt0,ipc
        pushsr  msp,kt0,q
;
        sub     msp,msp,29*4        ;push gr96-gr124
        mtsrim  cr,29-1
        storem  0,0,gr96,msp
```

The register stack must now be brought into a valid condition, if is not already in a valid condition. Valid is defined as consistent with the conditions supporting a function call prologue. As described in the previous section 5.3, *Asynchronous Context Switching*, the stack may not be valid if a **SPILL**, **FILL** or **far–longjmp** is interrupted.

Unlike the asynchronous context save case, our intention is not to simply determine the active local registers for saving on the user's memory portion of the register stack, but to enable the user to continue making function calls with the existing stack. That is, the C language signal handler will appear to have been called in the normal manner, rather than as a result of an interrupt.

```
                ; Register stack fixup
R_fixup:
        const   kt0,WS              ;WindowSize
        add     kt0,msp,CTX_RAB
        load    0,0,kt2,kt2         ;interrupted rab
        sub     kt1,rfb,kt2         ;determine if
        cpgeu   kt1,kt1,kt0         ;rfb-rab>=WindoSize
        jmpt    kt1,nfill           ;jmp if spill
                                    ;or valid stack
        add     kt1,gr1,8           ;check if
        cpgtu   kt1,kt1,rfb         ; gr1+8 > rfb
        jmpt    kt1,nfill           ;yes, long-longjmp
         nop
;
ifill:                              ;here for interrupted FILL restart
        add     kt1,msp,CTX_CHC
        const   kt0,0
        push    kt1,kt0             ;resave CHC=0
        add     kt0,FillAddrReg,4
        add     kt1,msp,CTX_PC0
        push    kt1,kt0             ;resave PC0,PC1
        push    kt1,FillAddrReg
        add     kt1,msp,CTX_RAB
        push    kt1,rab             ;resave rab=rfb-512
;
```

```
nfill: ;move gr1 into valid range
        cpgtu   kt0, gr1, rfb    ;if gr1 > rfb
        jmpt    kt0, lower       ;far-longjmp case
        cpltu   kt0, gr1, rab    ;if gr1 < rab then
        jmpf    kt0, sendsig     ;interrupted spill
         nop
raise:
        sll     gr1, rab, 0
        jmp     sendsig
         nop
lower:
        sll     gr1, rfb, 0
        jmp     sendsig
         nop
```

Now use the signal number to determine the address of the corresponding signal handler. The code below assumes there is an array of signal handlers. The first entry of the array is held at memory address **SigArray**.

```
sendsig:            ;prepare to leave Supervisor mode
        add     kt0,msp,CTX_SIGNUMB
        load    0,0,gr96,kt0     ;get signal numb.
        sub     kt2,gr96,1       ;handler index...
        sll     kt2,kt2,2        ; ...in words
        const   kt1,SigArray
        consth  kt1,SigArray
        add     kt2,kt2,kt1
        load    0,0,gr97,kt2     ;handler adds.
;
        mtsrim  cps,FREEZE       ;enter Freeze mode
        const   kt1,_trampoline
        add     kt0,kt1,4
        mtsr    pc1,kt1          ;return to user
        mtsr    pc0,kt0          ;and process signal
        iret
```

Via an IRET, execution is continued in User mode procedure **trampoline**. This procedure is often located in the memory page containing the PCB structure. Using User accessible global registers *gr96* and *gr97*, two parameters, the signal number and a pointer to the signal handler routine, are passed to the trampoline code. The handler routine is called, passing to it the signal number and a pointer to the saved context.

```
;User mode entry to signal handler
_trampoline:                    ;Dummy Call
        sub     gr1,gr1,6*4      ;space for C-call
        asgeu   V_SPILL,gr1,rab
        add     lr1,gr1,6*4
        add     lr0,gr97,0       ;copy handler()
        add     lr2,gr96,0       ;copy signal #
        add     lr3,msp,0        ;pass CTX pointer
;
```

```
        calli   lr0,lr0          ;call handler()
          nop
;
        add     gr1,gr1,6*4      ;restore stack
          nop
        asleu   V_FILL,lr1,rfb
        const   tav,SYS_SIGRETURN
        asneq   V_SYSCALL,gr1,gr1 ;system call
```

After the signal handler returns, the interrupted context is restored via the *sigreturn* system call. The supervisor mode code used to implement the restoration process is shown in the section titled *Restoring Context* (section 5.10). At the time of the system call trap, the memory stack pointer, *msp*, must be pointing to the structure containing the saved context. The system call code checks relevant register data to ensure that the User is not trying to gain Supervisor access permissions as a result of manipulating the context information during the signal handler execution. (Note, it is likely that assembly code library supporting the *sigreturn* system call shall copy the *lr2* parameter value to the *msp* register before issuing the system call trap.)

5.6   INTERRUPTING SUPERVISOR MODE

A user program may be in the process of executing a system call when an interrupt occurs. This interrupt may require C level handler processing. In some respects this is similar to a user program dealing with a C level signal handler; however, there are some important differences. A User mode signal handlers may chose not run to completion by doing a **longjmp** out of the signal handler. Also, signal handlers process User mode data. Supervisor mode interrupt handlers always run to completion and process data relevant to the Supervisor's support task rather than the current User mode task.

Because user task is being interrupted whilst operating in Supervisor mode, the complete processor state must be saved in a similar way to an asynchronous context switch. The context information can not be stored in the current user's PCB because it is used to hold the User mode status when Supervisor mode is entered via a system call.

User programs usually switch stacks when executing system calls. The user's system stack is not accessible to the User mode program. This keeps Supervisor information that appears on the stack during system call execution hidden from the user. The user's system stack can be used to support C function calls during interrupt handler processing. Alternatively, an interrupt processing stack can be used. Keeping a separate interrupt stack for Supervisor mode interrupt processing enables a smaller system mode User stack to be supported, as the interrupt processing does not cause the system stack to grow further. Remember, the per-user system stack is already in use because the user was processing a system call when the interrupt occurred.

The **interrupt_common** entry point to the interrupt handler shown in *Asynchronous Context Switch* (section 5.3) needs to be expanded to distinguish between interrupting User mode and interrupting Supervisor mode. The appropriate processing requirement is determined by examining the OPS register in the interrupt handler. The label **user_interrupt** should be used to select the code for an interrupt of User mode code.

```
interrupt_common:                   ;examine processor mode interrupted
        mfsr    it1,ops             ;get OPS special
        sll     it1,it1,27          ;check SM bit
        jmpf    user_interrupt      ;User mode inter.
         nop
```

The following code assumes Supervisor mode interrupts are not nested, because the current context is pushed onto the interrupt processing stack which is assumed empty. If interrupts are to be nested, then the context should be pushed on the current memory stack once it has been determined that the *msp* has already been assigned to the interrupt memory stack. IM_STACK and IR_STACK are the addresses of the bottom of the interrupt memory and register stacks respectively.

```
        .equ    WS,512              ;Window Size

        .macro  const32,reg,data
        const   reg,data            ;zero high, set low
        consth  reg,data            ;high 16-bits
        .endm

supervisor_interrupt:               ;process Supervisor mode interrupt
        const32 it1,IM_STACK        ;interrupt M-satck
        push    it1,it0             ;stack signal id
        push    it1,gr1
        const   it0,WS
        sub     rab,rfb,it0         ;set rab=rfb-512
;
        pushsr  it1,it0,pc0         ;push specials
        pushsr  it1,it0,pc1
        pushsr  it1,it0,pc2
        pushsr  it1,it0,cha
        pushsr  it1,it0,chd
        pushsr  it1,it0,chc
        pushsr  it1,it0,alu
        pushsr  it1,it0,ops
        mtsrim  cps,DISABLE         ;remove freeze
        push    it1,tav
;
        mtsrim  chc,0               ;clear CHC
;
        push    it1,lr1             ;push R-stack
        push    it1,rfb             ; support
        push    pcb,msp             ;push M-stack pntr.
        add     msp,it1,0           ;use msp pointer
;
```

```
        mtsrim  cps,ENABLE          ;enable interrupts
    ;
        push    msp,FPStat0         ;floating point
        push    msp,FPStat1
        push    msp,FPStat2
    ;
        pushsr  msp,kt0,ipa         ;more specials
        pushsr  msp,kt0,ipb
        pushsr  msp,kt0,ipc
        pushsr  msp,kt0,q
    ;
        sub     msp,msp,29*4        ;push gr96-gr124
        mtsrim  cr,29-1
        storem  0,0,gr96,msp
```

There is no need to save any of the register cache data. The register stack support registers are updated with the initial values of the supervisor interrupt stack. If nested high level handler interrupts are to be supported, see the following *Optimizations* section. The *gr1* register stack pointer is then set to the top (*rab*) of the cache, indicating the cache is fully in use. The new activation record size pointer, *lr1*, is then set to the bottom of the cache *(rfb)*. This ensures that when the interrupted C level service function returns, the cache will be repaired to exactly the position at which the interrupt occurred. This is particularly important if a Supervisor mode **FILL** was interrupted. The user's system mode register data will be spilled onto the interrupt stack, but this creates no problem.

```
        const32 rab,IR_STACK-WS
        add     gr1,rab,0           ;prepare interrupt
        const32 rfb,IR_STACK        ; R-stack support
        add     lr1,rfb             ; registers
    ;
    ;call appropriate C-level interrupt handler
```

5.6.1 Optimizations

The code shown above does not attempt to determine the region of cache registers currently in use. This means that the first C level procedure call in the interrupt handler will result if a cache spill trap occurs.

By determining the region of the cache currently in use and by bringing the register stack into a valid condition, any available cache registers can be made immediately available to the interrupt handler C routines. The code following the label **R_fixup:** in the previous *User Mode Signals* section (section 5.5) does bring the stack into a valid condition and can be used to replace the code shown above. Once the stack support registers are restored to a valid state, the *stack–cut–across* method described in the *User System Calls* section (section 5.7) can *attach* the cache to the interrupt register stack.

It is possible that while processing an interrupt (which means the processor is already in Supervisor mode) an additional interrupt occurs. If an operating system supports nested interrupts, then the code in the *Interrupting Supervisor Mode* section (section 5.6) will be executed again. This overhead can be avoided by following the *Interrupt Queuing Model* method described in section 4.3.12 of the *Interrupts and Traps* chapter.

The method relies on supporting only *lightweight* interrupt nesting. The code in this section is entered only once to start the execution of a C level interrupt processing *Dispatcher*. Each interrupt adds a interrupt request descriptor (bead) on to a queue of descriptors (string of beads). The dispatcher removes the requests and processes the interrupt until the list becomes empty. Lightweight interrupts enable the external device to be quickly responded to, although the dispatcher may not complete the processing till some time later.

5.7 USER SYSTEM CALLS

User programs usually switch stacks when executing system calls. The user's system stack is not accessible to the User mode program. This keeps Supervisor information which appears on the stack during system call execution hidden from the user.

Synchronous context switching generally happens as a result of a system call. However, system calls are also used to request the operating system to obtain information for a user which is only directly obtainable with Supervisor access privileges. The user's state must be saved to the PCB structure in a similar way to a synchronous context save. This makes the global and special registers available for Supervisor mode C function use. There is no need to save the register cache until a full context switch is known to be required.

```
        .equ    SIG_SYNC, -1
        .equ    ENABLE,(SM|PD|PI)
        .equ    DISABLE,(ENABLE|DI|DA)

syscall:                            ;V_SYSCALL trap handler
        const   it0,SIG_SYNC        ; assumes no
        push    pcb,it0             ; outstanding DERR
        push    pcb,gr1             ;push gr1
        push    pcb,rab             ;push rab
        pushsr  pcb,it0,pc0         ;push specials
        pushsr  pcb,it0,pc1
        sub     pcb,pcb,3*4         ;space pc2,cha,chd
        const   it0,0
        push    pcb,it0             ;push CHC=0
        sub     pcb,pcb,1*4         ;space for alu
        pushsr  pcb,ops             ;push OPS
        mtsrim  cps,DISABLE         ;remove freeze
        sub     pcb,pcb,1*4         ;space for tav
```

```
;
        push    pcb,lr1         ;stack support
        push    pcb,rfb         ;push rfb
        push    pcb,msp         ;push M-stack pnt.
;
        mtsrim  cps,ENABLE      ;enable interrupts
;
        push    pcb,FPStat0     ;floating point
        push    pcb,FPStat1
        push    pcb,FPStat2
;
;Assume the same gr112-gr115 data is shared
;by all users and the supervisor, and
;therefor will not push gr112-gr115.
;
;Align pcb for system call return
        sub     pcb,pcb,(4+(124-96+1))*4
```

The system call code can continue to use the cache attached to the user's system mode registers stack. To do this the current top of stack position, *gr1*, must be maintained. The register stack support registers are relocated to the system stack, maintaining the existing stack position offset. The following code performs this *stack cut–across* operation. It assumes the system call is made from a valid stack condition. However, it includes bounds protection because operating systems can never completely rely on users always maintaining valid stack support registers.

```
        sub     gr96,rfb,gr1    ;determine rfb-gr1
        andn    gr96,gr96,3     ;stack is double word aligned
        const   gr97,(128*4)    ;max allowed value for
        cpleu   gr97,gr96,gr97  ; rfb-gr1 is 128*4
        jmpt    gr97,$1         ;jump if normal register usage
         const  gr97,0x1fc      ;mask for page displacement math
        const   gr96,512        ;limit register use to allowed max

$1:     and     gr1,gr1,gr97    ;determine gr1 displacement within
        const   gr97,SR_STACK-1024; 512-byte page
        consth  gr97,SR_STACK-1024;
        add     gr1,gr1,gr97    ;gr1=SR_STACK-1024+displacement
        add     rfb,gr1,gr96    ;rfb=(new gr1)+
        const   gr97,(128*4)    ; min(512,rfb-gr1))
        sub     rab,rfb,gr97    ;set rab=rfb-512
        add     lr1,rfb,0       ;ensure all User mode registers
                                ; restored
```

The technique relies on keeping bits 8–2 of the stack pointer, *gr1*, unchanged. In other words, the *lr0* register has the same position in the cache after the memory resident stack portion has been exchanged. This is achieved by calculating the address displacement of *gr1* within a 512–byte page size. The *gr1* displacement remains the same if the memory resident portion of the register stack has been exchanged. SM_STACK and SR_STACK are the addresses of the bottom of the per–user system memory and register stacks respectively (see Figure 5-5).

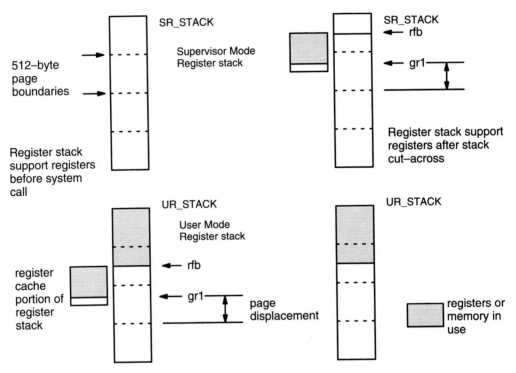

Figure 5-5. Register Stack Cut–Across

Once stack cut–across has been completed, a call to the C level system call handler can be issued. The C code may get its incoming parameters from the register stack, or the system call trap handler code may copy the parameters from the local registers to memory locations accessible by the Supervisor mode C handler.

```
;copy lr2,... arguments to memory locations
     add      gr96,tav,0      ;save service numb.
     sub      gr1,gr1,4*4     ;new stack frame
     asgeu    V_SPILL,gr1,rab
     add      lr1,gr1,4*2     ;ensure lr1 restore
     const32  lr0,_syscall    ;C handler
     calli    lr0,lr0         ; call
     add      lr2,gr96,0      ;pass service numb.
```

The C system call handler may place its *return* values in known memory locations, rather than global registers *gr96–gr111*. If this is the case, then the values shall have to be copied to the normal return registers. System calls indicate their successful or unsuccessful completion to their callers by setting register *tav (gr121)* to TRUE or FALSE; the high level handler achieves this by modifying the *gr121* register location in the PCB before the system call return code is executed. A FILL assertion is used to repair the cache to the position at which the system call was issued.

```
        add      gr1,gr1,16        ;restore system
        nop                        ; call frame lr1
        asleu    V_FILL,lr1,rfb    ;restore all cache
    ;copy return values from memory to gr96,...
        jmp      resume            ;restore context
        nop
```

Because a User mode signal handler may use the system call mechanism to issue a *sigreturn*, it is possible an asynchronous context restore may be required in place of the *normal* synchronous context restore associated with a system call. Label **resume** is jumped to and is described in the *Restore Context* section (section 5.10). If an asynchronous context is being restored, then a pointer to the context being restored will have been passed to the *sigreturn* system call. The high level C handler will have copied this data over the PCB data stored at the time of the system call trap entry. The C handler must change the SIG_SYNC value stored in the PCB by the system call trap handler. This will cause the **resume** code to perform an asynchronous rather than synchronous context restore.

5.8 FLOATING–POINT ISSUES

The example code presented saves only three supervisor accessible global registers under the heading *floating–point support*. These registers are typically *ks*13–*ks*15. This is sufficient to save and restore floating–point context when an Am29000 processor is being used with trapware emulation. This is only true if interrupts are turned off during floating–point trapware execution. If floating–point trapware is interruptible, then the Am29000 trapware support registers (typically *it0–it3* and *kt0–kt11*) would have to be saved.

When an Am29027 floating–point coprocessor is used, either inline or via trapware support, the complete state of the coprocessor must be saved. This requires an additional 35 words space in addition to the three Am29000 global support registers.

Some real–time operating systems may run floating–point trapware with interrupts off and chose to save no floating support registers at all. This will improve context switch times. User programs typically only change the rounding mode information in the support registers. If all user tasks run with the same rounding information, then there is no need to save and restore the three floating–point support registers.

The Am29050 directly executes floating point instructions without the need for trapware. It has four floating point support registers, special registers *sr160–162* and *sr164*. In fact, the three support registers required by the Am29000 are used to virtualize these Am29050 registers. Saving Am29050 floating point context would be achieved by saving these four registers and the four double word accumulator values. However, the Am29050 does not directly support integer DIVIDE and

---

DIVIDU instructions. The trapware which implements these instructions requires six support registers (typically *kt0–kt5*). If this trapware is interruptable, then these registers would also have to be saved.

5.9 DEBUGGER ISSUES

Debuggers such as AMD's MiniMON29K monitor have a special context switch requirement. They need to be able to switch context to the debugger from a running application or operating system without losing the contents of any processor register. One possibility is to reserve a global register in the range *gr64–gr95*, specifically for debugger support. But, most operating system developers are unwilling to give up a register.

A technique which avoids losing a register for operating system use is to use *gr4* to first store a single operating system register, and then use this register to start saving the rest of the processor context. The Am29000 does not have a *gr4* register but the ALU forwarding logic enables this technique to work. The code example below, taken from MiniMON29K, shows how the processor context save gets started. Note, **_dbg_glob_reg** is the memory address used by the debugger to save global registers.

```
            .macro  const32,reg,data
            const   reg,data         ;zero high, set low
            consth  reg,data         ;high 16-bits
            .endm

dbg_V_bkpt:
            const32 gr4,_dbg_glob_reg+96*4
            store   0,0,gr96,gr4     ;save gr96
            const32 gr96,_dbg_glob_reg+97*4
            store   0,0,gr97,gr96    ;save gr97
            add     gr96,gr96,4
            store   0,0,gr98,gr96    ;save gr98
    ;
            call    gr96,store_state
            const   gr97,V_BKPT
```

Label **dbg_V_bkpt** is the address vectored to by an illegal opcode (MiniMON29K uses these to implement breakpoints on the Am29000). When function **store_state** is reached, global registers *gr96–gr98* have already been saved.

The *gr4* user should be careful to remember that the Am29000 ALU forwarding logic only keeps the *gr4* register value *alive* for 1–cycle following its modification. Additionally, because emulators also make use of *gr4* in analyzing processor registers, it is not possible to use an emulator to debug the monitor entry code shown above.

5.10 RESTORING CONTEXT

The supervisor register *pcb* must point to the top of the process control block stack describing the previously saved context. A test of the *signal number* data located at the bottom of the PCB stack enables us to determine if the stack was saved synchronously or asynchronously. Restoring synchronously saved tasks can be achieved more quickly because there is less relevant data in the PCB stack.

```
resume:
        add     kt0,pcb,CTX_SIGNUMB
        load    0,0,kt0,kt0     ;sync/async save ?
        jmpt    kt0,sync_resume
        nop
```

Asynchronously saved states have a greater number of global registers to be restored. There are also additional special register values.

```
async_resume:
        mtsrim  cr,29-1         ;restore gr96-124
        sub     pcb,pcb,29*4
        loadm   0,0,gr96,pcb
;
        popsr   q,it0,pcb       ;restore specials
        popsr   ipc,it0,pcb
        popsr   ipb,it0,pcb
        popsr   ipa,it0,pcb
;
        jmp     fp_resume
        nop
```

Now that the context information, unique to an asynchronously saved state, has been restored, the context which is common between asynchronous and synchronous save states can be restored via a jump to **fp_resume**.

```
sync_resume:
        sub     pcb,pcb,9*4     ;space gr116-124
;
        sub     pcb,pcb,4*4     ;restore gr112-115
        mtsrim  cr,4-1
        loadm   0,0,gr112,pcb
;
        sub     pcb,pcb,16*4    ;space for gr96-111


fp_resume:
        pop     FPStat2,pcb     ;floating point
        pop     FPStat1,pcb
        pop     FPStat0,pcb
```

Now that most of the global and User mode accessible special registers have been restored, it is time to restore the register cache. In the case where they were

---

saved due to an asynchronous event, this requires care. First the register stack support registers must be restored.

```
.equ      DISABLE,(SM|PD|PI|DI|DA)

mtsrim    cps,DISABLE
pop       msp,pcb          ;M-stack support
pop       rfb,pcb          ;R-stack support
pop       lr1,pcb
add       kt1,pcb,11*4
pop       gr1,kt1
add       gr1,gr1,0        ;alu operation
pop       rab,kt1
```

By examining the register stack support pointers it is possible to determine if the process state was stored during a **SPILL** interrupt. In this case the saved *gr1* will be more than a window distance below *rfb*, this means [*gr1*]–[*rfb*] should not be restored. In the case of restoring an interrupted far–**longjmp**, the cache need not be restored.

```
.equ      WS,512           ;Window Size

;If User mode uses virtual addressing,
;restore PID field in MMU register
;to PID of incoming task.
          sub       kt0,rfb,rab      ;window size
          srl       kt0,kt0,2        ;convert to words
          cpleu     kt1,kt0,WS>>2    ;test for normal
          jmpt      kt1,rnorm        ; or FILL interrupt
          cpgtu     kt1,gr1,rfb      ;test for far-
          jmpt      kt1,rlljmp       ; longjmp interrupt
          nop
;
rspill:                            ;restore interrupted spill
          const     kt0,WS
          sub       kt1,rfb,kt0      ;determine rab

          add       kt0,gr1,0        ;save interrupted gr1
          add       gr1,kt1,0        ;set gr1=rfb-(window size)
          mtsrim    CR,(512>>2)-1
          mtsrim    cps,ENABLE&~PD   ;virtual data
          loadm     0,UA,lr0,kt1     ;load all of cache
          mtsrim    cps,ENABLE       ;physical data
          jmp       rlljmp
          add       gr1,kt0,0        ;restore interrupted gr1
```

When synchronously saved tasks are restored, or asynchronously saved tasks which were interrupted during either a normal register stack condition or an interrupted **FILL,** local registers [*gr1*]–[*rfb*] are restored to the cache.

```
rnorm: sub     kt0,rfb,gr1      ;determine number of bytes
       srl     kt0,kt0,2        ;adjust to words
```

```
sub      kt0,kt0,1
mtsr     CR,kt0
mtsrim   cps,ENABLE&~PD    ;virtual data
loadm    0,UA,lr0,gr1      ;restore R-stack cache
mtsrim   cps,ENABLE        ;physical data
```

Now that the local registers have been restored, all that remains to do is restore the remaining special registers. This requires applying Freeze mode with interrupts disabled during this critical stage.

```
rlljmp:
        pop      tav,pcb
        mtsrim   cps,FREEZE
        popsr    ops,it0,pcb     ;frozen specials
        popsr    alu,it0,pcb
        popsr    chc,it0,pcb
        popsr    chd,it0,pcb
        popsr    cha,it0,pcb
        popsr    pc2,it0,pcb
        popsr    pc1,it0,pcb
        popsr    pc0,it0,pcb
        iret
```

5.11 INTERRUPT LATENCY

Interrupt latency is an important issue for many real–time applications. I defined it as the time which elapses between identifying the interrupting devices request and performing the necessary processing to remove the request. Latency is increased by having interrupts disabled for long periods of time. Unfortunately it is desirable to have operating system code perform context switching with interrupts disabled.

Consider the case where a User mode process is interrupted and a signal is to be sent to the process. The operating system starts saving the interrupted process context on the user's memory stack. However, in the process of doing this an interrupt is generated by a peripheral device requiring Supervisor mode C level interrupt handler support. This second interrupt requires a context switch to the Supervisor mode interrupt stack. In the process of preparing the processor to run the C level handler, the context switch code may become confused about the state of the stack support registers as a result of partial changes made by the interrupted signal handler operating system code. Additionally, there is likely to be register usage conflict between the different operating system code support routines.

The status confusion and register conflict is avoided by disabling interrupts during the critical portions of the operating system code. The code shown in this chapter enables interrupts after the frozen special registers and stack support registers have been saved. This is insufficient to deal with the nested interrupt

---

situation described above. However, this does reduce interrupt latency, which is a concern to real–time 29K users. Some implementors may chose to move the enabling of interrupts to a later stage in the operating system support code — more specifically, to a point after register stack support registers have been assigned their new values. Register usage changes will also be required to avoid conflict.

Within the example code used throughout this chapter, interrupts can be enabled just after special register CHC has been saved (before *lr1* is pushed on the PCB). This low latency technique enables *lightweight* interrupt handlers to be supported during the operation of normally critical operating system code. Lightweight handlers typically only run in Freeze mode and can easily avoid register conflict if they are restricted to global registers *it0–it3*. Using the *Interrupt Queuing Model* described in section 4.3.12, a lightweight handler responds to the peripheral device interrupt. It tansfers any critical peripheral device data and clears the interrupt request. In doing so, it inserts an interrupt–descriptor into a queue of descriptors for later processing.

A Supervisor C level interrupt handler known as the Dispatcher removes queue entries and calls the appropriate handler to process them. If the operating system is interrupted in a non–critical region by a device requiring a Supervisor mode C level handler, then the dispatcher is immediately started. If the interrupt is in a critical region then the Dispatcher shall be started later when the current critical tasks have been completed. If the Dispatcher is already running when the interrupt occurred, then the associated interrupt descriptor shall wait in the queue until the Dispatcher removes it for processing.

The use of a Dispatcher and interrupt queuing helps to reduce interrupt latency via the use of lightweight interrupts when building queue entries. However, the method has some restrictions. It works where troublesome nested interrupt servicing can be partially delayed for later high level handler completion. But some interrupts can not be delayed. For example an operating system may be running with address translation turned on, and a TLB miss may occur for an operating system memory page which needs the support of a high level handler to page–in the data from a secondary disk device. In this case the interrupt must be completely serviced immediately. This is not a typical environment for 29K users in real–time applications. And even in many non–real–time operating system cases the operating system runs in physical mode or all instruction and data are known to be currently in physical memory. The trade–offs required in deciding when to enable interrupts and resolving register conflict are specific to each operating system implementation.

5.12 SELECTING AN OPERATING SYSTEM

I am often asked by engineers about to start a 29K project, what they should look for when selecting an operating system. There are a number of companies offering operating systems with a range of different capabilities; alternatively a home–grown system could be constructed. The material covered in this chapter and others should help in either constructing or selecting a suitable operating system. I would certainly advice seriously considering purchasing rather than constructing. The task may be enjoyable but probably more lengthy than most project time tables will allow.

There is usually no one right operating system. The choice depends on a number of criteria which may vary from project to project. The following list presents several questions which you need to ask yourself and possibly operating system vendors. You can decide the importance of each item with regard your project requirements.

- Are 3–bus family members as well as 2–bus members supported? If the Am29000 or Am29050 processors are to be used, and the data bus and instruction bus are not to be tied together, then the operating system must be clear about maintaining code and data in separate regions. The Harvard architecture, supported by 3–bus memory systems, typically achieves a 20% performance gain over 2–bus memory systems. Additionally, when 3–bus systems are supported, the operating system may require the support of a hardware bridge allowing the instruction memory to be reached (usually with access delays) via a data memory access.

- Are interruptible **SPILL** and **FILL** code supported? By running them with interrupts disabled the difficulties of performing repair of the register stack support registers can be avoided, should they be interrupted. However, they require the support of multi–cycle LOADM and STOREM instructions, which results in increased interrupt latency. Additionally, **SPILL** and **FILL** support with interrupts disabled, results in a larger overhead compared with trampolining to support routines; thus it is non–optimal as **SPILL**ing and **FILL**ing occur a lot more often then their interruption.

- Given that **SPILL** and **FILL** are interruptible, their operation is interdependent with the **longjmp()** library routine and the signal trampoline code. All four of these services most coordinate their manipulation of register stack support registers if interrupts are to reliably supported.

- Some operating systems support nested interrupts, others do not; without nested interrupt support, interrupt latency can be increased. The use of kernel threads to complete interrupt processing is one way to keep down latency. If interrupt handlers are to be written in a high level language such as C, it may be desirable to support Freeze mode handlers in C. This greatly reduces the interrupt support overhead, because the overhead of preparing the register stack for use by non–leaf procedures is relatively high.

- If the system is to support a high interrupt throughput, then processing interrupts with a Dispatcher will be more efficient. The Dispatcher can execute in assembly level or C level. If C, then the interrupted register stack condition need only be repaired once before entering the Dispatcher, rather than for every interrupt.

- Synchronous context switching times are greatly improved by only restoring the activation record of the procedure about to start execution. This can only be done for tasks which were synchronously switched out; but is a better method than restoring the register stack to the exact position in use at the time of the task context save.

- Operating systems each have their own system call interface which is usually a little different from HIF (see Appendix C). However, it may be still useful to have HIF services available. The HIF services can often be supported by translating them into the underlying operating system serves. The High C 29K and GNU library services generate HIF service calls. These libraries can be used with a non–HIF operating system; but care must be taken as library routines such as printf() are not reentrant. The OS–boot operating system, most often used with HIF conforming library services, does not support task switching, but other operating systems will, and the reentrant library procedure limitations will become a problem.

- Not all members of the 29K family support floating–point instructions directly in hardware. It is the operating system's responsibility to ensure that the desired floating–point emulation routines (trapware) are installed. The operating system vendor should also supply the appropriate transcendental library services (sin(), cos(), etc.) for the chosen processor.

  Floating–point instruction emulation is typically configured to operate with interrupts not enabled. This avoids the need to save interrupted floating–point context. However, the addition of floating–point environment saving, during application context switching, is a requirement for some systems and an unwanted burden for other systems. It is worth knowing the options an operating system supports in this area.

- It is often desirable and less expensive to purchase an operating system in linkable or binary form, rather than source. This makes it more difficult to make changes to the operating system code; this can be required to incorporate support for specialized peripheral devices. It is best that the operating system not consume all of the 32 global registers assigned for operating systems use (*gr64–gr95*). Additionally, linkable operating system images can use link–time register assignment rather than compile time. This enables the user to rearrange

---

the global register usage and utilize unassigned registers for peripheral support tasks.

- The 29K family has no hierarchical memory management unit policy built into the hardware. Support of the translation look–aside buffers is left to software. This offers great flexibility, but generates questions about the MMU support policy adopted by the operating system. Even if address translation is not supported by an operating system, it is still desirable to use the MMU hardware (where available) to support address access protection with one–to–one address translation.

- There is a movement in the operating system business, which includes real–time variants, to support POSIX conforming system calls. It may be worth knowing how, and to what extent, the operating system vendor plans to support POSIX.

- Support for debugging operating system activity and application code is very important. Often operating systems have weaknesses in this area. The Universal Debug Interface (UDI) has been influential in the 29K debug tool business. It offers flexibility in debug tool configuration, flexibility and selection. Debug tools are generally more available for DOS and UNIX based cross development environments.

5.13 SUMMARY

Typical RISC processors, including the 29K, require more complex system software. The manageability of such software development is very much a function of the particular RISC processor implementation. Increased knowledge of how the compiler utilizes the processor registers is required to achieve best performance. The availability of a large number of internal registers leads to improved operation speeds; although the performance gains are at the cost of a somewhat more complex application task context switch.

The use of interrupt processing via lightweight interrupts and signal handling methods, along with the relative infrequency of context switching, enable the system designer to implement a supervisor of generally much improved performance, vis–a–vis CISC processors. Fortunately, application developers can make use of RISC technology without having to solve the supervisor design problems themselves, as there are a number of operating system products available.

Chapter 6

Memory Management Unit

Address values generated by the program counter and data load and store operations appear on the Am29000 processor address bus. Certain members of the 29K family contain instruction caches, which eliminates the need for the processor to request instructions from external memory when the required instruction can be obtained from the cache. However, unless the Memory Management Unit (MMU) is in operation, address values will flow directly on to the pins assigned to the address bus.

The MMU enables address values to be translated, to some extent, into a different physical address. This means that the address values generated by a program need not directly correspond to the physical address values which appear on the chips address pins. The program generates *virtual addresses* for data and instructions which are located in physical memory at addresses determined by the MMU address translation hardware.

With the Am29000 processor, virtual address space is broken into pages of 1K byte, 2K byte, 4K byte or 8K byte size. The first page begins at address 0 and subsequent pages are aligned to page boundaries. The MMU does not modify the lower address bits used to address data within a page. For example, with a 4K page size, the lower 12 address bits are never modified. However, the MMU translates the upper 20 virtual address bits into a new 20–bit value. The translated upper 20–bits and the original lower 12–bits are combined to produce a 32–bit physical address value.

The use of an MMU enables a program to appear to have memory located over the complete 32–bit virtual address space (4G bytes). The physical memory system is, of course, much smaller. Virtually addressed pages are *mapped* (via address translation) into physical pages located in the available memory, typically 1M to 4M bytes. A *secondary memory* is used to store virtually address pages which are not currently located in the physical memory due to its limited size.

The secondary memory is typically a disk. When the MMU identifies the program's need to access data stored on a page currently *out* on disk, it must instruct the operating system to *page–in* the required page into the physical memory. The page may be located almost anywhere in physical memory, but the address translation capability of the MMU will make the page appear at the desired virtual address accessed by the program. In the process of paging–in from disk, the operating system may have to *page–out* to disk a page currently located in physical memory. In this way memory space is made available for the in–coming page.

Within the 29K family, the MMU unit is located on–chip, and is constructed using *Translation Look–Aside Buffers* (TLBs). This chapter describes in detail how the TLB hardware operates, and how it can be used to implement a virtual address capability. The TLBs provide other functions in addition to address translation, such as separate access permissions for data read, write and instruction execution. These important functions will be explained and highlighted in example code.

6.1   SRAM VERSUS DRAM PERFORMANCE

As already stated, secondary memory is typically disk. However, it is difficult to show example code relying on disk controller operation. The example code would be too large and too much time would be spent dealing with disk controller operation. This is not our intention. I have chosen to use SRAM devices for *physical* memory and DRAM and EPROM devices have been chosen to play the role of *secondary* memory.

SRAM devices are much faster than most DRAM memory system arrangements. Thus, by paging the program into SRAM, a very desirable speed gain should be obtained. Certainly the secondary memory capacity is limited to the typically 1M to 4M bytes made available by the DRAM and EPROM combination. But programs will execute from SRAM alone, which may be limited to as little as 128K bytes. For large programs this is likely to result in SRAM pages being paged out to secondary DRAM to make space available for incoming pages.

The SRAM will effectively be a memory cache for the secondary DRAM; the Am29000 processor MMU being used to implement a software controlled cache mechanism. The performance difference shown by programs executing from SRAM versus DRAM is large. Figure 6-1 shows the average cycles required per instruction execution for four well know UNIX utility programs. The influence of memory performance on these benchmarks is likely to be similar to that experienced by large embedded application programs. The DRAM memory system used is termed *4–1*. This terminology is used throughout this chapter. In this case it means the memory system requires four cycles for a random access and one cycle for a *burst–mode access*.

Burst–mode enables multiple instructions and data to be accessed consecutively after a single start address has been supplied. The first data or instruction word in the burst suffers the access penalties of a random access, but subsequent accesses are much less expensive in terms of access delay cycles. The external memory system is responsible for generating access addresses after the processor has supplied the start address for the burst. This can be simply achieved with an address latch and counter.

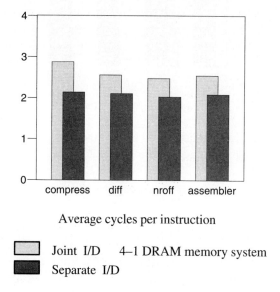

Average cycles per instruction

Joint I/D   4–1 DRAM memory system
Separate I/D

Figure 6-1. Average Cycles per Instruction Using DRAM

The Am29000 processor can execute a new instruction every cycle if supported by the memory system. Figure 6-1 shows that the desired 1 cycle per instruction is far from achievable by the utility programs using a 4–1 memory system. Certain members of the 29K family (the Am29000 and the Am29050 processors) support a 3–bus architecture. One bus is used for physical address values, and there are separate busses for instruction and data information. This bus structure allows simultaneous instruction and data transfer. Once the address bus has been used to supply the start address of an instruction burst, the address bus is free for use in random or burst–mode data accesses. Figure 6-1 shows performance values for both separate (separate I/D), and joint instruction and data (joint I/D) busses. It can be clearly seen that separate busses offer a significant performance gain. Figure 6-2 shows the average cycles per instruction for the same four benchmarks executing on a 2–1 memory system.

Implementing a 2–1 memory system at 25M Hz processor speeds, in particular obtaining a 2–cycle first access, requires SRAM memory devices. The results on Figure 6-2 show that 1–cycle per instruction is almost achieved when a separate instruction and data bus is used with 2–1 memory.

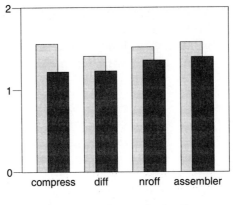

Average cycles per instruction

Joint I/D   2–1 SRAM memory system
Separate I/D

Figure 6-2. Average Cycles per Instruction Using SRAM

29K family members supporting separate busses do not have any means within the chip of reading data which is located in instruction memory. If instructions and data are to be located in the same memory pages, then an off–chip *bridge* must be constructed between the the data and instruction busses. Accessing data located in the instruction memory system via the bridge connected to the data bus, will require more access cycles than accessing data located in the data memory system connected to the data bus directly. The bridge could support accessing instructions located in data memory, but the performance penalties seem too great to implement. The bridge mechanism is acceptable if used for the occasional read of data located in EPROM attached to the instruction bus. It can also be used for reading, as data, an instruction which has caused an execute exception violation.

The construction of two memory systems, one for data and a second for instructions, is undesirable. But it does allow a performance gain. This chapter shall deal with an example system with a joint I/D. This is because the code example is simplified. A separate I/D memory system would require separate instruction and data memory caches and associated support data structures. A block diagram of the example system is shown in Figure 6-3.

Even with a joint I/D memory system it may still be necessary to build two memory systems to achieve a low number of cycles per instruction. This is because it is difficult to achieve single cycle burst–mode access with current memory devices at 25M Hz processor rates. Two memory systems are required and are used alternatively. This technique is often called *memory system interleaving*. One memory system supplies words lying on even word boundaries and the second memory system

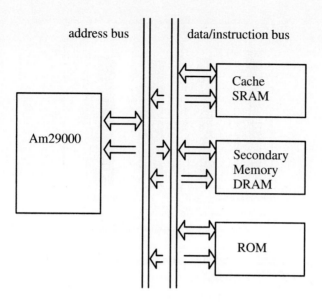

Figure 6-3. Block Diagram of Example Joint I/D System

supplies words lying on odd word boundaries. In this way each memory system has twice as many cycles to respond to consecutive memory accesses compared to a single memory system acting alone.

Interleaving can not guarantee a faster random or burst–mode first access, because the first access can not be overlapped with an another access in the way achievable by consecutive burst–mode accesses. However, some implementations may achieve some savings if the first access happens to fall to the memory system which did not provide the previous access.

With joint I/D systems, 4 cycle first access is very punishing on performance. This is because instruction bursts must be suspended when a data access occurs. To start a data access *costs* 4 cycles. After it has completed, the joint I/D bus can restart the instruction burst at a cost of 4 cycles. Thus accessing a single data word will effectively cost 8 cycles. The 4 cycle memory response latency is hidden by the branch target cache (BTC) for branches and calls but not interruption of contagious instruction execution. Separate I/D systems do not suffer to the same extent from memory latency effects, as the instruction bus can continue to supply instructions in parallel with the data bus operation. Members of the 29K family, such as the Am29030 processor, which only support joint I/D systems, have instruction cache memory on–chip rather than BTC memory. This will enable the effects of instruction stream interruption to be better hidden, as the on–chip cache can be used to restart the instruction stream after data access has occurred.

Figure 6-4 shows average cycles per instruction for the four benchmark programs running on various joint I/D memory systems. The 4–2 DRAM system does

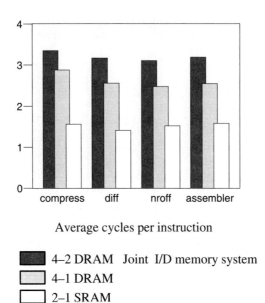

Average cycles per instruction

■ 4–2 DRAM   Joint I/D memory system
☐ 4–1 DRAM
☐ 2–1 SRAM

Figure 6-4.   Average Cycles per Instruction

not support single cycle burst–mode (2–cycle burst), and the performance reduction from a 4–1 DRAM system is apparent. The MMU and associated software will be used in the example system to construct a software controlled cache. The secondary memory shall be a 4–2 or 4–1 DRAM memory system. Programs shall be paged into a small 2–1 SRAM memory. If the paging activity can be kept to a minimum, it is possible that the effective average cycle per instruction will approach that of SRAM acting alone.

Current costs for DRAM devices are about $5 for 256kx4 DRAMs and $10.50 for 32Kx8 SRAMs. At these prices 1M byte of DRAM would cost $40 and 1M byte of SRAM $336. Prices will of course continue to fall on a per–byte basis. However, a large difference between SRAM and DRAM prices will remain, and SRAM memory system costs will remain an obstacle in obtaining the highest system performances. A 128K byte SRAM memory cache would cost $42. Using such a cache in conjunction with a secondary DRAM memory is a cost effective way of achieving high performance. Because the Am29000 processor implements TLBs and lightweight interrupts (see section 4.3.3) on–chip, it is an ideal processor to implement a software cache mechanism.

6.2 TRANSLATION LOOK–ASIDE BUFFER (TLB) OPERATION

The Am29000 processor has a number of special purpose support registers accessible only by the processor operating in Supervisor mode. Special register 2, know as the Current Processor Status (CPS) register has two bits which are used to enable or disable the MMU operation. Bit PI, if set, disables the MMU for all instruction accesses. Bit PD, if set, disables the MMU for all data accesses. When these bit fields are both set, program address values flow directly to the address unit unmodified. This is simply known as physical addressing.

By clearing both bits PI and PD, program instruction address values and data address values are presented to the MMU for translation and other checking. The Am29000 generates addresses early. This means addresses are presented to the MMU during instruction execution. The MMU completes the translation during the execution cycle, making the translated address available at the start of the next processor cycle. The MMU does not need to check every address value; all data access LOAD and STORE instruction addresses are translated. For instruction accesses, only JMP and CALL type instructions are translated, as well as whenever the current execution address crosses a page boundary. Figure 6-5 shows the probability of an instruction requiring an address translation for the four utility programs previously studied. Typically about 30% of instructions are shown to require address translations.

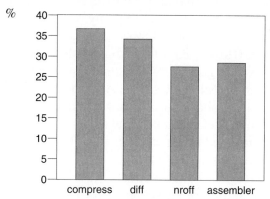

Joint I/D 2–1 SRAM memory system

Figure 6-5. Probability of a TLB Access per Instruction

The MMU is constructed using a 64 entry Translation Look–Aside buffer (TLB). Let's first deal with how the TLB registers are configured, and how address translation is performed. Later, the additional functions supported by the TLB registers will be studied. TLB registers are arranged in pairs which form a single TLB entry.

The Am29000 processor can support 1K, 2K, 4K, and 8K byte page sizes. Special register 13, the Memory Management Unit configuration register (MMU register), has a two bit field (PS) which is used to select the page size. For the following discussion let's assume the PS bits are set to give a page size of 4K bytes.

The lower 12 address bits will be unmodified by the MMU translation, they will flow directly to the address pins. The next five address bits (bits 12 to 16) will be used to select a TLB *set*. See Figure 6-6 for address field composition. If the page size had been 2K bytes then address bits 11–15 would be used to obtain five bits for TLB set selection. Whatever the page size, five bits are required to select from one of 32 TLB sets. The Am29000 processor has actually 64 TLB entries arranged as two per TLB set.

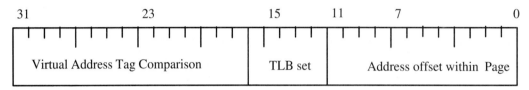

Figure 6-6. TLB Field Composition for 4K Byte Page Size

Each TLB entry contains an address translation for a single page. Therefore the MMU contains translations for a maximum 64 pages. It is possible the address requiring translation does not have a match with any of the current TLB entries, but this will be discussed later. The virtual address space is divided into 32 sets of equal sized pages (known as sets 0 to 31). Page 0 starting at address 0 belongs to set 0. Page 1 belongs to set 1 and so on. Pages 32, 64 and many more also belong to set 0. And likewise page 31, 63 and more belong to set 31. All addresses falling on pages which are members of the set must obtain an address translation from the TLB entrees which are associated with the set. This is know as *Set Associative Translation*. If a page address could be translated by an entry in any TLB, then the translation technique is known as *Fully Associative*.

Compared to full associative mechanisms, set associative translation requires less chip area to implement than full associative mechanisms, and can more easily operate at higher speeds. However, there are still many pages which *compete* with each other to get their address translation stored in a TLB assigned to the associated TLB set. For this reason the Am29000 processor supports two TLB entries per set. This is often expressed as "two columns per set". A page associated with a particular set can have its address translation located in any of the two possible TLB entries. This leads to the title: Two–way Set Associative Translation.

To determine which TLB entry has a valid entry for the page currently being translated, the upper address bits, 17–31 in our 4K byte page example, are compared with the the VTAG filed in the TLB entry. The VTAG contains the corresponding upper bits for the TLB entries current translation. If a mach occurs, and other TLB permission bit field requirements are also satisfied, then the TLB RPN field supplies the upper address bits for the now translated physical address. In our 4K page example the RPN (Real Page Number) field would supply upper address bits 12 to 31, which when combined with the page, offset bits 0 to 11, produce a 32–bit physical address. See Figure 6-7 for a block diagram of the TLB layout.

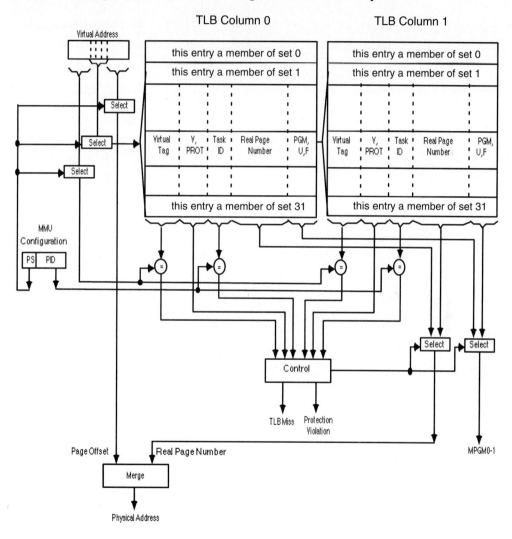

Figure 6-7. Block Diagram of Am29000 processor TLB Layout

TLB entries are constructed from fields requiring 64–bit storage. This results in 128 TLB registers supporting the 64 TLB entries (32 sets 2–*ways* per set). Two TLB

---

registers are required to describe a TLB entry. The first TLB register holds entry word 0 and a second register holds entry word 1. Figure 6-8 shows the TLB register layout.

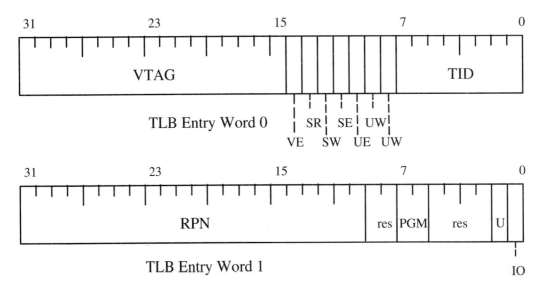

Figure 6-8. Am29000 Processor TLB Register Format

Now that the address translation mechanism has been discussed, the TLB entry fields can be examined in more detail. The VTAG and RPN fields have already been described. Word 0 contains access permission fields. First look at the TID field of word 0. For a TLB entry to match with the current translation, not only must the VTAG match with the upper virtual address bits, but the current process identifier (PID) must match with the task identifier in the TID field. The PID is located in an 8–bit field in the MMU configuration register.

Multi–tasking operating systems assign a unique PID to each task. Whenever a context switch occurs to a new task the MMU register is updated with the PID for the currently executing task. This enables the MMU to support multi–tasking without having to flush the TLB registers at every context switch. TLB entries are likely to remain until a task is again restored and the TLB entries reused. TLB entries are only valid if the VE bit is set, the VE bit for each TLB entry should be cleared before address translation is enabled.

When the processor is running in Supervisor Mode (the SM bit in the CPS register is set), then the current PID value is zero, regardless of the PID value located in the MMU register. Each TLB entry can separately enable read, write and execute permissions for accesses to the mapped page. The SE, SR and SW bits control access permissions for Supervisor accesses to the page. The UR, UW and UE bits control access permissions for the TID identified user.

If no currently valid mapping can be found in the two associated TLB entries, then a TLB miss trap occurs. There are four traps assigned to support address translation misses, two are reserved for the processor operating in Supervisor mode, and a additional two can be taken when a translation is not found when the processor is operating in User mode. Each mode has separate traps for instruction address translation and data address translation. A subsequent section describes the process of taking a trap.

Two additional traps are assigned to Supervisor and User mode protection violations. These occur when a TLB entry has a valid entry but the permission fields do not allow the type of access being attempted. For example unless the UW bit is set a User mode process can not write to the mapped page, even if all other TLB entry fields indicate a match with the translation address.

Now examine the bit fields of word 1. The IO bit is little used, it enables a virtual address to be associated with a physical page in I/O space. The U bit is maintained by the Am29000 processor. Whenever a TLB set is used in a valid translation the U bit associated with the set is updated to indicate which of the two TLB entries was used. In other words, the U bit selects the column within the set. The U bit is used to supply the most significant bit in the least–recently used (LRU) register. Special register 14 has a 6–bit field which is updated whenever an address translation fails and a TLB access trap occurs. The lower 5–bits of the LRU register are loaded with the TLB set number. Thus the LRU register supplies to the trap handler a recommendation for TLB entry replacement. The trap handler typically builds a new valid TLB entry at the recommended location before execution of the interrupted program is continued.

The 2–bit PGM field is not assigned a task by the Am29000 processor, these bits are placed on the PGM[1:0] out put pins when a translation occurs. Developers can place any information they wish in the PGM bits. These bits are particularly useful for multiprocessor applications when one processor wishes to signal other processors about page cache–ability information.

All data accesses have their translated address and corresponding PGM value presented on the the chip pins in the cycle following the cycle executing the LOAD or STORE instruction. Pages containing instructions have their corresponding PGM bits presented to the chip bins when a jump or call to an address within the page first occurred. However, if the target of the jump or call is found in the on–chip instruction cache and the address bus is currently in use when jump or call instruction is in execute, the PGM bits for the target instruction page will not be presented to the chip PGM[1:0] bins.

In this chapter, the software controlled cache code example shall use the PGM bits to store page–lock and page–dirty information in bits PGM[0] and PGM[1], respectively.

6.2.1 Taking a TLB Trap

The address translation performed by the MMU is determined by the trap handler routines which are used to update the TLB registers. When the current processor status register bits PD and PI are both clear, enabling the MMU hardware for both data and instruction address translation, the DA and FZ bits in the CPS register must also be cleared. Clearing these bits disables Am29000 special register freezing and enables traps to be taken.

When the MMU does not contain a match for the current address translation, a trap is taken by the processor. This also happens for valid translations not meeting permission requirements. The software executed by the trap handler must construct a TLB entry for the *failing* address from page table entries (PTEs) stored in memory. The TLB registers simply act as a cache for the currently–needed translations stored in off–chip data memory.

Many CISC–type processors have algorithms in the chip microcode for automatically updating the MMU hardware from more extensive data located in external data memory. Because the Am29000 does not implement this function in hardware, the user is free to construct a software algorithm for TLB reloading which best suits the memory management architecture. This increased flexibility outweighs any reduction in TLB register reload time that may occur for some configurations. The flexibility is what makes possible the software controlled cached described later.

When the Am29000 takes a trap the processor enters Supervisor mode with frozen critical support registers. This is known as Freeze mode. A more complete explanation is given in Chapter 4 *(Interrupts and Traps)*. The frozen special registers describe the state of the processor at the time of the address translation failure. Examining these registers enables the trap handler software to determine the necessary action and eventually restart the instruction in execute when the trap occurred. After the *trapware* routines have constructed the required TLB entry, the faulting instruction will be able to complete execution.

Later sections will deal with the trapware in detail for the example software controlled cache system. The interesting details of the trapware will be covered then. Since the code is memory architecture specific, the operation of the software controlled cache needs to be discussed first. This discussion is in the later section entitled *Software Controlled Cache Memory Architecture* (section 6.4).

6.3 PERFORMANCE EQUATION

Performance has been considered in terms of average number of cycles per instruction execution. This is a useful metric when considering memory system architectures. Figure 6-1, Figure 6-2 and Figure 6-4 give average cycles per user instruction execution ($A_{C/I}$). However, if a TLB miss occurs during instruction execution, a number of Supervisor mode trapware instructions will be required to prepare the

TLB registers before the user's code can continue. If TLB trapware is activated in support of too many instructions, then the effective number of cycles required per application instruction will increase.

The effective average cycles per instruction is given by: $A_{effective} = P\ A_{C/I}$ where $A_{C/I}$ is the average number of cycles per instruction for the program running in physical mode, without the MMU in operation. The multiplying factor, P, determines how much performance is reduced by the use of the MMU hardware. The value of P is given by:

$$P = 1 + \frac{P_{TLB/I}\quad P_{miss}\quad T_{cycles}}{A_{C/I}}$$

We shall look at the terms of this equation individually to determine their effect. Term $P_{TLB/I}$ is the probability an instruction shall cause a TLB access. Figure 6-5 showed average figures for $P_{TLB/I}$ observed with the four benchmark programs examined. Given that a TLB access occurs, we are then interested in the probability that an entry is not found and a miss trap is taken. This conditional probability is given by term P_{miss}, and Figure 6-9 shows average P_{miss} values for the four benchmark programs running on the software controlled cache system .

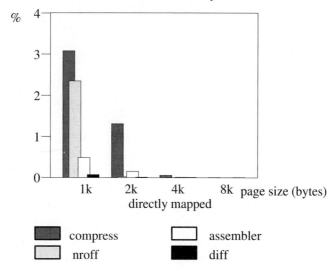

Figure 6-9.   TLB Miss Ratio for Joint I/D 2–1 SRAM System

What matters at present is we observe that TLB miss rates increase as we decrease page size. This is expected because smaller page sizes mean a smaller portion of the program's pages have mappings currently cached in the TLB registers. Given that the Am29000 processor has a fixed number of TLB entries, it is best to have large page sizes if TLB misses are to be reduced. However, the better granularity of small page sizes may lead to better physical memory utilization. An additional consideration is the size of pages transported from secondary memory such as disk or network connections. Secondary memory communication may be improved by better communication efficiencies. These efficiencies may be achieved with larger page sizes.

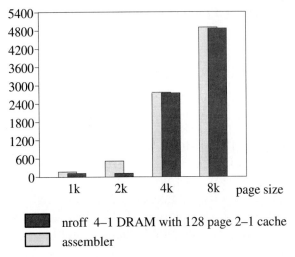

Figure 6-10. Average Cycles Required per TLB Miss

The final term of the T_{cycles} equation is the average number of cycles required to process a TLB miss. Figure 6-10 shows values for the four benchmark programs running on the cache system. When a TLB miss occurs for a page which is not currently located in the physical memory but in secondary memory, a large number of processor cycles is required to first transfer the page from secondary memory to physical memory and then build a valid TLB entry. As the page size increases the TLB miss trap handler execution time increases substantially.

The product, $P_{TLB/I}$ P_{miss} T_{cycles} gives the average number of cycles overhead added to each application instruction in order to support the MMU operation. After studying the software cache memory architecture, the effective number of cycles per instruction achieved will be reexamined and compared with the non–cache memory architecture performance.

6.4 SOFTWARE CONTROLLED CACHE MEMORY ARCHITECTURE

By studying a software controlled cache mechanism we can achieve three objectives: First, a better understanding of the non–TLB–cached page–table layout.

Second, further understanding of TLB trapware implementation detail. Thirdly, an awareness of software controlled cache benefits.

When a TLB miss occurs, the trap handler must determine the replacement TLB entry data. It does this by indexing a table of Page Table Entries (PTEs). Each PTE contains information on how to map a physical page into its corresponding secondary memory page. In our example system, the physical memory is SRAM and the secondary memory is DRAM. In fact, the secondary memory is physically addressable, but the execution of all programs from within the limited sized SRAM cache will be attempted, and the DRAM will only be accessed when a page–to or page–from secondary memory needs copying.

There are many different PTE table arrangements. Some systems have multiple layers of PTEs, where a higher level PTE points to tables of lower level PTEs. In multi–tasking systems, each task may have its own table of PTEs. And if the Supervisor code also executes with address translation, then it may also have a table of PTEs. To simplify our example system, we will assume the supervisor always runs in physical mode, and there is a single table of PTEs shared by all User mode programs. To evaluate the system performance, only single User mode tasks will be run, in particular the *nroff* and *assembler* utility programs.

PTEs need not have the same structure as TLB entries. They typically do not. This enables the memory management system to keep additional page information in memory and only cache critical data in the TLB registers. In addition it may be possible to compact information into a smaller PTE structure, which results in a substantial space saving in systems which keep extensive PTE tables permanently in physical memory (in our case SRAM). For the example system, PTEs shall have exactly the same format as TLB entries. The method has the benefit that TLB entries can be loaded from PTE memory location directly without additional processor cycles being expended in reformatting.

The PTE format will be 4–way set associative. The number of sets shall be limited by the amount of available SRAM cache memory, but a lower limit of 32, established by the Am29000, is required. Given a minimum page size of 1K bytes, the SRAM can not be smaller that 128K bytes (1K x 4 x 32). If the number of PTE sets is greater than 32, then the cache has more set resolution than the TLBs. In this case a TLB set caches entries for more than one PTE set, and the TLB VTAG field has more address resolution than the PTE VTAG field requires.

Each TLB entry indicates how the user's virtual address is mapped into an SRAM page number (given by the TLB RPN entry). The PTE entries must have a mapping relationship with DRAM memory pages and SRAM memory pages. The entries use the PTE RPN field to store the DRAM page number. PTEs also have a mapping relationship with SRAM pages. This enables the memory page maintained by the PTE to be moved between SRAM and DRAM. The PTE SRAM mapping is simple. PTEs and SRAM pages are stored consecutively in memory, as are SRAM pages. Given the PTE address, the corresponding SRAM page address can be found by determining the PTE address displacement from the PTE table base. The PTE displacement, multiplied by the page size, will locate the SRAM page relative to the base address of SRAM pages. Figure 6-11 outlines the system.

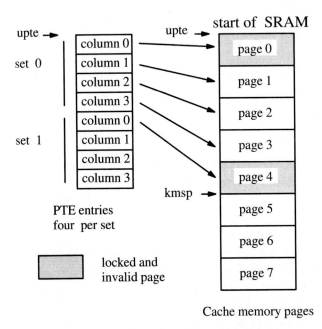

Figure 6-11. PTE Mapping to Cache Real Page Numbers

Because the PTE entries are not an exact cache of PTE entries, due to the RPN field differences, TLB register word 1 must be adjusted accordingly before the TLB register can be updated form the PTE entry.

The Am29000 C language calling convention reserves processor registers *gr*64–*gr*95 for operating system use. To improve trap handler performance a number of these registers are used by these critical routines. For temporary use, six registers are required, and for static information caching two registers are used. The particular registers used are described later along with the example code. The two static registers are of particular interest; they will give them synonyms *upte* and *kmsp*.

It is desirable to keep critical data and routines in SRAM memory. For example, the TLB miss handler routines should be stored in cache memory. Cached pages can be marked as *locked–in,* this will prevent them from being paged–out to DRAM. However, the SRAM is only intended to hold User mode application pages. Trap handlers and other critical operating system routines run in Supervisor mode, and in our example system, without address translation. In practice, a larger SRAM could be implemented and, say, half allocated for cache use; the other half being reserved for operating system code and data. This may not lead to the most efficient use of such an effective resource as SRAM. The problem can be overcome by marking certain PTE entries as invalid but locked. The SRAM pages corresponding to these PTE can then be accessed in non–translated address mode by Supervisor mode code.

Since the PTE table is frequently accessed by TLB trapware, it is important that quick access to the table is supported. For this reason register *upte* is initialized to point to the base of the PTE table, and the table is located in the first SRAM page. One SRAM page can contain 32 sets of PTE data. In multi–tasking systems, with each task having its own PTE table, the *upte* value is normally stored in a per–task data structure know as the Process Control Block (PCB), and the *upte* register is updated from the PCB data at each context switch.

The Am29000 takes traps very quickly, without expending a number of internal processor cycles preparing an interrupt processing context for the processor. This advantage over typical CISC processor operation enables the Am29000 to process the trap quickly in Freeze mode and return to the user's program. It is the Freeze mode processing capability of the Am29000 that makes a soft cache mechanism attractive. However, TLB miss handlers can not always complete their handling quickly in Freeze mode code. In such cases they must signal the operating system to continue with further processing, Freeze mode is departed, and Supervisor mode with freeze disabled is entered. Before Freeze mode can be exited, the frozen special registers must be stored on a Supervisor mode memory stack. They will have to be restored from this stack once the operating system completes the TLB miss processing. The operating system stack is located on page 4, which is in a different set from the PTE table. Operating system accessible register *kmsp* is used as a stack pointer.

Using the cache architecture described, the *nroff* and *assembler* utilities were observed running in a 128 page SRAM based system. The page–in activity is shown on Figure 6-12. It appears the two programs were too large to execute in 128K byte SRAM (1K byte page size). The paging activity is at a minimum with a 256K byte cache (2K byte page size). It is possible the increased paging activity is due to cache sets being only 4–way. In the case of *nroff*, it is more likely the page replacement algorithm was having difficulty in keeping the desired pages in the cache for such a large program.

As page sizes get larger, the probability of a TLB miss diminishes. Since the cache gets larger for a given SRAM of fixed number of pages, expect the probability of a page–in to increase as page size increases. Reflecting the fact that with large caches, a TLB miss causes a page–in and the TLB maintains a cached entry for the permanently resident page. Figure 6-13 gives the probability of a page–in given a TLB miss has occurred.

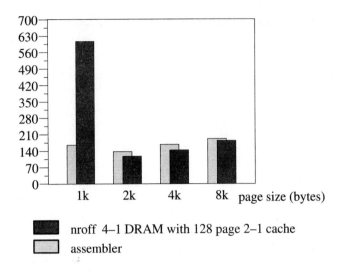

Figure 6-12.   Software Controlled Cache, K bytes paged–in

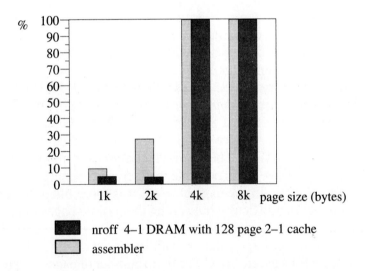

Figure 6-13.   Probability of a Page–in Given a TLB Miss

With the *nroff* utility, the probability actually reduces when the page size is increased from 1K byte to 2K byte. This is because of the cache–thrashing occurring with the 128K byte cache used with the 1K byte page size.

6.4.1 Cache Page Maintenance

The example software controlled cache system only supports User mode address translation. This means Supervisor mode TLB miss handlers will not be considered. TLB entries shall always enable instruction execution for each page, this eliminates support for the TLB instruction access protection violation trap. Pages will be initially marked as non–writeable, as will be seen this supports maintenance of the page–dirty bit. So in total, we need only deal with three traps: Instruction access miss, data access miss, and data access protection violation.

The Am29000 has 65 global registers (*gr1*, *gr64–gr127*), of these 32 are reserved for operating system use only (*gr64–gr95*). To improve the performance of the trapware, several of the operating system registers have been assigned TLB handler support functions. The following code uses register synonyms, so the actual register assignments can be easily changed.

```
.reg    it0,gr64        ;Freeze mode
.reg    it1,gr65        ;temporary regs
.reg    it2,gr66
.reg    it3,gr67

.reg    kt0,gr68        ;temporary regs
.reg    kt1,gr69

.reg    kmsp,gr93       ;supervisor M-stack
.reg    upte,gr95
```

The code shown within this chapter makes use of a number of macros for pushing and popping special registers to an external memory stack. These macros, *push*, *pushsr*, *pop* and *popsr*, were described in section 3.3.1 (*Useful Macro–Instructions*).

The example code can be used to construct a cache of various number of PTE entries (ways or columns) per set, and total number of sets. The constant definitions shown below are used to control the cache size.

```
.equ    PGSIZE,10           ;Page size
.equ    C_SETS,6            ;cache sets
.equ    C_COLUMNS,2         ;columns per sets
.equ    WSIZE,512           ;window size
.equ    SIG_ICMISS,1        ;signal I-miss
.equ    SIG_DCMISS,3        ;signal D-miss
.equ    SIG_PROTECT,5       ;signal W-protect
.equ    CTX_CHC,3*4         ;context offset

        .sect cache,bss
        .use cache
cache_adds:
    .block (1<<PGSIZE)*(1<<C_SETS)*(1<<C_COLUMNS)
```

The operating system code, which is not shown, is responsible of initializing support registers, *kmsp,* and *upte*. It must also mark the PTEs locked and invalid for

---

any SRAM pages which are not to be used for caching, but by the operating system. The example code uses pages 0 and 4 to store performance critical support data.

6.4.2 Data Access TLB Miss

When a read or write data access occurs for a page whose translation from virtual to physical address is currently not in the TLB registers, a TLB miss is taken. This causes execution to vector to trap number 9. The address of the trapware handler, **UDTLBMiss**, is at location 9 in the vector table. A miss may occur because the accessed page is currently not in the cache, or, more importantly, because the PTE mapping the cached page is currently not cached by the TLB registers. The PTEs for the appropriate set must be scanned to determine if the page is in the cache.

When a trap is taken, the Am29000 processor special support registers are frozen, their contents report the state of the processor at the time of the trap. Special register CHA contains the virtual address for the failing data access. Using the CHA value, the cache set is determined and the 4 PTE columns assigned to the set are scanned. The PTE valid bit must be set and the PTE VTAG field must match with the upper bits of the CHA address for a match to be found. Note, the example code does not compare the TID field; this would be necessary if the cache were supporting a multi–tasking operating system.

```
UDTLBmiss:
        mfsr    it0,cha
        const   kt1,SIG_DCMISS  ;signal number
        srl     it2,it0,PGSIZE  ;select cache set
        and     it2,it2,(1<<C_SETS)-1
        sll     it2,it2,3+C_COLUMNS
        add     it2,it2,upte    ;adds of 1st PTE
;
scan_columns:
        srl     it0,it0,PGSIZE+5
        sll     it0,it0,PGSIZE+5
        const   kt0,(1<<C_COLUMNS)-1
next_column:
        jmpt    kt0,not_cached
        sub     kt0,kt0,1       ;dec column count
        load    0,0,it1,it2     ;load word 0
        add     it2,it2,8       ;next PTE entry
        sll     it3,it1,31-14   ;test VE-bit
        jmpf    it3,next_column
        srl     it3,it1,PGSIZE+5;mask PTE VTAG
        sll     it3,it3,PGSIZE+5
        cpeq    it3,it0,it3     ;compare VTAG
        jmpf    it3,next_column
        mfsr    it3,LRU
        sub     it2,it2,4       ;adds word 1
```

If a PTE is found in the set which matches with the CHA address, then the TLB entry of the associated set, selected by the LRU register, is updated with the contents of the matching PTE. Field RPN of word 1 of the PTE is not filled with the secondary memory (DRAM) page number taken from the PTE, but with the page number of the SRAM cache page.

```
in_cache:
;Word 0 in it1,it2 points to PTE word 1
        load    0,0,it0,it2     ;load word 1
        mttlb   it3,it1         ;assign Word 0
        add     it3,it3,1
        and     it0,it0,0xc1    ;mask out RPN
        sub     it1,it2,upte    ;set offset;
        srl     it1,it1,3       ;set index;
        sll     it1,it1,PGSIZE  ;cache page offset
        add     it1,it1,upte    ;cache RPN
        or      it0,it1,it0     ;or in cache RPN
        mttlb   it3,it0         ;assign Word 1
        iret
```

When the required page is found in the cache, the TLB handler executes very quickly without ever leaving Freeze mode. After the TLB entry has been updated an IRET instruction causes execution to be restarted from the state defined by the frozen special registers. The trapware is arranged so the most frequently occurring events are processed first and suffer the lowest support overhead. However, if the page is not found in the cache (no matching PTE) then the trapware must call on the operating system to complete the necessary processing. It does this by sending a signal. The code following label **not_cached** pushes the contents of the special registers as well as other signal information onto a *signal frame* on the Supervisor memory stack. Execution is then forced to continue in Supervisor mode with non–translated addressing at **tlb_sig_handler.** The signal frame shall be used to repair the special registers after the *higher level* operating system support code has completed.

```
not_cached:
;Send a signal to the operating system
        push    kmsp,kt1        ;push signal number
        push    kmsp,gr1        ;push gr1
        push    kmsp,rab        ;push rab
        const   it0,WSIZE
        sub     gr1,rfb,it0     ;set gr1=rfb-WSIZE
        sub     rab,rfb,it0     ;set rab=rfb-WSIZE
        pushsr  kmsp,it0,pc0    ;push pc0
        pushsr  kmsp,it0,pc1
        pushsr  kmsp,it0,pc2
        pushsr  kmsp,it0,cha
        pushsr  kmsp,it0,chd
        pushsr  kmsp,it0,chc
        pushsr  kmsp,it0,alu
        pushsr  kmsp,it0,ops    ;push ops
;
        push    kmsp,tav        ;push tav
        cpeq    tav,kt1,SIG_ICMISS
```

```
        jmpt     tav,i_miss
         mfsr    tav,pc1          ;pass address
         mfsr    tav,cha
;
i_miss:
         mtsrim  chc,0            ;cancel load/store
         mtsrim  ops,0x70         ;set PD|PI|SM
;
         const   it1,tlb_sig_handler
         consth  it1,tlb_sig_handler
         add     it0,it1,4        ;trampoline signal
         mtsr    pc1,it1          ; handler
         mtsr    pc0,it0
         iret
```

The signal frame has a *signal number* field which is used to report the type of TLB trap which occurred. The layout of the frame is given in Figure 6-14. Global register *tav* (*gr121*) is used to pass the address causing the trap to occur. For a TLB data miss, the address is already contained in the CHA register, but copying it to *tav* is convenient because the signal handler code is also shared by other routines.

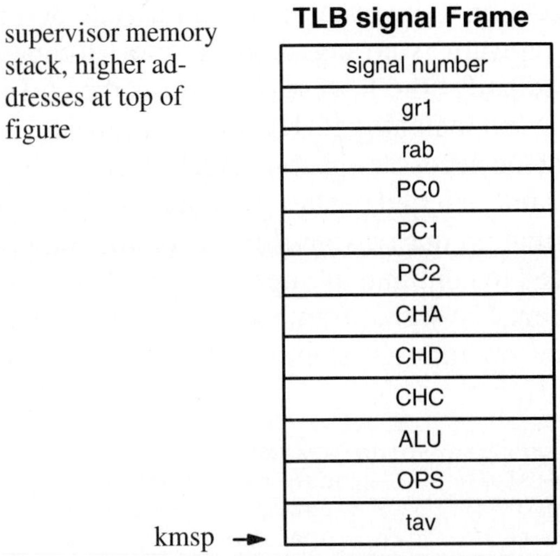

supervisor memory stack, higher addresses at top of figure

TLB signal Frame

signal number
gr1
rab
PC0
PC1
PC2
CHA
CHD
CHC
ALU
OPS
tav

kmsp →

Figure 6-14. TLB Signal Frame

6.4.3 Instruction Access TLB Miss

Instruction access TLB misses are dealt with in the same way as data access misses. Only the signal number is different and the faulting address is contained in special register PC1 rather than CHA. Register PC1 contains the address of the instruction in execute at the time of the failing address translation. Since cache pages contain both instructions and data, the same set of PTE apply for data and instruction address values. Via the interrupt vector table, the User mode instruction access trap number 8 causes execution to continue at address label **UITLBmiss**.

```
UITLBmiss:
        mfsr    it0,pc1
        const   kt1,SIG_ICMISS   ;signal number
        srl     it2,it0,PGSIZE   ;select cache set
        and     it2,it2,(1<<C_SETS)-1
        sll     it2,it2,3+C_COLUMNS;PTE set offset
        jmp     scan_columns
        add     it2,it2,upte     ;adds of 1st PTE
```

6.4.4 Data Write TLB Protection

The following signal handler code is responsible for moving pages from secondary DRAM to SRAM cache memory (paging–in). When pages are first paged–in they are given read and execute permissions only, unless the initial faulting access is due to a data write. At some time later during program execution, a write to the cached page may occur. When this happens, a data write protection trap is taken, and execution is vectored to address label **tlb_data_prot**.

In the same way as a data TLB miss, the associated PTE entries are scanned to find the matching entry. There must be a matching entry and, in addition, a cached TLB entry which is disallowing write access. Once the PTE has been found, the CHA address value is again used to find the associated TLB entry. Note, the LRU register can not be used because it is only updated on TLB misses. To find the TLB entry, the VTAG portion of the CHA address is compared with the only two possible TLB entries associated with the set.

```
        ;A write request to a read-only page has occurred.

tlb_data_prot:
        mfsr    it0,cha
        const   kt1,SIG_PROTECT ;signal
        srl     it2,it0,PGSIZE   ;select cache line
        and     it2,it2,(1<<C_SETS)-1
        sll     it2,it2,3+C_COLUMNS;PTE set offset
        add     it2,it2,upte     ;adds of 1st PTE
;
scan:
        srl     it0,it0,PGSIZE+5;adds VTAG
        sll     it0,it0,PGSIZE+5
        const   kt0,(1<<C_COLUMNS)-1
nxt_column:
        jmpt    kt0,not_cached
        sub     kt0,kt0,1        ;dec column count
        load    0,0,it1,it2      ;load word 0
        add     it2,it2,8        ;next PTE entry
        sll     it3,it1,31-14    ;test VE-bit
        jmpf    it3,nxt_column
```

```
        srl     it3,it1,PGSIZE+5  ;mask PTE VTAG
        sll     it3,it3,PGSIZE+5
        cpeq    it3,it0,it3       ;compare VTAG
        jmpf    it3,nxt_column
;
        mfsr    it3,cha           ;find TLB entry
        srl     it3,it3,PGSIZE-1;get TLB set
        and     it3,it3,0x3e
        mfsr    kt0,cha
        srl     kt0,kt0,PGSIZE+5;form adds VTAG
        sll     kt0,kt0,PGSIZE+5
mftlb   it0,it3 ;read Word 0
        srl     it0,it0,PGSIZE+5;form TLB VTAG
        sll     it0,it0,PGSIZE+5
        cpeq    it0,it0,kt0
        jmpt    it0,entry_found
        sub     it2,it2,8         ;PTE adds word 0
        add     it3,it3,64        ;Word 0 in set 1
```

Once the PTE and TLB entries have been found execution continues at label **entry_found**. Both entries must now be updated to set the UW bit enabling User mode write access. In addition, the PGM[1] bit used to keep a record of any data writes to the SRAM page is also set. This bit, known as the dirty–bit, will be used in the page–out algorithm. Once the TLB register reporting the access permission fault has been updated, an IRET instruction is used to restart the program using the contents of the still frozen special registers.

```
entry_found:
;Word 0 in it1, it2 points to PTE word 0
        const   kt1,0x200         ;UW-bit
        or      it1,it1,kt1
        store   0,0,it1,it2       ;store new word 0
        mttlb   it3,it1           ;assign Word 0
;
        add     it2,it2,4
        load    0,0,it0,it2       ;load  word 1
        add     it3,it3,1
        or      it0,it0,0x80      ;set PGM[1] dirty
        store   0,0,it0,it2       ;store new word 1
        and     it0,it0,0xc1      ;mask out RPN
        sub     it1,it2,upte      ;set offset
        srl     it1,it1,3         ;set index
        sll     it1,it1,PGSIZE    ;cache page offset
        add     it1,it1,upte      ;cahe RPN
        or      it0,it1,it0       ;or in cache RPN
        mttlb   it3,it0           ;assign Word 1
        iret
```

6.4.5 Supervisor TLB Signal Handler

When trapware code is unable to complete the necessary TLB update, for example, if the corresponding address is for a page not currently in the cache, the operating system receives a signal and information on its memory stack required to continue the TLB update process. An IRET instruction is used to *trampoline* to the signal handler address **tlb_sig_handler**. The IRET does not cause the faulting User mode instruction to restart, because after the frozen special registers are saved on the stack, the PC registers are loaded with the address of the signal handler. Additionally, the OPS status register is modified to cause Supervisor mode with non–translated address to commence after the IRET, rather than the interrupted User mode with address translation on.

A small number of support registers were required to support the trapware routines. The *higher level* signal handler code requires registers for its own operation. It is undesirable to use some of the remaining operating system registers in the *gr64–gr95* range to support this code. Global registers are a scarce resource and likely needed by other critical operating system tasks. The registers used by the trap handlers (*it0–it3*) are by convention used by all Freeze mode handlers, since during Freeze mode, interrupts are disabled and therefore there are no register access conflicts. However, the signal handler code runs with interrupts turned on. An interrupt occurring during signal processing would likely use the interrupt temporary registers (*it0–it3*), and therefor the signal handler must acquire additional registers for its operation. It does this by pushing some of the User mode assigned global registers (*gr96–gr127*) onto the Supervisor stack, just below the signal frame.

```
;Try and find an empty PTE entry in the column.
;Register tav has the offending address.

tlb_sig_handler:
        push    kmsp, gr96      ;get some registers
        push    kmsp, gr97
        push    kmsp, gr98
        push    kmsp, gr99
        push    kmsp, gr100
;
        mfsr    gr96,tmc        ;get random value
;
        srl     gr98,tav,PGSIZE ;select cache set
        and     gr98,gr98,(1<<C_SETS)-1
        sll     gr98,gr98,3+C_COLUMNS;PTE set offset
        add     gr98,gr98,upte  ;PTE column 0 address
;
        const   gr100,(1<<C_COLUMNS)-1
column_loop:
        jmpt    gr100,page_out
         and    gr96,gr96,((1<<C_COLUMNS)-1)<<3
        add     gr99,gr98,gr96  ;column wrap-around
        load    0,0,gr97,gr99   ;load word 0
        add     gr96,gr96,8     ;next PTE entry
        sll     gr99,gr97,31-14 ;test VE-bit
        jmpt    gr99,column_loop
         sub    gr100,gr100,1   ;dec column count
;
```

```
        sub     gr96,gr96,8
        call    gr100,store_locals;destroys gr96
        add     gr98,gr98,gr96   ;PTE adds of Word 0
page_in:                         ;Page-in code follows . . .
```

The four PTE entries associated with the set are then scanned to find an unused entry (i.e., the VE bit is not set). If all PTEs are marked valid, then execution continues at **page_out**. Once a empty entry is found a call to routine **store_locals** is made. This call causes all 128 local registers within the Am29000 processor to be copied onto the Supervisor memory stack just below the user's saved global registers. Note, when the set of four PTEs are scanned, a random column in the set is initially selected. This may initially reduce column scan times. After the local registers have been made available for signal handler use, execution continues at label **page_in**.

6.4.6 Copying a Page into the Cache

Once a PTE for the *in–coming* page has been selected the corresponding SRAM cache page can be easily determined with a little address–based calculation. Words 0 and 1 for the TLB entry are now formed and stored in the TLB selected by the LRU register. The TLB entry is also copied to the PTE location, with the one difference that PTEs have the DRAM page number in the RPN filed rather than the SRAM page number.

The Dirty bit, PGM[0] , is cleared and the page is marked for read and execute permissions, unless the signal is from a failing data write access; in this case, the page is marked dirty and write permission is granted. To determine if a write access failed, the channel control register CHC is checked for a valid data write access in progress. The CHC register is obtained by referencing the signal frame stored on the Supervisor memory stack. Fortunately, the LRU register did not need to be saved on the memory stack, because the LRU will remain unchanged during signal code execution. The LRU register is only updated when an address translation fails, this can not happen when the operating system is running in physical address mode.

The DRAM page is copied into SRAM memory in bursts of 128 words. Bursting is repeated several times depending on page size. Using long data bursts to transfer data is most efficient. The LOADM and STOREM instructions remain in execute until all their data has been transferred, which is only dependent on the access delay of the memory. Once the SRAM page has been filled, the user's local registers are repaired via a call to **load_locals** and a jump to **ret_usr** starts the process of restoring the processor to its state at the time of the trap.

```
page_in:
        srl     gr96,tav,PGSIZE+5;form VTAG
        sll     gr96,gr96,PGSIZE+5
        mfsr    gr97,mmu         ;get TID
        and     gr97,gr97,0xff
        or      gr96,gr96,gr97   ;or in TID
```

Programming the 29K RISC Family

```
;
        const    gr100,0x00        ;PGM[1]=0 clean
        const    gr97,512 + 5*4 + CTX_CHC
        add      gr97,kmsp,gr97    ;get chc
        load     0,0,gr97,gr97
        mtsrim   fc,31-0
        extract  gr97,gr97,gr97    ;rotate
        jmpf     gr97,i_page       ;test CV-bit
         const   gr99,0x4500       ;VE|UR|UE
        mtsrim   fc,1+31-15
        extract  gr97,gr97,gr97    ;rotate LS-bit
        jmpt     gr97,i_page       ;jump for
         nop                       ;data load
        const    gr99,0x4700       ;VE|UR|UW|UE
        const    gr100,0x80        ;PGM[1]=1 dirty
i_page:
        or       gr97,gr96,gr99    ;or in permissions
        store    0,0,gr97,gr98     ;store Word 0
        mfsr     gr96,lru
        mttlb    gr96,gr97         ;assign TLB word 0
;
        add      gr96,gr96,1
        add      gr98,gr98,4       ;PTE adds Word 1
        srl      gr97,tav,PGSIZE;
        sll      gr97,gr97,PGSIZE
        or       gr97,gr97,gr100;assign PGM[1]
        store    0,0,gr97,gr98     ;store Word 1
        sub      gr99,gr98,upte    ;set offset
        srl      gr99,gr99,3       ;set index
        sll      gr99,gr99,PGSIZE      ;cahe page offset
        add      gr99,gr99,upte    ;cache RPN
        mttlb    gr96,gr99         ;assign TLB word 1
;
        mtsrim   cr,128-1
        const    gr96,(1<<PGSIZE)/512;busrt count
        sub      gr96,gr96,2
        const    gr100,512
        srl      gr97,tav,PGSIZE ;get page address
        sll      gr97,gr97,PGSIZE
more_in:
        loadm    0,0,lr0,gr97      ;read in a block
        storem   0,0,lr0,gr99      ;copy out a block
        add      gr97,gr97,gr100   ;advance pointer
        jmpfdec  gr96,more_in
         add     gr99,gr99,gr100   ;advance pointer
;
        call     gr100,load_locals;destroys gr96
         nop
        jmp      ret_user
         nop
```

6.4.7 Copying a Page Out of the Cache

If a TLB miss occurs and all PTE entries for the associated set are marked valid, then a PTE must be selected and the corresponding SRAM page copied back to DRAM. This makes room for the page containing the miss addresses to be copied into the space made available by the out–going page. The PTEs for the set are scanned and if a non–dirty page is found, it is selected for *paging–out*. If all pages are marked dirty, then a jump to label **all_dirty** is taken, as further column scanning is required to determine if a page can be paged–out.

```
;All columns are in use. Select a column which is not locked and
not ;dirty for paging out.
;Register gr98 points to a random column in current set.

page_out:
        call    gr100,store_locals;destroys gr96
        add     gr98,gr98,4       ;pnts to PTE word 1
        mfsr    gr96,tmc          ;get random number
        const   gr100,(1<<C_COLUMNS)-1;column counter

dirty_loop:
        jmpt    gr100,all_dirty
        and     gr96,gr96,((1<<C_COLUMNS)-1)<<3
        add     gr99,gr98,gr96    ;column wrap
        load    0,0,gr97,gr99     ;load PTE word 1
        add     gr96,gr96,8       ;next TLBT entry
        sll     gr99,gr97,31-7    ;test PGM[1] dirty
        jmpt    gr99,dirty_loop
   sll  gr99,gr97,31-6            ;test PGM[0] locked
        jmpt    gr99,dirty_loop
        sub     gr100,gr100,1     ;dec column count
```

Once a PTE for the out–going page is selected, the two TLB entries for the associated set must be checked to determine if they are caching an entry for the selected PTE. If there is a valid TLB entry, then it must be marked invalid as the associated SRAM page is about to be assigned to a different virtual page address.

```
page_selected:
;Must first page-out selected cache page before filling the cache
;with the new selected page.
        sub     gr96,gr96,8
        add     gr98,gr98,gr96    ;adds of PTE Word 1
;
;Invalidate any processor TLB entries for the outgoing page.
;Could check VE bit in each TLB entry first.
        srl     gr96,gr97,PGSIZE+5;form VTAG
        sll     gr96,gr96,PGSIZE+5
        srl     gr100,gr97,PGSIZE-1;get TLB set
        and     gr100,gr100,0x3e
        mftlb   gr99,gr100        ;read Word 0
        srl     gr99,gr99,PGSIZE+5;form VTAG
```

```
        sll       gr99,gr99,PGSIZE+5
        cpeq      gr99,gr99,gr96
        jmpf      gr99,test_column_1
invalidate_tlb:
        const     gr99,0              ;clear TLB VE-bit
        jmp       tlb_clear
        mttlb     gr100,gr99
test_column_1:
        add       gr100,gr100,64   ;Word 0 in column 1
        mftlb     gr99,gr100
        srl       gr99,gr99,PGSIZE+5;form VTAG
        sll       gr99,gr99,PGSIZE+5
        cpeq      gr99,gr99,gr96
        jmpt      gr99,invalidate_tlb
        nop
```

It is during the page–out routine that the maintenance of a dirty–bit pays back its dividend. If the page is not dirty then there is no need to copy it back to DRAM, because the DRAM copy is exactly the same as the SRAM copy. If no writes have occurred to the page then the copy–out is avoided.

```
tlb_clear:
        sll       gr96,gr97,31-7   ;test dirty bit
        jmpf      gr96,page_in
        sub       gr98,gr98,4        ;gr98  pnts. word 0
        srl       gr97,gr97,PGSIZE;secondary mem RPN
        sll       gr97,gr97,PGSIZE
        sub       gr99,gr98,upte   ;set offset
        srl       gr99,gr99,3        ;set index
        sll       gr99,gr99,PGSIZE;cache page offset
        add       gr99,gr99,upte   ;cache RPN

        mtsrim    cr,128-1
        const     gr96,(1<<PGSIZE)/512;burst count
        sub       gr96,gr96,2
        const     gr100,512
```

The page–out routine, like the page–in routine makes use of burst–mode data copying to greatly speed up the processes of data moves.

```
more_out:
        loadm     0,0,lr0,gr99      ;read in a block
        storem    0,0,lr0,gr97      ;copy out a block
        add       gr97,gr97,gr100  ;advance pointer
        jmpfdec   gr96,more_out
        add       gr99,gr99,gr100  ;advance pointer
        jmp       page_in           ;gr98 pnts word 0
        nop
```

6.4.8 Cache Set Locked

The signal processing software, like the trapware, has its code ordered to deal with the most frequently occurring events first. This results in shorter processing

---

times. There is no need to burden the simpler tasks with overheads supporting the operation of less frequently occurring events. However, this does lead to some repetition in code for the most infrequent signal processing events. For example, if a page must be copied–out and all the pages are marked dirty, then the PTEs in the set must be scanned again to find a unlocked page. The selected page is then paged–out.

```
;All pages are dirty, page-out a non locked page

all_dirty:
        const   gr100,(1<<C_COLUMNS)-1;column counter
lock_loop:
        jmpt    gr100,cache_locked
         and    gr96,gr96,((1<<C_COLUMNS)-1)<<3
        add     gr99,gr98,gr96  ;column wrap
        load    0,0,gr97,gr99   ;load word 1
        add     gr96,gr96,8     ;next PTE entry
        sll     gr99,gr97,31-6  ;test PGM[0] lock
        jmpt    gr99,lock_loop
         sub    gr100,gr100,1   ;dec column count
;
        jmp     page_selected:
        nop
```

If all pages associated with the current set are marked locked, then the signal handler arranges to have the DRAM page mapped directly to the faulting virtual address. This reduces the access times for all data and instructions contained in the page. The algorithm does not try and restore the page to SRAM at a later date

```
;All columns for the current set are locked.
;Map the virtual address to non-cache secondary memory.

cache_locked:
        srl     gr96,tav,PGSIZE+5;form VTAG
        sll     gr96,gr96,PGSIZE+5
        mfsr    gr97,mmu        ;get TID
        and     gr97,gr97,0xff
        or      gr96,gr96,gr97  ;or in TID
        const   gr97,0x4700     ;VE|UR|UW|UE
        or      gr97,gr96,gr97  ;or in permissions
        mfsr    gr98,lru
        mttlb   gr98,gr97       ;assign Word 0
;
        add     gr98,gr98,1
        srl     gr96,tav,PGSIZE ;form RPN
        sll     gr96,gr96,PGSIZE
        mttlb   gr98,gr96       ;assign Word 1
```

6.4.9 Returning from Signal Handler

When the signal handler has completed its processing, the context of the processor at the time of the original TLB trap must be restored and execution continued.

First, the user's global registers, temporarily made use of by the operating system, must be restored from the Supervisor memory stack. Interrupts must be disabled and the processor state frozen while the special support registers are restored from the signal frame. Once this has been accomplished and the memory stack is restored to its pre–trap value, an IRET instruction is used to restart the instruction in execute at the time the translation trap was taken.

```
;Pop registers of supervisor mode stack and
;return to program causing the TLB miss.

ret_user:
        pop     gr100,kmsp
        pop     gr99,kmsp
        pop     gr98,kmsp
        pop     gr97,kmsp
        pop     gr96,kmsp
;
        mtsrim  cps,0x73        ;disable interrupts
        pop     tav,kmsp        ;restore tav
        mtsrim  cps,0x473       ;turn on FREEZE
        popsr   ops,it0,kmsp
        popsr   alu,it0,kmsp
        popsr   chc,it0,kmsp
        popsr   chd,it0,kmsp
        popsr   cha,it0,kmsp
        popsr   pc2,it0,kmsp
        popsr   pc1,it0,kmsp
        popsr   pc0,it0,kmsp
        pop     rab,kmsp        ;pop rab
        pop     it1,kmsp        ;pop rsp
        add     gr1,it1,0       ;alu operation
        add     kmsp,kmsp,4     ;discount signal
        iret
```

6.4.10 Support Routines

The example code used two support routines to copy the 128 32–bit local registers to and from the Supervisor memory stack. Most operating systems assign all of the local registers for use by the user's application code. The large number of registers effectively implements a data cache. The advantage to having several registers is that, unlike data memory, the register file supports simultaneous read and write access. In order to support maximum length data bursts on page transfers, the register file is made available to the signal processing routine.

```
;Push local registers onto Supervisor M-stack

store_locals:
        const   gr96,512        ;Window Size
        sub     kmsp,kmsp,gr96
        mtsrim  cr,128-1        ;save 128 registers
```

```
        jmpi    gr100           ;return
          storem 0,0,1r0,kmsp


;Pop local registers off Supervisor M-stack

load_locals:
        const   gr96,512        ;Window Size
        mtsrim  cr,128-1        ;load 128 registers
        loadm   0,0,1r0,kmsp
        jmpi    gr100           ;return
        add     kmsp,kmsp,gr96
```

6.4.11 Performance Gain

The benefits of using a software controlled cache to take advantage of limited SRAM availability should be seen in reduced average number of cycles per application instruction. Ideally the cache performance should approach that of a single large SRAM memory system. However, the cost of TLB and cache maintenance is not insignificant, especially when small page sizes are used. Figure 6-15 and Figure 6-16 show the effective average cycle times per instruction observed for a 128 page cache system. The cache memory was 2–1 and the secondary memory 4–1.

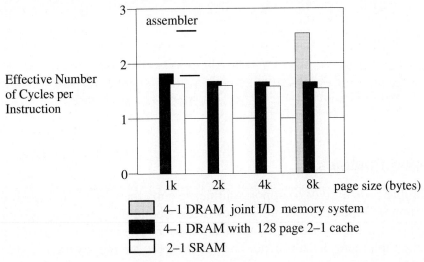

Figure 6-15. Cache Performance Gains with the Assembly Utility

Compare results for the smallest cache system of 128 1K byte cache pages. The effective performance is more divergent from the maximum achievable SRAM performance with this cache size. When the page size is 2K bytes or greater, the cache overhead reduces noticeably. With a DRAM–only system, an 8K byte page size would be selected to reduce TLB handler support overheads. This means the 128K

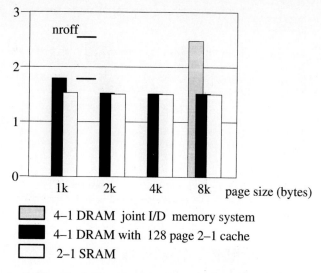

Figure 6-16. Cache Performance Gains with NROFF Utility

byte cache model should really be compared with the 8K byte DRAM only model. In this case, the cache achieved an average performance gain of 28% for the two utility programs tested.

Using a cache has some additional benefits for embedded systems. Often initialization code and data are placed in EPROM, which can be slow to access. When the EPROM is accessed, the associated page would be automatically copied to SRAM. Additionally, application read/write data which is not located in a uninitialized data (BSS) section, and therefore requires initialization before the application program commences, would be automatically initialized from the EPROM data pages. This will remove the burden from the operating system routines responsible for application environment initialization.

The software controlled cache benefits become larger when the secondary DRAM memory becomes relatively slower. Figure 6-17 shows a comparison of a 4–2 DRAM system with a 128 1K byte page SRAM. The benchmark programs show an average performance gain of 39.4%.

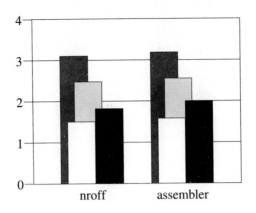

Effective Number of Cycles Per Instruction

Joint I/D memory system

■ 4–2 DRAM 8K pages
▨ 4–1 DRAM 8K pages
■ 4–2 DRAM with 128 1K byte page 2–1 cache
□ 2–1 SRAM   8K pages

Figure 6-17. Comparing Cache Based Systems with DRAM Only Systems

Chapter 7

Software Debugging

This chapter supports software engineers wishing to develop application code or operating system code for execution on a 29K RISC microprocessor.

Debugging tools which can be used in both a hardware and software debugging role, such as in–circuit emulators and logic analyzers, are not described; that is left to the individual tool manufacturer. The material presented concentrates on describing the operation of inexpensive tools based on the MiniMON29K debug monitor and Universal Debug Interface (UDI).

Also described are processor features which were specifically included in the design for the purpose of debugging. The precise details of how these features are configured to build a debug monitor such as MiniMON29K will not be described in detail. This chapter is not intended to show how debug tools are constructed, but rather to show how existing tools can be utilized and describe their inherent limitations. However, readers wishing to build their own tools will be able to glean the information required.

7.1   REGISTER ASSIGNMENT CONVENTION

The 29K processor calling convention divides the processor registers into two groups: those available to the run–time application, and hence used by compiler generated code, and those reserved for operating system use.

All the 29K processor's 128 local registers, used to implement the register stack cache, are allocated to application code use. In addition, 32 (*gr96–gr127*) of the 64 global registers are assigned to application use, and the remaining group of 32 (*gr64–gr95*) are for operating system use.

The processor does not assign any particular task to the global registers in the operating system group. However, over time a convention has evolved among 29K processor users. The subdivision of global registers *gr64–gr95* into sub groups was described in section 3.3 (page 117), and is widely adhered to; the methods presented in this chapter shall continue with the convention.

The subgroups are known as: The interrupt Freeze mode temporaries (given synonyms *it0–it3*); the operating system temporaries (*kt0–kt11*); and the operating system static support registers (*ks0–ks15*).

7.2 PROCESSOR DEBUG SUPPORT

7.2.1 Execution Mode

The processor is in Supervisor mode whenever the SM–bit in the Current processor Status register (CPS) is 1. If the SM bit is 0, the processor is executing in User mode. When operating in User mode the processor cannot access protected resources or execute privileged instructions.

Generally a processor maintains context information which refers to operating system status and various user processes. Operating in User mode is a means of preventing a User mode process from accessing information which belongs to another task or information that the operating system wishes to keep hidden.

If a User mode task breaks any of the privilege rules described in the processor's User Manual, then a protection violation trap is taken. Traps cause the operating system to regain control of execution. Typically the operating system will then send a software signal to the User mode process reporting its violation and possibly stopping its execution. The exact action which takes place is particular to each operating system implementation.

Besides preventing User mode programs from using processor instructions which are reserved for operating use only, an operating system can precisely control a processes access to memory and registers. This can be very useful when debugging User mode software. The following section describes the processor's memory management support. The register protection scheme is very simple. Special register RBP is used to restrict banks of global registers to Supervisor mode access only. Each bank consists of 16 registers and a 1 in each RBP bit position restricts the corresponding bank to Supervisor mode access only. Thus, it is normal to set RBP=0x3F, which allows User mode processes to access global registers *gr96* and higher. These are the only registers which can be affected by compiler generated code. Note however, global registers *gr0* and *gr1* which perform special support tasks are effected by compiler generated code and their access is not restricted by the RBP protection scheme.

7.2.2 Memory Access Protection

A number of the 29K processor family members are equipped with a Translation Look–aside buffer (TLB). It is intended for construction of a Memory Management Unit (MMU) scheme. A complete description of the TLB operation is given in *Memory Management Unit* (Chapter 6).

An MMU is normally used to provide virtual memory support. However, it can also play an important debugging role, even in embedded applications. Note, this function is not intended to be performed by the Region Mapping facility provided on some family members. The Region Mapping facility does not support the address space granularity supported by the TLB hardware. In addition, Region Mapping in some cases only allows address mapping to a limited region of physical memory. For example, on the Am29200 microcontroller, only the DRAM memory and not the ROM memory can be accessed in virtual address space.

When code is being developed, often an erroneous data reference will occur. If no memory is located at the particular address then the target memory system should generate a hardware access error (such as DERR or IERR on some family members). However, address aliasing often results in the access being performed on some other address location for which address decoding determines physical memory has been assigned. This kind of programming bug can be difficult to detect. Using the TLB, address access errors can be immediately detected and reported to the operating systems via access protection violations.

The OS–boot operating system, used by many customers, can provide memory access protection by mapping virtual address to physical addresses in a one–to–one format. This is adequate for many embedded applications where memory paging does not occur and application programs can be completely located in available memory. When an access violation occurs OS–boot informs the MiniMON29K monitor who reports the violation to the process controlling debugging. The details of this mechanism are described in later sections.

Whether you intend using OS–boot or some other operating system, it is likely you would benefit from using the on–chip TLB hardware to support a more powerful debug environment, via the detection of invalid memory references.

7.2.3 Trace Facility

Using the Trace Facility, a program can be executed one instruction at a time. This allows the execution of a program to be followed and the state of the processor to be examined and modified after each instruction has executed.

The 29K family has a four stage pipeline: Fetch, Decode, Execute and Write–back. Tracing is enabled by setting the Trace enable (TE) bit in the CPS register. When an instruction passes from the execute stage of the pipeline into the write–back stage, the TE bit is copied into the TP bit. The Trap Pending (TP) bit is also located in the CPS register, and when it becomes set the processor takes a trace trap.

The Supervisor mode code normally arranges for the vector table entry for the trace trap to cause the debug monitor to gain control of the processor.

The debug monitor, normally MiniMON29K, uses the IRET instruction to re-start program execution after the Trace trap handler has completed. Execution of an IRET causes the Old Processor Status register (OPS) to be copied into the CPS register before the next program instruction is executed. The TP bit in the OPS is normally cleared by the debug monitor before the IRET is executed. If the TE bit in the OPS is set then tracing of the restarted instruction sequence shall continue after executing the IRET.

Note, when the disable all (DA) bit in the CPS register is set the trace trap cannot be taken unless the processor supports Monitor mode (described below). Should the program being debugged issue an instruction such as ASNEQ, it will then take a trap and the DA bit will become set. The OPS and CPS registers will have the TP bit set but a trace trap will not be taken. This means that Freeze mode code (trap handlers which execute with the DA bit set) cannot be debugged by a software debug monitor unless the processor supports Monitor mode. Most members of the 29K processor family do not support Monitor mode.

7.2.4 Program Counter register PC2

The instruction following a branch instruction, known as the delay instruction, is executed regardless of the outcome of the branch. This performance improving technique requires that two registers be used to record the addresses of the instructions currently in the execute and decode stages of the processor pipeline. When a branch is taken the PC0 register contains the address of the target instruction as it enters the decode stage of the pipeline. Register PC1 always contains the address of the instruction in execute. When the target instruction of a branch enters decode the instruction in execute is the delay slot instruction following the branch.

Program counter registers PC0 and PC1 are required to restart the processor pipe–line in the event of a trap or an interrupt occurring. Many of the synchronous traps, such as a register access privilege violation, cause execution to be stopped with the address of instruction causing the violation held in PC1 (execute address). Asynchronous traps, such as an external interrupt, and instruction traps, such as AS-SERT instructions, cause the address of the instruction following the one in execute at the time of the interrupt to be held in the PC1 register. In fact when a trap or inter-rupt is taken the PC register values are frozen and used to restart program execution later. The frozen PC values are held in a 3 register PC–buffer. Of course, the actual PC registers continue to be used. Instructions such as MTSR and MFSR (move–to and move–from special register) can be used to modify the PC–buffer register values.

The address of the instruction previously in execute and now in write–back is held in the PC2 register. This is very convenient because a debugger can determine the instruction which was in execute at the time the interrupt or trap occurred. The trace trap is an asynchronous trap, and thus after the trap is taken the next instruction about to execute is addressed by PC1. Some family members support Instruction Breakpoint registers, which can be used to stop execution when a certain address reaches execute. When this occurs a synchronous trap is taken and the instruction is stopped before execution is completed.

Debug monitors, such as MiniMON29K, understand the operation of the PC registers and can use them to control program execution. When MiniMON29K is used with a processor which has no Breakpoint registers, a technique relying on temporarily replacing instructions with illegal opcode instructions is used to implement breakpoints. Illegal opcode instructions are used in preference to trap instructions because execution is stopped with the PC–buffer recording execution a cycle earlier. That is, the breakpoint address is in PC1 rather than PC2, as would happen with a trap instruction.

One further useful feature of the PC2 register occurs when breakpoints are set to the first instruction of a new instruction sequence — typically the first instruction of a procedure. When the breakpoint is *taken* and program execution is stopped, the PC2 register contains the address of the delay slot instruction executed before the new instruction sequence started. This is very useful in determining where a program was previously executing.

7.2.5 Monitor Mode

Monitor Mode only applies to the Am29050 processor. If a trap occurs when the DA bit in the CPS register is a 1, the processor starts executing at address 16 in instruction ROM space. Monitor Mode is not entered as a result of asynchronous events such as timer interrupts or activation of the TRAP(1–0) or INTR(3–0) lines.

On taking a Monitor Mode trap the Reason Vector register (RSN) is set by the processor to indicate the cause of the trap. Additionally, the MM bit in the CPS register is set to 1. When the MM bit is set, the shadow program counters (SPC0, SPC1, and SPC2) are frozen, in a similar way to the FZ bit freezing the PC0–PC2 buffer registers. Because the shadow program counters continue to record PC-BUS activity when the FZ bit is set, they can be used to restart Freeze Mode execution. This is achieved by an IRET or IRETINV instruction being executed while in Monitor Mode.

Monitor mode traps are used by monitors in the debugging of trap and interrupt handlers and are not intended for operating system use.

7.2.6 Instruction Breakpoints

Some members of the 29K processor family (notably the Am29050 processor) support Instruction Breakpoint registers. These registers can be used to stop a programs execution when an instruction at a specified address enters execute. The control mechanism for Breakpoints is flexible, allowing a User process ID to be specified.

Breakpoints can be assigned to Instruction space or ROM space. Both of these spaces normally contain instructions but the ROM space typically contains ROM rather than RAM memory devices. No matter which kind of memory device is utilized the Breakpoint registers can be used.

When a processor does not support Breakpoint registers, illegal instructions or traps are used to stop execution at desired address locations. Debug monitors are, however, unable to manipulate instructions which are located in ROM devices. Thus the main uses of the Breakpoint register is to support breakpoints when ROM devices are in use. Additionally, they are used in the rare case where a 3–bus Harvard architecture memory system is constructed without providing a means for the processor to read and write instruction space. In this case the processor will not be able to replace instructions at a breakpoint addresses with temporary illegal instructions.

The MiniMON29K debug monitor, described in detail later, must make some decision about the values to put in the breakpoint register fields: BTE (break on translation enable) and BPID. However, at the time a breakpoint is installed the debugcore does not know: first, if the operating system will run with address translation turned on; and second, the process identifier (PID) of the application process. Thus not until **dbg_iret** in the debugcore is called will the monitor fill–in these fields by examining the processor special registers OPS and MMU.

7.3   THE MiniMON29K DEBUGGER

Developers of software for embedded applications are used to working with emulators. They enable code to be down–loaded to application memory or installed in substitute overlay memory. This avoids having the development delays associated with running code from EPROM. The use of emulators may be a necessary stage in first getting the target hardware functional; for this task their ability to work with partially functioning hardware makes them indispensable. However, once the processor is able to execute out of target system memory and a communications channel such as a serial link is available, the need for an emulator is reduced. Emulators are expensive, and it is not always possible to make one available to each team member. The use of a debug monitor such as the MiniMON29K monitor during the software debug stage of a project is an economical alternative to an emulator.

The MiniMON29K monitor is not intended to be a standalone monitor. That is, it requires the support of a software module known as the Target Interface Process (TIP). The TIP executes on a separate host processor. The embedded 29K target processor communicates with the TIP via a serial link or other higher performance channel (see Figure 7-1). The User–Interface process, known as the Debugger Front

---

End (DFE), communicates with the TIP via the inter–process communication mechanism known as UDI which is described later.

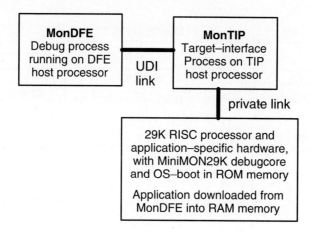

Figure 7-1. MinMON29k Debugger Components

Most monitors do not offer high level language support. Assembly code instructions must be debugged rather than the original, say C, code. Using GDB in conjunction with the MiniMON29K monitor enables source level code to be debugged, which is far more productive and necessary for large software projects. (More on this in the UDI section).

MiniMON29K has a small memory requirement, for both instruction memory and data memory of the target 29K system. The size is reduced by implementing much of the support code in the TIP host machine, and communicating with the target via high–level messages. The amount of communication required is reduced by incorporating sophisticated control mechanisms in the target debugcore.

Much of the following discussion in this section, is concerned with describing the operating principles of target hardware software components. Other Mini-MON29K components such as MonTIP and MonDFE are described in the later UDI sections.

7.3.1 The Target MiniMON29K Component

The embedded portion of the MiniMON29K monitor must be installed in target system ROM or down–loaded by the host via a shared memory interface. The target application code and additional operating system code can then be down–loaded via the message system. If changes to the code are required, then the message system can be used to quickly down–load new code without changing any ROM devices.

The software installed in the target hardware consists of a number of modules, described in Figure 7-2. When the embedded Am29000 processor is reset, the initial

---

operating system module, OS, takes control. This module initializes the processor and the other support modules. The monitor components are required to implement a message communications driver and a debug control core (debugcore).

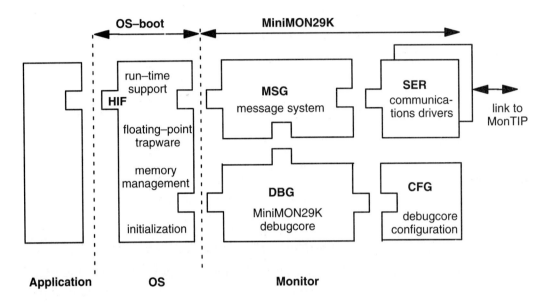

Figure 7-2. 29K Target Software Module Configuration

The operating system module is not part of the MiniMON29K monitor. This allows developers to build their own operating system or make use of a 3rd–party real–time executive product. However, AMD does supply processor initialization code and HIF system call support routines. HIF is an embedded system call interface specification, which many of the 29K processor support library services make use of. The AMD supplied operating system code is known as *OS–boot*, and it is normally supplied in the same ROM containing the MiniMON29K target component software. (All of the OS–boot and MiniMON29K 29K source code is freely available from AMD).

7.3.2 Register Usage

The debugcore, message driver and other MiniMON29K monitor modules do not require any processor registers to be reserved for their use. This means that all the processor registers are available for use by the operating system and application code.

What this really means is that any registers temporarily used by MiniMON29K code are always restored. The only exception to this occurs with global register *gr4* and the TE and TP bits of the CPS special register.

Global register *gr4* is implemented in some members of the 29K family but not reported in the relevant User Manual, as it is never used by application or operating system code. With family members which have no *gr4* register, the ALU forwarding logic can be used to keep a *temporary* register *alive* for 1 processor cycle following its modification. The *gr4* data is lost during the write–back stage when there is no real *gr4* register in the global register file. Note, software such as the MiniMON29K debugcore can be difficult to debug because emulators also make use of *gr4* in analyzing processor registers.

The TE and TP bits, located in the Current Processor Status register, *belong* to the MiniMON29K debugcore. However, the CPS register really belongs to the operating system and the OS should not modify the TE and TP bits which are maintained by the debugcore. When the operating system issues an IRET instruction it updates the CPS register with the contents of the OPS register. Normally the debugcore will set the TE bit in the OPS before the operating system performs an IRET. However, initially the operating system must call the support routine **dbg_iret()** to perform the IRET on behalf of the operating system. This gives the debugcore an opportunity to gain control of the TE bit.

7.3.3 The Debugcore

The TIP host processor controlling the target 29K processor sends messages via the available link to the debugcore module. The message system enables the host to examine and change registers and memory in the target hardware. Program execution can also be controlled via instruction breakpoints and single stepping instructions. Messages are provided specifically for controlling processor execution.

The debugcore decodes the messages, giving access to the 29K processor registers and the target system memory. However, it does not access the non–processor resources directly. The access control module supports the peek and poke functions shown below. These functions are used for all non–register space target hardware access. Note, all functions and data variables defined in the configuration Mini-MON29K module begin with the **cfg_** prefix.

```
void cfg_peek(to, from, count, space, size)


void cfg_poke(to, from, count, space, size)
```

The peek function is used to read from target space into temporary debug core BSS memory space. The poke function is used when writing to target space. The 'space' parameter is used to indicate the target address space, according to the received message parameters. Typical space field values would enable instruction space, data space or I/O space access. The 'size' field is used to indicate the size, in bytes, of the objects being transferred. The CFG module normally tries to make memory accesses in the size indicated. However, if a memory system does not support, say, byte–write access to ROM–space, then the CFG access functions can be configured to perform byte manipulation via word–sized memory accesses. By keeping the access functions separate, a user can configure the peek and poke functions for any special requirements without having to understand the debugcore module. Peek and poke functions are supplied for typical existing target hardware.

When the target processor stops executing operating system or application code, a context switch occurs into the debugcore context. The state of the processor is recorded when switching context, thus enabling execution to be resumed without any apparent interruption. The debugcore context may be entered for a number of reasons, such as: a message was received from the TIP host, an instruction breakpoint was encountered, a memory access violation occurred. Whenever the debugcore gains control a 'halt' message is sent to the TIP host processor. The TIP host and target can then exchange messages as necessary to analyses or change the state of the processor or memory.

7.3.4 Debugcore installation

It is very simple to install the debugcore with any operating system. Mainly, what is required is use of a number of Vector Table entries which are not normally required for operating system operation. And to call the debugcore initialization routine **dbg_control**(). Figure 7-3 shows the vector table entries required. The two most obvious entries are for trap number 0 (illegal opcode) and number 15 (trace trap). These table entries point to the debugcore entry labels **dbg_V_bkpt** and **dbg_V_trace**, respectively. Note, all the DBG module functions and data structure names begin with the **dbg_** prefix.

The operating system is responsible for inserting the necessary address labels into the vector table. Any vector table entries which are not required by the operating system can be *defaulted* to the debugcore, via the **dbg_trap** entry. When this entry is used, register *gr64* should contain the original trap number. It can be very useful to direct traps such as protection violation (number 5) and Data TLB protection Violation (number 13) into the debugcore. This is much better than just issuing a HALT instruction in the operating system. When a trap is taken into the debugcore a message is sent to the MonTIP process which will inform the DFE process when execution has halted. DFEs such as MonDFE and GDB understand the 29K trap number assignment and can report a trap number 13 as a User mode data protection violation (Segmentation fault in UNIX language).

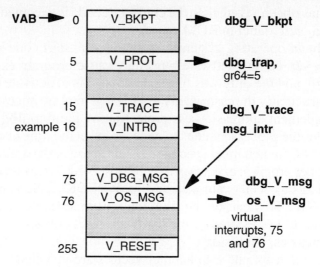

Figure 7-3. Vector Table Assignment for Debugcore

Initializing the vector table is part of what is known as the operating system cold–start code. The operating system start–up sequence is shown in Figure 7-4.

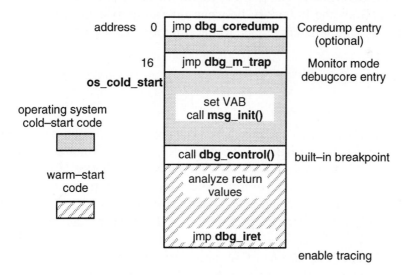

Figure 7-4. Processor Initialization Code Sequence

When the processor's power is applied, or when the *RESET pin is asserted, the CPU begins executing instructions at location 0 in ROM instruction space (ROM space and instruction space are the same in many 29K family members). Control is usually passed directly to the operating system cold–start code. To save the contents of all the processor's registers before the system is initialized, the user may modify the code in the operating system to jump to the debugger core–dump facility. Once the registers have been saved, then the cold–start code is executed by passing control to the **os_cold_start** label in ROM space.

Normally an operating system will begin cold–start code immediately at address 0. However, certain software bugs may cause program execution to become out–of–control, and the only way to regain control is to activate the processor reset pin. This is particularly the case when the TLB registers are not used by the operating system to implement address access protection. A jump to **dbg_coredump** at address 0, enables the processor states to be recorded at the time reset was asserted. By examining the PC and channel special registers some understanding of the cause of the loss of proper program execution may be observed. To restart execution after the core–dump data has been examined, a MiniMON29K RESET message must be issued by MonTIP. This causes the **dbg_trap_num** variable to be cleared and the processor state to be restored to the hardware reset condition before execution is started at address **os_cold_start**.

After the interrupt and trap handler vectors are installed, the cold–start code performs one–time initialization of target system hardware, then calls **msg_init()** to initialize the message system and and underlying communication drivers.

When the cold–start sequence is complete, a call is made to **dbg_control()** which initializes the debugcore. The point at which the entry point to the debugcore is made actually defines the boundary between operating system cold–start and warm–start code. The parameters passed to the function are shown below:

```
return_struct dbg_control(
int    dbg_trap_num,          /* lr2 value */
int*   os_info_p)             /* lr3 value */
```

It is called just like a C language routine. Local register *lr2* contains a copy of the value held at memory location **dbg_trap_num**. Register *lr3* contains the address of a data structure which describes the memory layout of the target system. The operating system is responsible for determining the amount and address range of available memory. Although this information is passed to the debugcore, it does not itself require this information. It merely keeps a record of the relevant data structure address so it can pass the information to the DFE process. Debug tool users interact with the DFE and generally like to know about the target memory availability. Figure 7-5 shows the layout of the structure passed to the debugcore. Note, where a 29K system is based on a single memory space containing both instructions and data, the **d_mem**, **i_mem** and **r_mem** parameters are the same.

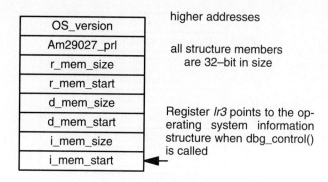

	higher addresses
OS_version	
Am29027_prl	all structure members
r_mem_size	are 32–bit in size
r_mem_start	
d_mem_size	
d_mem_start	Register *lr3* points to the op-
i_mem_size	erating system information structure when dbg_control()
i_mem_start	is called

Figure 7-5.   Operating System Information Passed to dbg_control()

The *lr2* parameter is required to know if a call to **dbg_coredump** has already been performed. Whenever the debugcore is entered the variable **dbg_trap_num** takes on the trap number causing debugcore invocation; for example number 15 when a trace trap occurs. When a core dump has been performed then trap number 255 is recorded. And when the debugcore is reentered with this number the state of the processor is not recorded again.

This is necessary because the call to **dbg_control()** appears as a built–in breakpoint. Whenever a breakpoint is taken the complete state of the processor is recorded, in effect a context switch into the debugcore occurs. The original context is restored when the debugcore receives a GO or STEP message from the MonTIP process. Whenever the debugcore gains control a HALT message is sent to MonTIP. Under DFE direction, MonTIP can then send messages to the debugcore to examine and change the saved processor status.

The debugcore records the return address for **dbg_control()** when it is first called. The address is important because it is the start of the operating system warm–start code. When an application program is down–loaded to the target hardware, an INIT message is normally sent. The message contains information extracted from the application COFF file. This information along with other operating system run–time support data is passed to the operating system when the **dbg_control()** function returns. As is normal for C procedures, the return information is placed in global registers starting with *gr96*. Figure 7-6 shows the format of the operating system warm–start data.

gr105	this register always 0
gr104	Operating system control info.
gr103	start of command line args (argv)
gr102	register stack size
g101	memory stack size
gr100	first instruction of User loaded code
gr99	end address of program data
gr98	start address of program data
gr97	end address of program text
gr96	start address of program text

Figure 7-6. Return Structure from dbg_control()

After the DFE (MonDFE for example) has been instructed to load a new program into memory, the return registers can be examined to verify their contents. Note, with some DFEs it is possible to load a COFF file without sending an INIT message. In this case the *return registers* are not affected and the PCs are not forced to the **dbg_control()** return address.

After loading a program a user will normally start execution, which causes the debugcore to switch out of context and restore the context described in the register shadow memory. If an INIT message was received then execution will commence in the operating system warm–start code. Otherwise, it continues from wherever the restored PC registers are located. Warm–start code normally examines the return structure values and prepares the operating system run–time support accordingly. For example, register *gr100* contains the start address of the down–loaded application program. The address value may be loaded in the PC–buffer registers before an IRET instruction is used to start program execution. However, it is important to note that the warm–start operation is entirely operating system dependent, and the code need pay no attention to the return structure information. The operation of OS–boot, normally supplied along with MiniMON29K, is described in a later section.

7.3.5 Advanced DBG and CFG Module Features

Normally the call to **dbg_control()** implies that a *built–in* breakpoint should be taken. This gives the user an opportunity to down–load an application program before execution is continued. However, by setting the call *lr2* parameter to V_NOBRK (254), no breakpoint will be taken and the call will return with no need for a GO message from MonTIP. This enables the debugcore to be initialized for operation, and is useful where there is no requirement to download an application program. Of course there are no call return values for the operating system warm–start to examine. The facility enables the debugcore to remain in a final system and only be called upon in a *emergency* such as memory access violation.

The CFG module is used to configure the operation of the DBG module. There is really no need to have the source code for the DBG module, only the CFG module. After configuring the CFG, it can be assembled and linked with the **.o** debug core modules (**dbg_core.o** and **dbg.o**). The CFG supplies the **cfg_peek()** and **cfg_poke()** functions, as well as defining the number of breakpoints supported and the size of the debugcore message send buffer. Note, however, that there is conditional assembly code in the CFG module for a wide range of target hardware systems. In practice configuring CFG normally means defining the correct symbol value during assembly.

Whenever the debugcore is entered, the routine **cfg_core_enter()** is called. This gives the debugcore user an opportunity to control the state of the processor during debugcore operation. For example, normally the debugcore runs with the on–chip timer turned off. This means no timer progress is made and no timer interrupts will occur while the debugcore is in context. The timer can be re–enabled by changing the code in **cfg_core_enter().** The supplied code also locks the processor cache (only with processor members supporting cache). This prevents application and operating system relevant data being displaced with debugcore information.

The debugcore is mainly written in the C language and makes use of application space processor registers during its operation. On taking, say, a breakpoint and entering the debugcore, all the processor registers are copied to *shadow* memory locations. Users examine and change the shadow values before they are returned to registers when the debugcore context is exited. It is possible that an external hardware device could generate an interrupt when the debugcore is *in–context* (interrupts may be enabled in the **cfg_core_enter()** procedure). This could cause some confusion as the interrupt handler may wish to modify some operating system assigned registers to record a change in the interrupting device status. The change would be lost when the debugcore exited. To overcome this problem, global registers *gr64–gr95* are not shadowed if memory location **dbg_shadow_os** contains a 0 (normally set to –1). This can be done in the **cfg_core_enter()** procedure.

When **dbg_shadow_os** is cleared, physical registers *gr64–gr95* are always accessed with MiniMON29K READ and WRITE messages. However, messages such as FIND and COPY operate on the shadow copies only, and this creates some minor restrictions in debugcore operation.

If **cfg_core_enter()** is modified to enable the on–chip timer to continue interrupting during debugcore operation, then memory location **dbg_shadow_timer** should also be set to 0 (normally –1). This prevents the TMR and TMC timer special registers from being restored from their corresponding shadow memory locations when the debugcore context is exited.

Interrupts must be enabled during debugcore operation if, say, an interrupt driven UART is being used for MiniMON29K message communication. It is sometimes possible to use the message system in a poll–mode (described in the following section), in this case interrupts can be disabled. Additionally, it may be possible to selectively enable device interrupts in **cfg_core_enter**(). However, care should be taken if any of the interrupts require C level context for interrupt processing. The debugcore continues to use the register stack in place at the time the debugcore was entered. The debugcore will not need to lower the stack support registers, but any C level interrupt handler may make temporary use of the stack (this is very much operating system dependent). Further, it is important that no attempt is made to reenter the debugcore, via, say, a memory access error during an interrupt service routine which interrupted the debucore operation.

7.3.6 The Message System

After the message system has been initialized with a call to **msg_init**(), the debugcore responds to MonTIP host messages appropriately and sends acknowledge messages to the host containing any requested data. The operating system can also make use of the message system to support application services such as access to the file system on the TIP host machine. The **msg_send**() function is used to request a single message be sent. A similar function is made available by the message system module on the TIP host processor.

```
int  msg_send(struct message *msg_pointer);
```

The function returns 0 if the message was accepted for sending and –1 if the message system is currently too busy. Variable **msg_sbuf_p** is maintained by MSG to point to the message buffer currently being sent. When this variable becomes 0, the message system is ready to send another message. The message buffer pointer passed to **msg_send**() is copied into **msg_sbuf_p** the contents of the buffer are not copied. Thus the user must be careful not to modify the buffer data until the message has been completely sent.

Messages are received by asking the message system to poll the message driver hardware until a message is available. Function **msg_wait_for**() is provided for this task. Alternatively, the message system can interrupt the operating system or the debugcore when a message is received from the TIP host processor. Received messages are normally located at address **msg_rbuf**. There is no danger of the receive buffer being over written by a new in–coming message, as the MonTIP always expects to receive a message before it will reply with a new message to the target.

7.3.7 MSG Operation

The MSG module may require the support of communications port specific driver modules, most notably the SER module. This module contains the code neces-

---

sary to talk to serial communication UARTs which support target and MonTIP connection. The MSG contains a number of shared memory communication drivers for IBM PC–AT plug–in cards, such as, the PCEB, EB29K, YARC and others.

Messages all have the same format, a 32–bit message number then a 32–bit length field, followed by any message related data. When the MSG determines that a new message has been received, and its message number is greater than 64, the operating system is interrupted (if interrupts are enabled), and execution continues at the address given in the vector table for entry number V_OS_MSG (76). In OS–boot this is address **os_V_msg**. This means that the operating system does not have to poll the message interface for service request completion. The message system can be used to support HIF services (see the later OS–boot section).

Received messages with identification numbers less than 64 are intended for the debugcore. The MSG causes the debugcore to be interrupted via vector table entry V_DBG_MSG (75). This causes execution to continue at address **dbg_V_msg**. When execution begins at this address, the processor state appears as if a hardware interrupt has just occurred while executing User mode code or an operating system service. The *virtual interrupt* mechanism is used to support this technique and is described below.

7.3.8 MSG Virtual Interrupt Mechanism

Consider what happens when a UART receives a character and an interrupt is generated:

1   The UART serial driver enters Freeze mode and execution continues at the address given in the vector table for the interrupt handler. (Note, it is the operating system cold–start code's responsibility to install the trap handler for this interrupt, even if a MiniMON29K SER module driver is used).

2   Next the SER driver saves some global registers to memory.

3   The driver *talks* to the UART, receives the character and places the new data into the **msg_rbuf** buffer at the location given by the pointer **msg_next_p**. The registers are restored and the pointer incremented.

4   The SER driver then jumps (virtual vectors) to address **msg_V_arrive** in the MSG module. This whole procedure appears to the message system as if the interrupt had been directed to **msg_V_arrive** when a character arrived in its buffer.

5   The MSG saves its own working register space and examines the size of the incoming message and decides if it is complete or if more data is required. If incomplete the registers are repaired and an IRET is issued. When complete, working registers are repaired and the PC–buffer registers are updated with address of the operating system handler or debugcore handler accessed from the vector table.

Using the sequence described above, messages arrive via a V_DBG_MSG or V_OS_MSG *virtual interrupt* directly to the appropriate message processing handler. The operating system and the debugcore need never be concerned about any registers used by the MSG or SER modules in the process of preparing the received message, as their temporary register usage is kept hidden.

When interrupts are being used, rather than polling for a new message to arrive, the **msg_wait_for**() function simply returns 0 indicating that no message is available. If the SER module is making use of polling and interrupts are turned off, then the **msg_wait_for**() function returns –1 when a complete new message is available in the **msg_rbuf.** In fact the MSG sets variable **msg_rbuf_p** to point to the just–received message buffer. The debugcore interrupt handler dereferences this pointer when accessing any received messages.

7.4   THE OS–BOOT OPERATING SYSTEM

MiniMON29K is a debugger. It does not initialize the processor, service interrupts, support HIF system calls or even install itself into the target system. All these tasks must be performed by an operating system. It does seem a rather grand title but OS–boot does perform these tasks. If a user does not build an operating system or buy an operating system from a third party then OS–boot may be adequate for their project needs.

AMD generally supplies OS–boot along with MiniMON29K for each 29K evaluation system. Because OS–boot supports the HIF system call services it is useful for running evaluation software. However, OS–boot is a simple operating system, it does not support multi–tasking or other grander operating system concepts. As well as supplying MiniMON29K and OS–boot in EPROM, users get the source to OS–boot, enabling them to make any necessary changes.

Typically, users will add operating system code to support additional peripheral devices. Or, use OS–boot as a means of launching into another more sophisticated operating system. This is described in more detail later. The technique is useful because it avoids the need to install MiniMON29K with the new operating system in EPROM. The new operating system need merely be down–loaded via MiniMON29K debugger messages into available target memory.

This section does not describe OS–boot in detail. It is mainly an overview of its operation. Hopefully users will gain an understanding of its relevance in the debug processes.

7.4.1 Register Usage

According to the register usage convention, an operating system is free to use global registers in the range *gr64–gr95*. OS–boot uses a good number of these registers. Many of the floating–point instructions and some integer instructions are not implemented directly by hardware with some members of the 29K family. This requires that *trapware* be used to support the *non–existing* instructions. The floating–point trapware included with OS–boot requires as much as 15 temporary registers and three static registers to support the trapware code. OS–boot is typically configured to assign registers *it0–kt14* (*gr64–gr78*) for temporary use and *ks13–ks15* (*gr93–gr95*) for static use.

The exact register assignment for OS–boot is determined by file **register.s** in the osboot directory. Other than trapware support, registers are required for run–time management and HIF services. These registers are typically allocated from the range *ks0–ks12* (*gr80–gr92*). There are a number of free registers for those requiring to add operating system support code.

7.4.2 OS–boot Operation

Operation begins at address label **os_cold_start**. The processor special registers, such as CPS and CFG, are initialized to enable the processor start–up sequence to commence. OS–boot does not contain very much cold–start code. However, the code is complicated by the incorporation of options enabling any member of the 29K family to be dealt with.

The vector table entries are constructed. Most of the unused entries are set to cause debugcore entry. Thus, should any unexpected trap or interrupt happen the debugcore will be able to report it. The vector table is normally placed at the start of data memory.

The memory system is then analyzed in the process of building the data structure passed to **dbg_control**(). In some cases this involves the operation of dynamic memory sizing code. The floating–point trap handlers are then prepared for operation. Initialization of floating–point support is a one–time operation, so it occurs before **dbg_control**() is called.

Before the cold–start operation is complete, additional vector table entries are made to support debugcore operation, entries such as V_TRACE. The message system is then initialized with a call to **msg_init**() and **dbg_control**() is called, indicating the completion of operating system cold–start code.

The return from **dbg_control**() causes execution of the operating system warm–start code to commence at address **warm_start**. The run time environment is now prepared. Much of this is concerned with memory management. The memory and register stack support registers are assigned values before any loaded application code starts. The warm–start code examines the return parameters from **dbg_control**() in preparing the run–time environment.

With 29K family members which have TLB hardware, OS–boot is normally configured to start application code execution in User mode with address translation turned on. Warm–start code gets the application code start address from return registers *gr100*. This address is loaded into the frozen PC–buffer registers and an IRET

---

used to depart the operating system supervisor mode code and enter the application code in User mode. Register *gr104* is used to select operating system warm–start options. If bit 31 is set then application code is started with no address translation enabled. (To use this feature set *gr104* to –1 after using the MonDFE *y* command to yank–in application code into target system memory.) Note, warm–start code does not issue an IRET instruction directly, it jumps to the debugcore service **dbg_iret**. This enables the debugcore to set the TE bit in the OPS register and so enable single stepping of the first application code instruction. Additionally the BTE and BPID fields of any breakpoint registers in use are also set by **dbg_iret**.

7.4.3 HIF Services

Once application code has started, operating system code will only be again called into play when: a floating–point trap occurs; a peripheral generates an interrupt; or when a HIF service is requested. HIF is a system call interface specification. OS–boot supplies the necessary support code which is accessed by a system call trap instruction. Many of the library calls, such as **printf**(), result in HIF trapware being called. HIF trapware support starts at address label **HIFTrap**.

HIF services are divided into two groups, those that can be satisfied by the 29K itself (such as the *sysalloc* service), and those that need MonTIP support (such as *open*). The HIF specification states that the service request number be placed in register *gr121*, if this number is less than 256 then MonTIP must assist. A request for MonTIP assistance, to say, open a file for writing, is accomplished by the operating system sending a MiniMON29K message to the TIP process. There are currently three types of messages used by the OS: HIF–request, CHANNEL1 (used when printing to *stdout*), and CHANNEL0_ACK (used when acknowledging data from *stdin*). Note, it is easy to extend the operating system message system usage and create new operating system message types. This may be useful if virtual memory paging was being supported by an operating system, where the MonTIP was acting as the secondary memory controller.

MonTIP replies to HIF MiniMON29K messages by sending messages to the debugcore to accomplish the requested task. It then sends a HIF_ACK message to the operating system acknowledging the completion of the requested service.

CHANNEL1 and CHANNEL0 messages are used by the operating system to support display and keyboard data passing between the application program and the user. Note these are the only operating system messages which the MonTIP passes via UDI to the MonDFE process. MonTIP responds to *stdout* service requests with CHANNEL1_ACK message, and supplies new keyboard input characters with a CHANNEL0 message sent to the operating system. (Note, some early versions of MonTIP did not make use of the operating system *_ACK messages, they used the debugcore instead. This created difficulties for multitasking operating systems. If you have this problem, please update your MonTIP program.)

Currently, the OS–boot implementation enters Wait mode after issuing a Mini-MON29K message. This is accomplished by setting the WM bit in the OPS register before using an IRET to *return* to application code from the HIF trap handler. Wait mode is exited when the message system interrupts the operating system in response to a MonTIP reply–message to the operating system. Because Wait mode is used OS–boot must run with interrupts turned on. However, the MiniMON29K debug-core has no such restriction and can operate in a poll–mode fashion.

7.4.4 Adding New Device Drivers

OS–boot is a very simple operating system and it does not offer support for additional I/O devices. However, the HIF specification states that file descriptors 0,1 and 2 are assigned to: standard in, standard out and standard error. Normally any open() library calls issued by an application program will result in the HIF *open* service returning a new file descriptor for a file maintained on the TIP host by MonTIP.

Target hardware can often have additional UART or parallel port hardware available for communication. If OS–boot is not completely replaced with a new OS, then these devices should be accessed via the normal library/HIF interface. OS–boot can be extended to include a driver to support any new peripheral device. Each device should be pre–allocated a file descriptor value starting with number 3. All access to peripherals can then be to the pre–allocated file descriptors. If the application code calls open() then the HIF *open* service should initially return 4, or some larger number depending on the number of peripheral devices added.

The Metaware libraries, supplied with the High C 29K compiler package, pre–allocate buffer and MODE settings for file descriptors 0, 1 and 2. Assuming no access to the library source file **_iob.c**, then calls to open() should be placed inside the **crt0.s** file. These open() calls should be for each of the pre–allocated file descriptors and will result in library initialization. The code inside **crt0.o** runs before the application main() code. Note, the MODE value for the open() calls may be restricted due to driver or peripheral limitations. And communication with the devices may be required in RAW mode rather than any buffered mode supported by the library when a device is opened in COOKED mode.

When library calls, or HIF calls such as _read() or _write(), are issued for the file descriptor associated with a peripheral the OS–boot trapware for the HIF services shall call upon the required device driver to perform the requested task.

7.4.5 Memory Access Protection

The OS–boot operating system includes an optional memory access protection scheme which is useful with embedded system debugging. It only functions with 29K family members which contain TLB hardware. When used, the operating system runs application programs in User mode with address translation turned on. Thus, all application addresses are virtual, but the memory management hardware is

---

configured to map virtual to physical addresses with a one–to–one scheme. No memory paging takes place and the entire program is at all times located in the available target system memory.

The benefit of the system is that *bad* addresses, generated by unexpected program execution, can be detected immediately. The operation of the 29K Translation Look–aside Buffer (TLB) used to construct the management scheme was briefly described in previous section 7.2.2 entitled *Memory Access Protection*. This section deals with the OS–boot code implementation. For more information about operation of TLB hardware see Chapter 6 (*Memory Management Unit*)

First consider the typical OS–boot memory configuration shown in Figure 7-7. Some 29K family members have a 3–bus architecture. This enables two memory systems to be utilized, one for instruction memory and the second for data memory. If instructions are to be accessed from data memory devices, or data placed in instruction memory, then a bridge must be built between the data and instruction memory busses. Note, a single address bus is shared by both memory systems. Typically, designers will build a bridge enabling instruction memory to be accessed from data memory address space. In such case the two addresses spaces do not overlap. However, without a bridge it is possible to have physical memory located in the different address spaces but the same address offset location.

Most of the newer 29K family members have a conventional 2–bus architecture, which results in instructions and data being located in the same memory devices located in a single address space. OS–boot caters for all the different memory configuration options, and this is reflected in the layout shown in Figure 7-7.

Operating system warm–start code knows the address regions allocated to a loaded application program by examining the data structure returned from the **dbg_control**() call. OS–boot actually saves the data to memory locations for future use, as we will see. Applications can be expected to access a limited number of regions out within the data region loaded from the application COFF file. This is required to support the memory allocation heap and the register and memory stacks. The allocated access regions are shown shaded in Figure 7-7. An attempt to access an address out within allowed regions will cause the debugcore to gain control of program execution.

During normal code execution, instruction and data TLB misses will occur. This requires that the TLB registers be refreshed with a valid address translation. OS–boot trap handlers are used to perform this task. If a *bad* address is generated the trap handlers must detect it.

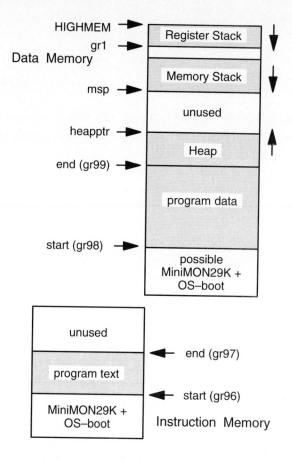

Note, Data and Instruction memory space may
overlap, or be only one single address space

Figure 7-7. Typical OS–boot Memory Layout

Two kinds of traps are expected: Instruction TLB misses and data TLB misses.
The trap handler for instruction misses is shown below. The return values from the
dbg_control(), shown in Figure 7-6, are stored by OS–boot in a structure at address
ret_struct. The PC1 value is compared with the start and end addresses of the loaded
program. If the PC1 address is within this range then a new valid TLB entry is built
and program execution restarted. If the address is out of the allowed range then a
jump to the debugcore entry point, **dbg_trap**, is taken.

```
UITLBmiss:
        mfsr    it0,pc1             ;PC address
        const   it1,ret_struct
        consth  it1,ret_struct
        load    0,0,it2,it1         ;TEXT start
```

```
            cpltu     it2,it0,it2        ;jump if
            jmpt      it2,UIinvalid      ;PC < start
             add      it1,it1,4
            load      0,0,it2,it1        ;TEXT end
            cpgtu     it2,it0,it2        ;jump if
            jmpt      it2,UIinvalid      ;PC > end
             const    it2,(VE|UE)
    one_to_one:
```

TLB register Word 0 has access control bits which separately enable Read, Write and Execution of data for the addressed page. The example code assumes that data and instructions are not located on the same page as pages containing instructions are marked for execution only.

```
    one_to_one:        ;it2 has RWE bits
            mfsr      it3,mmu            ;need page size
            srl       it3,it3,8          ;get PS bits.
            and       it3,it3,3          ;1k page min
            add       it3,it3,10+5       ;32-sets
            srl       it1,it0,it3        ;form
            sll       it1,it1,it3        ; VTAG
            or        it1,it1,it2        ;add RWE bits
            mfsr      it2,mmu            ;get PID
            and       it2,it2,0xFF
            or        it1,it1,it2        ;add PID bits
    ;
            sub       it3,it3,5          ;page size
            srl       it2,it0,it3        ;form
            sll       it2,it2,it3        ; RPN
    ;
            mfsr      it0,lru            ;select column
            mttlb     it0,it1            ;word 0
            add       it0,it0,1
            mttlb     it0,it2            ;word 1
            iret
    ;
    UIinvalid:
            jmp       dbg_trap           ;enter debugcore
             const    gr64,8
```

The data–miss trap handler is a little more complicated. The address under consideration appears in channel register CHA. The address is first tested to see if it is greater than the data region start address and less than the current heap pointer. The operating system maintained heap was initialized just above the end of the loaded program data region. If the address is not within this range then it is tested to determine if it is within the memory or register stack regions. The stacks are located at the very top of physical data memory.

```
    UDTLBmiss:
            mfsr      it0,cha            ;data address
```

```
        const   it1,ret_struct+8
        consth  it1,ret_struct+8
        load    0,0,it2,it1      ;DATA start
        cpltu   it2,it0,it2      ;jump if
        jmpt    it2,UDinvalid    ;adds < start
         cpltu  it2,it0,heapptr;adds < heapptr
        jmpt    it2,one_to_one
         const  it2,(VE|UR|UW)
stacks:
        const   it2,HIGHMEM
        consth  it2,HIGHMEM
        load    0,0,it2,it2      ;DATA end
        cpgeu   it2,it0,it2      ;jump if
        jmpt    it2,UDinvalid    ;adds >= end
         cpgeu  it2,it0,msp      ;jump if
        jmpt    it2,one_to_one ;adds>=msp
         const  it2,(VE|UR|UW)
;
UDinvalid:
        jmp     dbg_trap         ;enter debugcore
         const  gr64,9
```

The example trap handler marks data pages for read and write access only. If the CHA address does not fall within the allowed region, then a TLB entry is not built, and, normally, program execution not restarted. Instead, the debugcore is entered and the trap number passed.

7.4.6 Down Loading a New OS

One way to replace OS–boot with another operating system is to simply link the new operating system with the MiniMON29K modules and, if necessary, place the result in EPROM memory. However, many users like to keep the existing OS–boot/ MiniMON29K combination in place and down–load a new operating system using MiniMON29K messages. Assuming no changes are made to the supplied OS–boot, then, when the loaded OS's execution is started, with say a MonDFE *g* command, warm–start code will prepare for execution to begin at the first instruction of the new operating system. Generally a HIF *setrap* service call is made followed by an assertion of the assigned trap number. This allows Supervisor mode to be entered.

The new operating system must initially run in Supervisor mode to take over processor resources initially under OS–boot control. If the floating–point trap handlers are to remain installed, then the new operating system must be careful to remember their global register support requirement. If the new operating system is still supporting HIF services then it must also pay attention to the HIF trapware register usage. HIF traps will occur if any application code run by the new OS is linked with libraries intended for use with a HIF conforming operating system. However, often a new operating system will replace the HIF libraries with new libraries which do not call HIF, but make use of the system call services of the new operating system.

The HIF trapware code can be replaced with new code, whose register usage is better integrated with the new operating system, by the new system *taking over* the HIF vector table entry. If this is done, then it is likely that the operating system message interrupt handler will also be *taken over*. Unless the **os_V_msg** trap handler address is replaced, the message system will continue to call the OS–boot interrupt handler. And the associated operating system register usage should be taken into account.

The MiniMON29K message system is typically supported by low level driver code which is often interrupt driven. Most often this is a UART interrupt handler. The message system will not generate virtual interrupts if the low level handler vector table entry is taken over. This can be necessary because of interrupt overloading. For example, the Am29200 interrupt INT3 is used for all peripheral devices including the on–chip UART. A new operating system may wish to add support, for, say, DMA activity, which was not supported by OS–boot. This may require an interrupt handler activated by INTR3. If the MiniMON29K message system is to continue operation, then the new operating system must take over the INTR3 vector table entry. But, after the new operating system handler is complete it must jump to the original vector handler address rather than IRETing. This gives the message system low level interrupt handler an opportunity to run.

7.5   UNIVERSAL DEBUG INTERFACE (UDI)

Code development for an embedded processor is generally more costly than development of code of equivalent complexity intended for execution on a engineering workstation. The embedded application code can not benefit from an underlying support operating system such as UNIX. In some cases, developers may chose to first install a small debug support monitor, such as MiniMON29K, or third–party executive which can offer a somewhat improved development environment. In the process of getting an embedded support monitor running or developing application code to run directly on the processor, emulation hardware may be employed. The availability of debug tools and their configurability is an important factor when selecting a processor for an embedded project.

The architecture of the latest RISC processors may be simplified compared to their CISC predecessors, but the complexity of controlling the processor operation has not been reduced. The use of register stacks and instruction delay slots and other performance enhancing techniques has lead to increased use of high level programming languages such as C. The compiler has been given the responsibility of producing efficient assembly code, and the developer rarely deals with code which manipulates data at the processor register level. The increased productivity achievable by this approach is dependent on high level debug support tools.

Developers of products containing embedded processors are looking to RISC for future products offering increased capability. The greater performance relative to

---

RISC processor cost should make this possible. The suitability, cost and productivity of the tools available for code development are likely to be the major factor in deciding the direction ahead in preparing to tool–up for RISC.

The following sections describe the Universal Debug Interface (UDI), which is processor independent and enables greater debug tool configurability. A number of emulator and embedded monitor suppliers, as well as high level language debug tools suppliers, are currently configuring their tools to comply with the proposed UDI standard. Current implementations are targeted for RISC processor code development. UDI should ease the choice in selecting tools and, consequently, selecting RISC. This section shall concentrate on describing the Free Software Foundation's GDB C language source debugger's integration with UDI.

7.5.1 Debug Tool Developers

A debug tool developer typically arranges for their product to be available for a range of popular processors. This normally means rebuilding the tool with the knowledge required to understand the peculiarities of each processor. If an enhancement is made to the debugger user–interface, then normally the debugger source and the processor specific information must be recompiled and tested before customers are updated.

When developing code to run on an engineering workstation, the processor supporting the debugger execution is the same processor running the program being developed. This means the debugger can make use of operating system services such as ptrace() (see section 7.5.3), to examine and control the program being debugged. When developing code for an embedded application, the program being developed is know as the *Target Program* and executes on the *Target Processor* which is usually a different processor than the one supporting the debugger, known as the *Host Processor*. The host processor and target processor do not communicate via the ptrace() system call, but via whatever hardware communication path links the two processors. The portion of the debugger which controls communication with the target processor is known as the target interface module, and whenever a change or addition is required in the communications mechanism, the debugger must be once again recompiled to produce a binary executable which is specific to the target–processor and target–communications requirements.

When the chipmakers turn out their latest whiz–bang RISC processor, the tool developer companies are faced with considerable development costs in ensuring their tools function with the new architecture. It is not uncommon for the availability of debug tools to lag behind RISC chip introduction. Often tools are introduced with limited configuration options. For example, target processor communication may be according to a low level debug monitor protocol, or an in–circuit emulator (ICE) protocol. Each debugger product has its own target interface module; this module must

---

be developed for each debugger in order to communicate with the new target RISC processor.

An embedded application developer may have prior experience or a preference for a particular debug tool, but the only available communications path to the target may not be currently supported. This incompatibility may discourage the developer from choosing to use a new processor. It is desirable that debuggers share communication modules and be more adaptable to available target processor interfaces.

Ideally a debugger from one company should be able to operate with, say, an emulator from another company. This would make it possible for a customer to select a little used debugger with a popular target monitor or vice versa.

The goal of the Universal Debug Interface (UDI) is to provide a standard interface between the debugger developer and the target communications module, so the two can be developed and supplied separately. In fact, an applications developer could construct their own communications module, for some special hardware communications link, as long as it complied with the standard.

7.5.2 UDI Specification

If UDI were a specification at procedural level, then debugger developers and communication module developers would have to supply linkable images of their code so the debug tool combination could be linked by the intended user. This is undesirable because it would require a linked image for every tool combination. Additionally, the final linked program would be required to run on an single debug host. UDI actually relies on an interprocess communication (IPC) mechanism to connect two different processes. The debugger is linked into an executable program to run on the host processor, this process is known as the Debugger Front End (DFE). The communications module is linked as a separate process which runs on the same or a different host processor, this process is known as the Target interface Process(TIP). The two processes communicate via the UDI interprocess communication specification.

Two IPC mechanisms have so far been specified: one uses shared memory and is intended for DOS developers, the second uses sockets and is intended for UNIX and VMS developers. Of course, when the shared memory IPC implementation is used the DFE and TIP processes must both execute on the same host processor. Using sockets with Internet domain communication enables the DFE and TIP to each execute on separate hosts on a computer network. Thus an applications developer can, from the workstation on his desk, debug a target processor which is connected to a network node located in a remote hardware lab. Using sockets with UNIX domain addresses (the method used to implement UNIX pipes) enables both processes to run on the same host.

Some of the currently available UDI conforming debug tools are presented in Figure 7-8. The interprocess communications layer defined by UDI enables the applications developer to select any front end tool (DFE) with any of the target control tools (TIP).

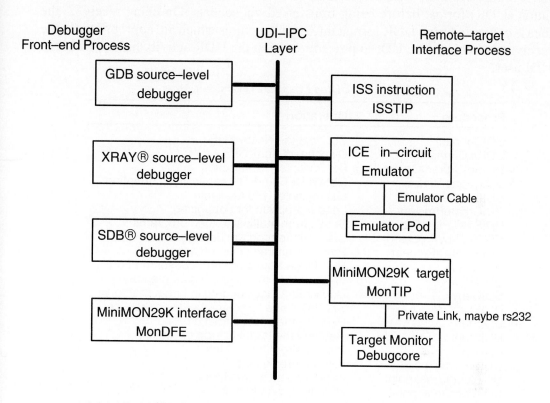

Figure 7-8. Currently Available Debugging Tools that Conform to UDI Specification

Because developers of UDI conforming tools must each have code which interfaces with the IPC mechanism according to the UDI protocol, the UDI community freely shares a library of code know as the UDI–p library. This code presents a procedural layer which hides the IPC implementation. For example, consider the following procedure:

The DFE code calls the UDIRead function which *transports* the function call to the TIP process. The TIP code developer must resolve the function request, by adding code which is specific to controlling the particular target. The IPC layer is effectively transparent, the TIP developer is unaware that the procedure caller is from a different process, possibly on a different host machine. Table 7-1 lists most of the UDI–p procedures available.

Because the DFE and TIP processes may be running on different machines, care must be taken when moving data objects between hosts. An "int" sized object on the DFE supporting machine may be a different size from an "int" on the TIP supporting machine. Further, the machines may be of different endian. The UDI–p procedures make use of a machine independent data description technique similar to the XDR library available with UNIX. Data is converted into a universal data representation (UDR) format before being transferred via sockets. On being received, the data is converted from UDR format into data structures which are appropriate for the receiving machine. The UDI–p procedures keep the UDR activity hidden from the UDI user.

Table 7-1.   UDI–p Procedures (Version 1.2)

Procedure	Operation
UDIConnect	Connect to selected TIP
UDIDisconnect	Disconnect from TIP
UDISetCurrentConnection	For multiple TIP selection
UDICapabilities	Obtain DFE and TIP capability information
UDIEnumerateTIPs	List multiple TIPs available
UDICreateProcess	Load a program for debugging
UDISetCurrentProces	Select from multiple loaded programs
UDIDestroyProcess	Discontinue program debugging
UDIInitializeProcess	Prepare runtime environment
UDIRead	Read data from target–processor memory
UDIWrite	Write data to target–processor memory
UDICopy	Duplicate a block of data in target memory
UDIExecute	Start/continue target–processor execution
UDIStep	Execute the next instruction
UDIStop	Request the target to stop execution
UDIWait	Inquire about target status
UDISetBreakpoint	Insert a breakpoint
UDIQueryBreakpoint	Inquire about a breakpoint
UDIClearBreakpoint	Remove a breakpoint

In later sections of this chapter, the development of a UDI conforming GDB, a source level debugger from the Free Software Foundation, is discussed in more detail. GDB is an example of a DFE process. As an example of a TIP process, we shall look at the MiniMON29K monitor and the Instruction Set Simulator from AMD. Most users of GDB will have some knowledge of the ptrace() system call which enables GDB to examine the state of the process being debugged. A brief description of ptrace() is beneficial along with further explanation of its unsuitability for embedded application software development.

7.5.3 P–trace

UNIX system call, ptrace(), provides a means by which a process may control the execution of another process executing on the same processor. The process being debugged is said to be "traced". However, this does not mean that the execution path of a process is recorded in a "trace buffer" as is the case with many processor emula-

---

Programming the 29K RISC Family

tors. Debugging with ptrace() relies on the use of instruction breakpoints and other hardware or processor generated signals causing execution to stop.

```
ptrace(request, pid, addr, data)
```

There are four arguments whose interpretation depends on the request argument. Generally, *pid* is the process ID of the traced process. A process being debugged behaves normally until it encounters some signal whether internally (processor) generated, like illegal instruction, or externally generated, like interrupt. Then the traced process enters a stopped state and the tracing process is notified using the wait() system call. When the traced process is in the stopped state, its core image can be examined and modified using the ptrace() service. If desired, another ptrace() request can then cause the traced process either to terminate or to continue. Table 7-2 lists the ptrace() request services available.

Table 7-2. ptrace() Services

Request	Operation
TraceMe	Declare that the process is being traced
PeekText	Read one word in the process's instruction space
PeekData	Read one word in the proceses's data space
PeekUser	Examine the processes–control data structure
PokeText	Write one word in process's text space
PokeDate	Write one word in process's data space
PokeUser	Write one word in process–control data structure
Cont	Startup process execution
Kill	Terminate the process being debugged
SingleStep	Execute the next instruction
GetRegs	Read processor register
SetRegs	Write processor register
ReadText	Read data from process's instruction space
ReadData	Read data from process's data space
WriteText	Write data into process's instruction space
WriteData	Write data into process's data space
SysCall	Continue execution until system call

Because both the process with the user–interface controlling the debugging, and the application process being debugged, may not be executing on the same processor, it is not possible to use the ptrace() system call mechanism to debug embedded application software. The debugger process (DFE) must run on a separate processor and communicate with the processor supporting execution of the application code.

The Free Software Foundation's source level debugger, GDB, makes use of the ptrace() system call. However, it can alternatively use a collection of procedures which support communication to a remote processor. These procedures implement the necessary protocols to control the hardware connecting the remote processor to the "host" debug processor. By this means, GDB can be used to debug embedded application software running on application specific hardware. The following section discusses the method in more detail.

7.5.4 The GDB–UDI Connection

GDB can, in place of ptrace(), make use of a procedural interface which allows communication with a remote target processor. Newer versions of GDB (version 3.98 and later) achieve this via procedure pointers which are members of a *target_ops* structure. The procedures currently available are listed in Table 7-3. According to GDB configuration convention, the file *remote–udi.c* must be used to implement the remote interface procedures. In the case of interfacing to the IPC mechanism used by UDI, the procedures in Table 7-3 are mapped into the UDI–p procedures given in Table 7-1. With the availability of the UDI–p library, it is a simple task to map the GDB remote interface procedures for socket communication with a remote target processor.

Table 7-3.   GDB Remote–Target Operations

Function	Operation
to_open()	Open communication connection to remote target
to_close()	Close connection to remote target
to_attach()	Attach to a loaded and running program
to_detach()	Detach for multitarget debugging
to_start()	Load program into target–system memory
to_wait()	Wait until target–system execution stops
to_resume()	Startup/Continue target–system execution
to_fetch_register()	Read target–system processor register(s)
to_store_register()	Write register(s) in target–system processor
to_xfer_memory()	Read/Write data to target–system memory
to_insert_breakpoint()	Establish an instruction break address
to_remove_breakpoint()	Remove a breakpoint
to_load()	Load a program into target–processor memory

7.5.5 The UDI–MiniMON29K Monitor Connection, MonTIP

MiniMON29K monitor code can not function without the support of a software module located in a support processor; the software module is known as the target interface process (TIP). The 29K target processor communicates with the processor running the TIP process via a serial link or other higher performance channel. This link supports a message system which is private to the MiniMON29K monitor, by that I mean it is completely independent of the UDI protocol. (See Figure 7-1.)

MiniMON29K must be installed in target system ROM memory or down–loaded by the TIP host via a shared memory interface. The target application code, and additional operating system code, can then be down–loaded via the message system. If changes to the code are required, then the message system can be used to quickly down–load new code without changing any ROM devices.

The MiniMON29K TIP process, **montip**, converts UDI service requests into MiniMON29K messages. The **montip** program which runs on UNIX machines, typically communicates with the target using an rs232 link. When run on DOS machines, it may communicate using an rs232 connection or a PC plug–in board shared memory scheme. Note, UNIX machines can be also used to debug PC plug–in cards; the **pcserver** program, run on DOS machines, enables the PC serial port to be connected to a UNIX machine. The MiniMON29K messages, transferred to the DOS host via plug–in card shared memory, are sent to the TIP host via the rs232 connection. The **montip** program supports several command–line options, as shown below. Not all are applicable to both DOS and UNIX host machines.

```
montip -t target [-r OS-boot]  [-m msg_log]  [-com serial_port]
       [-re msg_retries]  [-mbuf msg_bufsize]  [-bl msg_loopcount]
       [-to timeout]  [-seg PC_seg_addr]  [-port PC_port_base]
       [-baud baudrate]  [-le]  [-R|P]
```

A explanation of the command line options can be obtained by just entering **montip** on your TIP host machine. When the **montip** process is started it *advertises* its readiness to service UDI requests. A DFE process will typically connect to the TIP process and a debug session will commence. Alternatively, there is no need to first start the TIP process. When a DFE process is started, such as **mondfe**, it will look for the advertised TIP; if the TIP process is not found the DFE will automatically start the TIP. This is how **montip** is normally started. The start–up **montip** parameters are taken from the "UDI Configuration File". The format of this file is explained in the following section discussing **mondfe**.

7.5.6 The MiniMON29K User–Interface, MonDFE

The MiniMON29K DFE process, **mondfe**, is a primitive 29K debugger. It provides a basic user–interface for the MiniMON29K product. It is fully UDI compliant (at least UDI version 1.2); and it can be used with any of the available TIP processes such as **isstip**, **mtip**, **montip**, etc. It is very easy to operate but has less debugging capability compared to other DFEs, such as **gdb**, **xray29u**, etc.; for example it does not support symbolic debugging.

It is very useful for simply loading application programs and starting their execution where no debugging support is required. Its simple command set also makes it easy to learn; when running, simply type the *h* command to obtain a complete list of available commands. The *h* command can also be used to explain each command's operation; for example, "*h s*" will explain the operation of the *set* command. Several command–line options are supported.

```
mondfe  [-D]  -TIP tip_id  [-q]  [-e echo_file]  [-c command_file]
        [-ms mem_stack_size]  [-rs reg_stack_size]  [-le]
        [-log logfile]  [pgm_name [arg_list]]
```

A list of command line options can be had by entering **mondfe** on your DFE host processor. The process is typically started by entering a command such as "modfe –D –TIP serial". The "–D" option causes an interactive debug session to commence. The UDI conforming TIP process communicating with **mondfe** is identified by the "–TIP serial" command line option.

DFEs and TIPs establish communication via a UDI Configuration File. On UNIX machines this file is called *udi_soc*; on DOS machines it is called *udiconfs.txt*. The Configuration File is found by first looking in the current working directory. If not found, the file given by environment variable UDICONF is searched for. Lastly, the executable PATH is searched. The format of these files is very similar, on UNIX:

```
session_id  AF_UNIX  socket_name     tip_exe tip_parameters
session_id  AF_INET  host_name       port    <not required>
```

The first column gives the session_id, which is used to select the appropriate line. The *serial* key–word used with the "–TIP" option in the example, is compared with the *session_id* for each line in the Configuration File. The first matching line provides all the necessary data for connecting to a TIP process which is already running; or, if necessary, starting TIP process execution.

The second column gives the socket domain used by the socket IPC mechanism connecting the two processes. Two domains are supported. The AF_UNIX domain indicates both processes reside on the same host processor. Use of the AF_INET domain indicates the TIP process is on another networked host machine. In such a case, the host name and socket port number are supplied in the following columns. The UDI specification does not support DFEs starting TIP processes on remote hosts. When the AF_INET domain is used to connect to the TIP, the TIP process must be first up and running before connection is attempted.

When the AF_UNIX domain is used, the third column gives the name of the socket used by the TIP to advertise its UDI services. If the DFE is unable to connect to the named socket, it will assume the TIP is not running. In such a case the remaining line information gives the name of the TIP executable and the start–up parameters. Below is example *udi_soc* file contents.

```
mon         AF_UNIX  mon_soc     montip -t serial -baud 38400 -com /dev/ttya
serial      AF_UNIX  *           montip -t serial -baud 9600 -com /dev/ttya
iss         AF_UNIX  iss_soc     iss -r ../../src/osboot/sim/osboot
pcserver    AF_UNIX  pc_soc      pcserver -t serial -baud 9600 -com /dev/ttya
cruncher    AF_INET  hotbox      7000
```

The relative path names given with **montip** start–up parameters, are relative to: <montip executable directory>/../lib . The path given with the "–r" option is required to find the OS–boot code for 29K start–up. When the DFE is always used to automatically start the TIP process, a "*" can be used for the socket name field. This causes the DFE to generate a random name for the socket file. This file will be removed when the DFE and TIP discontinue execution at the end of the debug session.

The DOS Configuration File (*udiconfs.txt*) format is a little simpler. There are only three entry fields, as shown by the example below:

```
mon        montip.exe -t serial -baud 38400
serial     montip.exe -t serial -baud 9600
sim        iss.exe    -r ..\..\src\osboot\sim\osboot
eb29K      montip.exe -t eb29K -r ..\..\src\minimon\eb29K\mon.o
yarcrev8   montip.exe -t yarcrev8 -r ..\..\src\minimon\yarcrev8\mon.os
```

The first field is again the session identifier. The second and third fields contain the TIP executable file name and its start–up option switches. All DFEs have some kind of command–line or interactive command which allows the *session_id* value to be entered. The DFE then reads the UDI Configuration File to determine the TIP with which communication is to be established. Most DFEs (**mondfe** has the *disc* command) have a command which enables the DFE to disconnect from the TIP, cease to execute but leave the TIP running. Because the TIP is still *alive* and ready to service UDI requests, a DFE can start–up later and reconnect with the TIP. However, typically the DFE and TIP processes are terminated at the same time.

7.5.7 The UDI – Instruction Set Simulator Connection, ISSTIP

An Instruction Set Simulator, **isstip**, is available for DOS and UNIX type hosts. The **isstip** process is fully UDI conforming and can be used by any DFE. Because of existing contract limitations, AMD normally ships **isstip** in binary rather than source form. Using the simulator along with, say the **gdb** DFE, is a convenient and powerful way of exercising 29K code without ever having to build hardware. Thus, software engineers can use the simulator while a project's hardware is still being debugged.

The Instruction Set Simulator can not be used for accurate application benchmarking, as the system memory model can not be incorporated into the simulation. AMD supplies the architectural simulator, **sim29**, for that purpose (see Chapter 1). The simulator supports several command line options, as shown below. For an explanation of these options, enter **isstip** or **man isstip,** on your TIP host machine.

```
isstip [-r osboot_file]  [-29000|-29050|-29030|-29200] [-t] [-tm]
       [-id <0|1>] [-sp <0|1>] [-st  <hexaddr>] [-ww] [-le] [-p|v]
```

With the *–r* option, the *osboot_file* is loaded into memory at address 0. This is useful for installing operating systems like OS–boot before application code starts executing. With processors which support separate Instruction and ROM memory spaces, the *osboot_file* is loaded into ROM space. If the *–r* option is not used, the simulator will intercept HIF service calls and perform the necessary operating system support service. The simulator always intercepts HIF services with service numbers 255 and less regardless of the *–r* option. These HIF services are provided directly by the simulator.

The simulator is very useful for debugging Freeze mode code. 'l allow single stepping through Freeze mode code which is not possible with ⌐al processor unless it supports Monitor mode. Freeze mode code is normally supplied in the optional *osboot_file*. Thus, the *–r* option must be used to enable Freeze mode debugging. Additionally, to enable debugging of Freeze mode timer interrupts the *–tm* option must also be selected to enable timer interrupt simulation. The simulator normally intercepts floating–point traps and performs the necessary calculation directly. Simulation speeds are reduced if floating–point trapware is simulated. However, if the trapware is to be debugged the *–t* option must be used to enable trapware simulation.

When the **isstip** process is started it *advertises* its readiness to service UDI requests. A DFE process will typically connect to the TIP process and a debug session will commence. However, it is more typical to get the DFE to start the TIP. The **mondfe** process starts the TIP during the DFE start–up process. The **gdb** DFE starts the TIP after the *target* **gdb** command is used. The start–up **isstip** parameters are taken from the "UDI Configuration File". The format of this file is explained in the previous section discussing **mondfe**.

7.5.8 UDI Benefits

A number of debug tool developers are currently, or will be shortly, offering tools which are UDI compliant. Typically the DFEs are C source level debuggers. This is not surprising, as the increased use of RISC processor designs has resulted in a corresponding increase in software complexity. The use of a high level language, such as C, is more productive than developing code at machine instruction level. And further, the use of C enables much greater portability of code among current and future projects. The low cost of GDB makes it an attractive choice for developers.

Target processors and their control mechanisms are much more varied than Debugger Front Ends (DFEs). I have briefly described the MiniMON29K TIP, which is a process which controls the execution of a 29K processor. A small amount of code known as the debugcore is placed in processor ROM memory and enables examination of the processor state. The MiniMON29K TIP communicates with the debugcore via a hardware link which is specific to the embedded application hardware.

Other TIPs already exist and more are under development. There is a 29K simulator (ISS) which runs on UNIX and DOS hosts. The DFE communicating with the simulator TIP is unaware that the 29K processor is not present, but being simulated by a process, executing on, say, a UNIX workstation. There are also tool developers constructing TIP programs to control processor emulators. This will make possible a top–of–the–line debug environment.

UDI makes possible a wider tool choice for application code developers. Debugger front end tools are supplied separately from target control programs. The user can consider cost, availability and functionality when selecting the debug environment. This level of debug tool configurability has not been available to the embedded application development community in the past.

Because debuggers like GDB are available in source form, developers can add additional debug commands, such as examination of real–time operating system performance. This would require adding operating system structural information into GDB. When the debugger front end and, for example, an emulator interface module, are supplied as a single executable, adding new commands is not possible. Via the use of Internet sockets the debugger may execute on a different networked host than the node supporting the emulator control process.

7.5.9 Getting Started with GDB

To demonstrate the operation of GDB debugging a program running on an Am29000 processor, the program below was compiled using the Free Software Foundation's GCC compiler. The example is simple, but it does help to understand the GDB–MiniMON29K monitor debug mechanism. A stand–alone Am29000 processor development card was used. It contains a UART and space for RAM and EPROM devices. The MiniMON29K monitor modules were linked with a HIF operating system support module (OS–boot) and an Am85C30 UART message driver module [AMD 1988]. The linked image was installed in EPROM devices in the target hardware. A serial cable was then used to connected the UART to a port on a SUN–3/80 workstation.

The demonstration could have been equally as well been performed on a 386–based IBM–PC; the target hardware being connected via a PC serial port. Alternatively, there are a number of manufactures building evaluation cards which support a dual–ported memory located on a PC plug–in card containing the RISC processor. The 386 communicates with the target processor via a shared memory interface. This requires a TIP which can communicate via shared memory with the debugcore running on the target hardware. A number of such TIP control processes have been built. A board developer has only to implement the TIP portion of the debug mechanism to gain access to a number of debuggers such as GDB which are UDI conforming.

The demonstration program, listed below, simply measures the number of characters in the string supplied as a parameter to the main() function.

```
main(argc, argv)                    /* program measure.c */
int    argc;
char   *argv[];
{
       int len;
       if(argc < 2) return;
       len = strlen(argv[1]);
    printf("length=%d\en", len);
```

```
}

int     strlen(s)
char    *s;
{
        int n;
        for (n = 0; *s != '\0'; s++)
        n++;
        return(n);
}
```

GDB was started running on the UNIX machine. The **target** command was used to establish communication with the debugcore running in the standalone development card. The UDI Configuration file was used to establish DFE and TIP communication. The format of the Configuration File was described in section 7.5.6. The UDI *session_id* for the example shown is *monitor*. The list below presents the response seen by the user. The keyboard entries made by the user are shown in bold type.

```
gdb
GDB is free software and you are welcome to distribute copies of
it  under certain conditions; type "show copying" to see the
conditions. There is absolutely no warranty for GDB; type "show
warranty" for details. GDB 4.5.2, Copyright 1992 Free Software
Foundation, Inc.

(gdb) target udi monitor measure
Remote debugging Am29000 rev D Remote debugging an Am29000
connected via UDI socket,  DFE-IPC version 1.2.1  TIP-IPC version
1.2.1  TIP version 2.5.1  MONTIP UDI 1.2 Conformant
```

Once communication had been established, a breakpoint was set at the entry to the strlen() function. Execution was then started using the **run** command. GDB informs the user that the program is being loaded. This is accomplished by the TIP sending messages to the debug core, which transfers the accompanying message data into Am29000 processor memory before Am29000 processor execution commences.

```
(gdb) symbol measure
Reading in symbols for measure.c...done.

(gdb) break strlen
Breakpoint 1 at 0x10200: file measure.c, line 14.

(gdb) run measure_my_length
Loading TEXT section at 0x10000 (24408 bytes) ...
Loading DATA section at 0x80003000 (4096 bytes) ...
Clearing BSS section at 0x80004000 (0 bytes) ...
Breakpoint 1, strlen(s=0x80004013 "measure_my_length")
                                    (measure.c line 17
17          for (n = 0; *s != '\0'; s++)
```

The program runs until the requested breakpoint is encountered. At this point a source code listing was requested. Typically, debug monitors do not allow source code to be viewed. The use of GDB makes this important advantage available to the embedded software developer.

```
(gdb) list
11
12      int  strlen(s)
13      char    *s;
14      {
15              int n;
16
17              for (n = 0; *s != '\0'; s++)
18              n++;
19              return (n);
20      }
```

The user then examined the call–stack history using the **info stack** command. This is currently inefficiently implemented. GDB uses the to_xfer_memory() proce-dure to send read messages to the target debugcore. Examining the instruction mem-ory in this way is much less efficient than requesting the debugcore to search back through its own memory for procedural tag words. Each procedure has a non–ex-ecutable trace–back tag word, or two, placed before the first instruction of the proce-dure (see Chapter 3). Tag words enable debuggers to quickly gain information about a procedure frame, and hence variable values. Adding the procedural "hook" to GDB to make use of the MiniMON29K monitor FIND service would greatly reduce message traffic, and improve the users response time for the **info stack** command.

```
(gdb) info stack
#0   strlen (s=0x80004013 "measure_my_length") (measure.c line 17)
#1   0x101ac in main (argc=2, argv=0x80004000) (measure.c line 8)
```

GDB enables single stepping of source code with the **step** or **next** commands. The listing shows a source–level step request followed by the printing of procedural variables "n" and "s". With large embedded programs it is important to be able to debug at source–level, and examine variables without having to look at cross–listing mapping tables to find the address associated with a variables memory location. Typically small embedded debug monitors do not support this kind of debugging.

```
(gdb) step
17              for (n = 0; *s != '\0'; s++)

(gdb) print n
$1 = 0

(gdb) print s
$2 = (unsigned char *) 0x80004013 "measure_my_length"
```

Embedded applications often deal with controlling special purpose hardware devices. This may involve interrupt handlers and assembly–level code which operates with processor registers reserved for the task. GDB does support examination of assembly code and registers by name. The listing below shows disassembly from the current PC location (PC1 on the Am29000 processor). The **si** command was then used to single step at machine instruction level. The **cont** command caused execution to continue to completion, as no further breakpoints were encountered.

The result of the printf() function call can finally be seen. This function relies on the operating system making use of MiniMON29K monitor messages. The HIF–OS write() system call, like the debugcore, sends the required message to the host processor. However, in the case of operating system messages, the message is not normally sent to the GDB module but to the HIF–OS support module. An exception is made in the case of a read() or write() to the standard–in or –out channel. Related messages are relayed via UDI to GDB which must control both the displaying of received data on the screen and sharing the keyboard between the application and the debugger itself.

```
(gdb) x/4i $pc
0x10228 <strlen+64>:          sub gr117,lr1,8
0x1022c <strlen+68>:          load 0,0x0,gr118,gr117
0x10230 <strlen+72>:          add gr118,gr118,1
0x10234 <strlen+76>:          store 0,0x0,gr118,gr117

(gdb) si
0x1022c
        18                    n++;

(gdb) p/x $pc
$3 = 0x0001022c

(gdb) p/cont
Continuing.
length=17
```

7.5.10 GDB and MiniMON29K Summary

GDB is a powerful debug tool which can be applied to the problem of developing software for embedded applications. The MiniMON29K monitor debugcore and message handling modules enable GDB to be simply incorporated in a wide range of embedded systems. The MiniMON29K monitor has only a small memory requirement and does not require processor registers to be reserved for its use.

Users are free to incorporate their own real–time operating system, or alternatively make use of the HIF operating system module. Because GDB is available in source form, it can be extended to understand real–time operating system support data structures. Purchasers of third party executives, or those who choose to build their own, should not find it difficult to extend GDB to analyze the real–time operating system control parameters, via the Universal Debugger Interface standard.

The increased complexity of many applications being solved by RISC processor designs have a corresponding increase in software complexity. The low cost of GDB and its associated productivity make it an attractive choice for developers.

Appendix A

HIF Service Calls

A.1   Service Call Numbers And Parameters

This section describes in detail each HIF 2.0 service. Service calls use local registers to pass parameters to the operating system, global registers are used to return results. Example code sequences are given for each service. However, user code does not normally invoke HIF services directly. It is more likely an assembly language *glue* routine or other library routine will be used to access the service. AMD supplies libraries of the necessary glue code. Chapter 2 introduced the HIF concepts and has an overview of its services.

Service 1 – exit

Terminate a Program

Description

This service terminates the current program and returns a value to the system kernel, indicating the reason for termination. By convention, a zero passed in *lr2* indicates normal termination, while any non-zero value indicates an abnormal termination condition. There are no returned values in registers *gr96* and *gr121* since this service does not return.

Register Usage

Type	Regs	Contents	Description
Calling:	*gr121*	1 (0x1)	Service number
	lr2	exitcode	User-supplied exit code
Returns:	*gr96*	undefined	This service call does not return
	gr121	undefined	This service call does not return

Example Call

```
        const   lr2, 1          ;exit code = 1
        const   gr121,1         ;service = 1
        asneq   69,gr1,gr1      ;call the operating system
```

In the above example, the operating system kernel is being called with service code 1 and an exit code of 1, which is interpreted according to the specifications of the individual operating system. The value of the exit code is not defined as part of the HIF specification.

In general, however, an exit code of zero (0) specifies a normal program termination condition, while a non-zero code specifies an abnormal termination resulting from detection of an error condition within the program.

Programs can terminate normally by falling through the curly brace at the end of the **main** function in a C language program. Other languages may require an explicit call to the kernel's **exit** service.

Service 17 – open   Open a File

Description

This service opens a named file in a requested mode. Files must be explicitly opened before any **read**, **write**, **close**, or other file positioning accesses can be accomplished. The **open** service, if successful, returns an integer token that is used to refer to the file in all subsequent service requests. In many high-level languages the returned token is referred to as a file descriptor. File names are generally not portable from one implementation to another. In some cases, names can be made more portable by limiting them to six or fewer upper-case alphabetic characters, or by using the **tmpnam** HIF service (33) to create names that conform to the current implementation's file system requirements.

Environment variables can also be used to specify legal file names for application programs wishing to conform to the requirements of a particular HIF implementation. The **getenv** service (65) provides the means to associate a file name or pathname with a mnemonic reference. This is the most portable means to specify pathnames for implementations that incorporate the **getenv** service.

The HIF specification intentionally refrains from defining the constituents of a legal pathname, or any intrinsic characteristics of the implemented file system. In this regard, the only requirement of a HIF-conforming kernel is that when the **open** service is successfully performed, that the routine returns a small integer value that can be used in subsequent input/output service calls to refer to the opened file.

Register Usage

Type	Regs	Contents	Description
Calling:	*gr121*	17 (0x11)	Service number
	lr2	pathname	A pointer to a filename
	lr3	mode	See parameter descriptions below.
	lr4	pflag	See parameter descriptions below.
Returns:	*gr96*	fileno	Success: $\geq$ 0 (file descriptor)
			Failure: $<$ 0
	gr121	0x80000000	Logical TRUE, service successful
		errcode	Error number, service not successful (implementation dependent)

Parameter Descriptions

Pathname is a pointer to a zero-terminated string that contains the full path and name of the file being opened. Individual operating systems have different means to

---

specify this information. With hierarchical file systems, individual directory levels are separated with special characters that can not be part of a valid filename or directory name. In UNIX-compatible file systems, directory names are separated by forward slash characters, / (e.g., */usr/jack/files/myfile*); where *usr*, *jack*, and *files* are succeedingly lower directory levels, beginning at the root directory of the file system. The name *myfile* is the filename to be opened at the specified level. The individual characteristics of files and pathnames are determined by the specifications of a particular operating system implementation.

The *mode* parameter is composed of a set of flags, whose mnemonics and associated values are listed in Table A-1.

Table A-1. HIF Open Service Mode Parameters

Name	Value	Description
O_RDONLY	0x0000	Open for read only access
O_WRONLY	0x0001	Open for write only access
O_RDWR	0x0002	Open for read and write access
O_APPEND	0x0008	Always append when writing
O_NDELAY	0x0010	No delay
O_CREAT	0x0200	Create file if it does not exist
O_TRUNC	0x0400	If the file exists, truncate it to zero length
O_EXCL	0x0800	Fail if writing and the file exists
O_FORM	0x4000	Open in text format

The O_RDONLY mode provides the means to open a file and guarantee that subsequent accesses to that file will be limited to **read** operations. The operating system implementation will determine how errors are reported for unauthorized operations. The file pointer is positioned at the beginning of the file, unless the O_APPEND mode is also selected.

The O_WRONLY mode provides the means to open a file and guarantee that subsequent accesses to that file will be limited to **write** operations. The operating system implementation will determine how errors are reported for unauthorized operations. The file pointer is positioned at the beginning of the file, unless the O_APPEND mode is also selected.

The O_RDWR mode provides the means to open a file for subsequent **read** and **write** accesses. The file pointer is positioned at the beginning of the file, unless the O_APPEND mode is also selected.

If O_APPEND mode is selected, the file pointer is positioned to the end of the file at the conclusion of a successful **open** operation, so that data written to the file is added following the existing file contents.

Ordinarily, a file must already exist in order to be opened. If the O_CREAT mode is selected, files that do not currently exist are created; otherwise, the **open** function will return an error condition in *gr121*.

If a file being opened already exists and the O_TRUNC mode is selected, the original contents of the file are discarded and the file pointer is placed at the beginning of the (empty) file. If the file does not already exist, the HIF service routine should return an error value in *gr121*, unless O_CREAT mode is also selected.

The O_EXCL mode provides a method for refusing to **open** the file if the O_WRONLY or O_RDWR modes are selected and the file already exists. In this case, the kernel service routine should return an error code in *gr121*.

O_FORM mode indicates that the file is to be opened as a text file, rather than a binary file. The nominal standard input, output, and error files (file descriptors 0, 1, and 2) are assumed to be open in text mode prior to commencing execution of the user's program.

When opening a FIFO (interprocess communication file) with O_RDONLY or O_WRONLY set, the following conditions apply:

- If O_NDELAY is set (i.e., equal to 0x0010):

  —A read-only open will return without delay.

  —A write-only open will return an error if no process currently has the file open for reading.

- If O_NDELAY is clear (i.e., equal to 0x0000):

  —A read-only open will block until a process opens a file for writing.

  —A write-only open will block until a process opens a file for reading.

When opening a file associated with a communication line (e.g., a remote modem or terminal connection), the following conditions apply:

- If O_NDELAY is set, the open will return without waiting for the carrier detect condition to be TRUE.

- If O_NDELAY is clear, the open will block until the carrier is found to be present.

The optional *pflag* parameter specifies the access permissions associated with a file; it is only required when O_CREAT is also specified (i.e., create a new file if it does not already exist). If the file already exists, *pflag* is ignored. This parameter specifies UNIX-style file access permission codes (*r*, *w*, and *x* for read, write, and execute respectively) for the file's owner, the work group, and other users. If *pflag* is −1, then all accesses are allowed. See the UNIX operating system documentation for additional information on this topic.

Example Call

```
path:       .ascii   "/usr/jack/files/myfile\0"
            .set     mode,O_RDWR|O_CREAT|O_FORM
            .set     permit,0x180

fd:         .word    0                      ;
            const    lr2,path               ;address of pathname
            consth   lr2,path               ;
            const    lr3,mode               ;open mode settings
            const    lr4,permit             ;permissions
            const    gr121,17               ;service = 17 (open)
            asneq    69,gr1,gr1             ;perform OS call
            jmpf     gr121,open_err         ;jump if error on open
             const   gr120,fd               ;set address of
            consth   gr120,fd               ;file descriptor
            store    0,0,gr96,gr120         ;store file descriptor
```

In the above example, the file is being opened in read/write text mode. The UNIX permissions of the owner are set to allow reading and writing, but not execution, and all other permissions are denied. As indicated above in the parameter descriptions, the file permissions are only used if the file does not already exist. When the **open** service returns, the program jumps to the **open_err** error handler if the open was not successful; otherwise, the file descriptor returned by the service is stored for future use in **read**, **write**, **lseek**, **remove**, **rename**, or **close** service calls.

As described in the introduction to these services, the HIF can be implemented to several degrees of elaboration, depending on the underlying system hardware, and whether the operating system is able to provide the full set of kernel services. In the least capable instance (i.e., a standalone board with a serial port), it is likely that only the O_RDONLY, O_WRONLY and O_RDWR modes will be supported. In more capable systems, the additional modes should be implemented, if possible.

If an error is encountered during the execution of an **open** call, no file descriptor will be allocated.

Service 18 – close   Close a File

Description

This service closes the open file associated with the file descriptor passed in *lr2*. Closing all files is automatic on program exit (see **exit**), but since there is an implementation-defined limit on the number of open files per process, an explicit **close** service call is necessary for programs that deal with many files.

Register Usage

Type	Regs	Contents	Description
Calling:	*gr121*	18 (0x12)	Service number
	lr2	fileno	File descriptor
Returns:	*gr96*	retval	Success: = 0 Failure: < 0
	gr121	0x80000000 errcode	Logical TRUE, service successful Error number, service not successful (implementation dependent)

Example Call

```
fd:        .word   0

           const    gr96,fd          ;set address of
           consth   gr96,fd          ;file descriptor
           load     0,0,lr2,gr96     ;get file descriptor
           const    gr121,18         ;service = 18
           asneq    69,gr1,gr1       ;and call the OS
           jmpf     gr121,clos_err   ;handle close error
            nop                      ;
```

The above example illustrates loading a previously stored file descriptor (*fd*, in this case) and calling the kernel's **close** service to close the file associated with that descriptor. If an error occurs when attempting to close the file, the kernel will return an error code in *gr121* (the content of that register will not be TRUE) and the program will jump to an error handler; otherwise, program execution will continue. The file will be closed and the file descriptor deallocated, even when an error is encountered.

Service 19 – read

Read a Buffer of Data from a File

Description

This service reads a number of bytes from a previously opened file (identified by a small integer file descriptor in *lr2* that was returned by the **open** service) into memory starting at the address given by the buffer pointer in *lr3*. Register *lr4* contains the number of bytes to be read. The number of bytes actually read is returned in *gr96*. Zero is returned in *gr96* if the file is already positioned at its end-of-file. If an error is detected, a small positive integer is returned in *gr121*, indicating the nature of the error.

Register Usage

Type	Regs	Contents	Description
Calling:	*gr121*	19 (0x13)	Service number
	lr2	fileno	File descriptor
	lr3	buffptr	A pointer to buffer area
	lr4	nbytes	Number of bytes to be read
Returns:	*gr96*	count*	*See **Return Value** table, below.
	gr121	0x80000000	Logical TRUE, service successful
		errcode	Error number, service not successful (implementation dependent)

The value returned in register *gr96* can be interpreted differently, depending on the current operating mode of the file identified by the *fileno* parameter. The operating mode is established or changed by invoking the **ioctl** service (24). The Return Value table shows how the Return Value in *gr96* should be interpreted for various operating modes.

Return Value

Count	Non-ASYNC	ASYNC	NBLOCK
gr96 > 0	count	n/a	count
gr96 = 0	EOF	success	EOF
gr96 < 0	fail	fail	if = −1 & gr121 = EAGAIN, no data is available. Otherwise, fail.

In the Return Value table, for normal synchronous **read** service requests, the return value contains a *count* of the number of bytes read (if *gr96* > 0), end-of-file (if

$gr96 = 0$), or an indication that the operation failed ($gr96 < 0$). For ASYNC mode, the operation is only scheduled by invoking the **read** service, so the return value in $gr96$ merely indicates that the request succeeded or failed. Non-blocking **read** requests indicate that data is to be returned if available; otherwise, the service is to return control to the user process with an indication that the operation would block if allowed to continue. When $gr96$ contains the value -1, and the *errcode* value in register $gr121$ is EAGAIN, then no data is available to be read. If $gr96$ contains any other negative value, or if register $gr121$ contains any other error code, the service request was not accepted.

If the operating mode of the file descriptor referenced by the **read** service has previously been set to ASYNC using the **ioctl** service, the **iowait** service should be used to test the completion status of this operation, and to access the number of bytes that have been transferred. If a previously issued asynchronous **read**, **write**, or **lseek** operation is not complete, the current **read** request will return a failure status. Only one outstanding request is allowed.

If the operating mode has previously been set to NBLOCK (non-blocking), the *count* value returned in $gr96$ will only reflect the number of bytes currently available in the buffer. NBLOCK mode only applies to terminal-like devices.

Example Call

```
fd:        .word   0
buf:       .block  256
           const   gr119,fd
           consth  gr119,fd
           load    0,0,lr2,gr119       ;get file descriptor
           const   lr3,buf             ;set buffer address
           consth  lr3,buf             ;
           const   lr4,256             ;specify buffer size
           const   gr121,19            ;service = 19
           asneq   69,gr1,gr1          ;call the OS
           jmpf    gr121,rd_err        ;handle read errors
           nop
```

The example call requests the HIF to return 256 bytes from the file descriptor contained in the variable: *fd*. If the call is successful, *gr121* will contain a TRUE value and *gr96* will contain the number of bytes actually read. If the service fails, *gr121* will contain the error code.

Service 20 – write

Write a Buffer of Data to a File

Description

This service writes a number of bytes from memory (starting at the address given by the pointer in *lr3*) into the file specified by the small positive integer file descriptor that was returned by the open service when the file was opened for writing. Register *lr4* contains the number of bytes to be written. The number of bytes actually written is returned in *gr96*. If an error is detected, *gr121* will contain a small positive integer on return from the service, indicating the nature of the error.

Register Usage

Type	Regs	Contents	Description
Calling:	gr121	20 (0x14)	Service number
	lr2	fileno	File descriptor
	lr3	buffptr	A pointer to the buffer area
	lr4	nbytes	Number of bytes to be written
Returns:	gr96	count*	*See **Return Value** table, below.
	gr121	0x80000000	Logical TRUE, service successful
		errcode	Error number, service not successful (implementation dependent)

The value returned in register *gr96* can be interpreted differently, depending on the current operating mode of the file identified by the *fileno* parameter. The operating mode is established or changed by invoking the **ioctl** service (24). The following table shows how the Return Value in *gr96* should be interpreted for various operating modes.

Return Value

Count	Non-ASYNC	ASYNC	NBLOCK
$gr96 = lr4$	success	n/a	(NBLOCK mode is not illegal for **write** requests, but
$0 \leq gr96 < lr4$	fail	=0, success	requests are performed in either synchronous or
$gr96 < 0$	extreme	fail	ASYNC mode. Return values are interprete accordingly.)

In the Return Value table, for normal synchronous **write** service requests, the return value contains a *count* of the number of bytes written. If the value returned in *gr96* is equal to the *nbytes* argument passed to the service in *lr4*, the write operation was successful. Any other return value indicates that an error occurred. If *gr96* contains a value between 0 and the value of *nbytes*, the failure is not catastrophic. Negative values returned in *gr96* indicate extreme errors.

For ASYNC mode, the operation is only scheduled by invoking the **write** service, so the return value in *gr96* merely indicates that the request succeeded or failed. A return value of 0 in *gr96* indicates that the asynchronous write operation was successfully scheduled.

Non-blocking **write** requests are performed in either synchronous or asynchronous mode, depending on whether the ASYNC operating mode was selected. NBLOCK mode is ignored, the return value in *gr96* is interpreted according to the values shown for Non-ASYNC and ASYNC modes in the table.

Example Call

```
fd:        .word   0
buf:       .block  256
           const   gr96,fd            ;set address of
           consth  gr96,fd            ;file descriptor
           load    0,0,lr2,gr96       ;get file descriptor
           const   lr3,buf            ;set buffer address
           consth  lr3,buf            ;
           const   lr4,256            ;specify buffer size
           const   gr121,20           ;service = 20
           asneq   69,gr1,gr1         ;call the OS
           jmpf    gr121,wr_err       ;handle write errors
            const  gr120,num          ;set address of
           consth  gr120,num          ;"num" variable
           store   0,0,gr96,gr120     ;store bytes written
```

The example call writes 256 bytes from the buffer located at *buf* to the file associated with the descriptor stored in *fd*. If errors are detected during execution of the service, the value returned in *gr121* will be FALSE. In this case, the **wr_err** error handler will be invoked. The number of bytes actually written is stored in the variable *num*.

Service 21 – lseek

Description

This service positions the file associated with the file descriptor in *lr2*, *offset* number of bytes from the position of the file referred to by the *orig* parameter. Register *lr3* contains the number of bytes offset and *lr4* contains the value for *orig*. The parameter *orig* is defined as:

0 = Beginning of the file
1 = Current position of the file
2 = End of the file

The **lseek** service can be used to reposition the file pointer anywhere in a file. The offset parameter may either be positive or negative. However, it is considered an error to attempt to seek in front of the beginning of the file. Any attempt to seek past the end of the file is undefined, and is dependent on the restrictions of each implementation.

Register Usage

Type	Regs	Contents	Description
Calling:	*gr121*	21 (0x15)	Service number
	lr2	fileno	File descriptor
	lr3	offset	Number of bytes offset from orig
	lr4	orig	A code number indicating the point within the file from which the offset is measured
Returns:	*gr96*	where*	*See **Return Value** table,
	gr121	0x80000000	Logical TRUE, service successful
		errcode	Error number, service not successful (implementation dependent)

The value returned in register *gr96* can be interpreted differently, depending on the current operating mode of the file identified by the *fileno* parameter. The operating mode is established or changed by invoking the **ioctl** service (24). The Return Value table shows how the Return Value in *gr96* should be interpreted for various operating modes.

Return Value

Count	Non-ASYNC	ASYNC	NBLOCK
$gr96 \geq 0$	where	n/a	(NBLOCK mode is not illegal for **lseek** requests, but requests are performed in either synchronous or ASYNC mode. Return values are interpreted accordingly.)
$gr96 < 0$	fail	fail	

In the Return Value table, for normal synchronous **lseek** service requests, the return value contains the current position in the file, if the value is greater than or equal to 0. Negative values returned in $gr96$ indicate that the request was not accepted.

The file position returned by the **lseek** service in $gr96$ (*where*) is always measured from the beginning of the file. A value of 0 refers to the beginning, and any other positive non-zero value refers to the current position in the file. To determine the size in bytes for a particular file, an **lseek** request with an *offset* value of 0 and an *orig* value of 2 will position the file to its end and return the byte position of the end-of-file, which is an accurate measure of the size of the file.

Asynchronous **lseek** requests are allowed if the operating mode for the file descriptor associated with the request has been set to ASYNC. In this case, the file position returned in $gr96$ (*where*) will not be relevant. The **iowait** service call should be used to determine the final file position when the seek operation is complete.

If a previously issued **read** or **write** request is still in progress when an **lseek** is issued, a failure status will be returned for the **lseek** request. Only one request can be pending at a time. To properly handle this situation, the **iowait** service should be used to ensure the completion of an outstanding **read** or **write** before issuing the **lseek** service request.

Example Call

```
fd:      .word   6                        ;file descriptor = 6

         const   gr96,fd                  ;set address of
         consth  gr96,fd                  ;file descriptor
         load    0,0,lr2,gr96             ;get file descriptor
         consth  lr3,23                   ;offset argument = 23
         consth  lr4,0                    ;origin argument = 0
         const   gr121,21                 ;service = 21
         asneq   69,gr1,gr1               ;call the OS
         jmpf    gr121,seek_err           ;seek error if false
          nop
```

The call example shows how a file can be positioned to a particular byte address by specifying the *orig*, which is the starting point from which the file position is adjusted, and the offset, which is the number of bytes from the *orig*, to move the file pointer. In this case, the file identified by file descriptor 6 is being repositioned to byte 23, measured from the beginning of the file (origin = 0).

The file descriptor, *offset*, and *orig* values are loaded and **lseek** is called to perform the file positioning operation. If an error occurs when attempting to reposition the file, the value returned in *gr121* is FALSE, and contains an error code that indicates the reason for the error. Upon return, *gr96* also contains the file position measured from the beginning of the file.

Remove a File

Description

This service deletes a file from the file system. Register *lr2* contains a pointer to the pathname of the file. The path must point to an existing file, and the referenced file should not be currently open. The behavior of the remove service is undefined if the file is open. Any attempt to remove a currently open file will have an implementation-dependent result.

Register Usage

Type	Regs	Contents	Description
Calling:	*gr121*	22 (0x16)	Service number
	lr2	pathname	A pointer to string that contains the pathname of the file
Returns:	*gr96*	retval	Success: = 0 Failure: < 0
	gr121	0x80000000 errcode	Logical TRUE, service successful Error number, service not successful (implementation dependent)

Example Call

```
path:      .ascii  "/usr/jack/files/myfile\0"

           const   lr2,path          ;set address of file
           consth  lr2,path          ;pathname.
           const   gr121,22          ;service = 22
           asneq   69,gr1,gr1        ;call the OS
           jmpf    gr121,rem_err     ;jump if error
            nop
```

In the example call, a file with a UNIX-style pathname stored in the string named path is being removed. The address (*pointer*) to the string is put into *lr2* and the kernel service 22 is called to remove the file. If the file does not exist, or if it has not previously been closed, an error code will be returned in *gr121*; otherwise, the value in *gr121* will be TRUE.

Service 23 – rename

Description

This service moves a file to a new location within the file system. Register *lr2* contains a pointer to the file's old pathname and *lr3* contains a pointer to the file's new pathname. When all components of the old and new pathnames are the same, except for the filename, the file is said to have been renamed. The file identified by the old pathname must already exist, or an error code will be returned and the rename operation will not be performed.

Register Usage

Type	Regs	Contents	Description
Calling:	*gr121*	23 (0x17)	Service number
	lr2	oldfile	A pointer to string containing the old pathname of the file
	lr3	newfile	A pointer to string containing the new pathname of the file
Returns:	*gr96*	retval	Success: = 0 Failure: < 0
	gr121	0x80000000 errcode	Logical TRUE, service successful Error number, service not successful (implementation dependent)

Example Call

```
old:     .ascii  "/usr/fred/payroll/report\0"
new:     .ascii  "/usr/fred/history/june89\0"

         const   lr2,old         ;set address of old pathname
         consth  lr2,old
         const   lr3,new         ;set address of new pathname
         consth  lr3,new
         const   gr121,23        ;service = 23 (rename)
         asneq   69,gr1,gr1      ;call the OS
         jmpf    gr121,ren_err   ;jump if rename error
         nop
```

The example call moves a file from its old path (renaming it in the process) to its new pathname location. The file will no longer be found at the old location.

Service 24 – ioctl

Description

This service establishes the operating mode of the specified file or device. It is intended primarily to be applied to terminal-like devices; however, certain modes apply to mass-storage files, or to other related input/output devices.

Register Usage

Type	Regs	Contents	Description
Calling:	*gr121*	24 (0x18)	Service number
	lr2	fileno	File descriptor number to be tested
	lr3	mode	Operating mode.
Returns:	*gr121*	0x80000000	Logical TRUE, service successful
		errcode	error number, service not successful EHIFNOTAVAIL if service not implemented (implementation dependent)

Parameter Descriptions

In the above interface, local register *lr2* is expected to contain a legal file descriptor, *fileno*, assigned by the HIF **open** service (HIF service number 17). The *mode* parameter establishes the desired operating mode, which is selected from one or more of the following:

0x0000	COOKED	Process I/O data characters
0x0001	RAW	Do not process I/O data characters
0x0002	CBREAK	Process only I/O signals
0x0004	ECHO	Echo read data
0x0008	ASYNC	Asynchronous data read
0x0010	NBLOCK	Non-blocking data read

Multiple *mode* values are possible; however, COOKED, RAW, and CBREAK modes are mutually exclusive. Other *mode* values can be combined with these by logically ORing them to form a composite *mode* value. Certain of these *mode* values do not apply to every open file descriptor. For example, the ASYNC mode is used to establish a data input mode that will cause a **read**, **write**, or **lseek** operation, once initiated, to complete at a later time. With the ASYNC mode set, a **read** or **write**

---

request will immediately return after passing the buffer address and file descriptor to the operating system, leaving the scheduling of the operation up to the HIF implementation. **lseek** operations can also be serviced in ASYNC mode. The completion status of these operations can be tested by issuing an **iowait** service request (HIF service number 25). When a **read** or **write** operation is issued for a file descriptor whose operating mode is ASYNC, the *count* returned in *gr96* will be 0 if the operation was accepted, or less than 0 if the operation was rejected. An **iowait** service should be issued to ascertain the number of bytes that have been transferred upon completion of the operation.

The default I/O processing mode is COOKED (0x0000), which implies that the HIF implementation examines input and output data characters as they are received, or before they are sent, and may perform some alteration of the data. Specific alterations are not explicitly indicated in this specification; however, it is common to perform end-of-line processing for files whose operating mode is COOKED. ASCII carriage-return and line-feed translations are common, as may be the translation of ASCII TAB characters to a number of equivalent spaces. When RAW mode is selected, no translation of input or output characters will be performed by HIF-conforming implementations.

Normally, when a **read** operation is issued for a terminal-like device by the application program, the processor will block any further execution of the subject program until the data has been transferred. The NBLOCK mode is intended to specify for terminal-like devices that subsequent **read** operations be executed without suspending (blocking) further CPU operation. This is particularly relevant to **read** operations when RAW mode is also selected. If NBLOCK mode has been specified, a subsequent **read** operation will return (in *gr96*) the number of characters currently available, or –1 if none are available. NBLOCK mode is not meaningful for **write** operations, but they are handled in the same fashion as synchronous or asynchronous operations, depending on whether ASYNC mode was specified.

RAW mode delivers the characters to/from the I/O device without conversion or interpretation of any kind.

If COOKED mode has been selected, line-buffering is implied. If NBLOCK is also selected, a subsequent **read** operation will return –1 for the *count*, unless an entire line of input is available.

The ECHO mode applies only to the standard input device (file descriptor = 0), and makes provision to automatically echo data received from that device to the standard output device (file descriptor = 1). ECHO mode is undefined for any other file descriptor.

The CBREAK mode is intended for file descriptors that refer to serial communication channels. CBREAK mode specifies that I/O signal inputs will be processed, which could alter the data stream.

The NBLOCK and ASYNC settings are not necessarily mutually exclusive. There may be occasions where this is a legal mode. NBLOCK specifies that subsequent **read**, **write**, or **lseek** operations not block until completion. If a **read** is requested, for example, and no data is currently available, the **read** service will return −1 (with an *errcode* value in *gr121* of EAGAIN), rather than blocking further execution until data becomes available. ASYNC mode simply allows an operation, once invoked, to proceed asynchronously with other operations, if the HIF implementation provides this capability.

If the above *mode* settings are not implemented, the EHIFNOTAVAIL error code should be returned to the user if the **ioctl** service is invoked.

Although the *mode* parameter occupies a 32-bit word, only the low-order 16-bits are reserved. The upper 16-bits are available for implementation-dependent mode settings, and are not part of this specification.

Example Call

```
fd:        word    0                   ;variable to contain the file
                                       ;descriptor
           const   gr120, fd           ;Get fd address
           consth  gr120, fd
           load    0,0,lr2,gr120       ;load file descriptor
           const   lr3,0x0010          ;NBLOCK mode
           const   gr121,24            ;service = 24
           asneq   69,gr1,gr1          ;call the OS
           jmpf    gr121,io_err        ;jump if failure
            nop
```

In the example call, a previously assigned file descriptor is passed to the service, in order to specify that subsequent read requests not block if data is not available. If an error occurs when servicing this request, *gr121* will be set to FALSE and the program will jump to an error handling routine (**io_err**) when the service returns.

Description

This service is used in conjunction with the **ioctl** (ASYNC mode) and **read, write**, or **lseek** services to test the completion of an asynchronous input/output operation and, optionally, to wait until the operation is complete. The **iowait** service is called with the file descriptor returned by the **open** service when the file was originally opened. The *mode* parameter specifies whether the **iowait** will block until the operation is complete, or immediately return the completion status in the result register (*gr96*). If the operation was complete, *gr96* will contain the number of bytes transferred for **read** or **write** service requests (*count*), or the ending file position (measured from the beginning of the file) for **lseek** service requests (*where*).

If no previous asynchronous (**ioctl** ASYNC mode) **read, write**, or **lseek** service is pending for the specified file descriptor, or if an unrecognized mode value is provided, the **iowait** service will return an error status in *gr121*.

Register Usage

Type	Regs	Contents	Description
Calling:	*gr121*	25 (0x19)	Service number
	lr2	fileno	file descriptor, as returned by **open** (17).
	lr3	mode	1 = non-blocking completion test 2 = wait until read operation complete
Returns:	*gr96*	count *	* See **Return Value** table
	gr121	0x80000000 errcode	Logical TRUE, service successful error number, service not successful (implementation dependent)

The value returned in register *gr96* can be interpreted differently, depending on the value specified in the *mode* parameter (in register *lr3*) of the service request. The Return Value table shows how the return value in *gr96* should be interpreted for non-blocking and blocking completion tests.

Return Value

Count	Blocking Tests read/write	lseek	Non-blocking Tests read/write	lseek
$gr96 > 0$	count	where	count	where
$gr96 = 0$	EOF	where	EOF	where
$gr96 < 0$	fail	fail	If $= -1$ & $gr121 =$ EAGAIN, there is no data available; otherwise, fail.	

In the Return Value table, for blocking completion tests, the return value specifies the status of the completed operation. If the operation was a **read** or **write** service request, the *count* value specifies the number of bytes actually transferred ($gr96 > 0$), an end-of-file condition was reached ($gr96 = 0$), or that a failure occurred ($gr96 < 0$). For **lseek** requests, the return value specifies the current position of the file, unless the value is negative, in which case a failure occurred.

The return value for non-blocking completion tests of **read** and **write** service requests is interpreted the same as for blocking completion tests, except for the case where the value in *gr96* is equal to –1. In this case, and if the *errcode* in register *gr121* is EAGAIN, then no data is currently available. Any other negative return value or error code signals a failure condition.

The **iowait** service reports errors that may have occurred in the outstanding asynchronous operation— subsequent to its original issue—as well as errors in the **iowait** call itself.

Example Call

```
fd:        .word   0                  ;file descriptor
           const   lr3,1              ;non-blocking completion
           const   gr121,25           ;service = 25 (iowait)
loop:      const   gr120,fd           ;load file descriptor adds.
           consth  gr120,fd           ;
           load    0,0,lr2,gr120      ;get file descriptor
           asneq   69,gr1,gr1         ;call the OS
           jmpf    gr121,wait_err     ;handle wait error
            const  lr3,1              ;non-blocking completion
           jmpt    gr96,loop          ;wait until op. complete
            const  gr121,25           ;service = 25 (iowait)
```

In the example call, the file descriptor (*fileno*) is loaded into *lr2*, non-blocking mode is selected, and the **iowait** service is invoked. If the service returns an error status in *gr121*, the program will jump to the **wait_err** label. If the operation is accepted, *gr96* will contain the completion status upon return from the service. This example jumps to reinvoke the service if the operation is not yet complete. This is equivalent to issuing a **iowait** service with a *mode* value of 2, specifying that the operation should block until the operation is complete. A more complex program might perform some useful work before re-trying the operation.

Service 26 – iostat   Input/Output Status

Description

This service returns the status corresponding to a file descriptor assigned by the **open** service. If the specified file descriptor is not legal, an error code will be returned in *gr121*; otherwise, *gr121* will contain a TRUE result, and *gr96* will contain the requested status. Two status values are defined:

| 0x0001 | RDREADY | Input device ready and data available |
| 0x0002 | ISATTY | File descriptor refers to terminal-like device (TTY) |

Application programs frequently need to determine if data is currently available to be read for a terminal-like device. If the RDREADY status is returned, at least one byte of data is available to be read from the device.

The ISATTY status indicates that the device associated with the file descriptor refers to a terminal-like peripheral, rather than a mass-storage file or other peripheral device. The **iostat** service can be used to determine if a standard output device (file descriptors 1 or 2) refers to a terminal, or if output is being redirected to a mass-storage file.

The RDREADY and ISATTY status values are *not* mutually exclusive; either or both results may be present. Although the status is returned in a 32-bit word, only the lower 16 bits are reserved for HIF-conforming reply values. The upper 16 bits are available for implementation-specific status results.

Register Usage

Type	Regs	Contents	Description
Calling:	*gr121*	26 (0x19)	Service number
	lr2	fileno	File descriptor number
Returns:	*gr96*	iostat	Input status 0x0001= RDREADY 0x0002= ISATTY
	gr121	0x80000000 errcode	Logical TRUE, service successful error number, service not successful (implementation dependent)

Example Call

```
const   lr2,0              ;set file descriptor = 0
const   gr121,26           ;service = 26
asneq   69,gr1,gr1         ;call the OS
jmpf    gr121,fail         ;handle failure
sll     gr120,gr96,30      ;test ISATTY status bit
jmpf    gr120,not_tty      ;jump if not a tty
 nop
```

In the example call, the program calls the **iostat** service to determine if the device associated with file descriptor 0 is a **tty-like** device. If the service returns an error indication in *gr121*, the program jumps to the **fail** label; otherwise, the *iostat* value returned in *gr96* is shifted to put bit-1 of the result into the sign-bit of *gr120*, which is tested to determine if the file descriptor refers to a **tty-like** device. If not, the program jumps to the **not_tty** label.

Service 33 – tmpnam   Return Temporary Name

Description

This service generates a string that can be used as a temporary file pathname. A different name is generated each time it is called. The name is guaranteed not to duplicate any existing filename. The argument passed in *lr2* should be a valid pointer to a buffer that is large enough to contain the constructed file name. User programs are required to allocate a minimum of 128 bytes for this purpose.

If the argument in *lr2* contains a NULL pointer, the HIF service routine should treat this as an error condition and return a non-zero error number in global register *gr121*.

The HIF specification sets no standards for the format or content of legal pathnames; these are determined by individual operating system requirements. Each implementation must undertake to construct a valid filename that is also unique.

Register Usage

Type	Regs	Contents	Description
Calling:	*gr121*	33 (0x21)	Service number
	lr2	addrptr	A pointer to buffer into which the filename is to be stored
Returns:	*gr96*	filename	Success: pointer to the temporary filename string. Failure: = 0 (NULL pointer)
	gr121	0x80000000 errcode	Logical TRUE, service successful Error number, service not successful (implementation dependent)

Example Call

```
fbuf:      .block  21                      ;buffer size = 21 bytes

           const   lr2,fbuf                ;set buffer pointer
           consth  lr2,fbuf                ;
           const   gr121,33                ;service = 33
           asneq   69,gr1,gr1              ;call the OS
           jmpf    gr121,tmp_err           ;jump if error
            nop
```

In the example call, the **tmpnam** service is called with a pointer to *fbuf*, which has been allocated to hold a name that is up to 21 bytes in length. If the service is able

---

to construct a valid name, the filename will be stored in *fbuf* when the service returns. If the content of *gr121* on return is not TRUE, the program fragment jumps to **tmp_err** to handle the error condition.

Service 49 – time   Return Seconds Since 1970

Description

   This service returns, in register *gr96*, the number of seconds elapsed since midnight, January 1, 1970, as an integer 32-bit value. It is assumed that the kernel service will have access to a counter, whose contents can be preloaded, that measures time with at least a one-second resolution, for this purpose.

   The time value returned by this service is Greenwich Mean Time (GMT). The conversion to local time should be accomplished by a separate function that uses the value returned by the **time** service and the time-zone information from the **gettz** (Get time zone) service call to compute the correct local time.

Register Usage

Type	Regs	Contents	Description
Calling:	*gr121*	49 (0x31)	Service number
Returns:	*gr96*	secs	Success: $\neq 0$ (time in seconds) Failure: $= 0$
	gr121	0x80000000 errcode	Logical TRUE, service successful Error number, service not successful (implementation dependent)

Example Call

```
secs:      .word   0

           const   gr121,49          ;service = 49
           asneq   69,gr1,gr1        ;call the OS
           jmpf    gr121,tim_err     ;jump if error
            const  gr120,secs        ;set the address
           consth  gr120,secs        ;for storing 'secs'
           store   0,0,gr96,gr120    ;store the seconds
```

   In the example call, the kernel service **time** is being called. If the value returned in *gr121* is TRUE, the number of seconds returned in *gr96* is stored in the *secs* variable; otherwise, the program jumps to **tim_err** to determine the cause of the error.

Service 65 – getenv

Get Environment

Description

This service searches the system environment for a string associated with a specified symbol. Register *lr2* contains a pointer to the symbol name. If the symbol name is found, a pointer to the string associated with it is returned in *gr96*; otherwise, a NULL pointer is returned.

In UNIX-hosted systems, the *setenv* command allows a user to associate a symbol with an arbitrary string. For example, the command *setenv TERM vt100* defines the string *vt100* to be associated with the symbol named *TERM*. Application programs can use this association to determine the type of terminal connected to the system, and, therefore, use the correct set of codes when outputting information to the user's screen. To access the string, **getenv** should be called with *lr2* pointing to a string containing the *TERM* symbol name. The address returned in *gr96* will point to the corresponding vt100 string if *TERM* is found. In UNIX-hosted systems, entering a different *setenv* command lets the user select a different terminal name without requiring recompilation of the application program.

Operating system implementations that do not include provisions for environment variables should always return a NULL value in *gr96* when this service is requested.

Register Usage

Type	Regs	Contents	Description
Calling:	*gr121*	65 (0x41)	Service number
	lr2	name	A pointer to the symbol name
Returns:	*gr96*	addrptr	Success: pointer to the symbol name string Failure: = 0 (NULL pointer)
	gr121	0x80000000 errcode	Logical TRUE, service successful Error number, service not successful (implementation dependent)

Example Call

```
mysym:    .ascii  "MYSYMBOL\0"
strptr:   .word   0

          const   lr2,mysym          ;set address of symbol to
          consth  lr2,mysym          ;be located in environment
          const   gr121,65           ;service = 65
          asneq   69,gr1,gr1         ;call the OS
          jmpf    gr121,env_err      ;jump if error
           const  gr120,strptr       ;set address of
          consth  gr120,strptr       ;string pointer
          store   0,0,gr96,gr120     ;store string pointer
```

The example call program calls the operating system **getenv** service to access a string associated with the environment variable *MYSYMBOL*. If the symbol is found, a pointer to the string associated with the symbol is returned in *gr96*. If the call is not successful (i.e., *gr121* holds a FALSE boolean value upon return), the program jumps to **env_err** to handle the error condition.

Service 67 – gettz   Get Time Zone

Description

This service obtains time zone information from the operating system. No arguments are required. The service returns in *gr96* an integer number of minutes of time, specifying the correction to Greenwich Mean Time (GMT) for localities west of Greenwich, England. A negative return value in *gr96* indicates a failure, or that time zone information is unavailable. A value is also returned in *gr97*. If Daylight Savings Time is currently in effect, *gr97* will contain the value 1 when the service returns; if it is not in effect, *gr97* will contain the value 0. If this information is not available, or if the service fails, *gr97* will contain a negative value.

Register Usage

Type	Regs	Contents	Description
Calling:	*gr121*	67(0x42)	Service number
Returns:	*gr96*	zonecode	Success: ≥ 0 (minutes west of GMT) Failure: < 0 (or information unavailable)
	gr97	dstcode	Success: $= 1$ (Daylight Savings Time in effect) $= 0$ (Daylight Savings Time not in effect)
	gr121	0x80000000	Logical TRUE, service successful error number, service not successful (implementation dependent)

If the result returned in *gr96* (*zonecode*) contains a value greater than 1,440 (60 minutes x 24 hours), then 1,440 should be subtracted from the result, which relates to minutes east of Greenwich.

Example Call

```
timzone: .word   0
dstflag: .word   0

         const   gr121,67            ;service = 67
         asneq   69,gr1,gr1          ;call the OS
         jmpf    gr121,tz_err        ;jump if error
         const   lr2,timzone         ;the adds. to storetimezone
         consth  lr2,timzone
         store   0,0,gr96,lr2        ;store the timezone correction
         const   lr2,dstflag         ;the addres to store daylight
         consth  lr2,dstflag         ;savings
         store   0,0,gr97,lr2        ;store daylight savings flag
```

In the example call, the **gettz** service is called to access the current time zone correction value. Upon return, *gr121* is tested to determine if the service was successful. If not, the program jumps to an error handling routine called **tz_err**. If the service was successful, the values returned in *gr96* and *gr97* are stored in local variables called **timzone** and **dstflag**, respectively.

Service 257 – sysalloc
Allocate Memory Space

Description

This service allocates a specified number of contiguous bytes from the operating-system-maintained heap and returns a pointer to the base of the allocated block. Register *lr2* contains the number of bytes requested. If the storage is successfully allocated, *gr96* contains a pointer to the block; otherwise, *gr121* contains an error code indicating the reason for failure of the call.

Register Usage

Type	Regs	Contents	Description
Calling:	*gr121*	257 (0x101)	Service number
	lr2	nbytes	Number of bytes requested
Returns:	*gr96*	addrptr	Success: pointer to allocated bytes, Failure: = 0 (NULL pointer)
	gr121	0x80000000	Logical TRUE, service successful
		errcode	Error number, service not successful (implementation dependent)

Example Call

```
blkptr:    .word    0

           const    lr2, 1200        ;request 1200 bytes
           const    gr121,257        ;service = 257
           asneq    69,gr1,gr1       ;call the OS
           jmpf     gr121,alloc_err  ;jump if error
            const   gr120,blkptr     ;set address to store
           consth   gr120,blkptr     ;pointer
           store    0,0,gr96,gr120   ;store the pointer
```

The example call requests a block of 1200 contiguous bytes from the system heap. If the call is successful, the program stores the pointer returned in *gr96* into a local variable called *blkptr*. If *gr121* contains a boolean FALSE value when the service returns, the program jumps to **alloc_err** to handle the error condition.

Service 258 – sysfree   Free Memory Space

Description

This service returns memory to the system starting at the address specified in *lr2*. Register *lr3* contains the number of bytes to be released. The pointer passed to the **sysfree** service in *lr2* and the byte count passed in *lr3* must match the address returned by a previous **sysalloc** service request for the identical number of bytes. No dynamic memory allocation structure is implied by this service. High-level language library functions such as **malloc()** and **free()** for the C language are required to manage random dynamic memory block allocation and deallocation, using the **sysalloc** and **sysfree** kernel functions as their basis.

Register Usage

Type	Regs	Contents	Description
Calling:	*gr121*	258 (0x102)	Service number
	lr2	addrptr	Starting address of area returned
	lr3	nbytes	Number of bytes to release
Returns:	*gr96*	retval	Success: = 0
			Failure: < 0
	gr121	0x80000000	Logical TRUE, service successful
		errcode	Error number, service not successful (implementation dependent)

Example Call

```
blkptr:   .word   0
          const   gr120,blkptr    ;set address of previously
          consth  gr120,blkptr    ;block pointer
          load    0,0,lr2,gr120   ;fetch pointer to block
          const   lr3,1200        ;set number of bytes to release
          const   gr121,258       ;service = 258
          asneq   69,gr1,gr1      ;call the OS
          jmpf    gr121,free_err  ;jump if error
           nop                    ;
```

The example calls **sysfree** to deallocate 1200 bytes of contiguous memory, beginning at the address stored in the *blkptr* variable. If the call is successful, the program continues; otherwise, if the return value in *gr121* is FALSE, the program jumps to **free_err** to handle the error condition.

Service 259 – getpsize   Return Memory Page Size

Description

This service returns, in register *gr96*, the page size, in bytes, used by the memory system of the HIF implementation.

Register Usage

Type	Regs	Contents	Description
Calling:	*gr121*	259 (0x103)	Service number
Returns:	*gr96*	pagesize	Success: memory page size, one of the following: 1024,2048,4096,8192 Failure: < 0
	gr121	0x80000000 errcode	Logical TRUE, service successful Error number, service not successful (implementation dependent)

Example Call

```
pagsiz:  .word   0

         const   gr121,259        ;service = 259
         asneq   69,gr1,gr1       ;call the OS
         jmpf    gr121,pag_err  . ;jump if error
          const  gr120,pagsiz     ;set address to
         consth  gr120,pagsiz     ;store the page size
         store   0,0,gr96,gr120   ;store it!
```

The example calls the operating system kernel to return the page size used by the virtual memory system. If the call was successful, *gr121* will contain a boolean TRUE result and the program will store the value in *gr96* into the *pagsiz* variable; otherwise, a boolean FALSE is returned in *gr121*. In this case, the program will jump to **pag_err** to handle the error condition.

Service 260 – getargs

Return Base Address

Description

This service returns the base address of the command-line-argument vector, *argv*, in register *gr96*, as constructed by the operating system kernel when an application program is invoked.

Arguments are stored by the operating system as a series of NULL-terminated character strings. A pointer containing the address of each string is stored in an array whose base address (referred to as *argv*) is returned by the **getargs** HIF service. The last entry in the array contains a NULL pointer (an address consisting of all zero bits). The number of arguments can be computed by counting the number of pointers in the array, using the fact that the NULL pointer terminates the list.

Register Usage

Type	Regs	Contents	Description
Calling:	*gr121*	260 (0x104)	Service number
Returns:	*gr96*	baseaddr	Success: base address of argv Failure: = 0 (NULL pointer)
	gr121	0x80000000 errcode	Logical TRUE, service successful Error number, service not successful (implementation dependent)

Example Call

```
argptr:   .word   0
          const   gr121,260        ;service = 260
          asneq   69,gr1,gr1       ;call the OS
          jmpf    gr121,bas_err    ;jump if error
           const  gr120,argptr     ;set address where base
          consth  gr120,argptr     ;pointer is to be stored
          store   0,0,gr96,gr120   ;store the pointer
```

The example calls operating system service 260 to access the command-line-argument vector address. If the service executes without error, the program continues by storing the argument vector address in the variable *basptr*. If *gr121* contains a boolean FALSE value upon return, the program jumps to **bas_err** to handle the error condition.

Service 273 – clock   Return Time in Milliseconds

Description

This service returns the elapsed processor time in milliseconds. Operating system initialization procedures set this value to zero on startup. Successive calls to this service return times that can be arithmetically subtracted to accurately measure time intervals.

Register Usage

Type	Regs	Contents	Description
Calling:	*gr121*	273 (0x111)	Service number
Returns:	*gr96*	msecs	Success: $\neq$ 0 (time in milliseconds) Failure: = 0
	gr121	0x80000000 errcode	Logical TRUE, service successful Error number, service not successful (implementation dependent)

Example Call

```
time:     .word    0

          const    gr121,273          ;service = 273
          asneq    69,gr1,gr1         ;call the OS
          jmpf     gr121,clk_err      ;jump if error
          const    gr120,time         ;set the address where
          consth   gr120,time         ;time is to be stored
          store    0,0,gr96,gr120     ;store the time in ms.
```

The example calls the operating system kernel to get the current value of the system clock in milliseconds. On return, if *gr121* contains a boolean FALSE value, the program jumps to **clk_err** to handle the error; otherwise, the time in milliseconds is stored in the variable *time*.

The return value from the clock service does not include system I/O data transfer time incurred by HIF services with service numbers less than 256. The return value is related to the value returned by the cycles service, in that it is derived from the processor cycles counter, but scaled by the processor frequency and resolved to ms.

Service 274 – cycles

Return Processor Cycles

Description

This service returns an ascending positive number in registers *gr96* and *gr97*, that is, the number of processor cycles that have elapsed since the last processor initialization was applied to the CPU. It provides a mechanism for user programs to access the contents of the internal Am29000 processor timer counter register. The cycle count can be multiplied by the speed of the processor clock to convert it to a time value. *Gr97* will contain the most significant bits of the cycle count, while *gr96* will contain the least significant bits. HIF implementations of this service are required to provide a cycle count with a minimum of 42 bits of precision.

The implementor of this HIF service must, as best possible, eliminate system I/O data transfer time incurred by HIF services with service numbers less than 256. This will benefit the user when using this service to perform benchmarks across different hardware platforms. The user of this service should be aware that the return value may stick contain cycles used in support of operating system tasks.

Register Usage

Type	Regs	Contents	Description
Calling:	*gr121*	274 (0x112)	Service number
Returns:	*gr96*	cycles	Success: Bits 0–31 of processor cycles Failure:= 0 (in both *gr96* and *gr97*)
	gr97	cycles	Success: Bits 32 and higher of processor cycles Failure:= 0 (in both *gr96* and *gr97*)
	gr121	0x80000000 errcode	Logical TRUE, service successful Error number, service not successful (implementation dependent)

Example Call

```
cycles:   .word   0                    ;MSb of cycles
          .word   0                    ;LSb of cycles

          const   gr121,274            ;service = 274
          asneq   69,gr1,gr1           ;call the OS
          jmpf    gr121,cyc_err        ;jump if error
           const  gr120,cycles         ;set the address where the
          consth  gr120,cycles         ;count is to be stored
          store   0,0,gr97,gr120       ;store the MSb,
          add     gr120,gr120,4        ;increment the address,
          store   0,0,gr96,gr120       ;then store the LSb of cycles.
```

The example call program fragment calls the operating system service 274 to access the number of CPU cycles that have elapsed since processor initialization. The cycle count (in *gr96* and *gr97*) is stored in the two words addressed by the variable *cycles* if the service call is successful. If *gr121* contains a boolean FALSE value on exit, the program jumps to **cyc_err** to handle the error condition.

Service 289 – setvec   Set Trap Address

Description

This service sets the address for user-level trap handler services that implement the local register stack spill and fill traps. In addition, if the current HIF implementation supports program calls to set other trap vectors, this service provides that capability. It returns an indication of success or failure in register $gr121$. The method used to invoke these traps in user mode is described on page NO TAG of this specification, in the User-Mode Traps section.

The only vectors supported by this specification are 64 (spill) and 65 (fill). These vectors are invoked by operating system software, using the trampoline principles described in the section User-Mode Traps, and are not supported by the Am29000 processor hardware.

Extensions to this service, in implementations that support setting traps other than spill and fill, will return the previously installed trap address in register $gr96$, if the service is successful. For User Mode Traps, register $gr96$ reports only the success or failure of the service. In HIF implementations where the extended **setvec** service is available, programs can use the returned (previous) vector address to implement vector chaining.

Register Usage

Type	Regs	Contents	Description
Calling:	$gr121$	289 (0x121)	Service number
	$lr2$	trapno	trap number
	$lr3$	funaddr	address of trap handler
Returns:	$gr96$	trapaddr	For user mode traps: Success:= 0 Failure: < 0 For extended trap vectors: Success:previous trap address Failure: = 0
	$gr121$	0x80000000 errcode	Logical TRUE, service successful Error number, service not successful (implementation dependent)

Example Call

```
trpadr:   .word   0
          const   lr2,64           ;trap number = 64
          const   lr3,t64_hnd      ;set address of
          consth  lr3,t64_hnd      ;trap-64 handler
          const   gr121,289        ;service = 289
          asneq   69,gr1,gr1       ;call the OS
          jmpf    gr121,vec_err    ;jump if error
           const  gr120,trpadr     ;set address where to
          consth  gr120,trpadr     ;store the trap address
          store   0,0,gr96,gr120   ;and store it!
```

The example calls the **setvec** service to pass the address to be used for the trap 64 trap handler routine. If the service returns with *gr121* containing a boolean TRUE result, the program continues by storing the trap address returned in *gr96*; otherwise, the program jumps to **vec_err** to handle the error condition.

Service 290 – settrap

Set Trap Vector

Description

This service provides the means to install trap handler addresses directly into the vector table whose base address is pointed to by the Vector Area Base Address special-purpose register (VAB). The vector numbers that may legally be modified by this service are implementation dependent.

Implementations that do not intend to provide the ability to set trap addresses with this service should return the EHIFNOTAVAIL error code when this service is invoked. If certain vectors are restricted from being set by this service, the implementation should check the **trapno** parameter and return the EHIFNOTAVAIL error code for references to restricted trap vectors.

Register Usage

Type	Regs	Contents	Description
Calling:	*gr121*	290 (0x122)	Service number
	lr2	trapno	Vector number
	lr3	trapaddr	Address of trap handler
Returns:	*gr96*	trapaddr	Address of previous trap handler
	gr121	0x80000000	Logical TRUE, service successful
		errcode	Error number: EHIFNOTAVAIL if service not available (implementation dependent)

Example Call

```
oldtrap: .word    0                  ;placeholder for old address

         const    lr2,54             ;floating divide trap vector
         const    lr3,new_div        ;set new_div as the
         consth   lr3,new_div        ;trap handler address
         const    gr121,290          ;service number 290
         asneq    69,gr1,gr1         ;call the OS
         jmpf     gr121,trap_err     ;jump if error
          const   gr120,oldtrap      ;set address for saving
         consth   gr120,oldtrap      ;the old trap handler address
         store    0,0,gr96,gr120     ;save the old handler address
```

In the example call, a new handler for the floating-point division operation is being installed. If the implementation returns an error, the program jumps to the

---

trap_err label. If the service was successful and a new trap handler was installed, the previous handler address (if any) is stored into the **oldtrap** variable.

There is often a need for programs operating on dedicated hardware to enter supervisor mode. This can be accomplished by reserving a trap vector for that purpose and installing a trap handler routine to return control to the user in supervisor mode. The operation is effected by issuing an assert instruction that invokes the specified trap. User mode can be restored by clearing (setting to 0) the Supervisor Mode bit (4) of the Current Processor Status register (CPS).

Service 291 – setim   Set Interrupt Mask

Description

This service provides the means to set the interrupt mask (IM) field and the disable interrupts (DI) field of the current processor status register (CPS). This field enables the external interrupt pins INTR0–INTR3, according to the following encoding:

00	INTR0 enabled
01	INTR1–INTR0 enabled
10	INTR2–INTR0 enabled
11	INTR3–INTR0 enabled

These two bits provide for a priority-oriented enabling capability; however, the INTR0 interrupt can not be disabled through the IM field alone. The disable interrupts (*di*) parameter must be set to 1 to produce this effect. A *di* value of 0 will enable the selected interrupts, and a value of 2 will leave the DI-bit of the CPS unchanged. If this service is not implemented, an error code of EHIFNOTAVAIL should be returned by the software. The error code for an illegal value in registers *lr2* or *lr3* is implementation dependent.

Register Usage

Type	Regs	Contents	Description
Calling:	*gr121*	290 (0x122)	Service number
	lr2	mask	New mask field value
	lr3	di	0= Enable interrupts 1= Disable interrupts 2= Leave interrupt enable unchanged
Returns:	*gr96*	mask	Old mask field value
	gr121	0x80000000	Logical TRUE, service successful
		errcode	Error number: EHIFNOTAVAIL if service not available (implementation dependent)

Example Call

```
oldmask: .word    0                ;placeholder for old mask value
         const    lr2,0x10         ;mask = 10 (*INTR(2:0) enable)
         const    lr3,0x0          ;enable interrupts (di = 0)
         const    gr121,291        ;service number 291
         asneq    69,gr1,gr1       ;call the OS
         jmpf     gr121,mask_err   ;jump if error
          const   gr120,oldmask    ;set address for saving
         consth   gr120,oldmask    ;the old IM field value
         store    0,0,gr96,gr120   ;save the old IM field value
```

In the example call, the IM-field of the current processor status register is to be set to 10, enabling external interrupt pins INTR0, INTR1, and INTR2. If this service is not available, or if the value in *lr2* is illegal, the service will return an error code, in which case the program jumps to the **mask_err** label. If the service execution is successful, the previous contents of the IM field is stored in the **oldmask** variable.

Service 305 – query   Return Version Information

Description

This service returns version information, or capabilities of the HIF implementation, as requested. On entry, the requested capability is passed as an argument in *lr2*. The service returns the requested information, or indicates that it is unavailable, in *gr96*.

Register Usage

Type	Regs	Contents	Description
Calling:	*gr121*	305 (0x131)	Service number
	lr2	capcode	Capabilities code
			0 = Request HIF version
			1 = Request CPU version & family code
			2 = Request Am29027 arithmetic accelerator version
			3 = Request CPU clock frequency
			4 = Request memory environment

For *lr2* = 0 (HIF version)

Returns:	*gr96*	hifvers	Success: ≥ 0 (encoded version information). The version number is returned as two 4-bit fields in the low-order 8 bits of the return value. The two fields are separated by an implied decimal point (e.g., 0x20 means HIF V2.0). Failure: < 0 (or unavailable)

For *lr2* = 1 (CPU version and family code)

Returns:	*gr96*	cpuvers	Success: ≥ 0 (encoded version/family). The high-order 8 bits of the configuration register (CFG), known as the processor release level (PRL) are moved to the low-order 8 bits of *gr96*, as two 4-bit fields. Failure: < 0 (or unavailable)

For *lr2* = 2 (Am29027 coprocessor version)

Returns:	*gr96*	027vers	Success: ≥ 0 (encoded version information). The high-order 8 bits of the accelerator's precision register form the arithmetic accelerator release level (ARL) and are moved to the low-order 8 bits of *gr96*, as two 4-bit fields.
			Failure: < 0 (or unavailable)

For *lr2* = 3 (CPU clock frequency)

Returns:	*gr96*	clkfreq	Success: > 0 (frequency in Hertz)
			Failure: $= 0$ (or unavailable)

For *lr2* = 4 (Memory environment)

	gr96	memenv	Success: > 0 (memory environment)
		BYTEW	0x1 byte-write available
		DWSET	0x2DW-bit set
		IREAD	0x4 Instruction memory readable
			Failure: ≤ 0 (or unavailable)

For all requests

Returns:	*gr121*	0x80000000	Logical TRUE, service successful
		errcode	error number, service not successful (implementation dependent)

In addition to the Return Usage table requests, negative **capcode** values in register *lr2* are available for implementation-dependent encoding of **query** requests. All positive values in register *lr2* are reserved for future expansion of the HIF **query** service.

Example Call

```
vers:     .word   0
          const   lr2,0            ;request HIF version
          const   gr121,305        ;service = 305
          asneq   69,gr1,gr1       ;call the OS
          jmpf    gr121,qry_err    ;handle query error
           const  lr2,vers         ;address to store version info
          consth  lr2,vers
          store   0,0,gr96,lr2     ;store the HIF version number
```

In the example call, a request code of 0 is loaded into *lr2* and the service is called. Upon return, if the value in *gr121* is FALSE, indicating failure, the program jumps to an error routine. If *gr121* is TRUE, then the program stores the returned HIF version information into the variable called **vers**.

Service 321 – signal   Register Signal Handler

Description

    This service provides the means to register (or un-register) a specified user signal handler. Local register *lr2* contains the address of the user signal handler routine on entry. This routine is expected to handle the signals shown in Table A-2, below. Sections 2.5, 4.4 and Appendix B, contain additional information on writing signal handlers for complex environments.

    The HIF service returns the address of the previously installed handler in *gr96*. If no previous handler was installed, *gr96* will contain a NULL pointer (*gr96* = 0). Signal handlers may perform any appropriate processing, but only the services with service numbers above 256 are guaranteed to be available. Calls to services with numbers below 256 may result in unpredictable behavior when returning to the interrupted program—unless the service executes a **longjump**(), which avoids execution of the interrupt return service (see Table A-3).

    To un-register a signal handler, local register *lr2* must contain a value of 0 (NULL) on entry. When a handler is un-registered in this manner, signal handling will revert to the default behavior established by the operating system.

    When one of the (SIGINT or SIGFPE) signals occurs, the HIF implementation must preserve: the signal number that occurred; the register stack pointer (*gr1*); the register allocate bounds (*gr126*); the program counters, PC0–PC2; the channel registers (*CHA*, *CHD*, and *CHC*); the ALU register; the old processor status, OPS; and the contents of *gr121*. These registers are saved in the user memory stack. The HIF implementation must be careful not to disturb values in registers that have not been saved on the user's stack. Global register *gr125* should contain the address of the last saved value in the HIF Signal Stack (e.g., *gr121*) at the conclusion of this phase. Figure A-1 illustrates the required user stack format for saved registers.

Table A-2. Default Signals Handled by HIF

Mnemonic	Value	Description
SIGINT	2	User interrupt (e.g., from keyboard)
SIGFPE	8	Floating–point exception

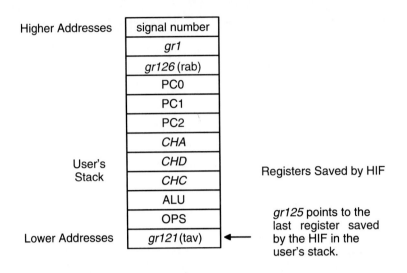

Higher Addresses	signal number
	gr1
	gr126 (rab)
	PC0
	PC1
	PC2
	CHA
User's	CHD
Stack	CHC
	ALU
	OPS
Lower Addresses	gr121 (tav)

Registers Saved by HIF

gr125 points to the last register saved by the HIF in the user's stack.

Figure A-1. HIF Register Preservation for Signals

It is at this point that execution of the HIF invokes the handler specified by the **newsig** parameter to the **signal** service. The handler is invoked with the processor mode set to the mode of the interrupted program (either user or supervisor). Depending on the nature of the interrupt (SIGINT or SIGFPE) and the complexity of the handler, additional registers may need to be saved. In this case, the handler must preserve: the values in the indirect pointers IPA, IPB, and IPC; the contents of the Q register; the stack frame pointer, *lr1*; and the local register stack free bounds in *rfb* (*gr127*). In addition, because high-level languages use global registers *gr96–gr124* as temporaries, the user signal handler may have to save these as well.

User signal handlers can be grouped into three levels of complexity, depending on the implementation:

1. The least complex are handlers which have no intention of returning control to the user. In this case, only a few additional registers may need to be saved (if any).

2. Floating-point error handlers are often more complex, where some of the user's context needs to be saved. In this case, probably only the indirect pointers (IPA–IPC), the Q register, and *gr125* need be preserved. After the error has been handled, the handler will issue one of the signal return services listed in Table A-3 to return control to the user's program.

3. The most complex handlers will be those that need to return to the user program at the C-level of context. If the handler intends to pass control to a user-

provided signal routine (e.g., to handle SIGINT), then it may be necessary to preserve all of the registers indicated in the figure above. In addition, handlers that intend to return control at the C-level of context will need to make provision for completing any interrupted SPILL or FILL operations or complete a long-jump that may be in progress. Fortunately, AMD supplies the necessary code in library routines supplied with most tool products (see Appendix B).

Before execution of the signal handler, the HIF conforming operating system is responsible for clearing the Channel Control (CHC) register (setting it to 0), to prevent restarting a load or store multiple operation that may have been interrupted. The proper contents of this register will be restored by the HIF when the handler issues one of the service requests listed in Table A-3.

Once a signal handler is invoked by one of the signals listed in Table A-2, and when it has finished, it will usually return to the operating system by invoking one of the signal return services shown in Table A-3, below, with register *gr125* pointing to the last saved register in the HIF-saved-registers (i.e., *gr121*), as shown in Figure A–1. More complex implementations may make other arrangements for returning to the user program's context. Sample code for saving and restoring the necessary registers is shown in section 4.4 and Appendix B.

The handler is responsible for determining the appropriate action for each type of interrupt (SIGINT or SIGFPE), and must return control to the operating system using one of the services listed in Table A-3, after first restoring the indirect pointers (IPA–IPC), the Q register, and with *gr125* pointing to the last saved register in the user's stack (assuming the suggested approach for preserving registers is followed).

Table A-3.   HIF Signal Return Services

Service	Name	Description
322	sigdfl	Perform default signal handling
323	sigret	Return to location indicated by PC1
324	sigrep	Return to location indicated by PC2
325	sigskp	Return to location indicated by PC0

Register Usage

Type	Regs	Contents	Description
Calling:	*gr121*	321 (0x141)	Service number
	lr2	newsig	Address of signal handler, or NULL pointer
Returns:	*gr96*	oldsig	Old handler address
	gr121	0x80000000	Logical TRUE, service successful
		errcode	Error number, service not successful (implementation dependent)

Example Call

```
oldhdlr: .word   0

         const   lr2,user_sigs      ;address of user signal handler
         consth  lr2,user_sigs
         const   gr121,321          ;service = 321
         asneq   69,gr1,gr1         ;call the OS to install handler
         jmpf    gr121,sig_err      ;jump to handle error
          const  gr120,oldhdlr      ;setup address to store old
         consth  gr120,oldhdlr      ;handler address
         store   0,0,gr96,gr120     ;store the old handler address
```

In the example call, a user signal handler whose entry point name is **user_sigs** is installed. When the service returns, if *gr121* contains a FALSE value, the program jumps to an error routine; otherwise, the address of the previously installed handler returned in *gr96* is stored in the local variable **oldhdlr**.

Service 322 – sigdfl   Perform Default Signal Action

Description

This service is called only from within a user signal handler installed using the **signal** (321) service. The function of this service is to instruct the HIF to perform the predetermined default action for the specified signal. The operating system is responsible for establishing the appropriate default action.

Register Usage

Type	Regs	Contents	Description
Calling:	*gr121*	322 (0x142)	Service number
	gr125	sigptr	Pointer to HIF Signal Stack containing preserved registers (See **signal** (321) for further information.)
Returns:	Does not return		

Example Call

```
const   gr121,322        ;service = 322
asneq   69,gr1,gr1       ;call the OS
```

Since this service does not return, no attempt is made to test returned values or store results.

Service 323 – sigret   **Return From Signal Interrupt**

Description

This service is called only from within a user signal handler installed using the **signal** (321) service. The function of this service is to return from the latest signal interrupt, to the location specified by the value in program counter PC1 at the time the signal occurred. Once invoked, this service does not return to the user signal handler.

Register Usage

Type	Regs	Contents	Description
Calling:	*gr121*	323 (0x143)	Service number
	gr125	sigptr	Pointer to HIF Signal Stack containing preserved registers (See **signal** (321) for further information.)
Returns:	Does not return		

Example Call

```
        const   gr121,323        ;service = 323
        asneq   69,gr1,gr1       ;call the OS
```

Since this service does not return, no attempt is made to test returned values or store results.

Service 324 – sigrep   Return From Signal Interrupt

Description

This service is called only from within a user signal handler installed using the **signal** (321) service. The function of this service is to return from the latest signal interrupt to the location specified by the value in program counter PC2 at the time the signal occurred. Once invoked, this service does not return to the user signal handler.

Register Usage

Type	Regs	Contents	Description
Calling:	*gr121*	324 (0x144)	Service number
	gr125	sigptr	Pointer to HIF Signal Stack containing preserved registers (See **signal** (321) for further information.)
Returns:	Does not return		

Example Call

```
        const   gr121,324        ;service = 324
        asneq   69,gr1,gr1       ;call the OS
```

Since this service does not return, no attempt is made to test returned values or store results.

Service 325 – sigskp
Return From Signal Interrupt

Description

This service is called only from within a user signal handler installed using the **signal** (321) service. The function of this service is to return from the latest signal interrupt to the location specified by the value in program counter PC0 at the time the signal occurred. Once invoked, this service does not return to the user signal handler.

Register Usage

Type	Regs	Contents	Description
Calling:	*gr121*	325 (0x145)	Service number
	gr125	sigptr	Pointer to HIF Signal Stack containing preserved registers (See **signal** (321) for further information.)
Returns:	Does not return		

Example Call

```
        const   gr121,325       ;service = 325
        asneq   69,gr1,gr1      ;call the OS
```

Since this service does not return, no attempt is made to test returned values or store results.

Service 326 – sendsig   Send Signal

Description

This service provides the means to send a signal to the current process, to support signal testing. A single parameter, *sig*, specifies the signal number to be sent.

Register Usage

Type	Regs	Contents	Description
Calling:	*gr121*	326 (0x141)	Service number
	lr2	sig	Signal number to be sent to current process
Returns:	*gr121*	0x80000000	Logical TRUE, service successful
		errcode	Error number, service not successful EHIFNOTAVAIL if service not implemented. (implementation dependent)

Example Call

```
const   lr2,SIGFPE        ;floating-point exception
const   gr121,326         ;service = 326
asneq   69,gr1,gr1        ;call the OS
jmpf    gr121,send_err    ;handle signaling error
 nop
```

In the above example, a floating-point exception error signal is being sent to the current process. It is presumed that a signal handler for the SIGFPE (floating-point exception) error has been previously installed (see **signal** service) and is being tested.

A.2 Error Numbers

HIF implementations are required to return error codes when a requested operation is not possible. The codes from 0–10,000 are reserved for compatibility with current and future error return standards. The currently assigned codes and their meanings are shown in Tables A–4 through A–9. If a HIF implementation returns an error code in the range of 0–10,000, it must carry the identical meaning to the corresponding error code in this table. Error code values larger than 10,000 are available for implementation-specific errors.

Table A-4. HIF Error Numbers Assigned

Number	Name	Description
0		Not used.
1	EPERM	Not owner
		This error indicates an attempt to modify a file in some way forbidden except to its owner.
2	ENOENT	No such file or directory
		This error occurs when a file name is specified and the file should exist but does not, or when one of the directories in a pathname does not exist.
3	ESRCH	No such process
		The process or process group whose number was given does not exist, or any such process is already dead.
4	EINTR	Interrupted system call
		This error indicates that an asynchronous signal (such as interrupt or quit) that the user has elected to catch occurred during a system call.
5	EIO	I/O error
		Some physical I/O error occurred during a read or write. This error may in some cases occur on a call following the one to which it actually applies.
6	ENXIO	No such device or address
		I/O on a special file refers to a sub-device that does not exist or is beyond the limits of the device.
7	E2BIG	Arg list is too long
		An argument list longer than 5120 bytes is presented to executive.
8	ENOEXEC	Exec format error
		A request is made to execute a file that, although it has the appropriate permissions, does not start with a valid magic number.
9	EBADF	Bad file number
		Either a file descriptor refers to no open file, or a read (write) request is made to a file that is open only for writing (reading).

Number	Name	Description
10	ECHILD	No children
		Wait and the process has no living or unwaited for children.
11	EAGAIN	No more processes
		In a fork, the system's process table is full, or the user is not allowed to create any more processes.
12	ENOMEM	Not enough memory
		During an executive or break, a program asks for more memory than the system is able to supply or else a process size limit would be exceeded.
13	EACCESS	Permission denied
		An attempt was made to access a file in a way forbidden by the protection system.
14	EFAULT	Bad address
		The system encountered a hardware fault in attempting to access the arguments of a system call.
15	ENOTBLK	Block device required
		A plain file was mentioned where a block device was required, such as in mount.
16	EBUSY	Device busy
		An attempt was made to mount a device that was already mounted, or an attempt was made to dismount a device on which there is an active file (open file, current directory, mounted-on file, or active text segment).
17	EEXIST	File exists
		An existing file was mentioned in an inappropriate context (e.g., link).
18	EXDEV	Cross-device link
		A hard link to a file on another device was attempted.
19	ENODEV	No such device
		An attempt was made to apply an inappropriate system call to a device, for example, to read a write-only device, or the device is not configured by the system.
20	ENOTDIR	Not a directory
		A non-directory was specified where a directory is required, for example, in a path name or as an argument to *chdir*.
21	EISDIR	Is a directory
		An attempt to write on a directory.

Number	Name	Description
22	EINVAL	Invalid argument
		This error occurs when some invalid argument for the call is specified. For example, dismounting a non-mounted device, mentioning an unknown signal in signal, or specifying some other argument that is inappropriate for the call.
23	ENFILE	File table overflow
		The system's table of open files is full, and temporarily no more open requests can be accepted.
24	EMFILE	Too many open files
		The configuration limit on the number of simultaneously open files has been exceeded.
25	ENOTTY	Not a typewriter
		The file mentioned in **stty** or **gtty** is not a terminal or one of the other devices to which these calls apply.
26	ETXTBSY	Text file busy
		The referenced text file is busy and the current request can not be honored.
27	EFBIG	File too large
		The size of a file exceeded the maximum limit.
28	ENOSPC	No space left on device
		A write to an ordinary file, the creation of a directory or symbolic link, or the creation of a directory entry failed because no more disk blocks are available on the file system.
29	ESPIPE	Illegal seek
		A seek was issued to a socket or pipe. This error may also be issued for other non-seekable devices.
30	EROFS	Read-only file system
		An attempt to modify a file or directory was made on a device mounted read-only.
31	EMLINK	Too many links
		An attempt was made to establish a new link to the requested file and the limit of simultaneous links has been exceeded.
32	EPIPE	Broken pipe
		A write on a pipe or socket was attempted for which there is no process to read the data. This condition normally generates a signal; the error is returned if the signal is caught or ignored.
33	EDOM	Argument too large
		The argument of a function in the math package is out of the domain of the function.

Number	Name	Description
34	ERANGE	Result too large
		The value of a function in the math package is unrepresentable within machine precision.
35	EWOULDBLOCK	Operation would block
		An operation that would cause a process to block was attempted on an object in non-blocking mode.
36	EINPROGRESS	Operation now in progress
		An operation that takes a long time to complete was attempted on a non-blocking object.
37	EALREADY	Operation already in progress
		An operation was attempted on a non-blocking object that already had an operation in progress.
38	ENOTSOCK	Socket-operation on non-socket
		A socket oriented operation was attempted on a non-socket device.
39	EDESTADDRREQ	
		Destination address required
		A required address was omitted from an operation on a socket.
40	EMSGSIZE	Message too long
		A message sent on a socket was larger than the internal message buffer or some other network limit.
41	EPROTOTYPE	Protocol wrong type for socket
		A protocol was specified that does not support the semantics of the socket type requested.
42	ENOPROTOOPT	Option not supported by protocol
		A bad option or level was specified when accessing socket options.
43	EPROTONOSUPPORT	
		Protocol not supported
		The protocol has not been configured into the system, or no implementation for it exists.
44	ESOCKTNOSUPPORT	
		Socket type not supported
		The support for the socket type has not been configured into the system, or no implementation for it exists.
45	EOPNOTSUPP	Operation not supported on socket
		For example, trying to accept a connection on a datagram socket.
46	EPFNOSUPPORT	
		Protocol family not supported
		The protocol family has not been configured into the system or no implementation for it exists.

Number	Name	Description
47	EAFNOSUPPORT	Address family not supported by protocol family
		An address was used that is incompatible with the requested protocol.
48	EADDRINUSE	Address already in use
		Only one usage of each address is normally permitted.
49	EADDRNOTAVAIL	Cannot assign requested address
		This normally results from an attempt to create a socket with an address not on this machine.
50	ENETDOWN	Network is down
		A socket operation encountered a dead network.
51	ENETUNREACH	Network is unreachable
		A socket operation was attempted to an unreachable network.
52	ENETRESET	Network dropped connection on reset
		The host you were connected to crashed and rebooted.
53	ECONNABORTED	Software caused connection abort
		A connection abort was caused internal to your host machine.
54	ECONNRESET	Connection reset by peer
		A connection was forcibly closed by a peer. This normally results from a loss of the connection on the remote socket due to a timeout or a reboot.
55	ENOBUFS	No buffer space available
		An operation on a socket or pipe was not performed because the system lacked sufficient buffer space or because a queue was full.
56	EISCONN	Socket is already connected
		A connect request was made on an already connected socket; or a *sendto* or *sendmsg* request on a connected socket specified a destination when already connected.
57	ENOTCONN	Socket is not connected
		A request to send or receive data was disallowed because the socket was not connected and (when sending on a datagram socket) no address was supplied.
58	ESHUTDOWN	Cannot send after socket shutdown
		A request to send data was disallowed because the socket had already been shut down with a previous shutdown call.
59	ETOOMANYREFS	Too many references; cannot splice.

Number	Name	Description
60	ETIMEDOUT	Connection timed out
		A connect or send request failed because the connected party did not properly respond after a period of time. (The timeout period is dependen on the communication protocol.)
61	ECONNREFUSED	
		Connection refused
		No connection could be made because the target machine actively refused it. This usually results from trying to connect to a service that is inactive on the foreign host.
62	ELOOP	Too many levels of symbolic links
		A pathname lookup involved more than the maximum limit of symbolic links.
63	ENAMETOOLONG	
		File name too long
		A component of a pathname exceeded the maximum name length, or an entire pathname exceeded the maximum path length.
64	EHOSTDOWN	Host is down
		A socket operation failed because the destination host was down.
65	EHOSTUNREACH	
		Host is unreachable
		A socket operation was attempted to an unreachable host.
66	ENOTEMPTY	Directory not empty
		A non-empty directory was supplied to a *remove* directory or **rename** call.
67	EPROCLIM	Too many processes
		The limit of the total number of processes has been reached. No new processes can be created.
68	EUSERS	Too many users
		The limit of the total number of users has been reached. No new users may access the system.
69	EDQUOT	Disk quota exceeded
		A write to an ordinary file, the creation of a directory or symbolic link, or the creation of a directory entry failed because the user's quota of disk blocks was exhausted; or the allocation of an *inode* for a newly created file failed because the user's quota of *inodes* was exhausted.
70	EVDBAD	RVD related disk error
1001	EHIFNOTAVAIL	HIF service not available.
		The requested HIF service is not implemented or is not available to the user program making the request.
1002	EHIFUNDEF	HIF service is undefined
		The HIF service referenced by the program is undefined. No valid HIF service with that service number exists.

Appendix B

HIF Signal Processing

B.1   User Trampoline Code

The following 29K assembly language code is a listing of the User mode code required to complete signal handler preparation tasks necessary for an HIF compliant operating system. When address **sigcode** is reached, the operating system has already saved the portion of the interrupt context frame down to the *tav* register onto the user's memory stack (see section 4.4). This source code is contained in library files delivered with the High C 29K product, and is listed here for reference and to aid comprehension of the way different code fragments fit together in a real implementation.

Implementors who do not wish to use an array of signal handlers, but a single C–level handler function, can change the code in the *call C–level* section. They need not access the **SigEntry** array to obtain the address of their handler function.

```
        .file   "signal.s"
; SigEntry is the address of an array of C-level user code signal
; handlers. They must return to the top-level before doing a
; sigret() return function. Nested signals are supported.

        .extern V_SPILL,V_FILL
        .extern fill_handler        ;In crt0.s

        .align 4
        .comm   WindowSize,4
        .data
```

```
SigEntry:
        .word   0                       ;reserved
        .word   0                       ;adds. of #2 SIGINT handler
        .word   0                       ;reserved
        .word   0                       ;reserved
        .word   0                       ;reserved
        .word   0                       ;reserved
        .word   0                       ;reserved
        .word   0                       ;adds. of #8 SIGFPE handler
        .word   0                       ;reserved
        .word   0                       ;reserved
        .word   0                       ;reserved
        .word   0                       ;reserved
        .word   0                       ;reserved
        .word   0                       ;reserved #14 SIGALARM
    .rep 32 -14
        .word   0                       ;reserved
    .endr


;---------------------------------------------------------- Macros
    .macro push,sp,reg
        sub     sp,sp,4         ;decrement pointer
        store   0,0,reg,sp      ;store on stack
    .endm
;
    .macro pushsr,sp,reg,sreg
        mfsr    reg,sreg        ;copy from special register
        sub     sp,sp,4         ;decrement pointer
        store   0,0,reg,sp      ;store on stack
    .endm
;
    .macro      pop,reg,sp
        load    0,0,reg,sp      ;get from stack
        add     sp,sp,4         ;increment pointer
    .endm
;
    .macro      popsr,sreg,reg,sp
        load    0,0,reg,sp      ;get from stack
        add     sp,sp,4         ;increment pointer
        mtsr    sreg,reg        ;move to special register
    .endm


        .reg    v0,gr96
        .reg    v1,             gr97
        .reg    v2,             gr98
        .reg    v3,             gr99
```

```
;================================================== Process Signal
; About to deliver a signal to a user mode signal handler.
; The state of all the registers (except for msp,chc and rab)
; is the same as when the process was interrupted.
;
; We must make the stack and window consistent before calling the
; handler. The orignal rab value is on the stack. The interrupt
; handler placed rfb-Windowsize in rab. This is required to
; support nested interrupts.
;
; Note that the window becomes inconsistent only during certain
; critical sections in spill,fill,longjmp and sigcode.
;     rfb - rab > windowsize => we are in spill
;     rfb - rab < windowsize => we are in fill
;     gr1 + 8   > rfb         => we are in long-longjmp case
; In case of spill,fill and lonjmp; rab is modified first,
; so if we are in one of these critical sections,
; we set rab to rfb - WINDOWSIZE.
;
        .equ    SIGCTX_UM_SIZE,   39*4
        .equ    SIGCTX_RFB,(37)*4          ;User-Mode save
;
        .equ    SIGCTX_SM_SIZE,   12*4    ;Supervisor-Mode saved
        .equ    SIGCTX_SIG,(11)*4 + SIGCTX_UM_SIZE
        .equ    SIGCTX_GR1,(10)*4 + SIGCTX_UM_SIZE
        .equ    SIGCTX_RAB,(9)*4 + SIGCTX_UM_SIZE
        .equ    SIGCTX_PC0,(8)*4 + SIGCTX_UM_SIZE
        .equ    SIGCTX_PC1,(7)*4 + SIGCTX_UM_SIZE
        .equ    SIGCTX_PC2,(6)*4 + SIGCTX_UM_SIZE
        .equ    SIGCTX_CHC,(3)*4 + SIGCTX_UM_SIZE
        .equ    SIGCTX_OPS,(1)*4 + SIGCTX_UM_SIZE
        .equ    SIGCTX_TAV,(0)*4 + SIGCTX_UM_SIZE
;
        .global sigcode
;-------------------------------------------------------- sigcode
sigcode:
        push    msp,lr1             ;push R-stack support
        push    msp,rfb
        push    msp,msp             ;M-stack support
        sub     msp,msp,3*4         ;space for Floating Point
;
        pushsr  msp,tav,IPA         ;User mode specials
        pushsr  msp,tav,IPB
        pushsr  msp,tav,IPC
        pushsr  msp,tav,Q
;
        sub     msp,msp,29*4        ;push gr96-gr124
        mtsrim  cr,29-1
        storem  0,0,gr96,msp
```

```
;------------------------------------------------ R-Stack fixup
R_fixup:
        const   v0,WindowSize       ;get register cache size
        consth  v0,WindowSize
        load    0,0,v0,v0
        add     v2,msp,SIGCTX_RAB
        load    0,0,v2,v2           ;get interrupted rab value
        sub     v1,rfb,v2           ;determine rfb-rab<=WINDOW_SIZE
        cpgeu   v1,v1,v0            ;
        jmpt    v1,nfill            ;jmp if spill or normal interrupt
        add     v1,gr1,8
         cpgtu  v1,v1,rfb           ;interrupted longjmp can look like
        jmpt    v1,nfill            ;fill, test for long-longjmp
         nop                        ;interruption, jmp if gr1+8 > rfb
; Fixup signal stack to re-start interrupted fill
; backup pc1 -- this is needed for the partial fill case.
; Clear chc so an interrupted load/store does not restart.
; Reset rab to a window distance below rfb,rab shall be
; decremented again on re-starting the interrupted fill.
; The interrupt handler set rab=rfb-WindowSize.
;
ifill:
        add     v0,msp,SIGCTX_RAB + 4
        push    v0,rab              ;resave rab=rfb-512
        const   v2,fill +4
        consth  v2,fill +4
        push    v0,v2               ;resave PC0
        sub     v2,v2,4
        push    v0,v2               ;resave PC1
        const   v2,0
        sub     v0,v0,3*4           ;point to CHC
        push    v0,v2               ;resave CHC=0
;
nfill:
        cpgtu   v0,gr1,rfb          ;if gr1 > rfb then gr1 = rfb
        jmpt    v0,lower
         cpltu  v0,gr1,rab          ;if gr1 < rab then gr1 = rab
        jmpt    v0,raise
         nop
;------------------------------------------------ Dummy Call
sendsig:
        .equ    RALLOC,4*4          ;make space for function calls
        sub     gr1,gr1,RALLOC
        asgeu   V_SPILL,gr1,rab
        add     lr1,rfb,0           ;set lr1 = rfb
        add     v1,msp, SIGCTX_SIG
        load    0,0,lr2,v1          ;restore signal number
        sub     v1,lr2,1            ;get handler index
        sll     v1,v1,2             ;point to addresses
```

```
;------------------------------------------------------- call C-level
; Handler must not use HIF services other than the _sigret() type.
      const   v0,SigEntry
      consth  v0,SigEntry
      add     v0,v0,v1
      load    0,0,v0,v0          ;determine if handler registered
      cpeq    v1,v0,0
      jmpt    v1,NoHandler
       nop
      calli   lr0,v0             ;call C-level signal handler
       nop
;
;------------------------------------------------- default return
NoHandler:
      jmp     __sigdfl
       nop


;------------------------------------------------- support code
raise:        jmp            sendsig
      sll     gr1,rab,0
lower:        jmp            sendsig
      sll     gr1,rfb,0
;
;------------------------------------------------- repair_regs
      .macro  repair_regs
      mtsrim  cr,29-1            ;restore gr96-gr124
      loadm   0,0,gr96,msp
      add     msp,msp,29*4
;
      popsr   Q,tav,msp          ;restore special registers
      popsr   IPC,tav,msp
      popsr   IPB,tav,msp
      popsr   IPA,tav,msp
;
      add     msp,msp,3*4        ;space for Floating Point
                                 ;R-stack already repaired
      add     msp,msp,3*4        ;repair msp to User mode
 .endm                          ;signal entry value.


;------------------------------------------------- repair_R_stack
; The handler function may request a signal return OS
; service,therefor avoiding the FILL in the prologue of
; the handler function. The code below replaces the possibly
; omitted prologue,required to return the register stack to
; the position at which it was interrupted ('gr1 the
; is interrupted register stack pointer.)
; A single FILL may not be able to restore the complete stack
; as a FILL can only restore 126 registers.
```

```
;  if 'gr1 < 'rfb-512 Yes LB = 'rfb-512,(signaled during a SPILL)
;                No   LB = 'gr1,(interrupted cache < 126 regs)
;
;  if LB =< rfb Yes FILL from  rfb to 'rfb (partial cache FILL)
;               No  FILL from  LB  to 'rfb (complete cache FILL)
;
;  If this *FILL* where interrupted we have no means of restarting
;  it like an ordinary FILL. So we make sure no registers are
;  damaged by an interrupt by setting gr1=rab for the duration
;  of the *FILL*. this marks the cache as fully in use. A SPILL
;  would be generated by an Interrupt of the *FILL*.
;
   .macro  repair_R_stack
        add    gr96,msp,SIGCTX_GR1
        load   0,0,gr98,gr96         ;gr98 = interrupted 'gr1
        add    gr96,msp,SIGCTX_RFB
        load   0,0,gr99,gr96         ;gr99 = interrupted 'rfb
;
;  if 'gr1 < 'rfb-512 Yes LB = 'rfb-512,(signaled during a SPILL)
;                No   LB = 'gr1,(interrupted cache < 126 regs)
        const  gr97,512
        sub    gr97,gr99,gr97        ;'rfb-512
        cpltu  gr96,gr98,gr97        ;test 'gr1 < 'rfb-512
        jmpf   gr96,$1               ;initialise LB='gr1
         add   gr1,rab,0             ;mark cache all in use
        add    gr98,gr97,0           ;set LB='rfb-512
$1:                                  ;LB in gr98
;  if LB =< rfb Yes FILL from  rfb to 'rfb (partial cache FILL)
;                No  FILL from  LB  to 'rfb (complete cache FILL)
        cpleu  gr96,gr98,rfb         ;test LB =< rfb
        jmpf   gr96,$2               ;default complete fill LB->'rfb
         nop
;
        add    gr98,rfb,0            ;fill rfb->'rfb (partial)
$2:                                  ;lower fill adds.(LA) in gr98
        cpeq   gr96,gr99,rfb         ;test if 'rfb==rfb, jump if
        jmpt   gr96,$3               ; partial fill is zero in size
         const tav,(0x80<<2)         ;prepare for *FILL*
        or     tav,tav,gr98
        mtsr   IPA,tav               ;ipa= LA<<2
        sub    tav,gr99,gr98         ;cache fill LA->'rfb
        srl    tav,tav,2             ;convert to words
        sub    tav,tav,1
        mtsr   cr,tav
        loadm  0,0,gr0,gr98          ;fill from LA->'rfb
;
$3:     add    rfb,gr99,0            ;move rfb up to 'rfb
        sub    rab,gr97,0            ;assign rab to 'rfb-512
```

```
        add     gr96,msp,SIGCTX_GR1
        load    0,0,gr98,gr96      ;gr98 = interrupted 'gr1
        add     gr1,gr98,0         ;move gr1 up to 'gr1
        nop
    .endm
```

B.2   Library Glue Routines to HIF Signal Services

The following five assembly level routines are used by C language application programs to request HIF services supporting signals. The first four services are used to cause signal handler termination. Except for _sigdfl(), the difference between these services is in how the processor PC buffer registers will be restored. It is possible to restart an instruction or skip the instruction being executed at the time signal processing started (see Appendix A). The _sigdfl() routine is used to request the default HIF operating service return service. The action taken is operating system implementation dependent. The _sigsend() service can be used request a signal be sent to the HIF application. This is useful, as it enables a software generated signal to test–out the signal handling system.

```
;======================================================= _sigret()
        .global __sigret
__sigret:
        repair_R_stack
        repair_regs
        const   tav,323            ;HIF _sigret
        asneq   69,gr1,gr1
        halt                       ;commit suicide if returns


;======================================================= _sigdfl()
        .global __sigdfl
__sigdfl:
        repair_R_stack
        repair_regs
        const   tav,322            ;HIF _sigdfl
        asneq   69,gr1,gr1
        halt                       ;commit suicide if returns


;======================================================= _sigrep()
__sigrep:
        .global __sigrep
        repair_R_stack
        repair_regs
        const   tav,324            ;HIF _sigrep
```

```
        asneq   69,gr1,gr1
        halt                            ;commit suicide if returns


;====================================================== _sigskp()
        .global__sigskp
__sigskp:
        repair_R_stack
        repair_regs
        const   tav,325                 ;HIF _sigskp
        asneq   69,gr1,gr1
        halt                            ;commit suicide if returns


;====================================================== _sendsig()
; lr2 = signal number
        .global _raise
        .global__sendsig
_raise:
__sendsig:
        const   tav,326                 ;HIF sendsig
        asneq   69,gr1,gr1
        jmpi    lr0
         nop
```

B.3   The Library signal() Routine for Registering a Handler

The following code signal() routine is part of the HIF signal support library. It is used to enter the address of a handler routine which is called when the indicated signal occurs. Handler addresses are stored in an array, indexed by signal number. The signal trampoline code (see section B.1) looks–up the table when a signal occurs and calls the registered handler. The second routine, _signal(), is the assembly language glue routine used to request the HIF *signal* service.

```
;====================================================== signal()
; signal(sig_number, handler);
;
;       lr2 = signal number
;       lr3 = handler address
        .global _signal
_signal:
; the memory variable WindowSize must be initalised at the
; start when rfb and rab are a window size apart.
        const   v0,WindowSize           ;get register cache size
        consth  v0,WindowSize
        load    0,0,v1,v0
```

```
        cpeq    v1,v1,0
        jmpf    v1,WindowSizeOK
         sub    v1,rfb,rab              ;rfb-rab = WINDOW_SIZE
        store   0,0,v1,v0
WindowSizeOK:
        const   v1,SigEntry
        consth  v1,SigEntry
        sub     v3,lr2,1                ;get handler index
        sll     v3,v3,2                 ;pointer to addresses
        add     v1,v1,v3
        store   0,0,lr3,v1              ;save new handler
        const   lr2,sigcode
        consth  lr2,sigcode
        ;Fall through to __signal
;===================================================== _signal()
        .global __signal
__signal:
        const   gr96,RegSigHand         ;User mode accessible copy
        consth  gr96,RegSigHand         ; of handler address
        store   0,0,lr2,gr96
        const   tav,321                 ;HIF signal
        asneq   69,gr1,gr1
        jmpi    lr0
         nop

        .date
        .global RegSigHand
RegSigHand      .word           0
```

Appendix C

Software Assigned Trap Numbers

The 29K processor hardware assigns tasks to most traps below number 64. Debuggers and operating systems assign tasks to trap numbers 64 and above. Over time, a number of the available trap numbers have been utilized by various tools and products. Table C-1 below lists the widely known trap number assignments. Of course it is possible that a company may make changes to a product in this area.

When a trap number is required for a new operating system or support service, it is best to avoid current trap number usage. This may enable virtualizing the new service *on top* of existing operating systems. For example, the HIF system call number (69) is different from the 4.3bsd UNIX system call number (66); this enables the UNIX operating system to distinguish HIF service calls and support them along with native UNIX system calls.

Table C-1. Software Assigned Trap Numbers

Trap Name	Number	Description
V_BKPT	0	MiniMON29K instruction breakpoint trap, processor illegal opcode trap.
V_TRACE	15	Processor trace trap defined by hardware..
V_SPILL	64	Spill and fill support for high level
V_FILL	65	language calling convention.

continued

Table C-2. Software Assigned Trap Numbers (continued)

Trap Name	Number	Description
V_BSDCALL	66	4.3bsd UNIX system call.
V_SYSVCALL	67	System V UNIX system call
V_MINIXCALL	68	Minix system call.
V_HIFCALL	69	HIF system call.
V_BRKCALL	70	BitBlocks Inc. realtime kernel support.
V_KSPILL	72	Reserved for Supervisor mode
V_KFILL	73	spill and fill support.
V_DELAYED_TIMER	74	JMI Inc. C EXECUTIVE support
V_DBG_MSG	75	MiniMON29K debug message trap.
V_OS_MSG	76	MiniMON29K OS message trap.
V_GDB_BKPT	77	GDB breakpoint.
ADA_RTS_TRAP	80	Ada run–time system call (function code in *gr116*).
ADA_TDM_TRAP	81	Ada Target Debug Monitor (TDM) service request.
ADA_RAISE_TRAP	82	Used to raise an exception (raise code is in *gr90*).
ADA_CONSTRAINT_TRAP	83	Raise constraint error.
ADA_NUMERIC_TRAP	84	Raise numeric error.
ADA_PROGRAM_TRAP	85	Raise program error.
ADA_STORAGE_TRAP	86	Raise storage error.
ADA_TASKING_TRAP	87	Raise tasking error.
V_SVSCTRAP	80	Multiprocessor Toolsmiths Inc.
V_IOTRAP	81	pSOS operating system support.
V_IRETTRAP	82	
V_DEBUG	83	
V_RESET	255	Used by MiniMON29K to indicate processor reset.

References and Bibliography

[Aho et al. 1986]   Aho, A.V., R. Sethi, and J. D. Ullman. *Compilers: Principles, Techniques, and Tools*. Reading, MA: Addison-Wesley, 1986.

[Alsup 1990]   Mitch,A. *Motorola's 88000 Family Architecture,* IEEE Micro, June 1990.

[AMD 1988]   Advanced Micro Devices, Inc. *AZ85C30 Serial Communications Controller*, No. 07513C, 1988, Sunnyvale, CA.

[AMD 1989]   Advanced Micro Devices, Inc. *Am29000 Microprocessor User's Manual*, No. 10620B, 1989, Sunnyvale, CA.

[AMD 1991a]   Advanced Micro Devices, Inc. *Am29050 Microprocessor User's Manual*, No. 14778A, 1991, Sunnyvale, CA.

[AMD 1991b]   Advanced Micro Devices, Inc. *Am29030 and Am29035 Microprocessors User's Manual*, No. 15723B, 1991, Sunnyvale, CA.

[AMD 1991c]   Advanced Micro Devices, Inc. *29K Family Product Overview*, No. 157716A, 1991, Sunnyvale, CA.

[AMD 1992a]   Advanced Micro Devices, Inc. *Fusion29K Catalog*, No. 11426D, 1992, Sunnyvale, CA.

[AMD 1992b]   Advanced Micro Devices, Inc. *Am29200 Microcontroller User's Manual*, No. 16326B, 1992, Sunnyvale, CA.

[AMD 1992c]   Advanced Micro Devices, Inc. *High–Speed–Board Design Techniques*, No. 16356A, 1992, Sunnyvale, CA.

[AMD 1993a]   Advanced Micro Devices, Inc. *29K Family 1993 International Press Coverage Update* , No. 16695B, 1993, Sunnyvale, CA.

[AMD 1993b]   Advanced Micro Devices, Inc. *Fusion29K* News Letter, No. 12990, 1993. Sunnyvale, CA.

[AMD 1993c] Advanced Micro Devices, Inc. *29K RISC Design–Made–Easy*, No. 10344D, 1993. Sunnyvale, CA.

[Hill 1987] Hill,M.D. *Aspects of Cache Memory and Instruction Buffer Performance,* Ph.D. Dissertation, University of California at Berkeley, CA, USA, 1987.

[Intel 1986] Intel Corporation. *80386 Programmer's Reference Manual*, No. 230985–001, 1986 Santa Clara, CA.

[Intel 1989] Intel Corporation. *80960CA User's Manual*, No. 270710–001, 1989, Santa Clara, CA.

[Johnson 1987] Johnson, W. M. *System Considerations in the Design of the Am29000,* IEEE Micro, November 1987.

[Johnson 1991] Johnson, W. M. *Superscalar Microprocessor Design,* Prentice Hall, 1991

[Kane et al. 1981] Kane, G., D. Hawkins, L. Leventhal, *68000 Assembly Language Programming,* Osborne/McGraw–Hill, 1991

[Kane 1987] Kane, G. *.MIPS R2000 RISC Architecture.* Englewood Cliffs, NJ: Prentice-Hall, 1987.

[Lowel 92] Lowel,B. *The Am29000 as an Embedded Controller,* Dr. Dobbs Journal. March, 1992.

[Mann 1991a] Mann,D.P. *29K Family Context Switching,* Embedded Systems Programming, November 1991.

[Mann et al. 1991b] Mann,D.P. and B. Stewart *Register Usage Strategies,* The C Users Journal, November 1991.

[Mann 1991c] Mann,D.P. *RISC Performance Depends on Compiler,* Computer Technology Review, December 1991.

[Mann 1992a] Mann,D.P. *UNIX and the Am29000 Microprocessor,* IEEE Micro, February 1992.

[Mann 1992b] Mann,D.P. *Speed System Operation by Matching CPU to Need,* Electronic Design, Novenber 1992.

[MIPS 1986] MIPS Computer Systems, Inc. *MIPS Language Programmer's Guide,* 1986, Sunnyvale, CA.

[MIPS 1989] MIPS Computer Systems, Inc. *Performance Brief,* June 1989, Sunnyvale, CA.

[Motorola 1985] *MC68020 32–bit microprocesor User's manual,* Prentice Hall, 1995.

[Olson 1988] Olson,T. *Am29000 Performance Analysis,* AMD No. 10621A, 1988, Sunnyvale, CA.

[Olson 1989] Olson,T. *Intel 80960CA Benchmark Report Critque,* AMD No. 14178A, 1980, Sunnyvale, CA.

[Smith 1992a] Smith,M.R. *To DSP or Not to DSP,* The Computer Applications Journal, Aug 1992.

[Smith 1992b] Smith,M.R. *How RISCy is DSP,* IEEE Micro, December 1992.

Index

Numbers

2–bus vs 3–bus processors
  performance: 211
  performance simulation: 47

29K, features: 5

A

A (Absolute): 41

Activation Record: 64, 124, 162
  leaf procedures: 176
  overlapping: 181

Address space
  2–bus vs 3–bus processors: 40
  C language programming: 40
  coprocessor space: 39, 107
  I/O space: 107
  instruction space: 8
  off–chip: 39
  overlapping: 8
  ROM space: 8, 109
  virtual addressing: 40

Address translation: 209
  one–to–one mapping: 245, 266

alloca(): 82

Addressing modes: 66

Am29000
  architectural simulation: 52
  description: 7
  pre rev–D version: 109

Am29005, description: 10

Am29027: 10, 85, 107
  initialization: 70
  mode: 70

Am29030
  architectural simulation: 54
  description: 13
  evaluation: 15

Am29035
  architectural simulation: 54
  description: 15

Am29050
  architectural simulation: 52
  description: 10
  floating–point: 37
  instruction forwarding: 11
  Monitor mode: 139

Am29200
  architectural simulation: 55

DRAM access times: 55
  description: 16
  evaluation: 22
  INT3 interrupt: 268

Am29205
  architectural simulation: 55
  description: 23

ANSI library: 85

Application: 61

Architectural Simulation, sim29: 46

Arithmetic/logic Unit (ALU)
  freeze mode restrictions: 138
  special registers: 36
  status register: 100

as29: 128

Assembler syntax: 127

Assert instructions: 103

ASM29K assembler: 128

Asynchronous context switch: 184
  leaf procedures: 184

B

Barrel shift: 103

Benchmarks: 240

Boolian: 102

Branch
  conditions: 36
  instructions: 44, 111

Branch Target Cache (BTC)
  Am29050 variation: 11
  entry replacement: 10
  performance: 8
  pipeline stalling: 44

Breakpoint registers: 247

Bridge connecting Instruction and Data
  busses: 8, 38, 81, 212, 264

Burst–mode
  context switch: 182

in Freeze mode: 119
with 2–bus processors: 7

Byte Pointer (BP): 29

C

C language programming: 62
  address space: 39, 40
  interrupt handlers: 157
  interrupts: 170
  peripheral access: 40

C++: 79, 95

Cache Interface Register, (CIR): 34

Calling Convention: 61, 63
  Am29027: 126
  activation record: 64
  FILL: 66
  global registers: 67
  lr0 and lr1: 65
  memory stack pointer (msp): 65
  optimization: 176
  parameter passing: 65
  register assignment: 117
  register stack pointer (rsp): 65
  return value: 67
  SPILL: 66
  trace–back tags: 124

CE/CNTL: 42

cfront: 79

Channel Address Register (CHA): 29

Channel Control Register (CHC): 29
  CV and ML bits: 31

Channel Data Register (CHD): 29

Channel Operation: 31, 37
  Freeze mode restrictions: 138
  interrupt processing: 145
  LOADM and STOREM: 31
  restarting a channel access: 145
  task context switch: 177

CISC: 4

clock, HIF service: 75, 320

coff: 95

coff2hex: 97

Cold–start code: 253

close HIF service: 291

Common Object File Format (COFF): 94
   endian conversion: 96

Common sub–expression: 78, 116

Compare: 102

Compiler features: 78

Complex addressing: 100

CONST: 110

const32 macro instruction: 188

CONSTH: 110

Condition Code Accumulator: 25

Configuration Register (CFG): 29, 30
   data width (DW)–bit: 109

Constant instructions: 110

Context switch
   asynchronous task: 184
   burst–mode: 182
   interrupting: 203
   restoring context: 201
   synchronous task: 177

Coprocessor space: 107

Core–dump debugging: 254

CPBYTE: 102

CPBYTE (Compare Bytes): 102

Cross development: 78

crt0.s: 68, 69

Current Processor Status (CPS): 29, 30
   modification: 44, 124
   ROM enable bit (RE): 39, 133
   unaligned access (UA)–bit: 109

cvcoff: 96

Cygnus Support Inc.: 79

cycles, HIF service: 75, 321

D

Daemon: 153

Data forwarding: 46

Data movement instructions: 107

Data TLB miss: 228

Debugcore of MiniMON29K: 251

Debugger Front End (DFE): 270

Debugging
   breakpoint registers: 247
   concurrent operation: 257
   core–dump: 254
   Debugger Front End (DFE): 270
   GDB: 274, 282
   getting started with GDB: 279
   gr4: 200
   ISSTIP simulator: 277
   instruction breakpoints: 247
   MiniMON29K: 248, 282
   MonDFE: 275
   MonTIP: 274
   processor support: 244
   register usage: 250
   single stepping (trace): 245
   software: 243
   Target Interface Process (TIP): 270
   Trace–Back Tags: 281
   target and host endian compatibility: 272
   use of PC2: 246

Delay slot: 78

Delayed branching, definition: 32

Direct Memory Access (DMA): 20

Dispatcher: 153

DIVIDE: 100

Divide instructions: 100

DIVIDU: 100

DMAC: 122

DMSM: 123

DREQT1–0 pins: 40

E

Early address generation: 12

Early Address Generation pin (EARLYA): 15

Emulators: 248, 268

Endian
  COFF file format: 96
  selection: 30, 96

errno: 73

EXBYTE: 109

Exception opcode (EXOP): 37

Execution mode: 244

EXHW: 109

exit HIF service: 286

EXTRACT: 103

EZ030: 15

F

FALSE: 102

FILL: 66, 69, 83
  code dependencies: 158
  interruption: 166, 185
  restarting: 169
  trampoline code: 163
  User mode handler code: 165

Floating–point
  Am29050 trapware support: 199
  accumulator access: 107
  accumulators: 37, 122
  double–precision: 123
  emulation: 85, 100
  functional unit: 123
  global support registers: 199
  inline code: 85
  instruction emulation: 37, 85, 120, 121, 199
  instruction latency: 123
  instructions: 100, 110
  interrupting instruction emulation: 199
  libraries: 85
  operating system support: 199
  register file support: 123
  special registers: 36

support registers: 121
  trapware interruption: 206

Floating–Point Environment (FPE): 37

Floating–Point Status (FPS): 37

FMAC: 122

FMSM: 123

Free Software Foundation: 78, 79
  assembler: 128

Freeze mode
  debugging: 138, 278
  exiting: 124
  interrupt processing: 137
  operating restrictions: 137
  PC–buffer data: 124
  PC–buffer registers: 33
  saving frozen context: 141

Fully associative address translation: 216

Funnel shifter: 103
  count register (FC): 103

Fusion29K: 128

G

GCC compiler: 78

GDB: 274
  getting started: 279
  MiniMON29K: 282

General Purpose Registers: 25
  restricted access: 32

getargs, HIF service: 319

getenv, HIF service: 312

getpsize, HIF service: 318

gettz, HIF service: 314

Global Registers: 25, 26, 66
  addressing: 25
  available for use: 117
  restricted access: 32

GNU: 78
  See also Free Software Foundation

gr0: 119

gr1: 120
   base plus offset addressing: 27
   shadow copy: 121

gr2 and gr3: 25

gr4, debugging: 200

H

Half–word constant: 111

Harvard memory architecture: 110
   advantages: 7
   debugging: 248
   performance: 205

hc29: 80

High C 29K: 79
   compiler: 78

Hill [1987]: 13

Host Interface (HIF): 67
   clock: 320
   close: 291
   cycles: 321
   error numbers: 340
   exit: 73, 286
   floating–point support: 71
   getargs: 72, 319
   getenv: 312
   getpsize: 318
   gettz: 314
   interrupt handling: 86
   ioctl: 301
   iostat: 307
   iowait: 304
   lseek: 296
   open: 287
   open file descriptors: 70
   query: 329
   read: 292
   remove: 299
   rename: 300
   run–time services: 73
   sendsig: 339, 354

service numbers: 73, 285
setim: 327
settrap: 68, 325
setvec: 72, 323
sigdfl: 335, 353
signal: 91, 331, 354
signal processing: 347
signal return services: 161
sigrep: 337, 353
sigret: 336, 353
sigskp: 338
sysalloc: 82, 316
sysfree: 317
time: 311
time services: 75
tmpnam: 309
trapware specification: 70
write: 294

I

I/O space: 107

I0–I31 (Instruction Bus): 41

Illegal opcode: 247

INBYTE: 109

Indirect pointers: 26, 36, 119
   global register access: 27

Information Processing Techniques Corp.
   (IPT): 128

INHW: 109

initcopy(): 80

INITDATA: 80

Initialization of the processor: 127

Instruction cache memory: 13
   access: 34

Instruction–field uses: 43

Instruction breakpoints: 247

Instruction format: 41

Instruction forwarding: 11

Instruction scheduling: 79

Instruction set: 100

Instruction TLB miss: 230

Instructions
  arithmetic: 100
  assert: 103
  branch: 111
  compare: 102
  data movement: 107
  delayed effects: 123
  floating–point: 111
  logical: 103
  miscellaneous: 115
  rotate: 103
  shift: 103

Integer arithmetic: 100

Integer Environment (INTE): 37

Interleafed memory: 14, 212

Interrupts
  C language programming: 170
  cache of saved context: 89, 146
  compiler support: 87
  handling in C: 86
  interrupting Supervisor mode: 193
  interrupting User mode: 185
  LOADM and STOREM: 31
  latching signal lines: 147
  latency: 136, 203
  light weight processing: 196
  microcode: 6
  minimizing latency: 151
  nested processing: 144
  object oriented approach: 259
  overview: 131
  priorities: 148
  processor operation: 132
  queuing: 151
  reenabling interrupts: 145
  register stack consistency: 166, 186
  restoring saved context: 149
  return mechanism: 133
  saved context frame: 158
  signal processing: 91
  stages: 131
  table of vectors: 28
  timer handling: 139
  trampoline code: 91
  User mode handlers: 157

interrupt_handler: 87

ioctl HIF service: 301

iostat HIF service: 307

iowait HIF service: 304

IREQT pin: 39

ISSTIP: 277

J

Johnson
  [1987]: 7
  [1991]: 5

K

Kulus Inc.: 85

L

Large Return Pointer (lrp): 118

Laser beam printer: 21

Latency, instruction memory: 44

ld29: 80

Leaf procedure: 125, 176
  asynchronous context switch: 184

Least Recently Used Register (LRU): 219

lib29: 80

LibInit: 72

Libraries: 84

Light–weight interrupts: 184

Linking compiled code: 80

LOAD
  address generation: 11
  scheduling: 46

LOAD and LOADM: 107, 110
  consecutive: 110
  in Freeze mode: 138
  OPT–field: 40, 109
  physical access (PA)–bit: 107
  set byte pointer (SB)–bit: 110
  User mode access (UA–bit): 107, 179

Load forwarding: 31

Load/Store Count Remaining (CR): 29

LOADM, interruption: 31

Local Registers: 25, 26, 121
  addressing: 25

Logical instructions: 103

longjmp(): 82
  code dependencies: 158
  interrupt: 166
  operating system support: 171
  signals: 189

Loop invariant code: 116

Loop inversion: 116

lseek HIF service: 296

M

M (IMmediate): 41

Macro instructions: 118

main() called by crt0.s: 72

malloc(): 82

Mann
  [1991]: 61
  [1992a]: 173
  [1992b]: 144

Memory
  access latency: 8, 110
  access protection: 231, 245, 263
  bad memory access: 138
  bandwidth: 13
  cache: 6
  connecting Instruction and Data busses: 8
  Harvard architecture: 7
  instruction memory latency: 44
  interleafed: 15, 212
  joining Instruction and Data busses
    together: 212
  load forwarding: 32
  minimum access time: 14
  narrow read: 15
  programmable bus sizing: 16
  page boundary: 215
  page size: 209, 223
  performance: 210
  performance simulation: 46
  pipeline effects: 42
  pipeline mode: 10
  restarting access: 31
  SRAM: 210
  static column DRAM: 53
  unaligned access: 71, 103, 110
  video DRAM: 19

Memory glue logic: 110

Memory Management Unit (MMU)
  one–to–one mapping: 245
  operation: 209
  page size: 221
  page tables: 222
  page–in: 210
  page–out: 210
  process identifier (PID): 109
  registers: 33
  run–time overhead: 39
  translation look–aside registers: 38

Memory space: 24

Memory stack: 67

Memory stack pointer (msp): 65 10

Metaware Inc.: 79

MFACC: 107

Microtec Research Inc.: 80

MiniMON29K: 248
  29K target components: 249
  access control module CFG: 251
  advanced DBG and CFG features: 256
  concurrent debugging: 257
  core–dump debugging: 254
  debugcore: 251

debugcore installation: 252
down loading a new OS: 267
GDB: 282
GO and HALT commands: 255
interrupts: 257
MonDFE: 275
MonTIP: 274
MSG virtual interrupt mechanism: 259
message system (MSG): 258
pcserver: 275
poll mode interrupts: 263
register usage: 250 15

Mircotec Research Inc.: 128

Miscellaneous instructions: 115

Mode, of execution: 244

MonDFE: 275

Monitor mode
    debugging: 247
    description: 139

MonTIP: 274

Motorola [1985]: 62

MTACC: 107

MULTIPLU: 100

MULTIPLY: 100 22

Multiply
    floating–point: 36
    integer: 36

Multiply and accumulate: 122

Multiprocessor, MMU support: 219

munch29: 94, 95

N

Narrow Read: 15

Nested interrupts
    processing: 144
    reenabling interrupts: 145

nm29: 94

O

Objdump: 95

Old Processor Status (OPS): 29, 30

Olson
    [1988]: 2
    [1989]: 2

One–to–one mapping. *See* address translation

OP (operation code): 41

open HIF service: 287

Operating system
    cold–start code: 253
    context save area: 183
    floating–point support: 199
    interrupt latency: 203
    issues: 173
    OS–boot: 260
    register usage: 117, 174, 203
    selection: 204
    stack support: 193
    translation look–aside buffer support: 218
    warm–start code: 254

Operation code (OP): 41

OPT2–0 pins: 40

Optimization techniques: 116

OS–boot: 260
    adding new device drivers: 263
    floating–point support: 261
    HIF services: 262
    memory access protection: 263
    open file descriptors: 263
    operation: 261
    overlaying a new operating system: 267
    poll mode interrupts: 263
    register usage: 260
    warm–start and cold–start code: 254

P

Page size: 209

pcserver: 275

Performance: 240

average cycles per instruction: 213

Peripheral Interface Adapter (PIA): 20

Physical Address Cache (PAC): 11

Physical addressing: 215

Pipeline
data dependencies: 45
interlocks: 44
memory dependence: 42
operation: 44
stalling: 110

Pipeline mode addressing: 10

Popping: 119

printf(): 67
with OS–boot: 262

Process Control Block (PCB): 173, 225
layout: 183

Process identifier (PID): 107

Processor Revision Level (PRL): 30

Program Counter 0 (PC0): 29

Program Counter 1 (PC1): 29

Program Counter Registers (PC0, PC1, PC2):
32
debugging support: 246

Programmable Bus Sizing: 16

p–trace: 272

Pushing: 119

Q

Q special register: 36

QTC Inc.: 85

query, HIF service: 329

queuing interrupts: 154

R

RA Register: 42

rab, relationship to rfb: 185

RAM, initialization: 80

RAMInit(): 81

RB or I: 41, 42

RB register: 41

RC register: 41

rdcoff: 95

read HIF service: 292

Real–time clock: 157

Real–time operating system: 67

Reason Vector (RSN): 34, 139

Region mapping: 11
debugging: 245

Register Allocation Bound (rab): 63, 70

Register Bank Protect (RBP): 29, 32
setting: 244

Register cache: 63

Register file, multiport access: 25

Register Free Bound (rfb): 63, 69

Register space: 24

Register stack: 63
asynchronous context switch: 184
interrupt processing: 166
interrupted condition: 186
operation: 162, 163
stack cut–across: 197
stack pointer: 26, 63, 69
support: 103
the rfb anchor: 185

Registers
for interrupts: 118
for operating systems: 118
general purpose: 25
global: 25, 26
indirect access: 119
Local: 25, 26

remove HIF service: 299

rename HIF service: 300

Reserved instructions: 115

Reset mode: 127, 253

rfb, the anchor register: 165, 185

RI_text: 81

RISC: 3

ROM, programming: 96

ROM space: 109

romcoff: 81

Rotate instructions: 103

S

SA29200: 22

SA29205: 23

SAXPY: 123

Scalable Clocking: 14

Scheduling LOAD instructions: 46

sendsig: 170
   HIF service: 339, 354

Serialization: 27, 177

Set associative address translation: 216

setim, HIF service: 327

setjmp(): 82
   code dependencies: 158
   operating system support: 171

Settrap, HIF service: 325

setvec, HIF service: 323

Shadow Program Counter: 34, 139
   debugging: 247

Shift instructions: 103

SigArray: 192

sigcode: 167

sigdfl, HIF service: 335, 351, 353

SigEntry: 171, 347

Signal
   HIF service: 354

HIF support: 331

signal(): 91

signal_associate: 92

sigrep, HIF service: 337, 353

sigret, HIF service: 336, 353

sigskp, HIF service: 338

sim29: 46

Signal Processing: 122

Signals
   HIF services: 331
   HIF support: 347
   introduction: 158
   longjmp(): 189
   return services: 161, 199
   SigEntry: 347
   sigcode: 347
   signal(): 354
   signaling a User mode task: 189
   sigreturn service: 193
   table of handlers: 171, 192
   trampoline code: 167, 347
   trampoline code dependencies: 158

Simulation
   architectural, sim29: 46
   instruction set, isstip: 277

Single stepping execution: 245

Software controlled cache
   cache line locked: 237
   copying a page into the cache: 234
   copying a page out of the cache: 236
   description: 210
   memory architecture: 222
   page dirty bit: 232, 237
   page maintenance: 227
   performance equation: 220
   returning from signal handler: 238
   signal handler: 232
   support routines: 239

Special Register: 27
   accessing: 121
   ALU support: 36
   Am29030 extensions: 34

Am29050 extensions: 33
asynchronous context switch: 185
Configuration (CFG): 29, 30
Current Processor Status (CPS): 29, 30
channel registers (CHA, CHD, CHC): 31
channel control: 37
floating–point support: 36
indirect pointers, (IPA, IPB, IPC): 36
memory management unit: 33
Old Processor Status (OPS): 30
program counter, (PC0, PC1, PC2): 32
Q: 36
Register Bank Protect (RBP): 32
task context switch: 177
timer control (TMC, TMR): 32
User mode accessible: 34
Vector Area Base Address (VAB): 28, 29
virtualizing: 36

SPILL: 66, 69, 83
code dependencies: 158
interruption: 166, 185
trampoline code: 163
User mode handler code: 164

SRAM: 210

Stack cache: 63

Stack cut–across: 197

Stack Pointer: 26

Start label inside crt0.s: 69

Static Link Pointer (slp): 118

Stewart, [1991]: 61

Strength reduction: 78

STORE and STOREM: 107, 110
consecutive: 110
in Freeze mode: 138
OPT–field: 40, 109
set byte pointer (SB)–bit: 110
User mode access (UA–bit): 179

STOREM, interruption: 31

strpcoff: 96

Supervisor mode
accessing from C: 75

definition: 244
interrupt handlers: 135
interrupting: 193

synchronous context switch, description: 177

sysalloc: 82
HIF service: 316

Sysfree, HIF service: 317

System Calls
See also Host Interface (HIF)
description: 196
stack support: 193
task context switch: 177
performance gain: 240

T

Target Interface Process (TIP): 270

tav: 118

Threads: 205

time, HIF service: 75, 311

Timer Control Registers (TMC, TMR): 32

Timer Counter Register (TMC): 29

Timer interrupt: 157
handler: 139

Timer Reload Register (TMR): 29

tmpnam HIF service: 309

Tool selection: 269

tpc: 118

Trace: 245

Trace–Back Tags: 124, 281

Trampoline
code: 92, 347
interrupt processing: 160
signal handling: 192

Transcendental routines: 85, 206

Translation Look–Aside buffer (TLB)
data miss: 228
data write protection: 231
instruction miss: 230

line: 216
MMU construction: 210
miss rates: 221
one–to–one mapping: 245
operating system support: 218
operation: 215
registers: 38
set associative: 216
trapware: 220

Transparent routines: 120, 127

Trap, overview: 131

Trap 63: 116

TRUE: 73, 102

U

udiconfs.txt: 276

udi_soc: 276

Unaligned memory access: 103, 110

Universal Debug Interface (UDI): 268
benefits: 278
GDB: 274, 279
ISSTIP: 277
MonTIP: 274
p–trace: 272
specification: 270

tool developers: 269
udi_soc and udiconfs.txt configuration: 276

University Support Program: 129

User mode
definition: 244
interrupt processing: 157
interrupting: 185

Utility Programs: 94

V

Vector Area Base (VAB): 28
settrap HIF service: 325

Video DRAM: 19

Video imaging: 21

Video interface: 21

Virtual memory addressing
cache invalidation: 10
overlapping address space: 40

VN: 42

W

Warm–start code: 254

write HIF service: 294